JavaScript: Novice to Ninja 2nd Edition

by Darren Jones

Copyright © 2017 SitePoint Pty. Ltd.

Product Manager: Simon Mackie   **Technical Editor:** James Hibbard

English Editor: Katie Monk   **Cover Designer:** Alex Walker

Published by SitePoint Pty. Ltd.

48 Cambridge Street Collingwood
VIC Australia 3066
Web: www.sitepoint.com
Email: books@sitepoint.com

ISBN 978-0-9953826-2-6 (print)

ISBN 978-0-9953827-7-0 (ebook)
Printed and bound in the United States of America

About Darren Jones

Darren has been programming and building websites since the turn of the millennium. He wrote the book *Jump Start Sinatra* in 2013 and followed it up with the *Getting Started With Ruby* video tutorials for SitePoint Premium. He has also written a number articles for SitePoint's website.

He started using JavaScript much more often after the release of Node.js. He loves the power and flexibility of the language as well as the amazing ecosystem that has grown around it. At the moment he is working on using React and Redux to develop an interactive online math quiz.

He was born in the city of Manchester and still lives there, where he teaches mathematics and enjoys playing water polo.

About SitePoint

SitePoint specializes in publishing fun, practical, and easy-to-understand content for web professionals. Visit http://www.sitepoint.com/ to access our blogs, books, newsletters, articles, and community forums. You'll find a stack of information on JavaScript, PHP, Ruby, mobile development, design, and more.

To Helen - thanks for always being there for me.

Table of Contents

Preface

In the preface to the first edition of this book, I talked about the ubiquity of JavaScript and its exponential growth. This shows no signs of slowing down as the second edition is published. In fact, there is a new phenomenon known as "JavaScript fatigue" that is used to describe the unrelenting barrage of new JavaScript tools and methodologies that are constantly appearing. In my view, this shouldn't be viewed as a negative, it's just a sign that the JavaScript landscape is a fertile one, and that will mean an ever-expanding list of new tools and libraries. Most of these help to take the language forward and make it better, and eventually these ideas make it into the official language. There's now a new version of JavaScript scheduled for release every year. And, with each passing year, and each new version, the language becomes more powerful and mature, capable of building complex applications. It's still not perfect, but it's getting better all the time.

While I was halfway through writing this second edition, I read somewhere that print books about JavaScript programming are pointless because they are out of date by the time they are published. On the one hand, I can appreciate this. The first edition of this book didn't use ES6 notation, which seemed to be a good idea at the time as it had only just become a standard, and hardly any browsers supported it. But ES6 quickly gained traction due to Node.js, and tools such as Babel bypassed the need for browser support. This meant that some of the code in the first edition appeared dated almost immediately after it was published. In this edition, I tried to avoid this happening by using the most up-to-date notation of the language, and removing most of the references to browser support. And, on the other hand, it doesn't matter, because, despite the unrelenting pace the JavaScript world moves at, the basic principles of programming don't change. This book is as much about learning to program as it is about learning JavaScript and, as in the first edition, it will teach you about fundamental programming principles. The way they are implemented might change, but the basic theory remains the same. I feel that JavaScript is an excellent choice of language for learning these techniques, particularly because of how easy it is to access – you can run a program from within your browser, without the need for installing any special software!

It's an exciting time to be programming JavaScript, and it's never too late to learn. In fact, if you are only just beginning to learn, you are lucky, as you'll be able to ignore all its baggage from the past and focus on the exciting language it has become. Whatever level you're at, I hope you get something from this book and enjoy programming in the language of the web!

The aim of this book is to introduce you to programming using the JavaScript language, eventually helping you to develop into a JavaScript ninja.

This is an exciting time to be learning JavaScript, having finally outgrown its early reputation as a basic scripting language used to produce cringeworthy effects on web pages. Today, JavaScript is used to produce professional and powerful web applications. Modern browsers are now capable of running JavaScript code at lightning speed, and Node.js has helped to revolutionize it by facilitating its use in other environments. This has led to a much more professional and structured approach to building JavaScript applications, where it is now considered a fully-fledged programming language. In short, JavaScript has grown up.

JavaScript has a number of cool features that make it stand out from other languages, such as callbacks, first-class functions, prototypal inheritance, and closures. Its event-based model also makes it a very good choice for modern web application development. JavaScript's ace in the pack, though, is something of which every language is envious — its *ubiquity*. JavaScript is available almost everywhere; anybody who has access to a browser can use it. And this is increasing every year as it becomes more readily available outside the browser environment. This translates into JavaScript's reach being immense: it is already the [most popular language on GitHub I can only see JavaScript growing even more popular in the future as it becomes the language of choice for the Internet of Things — helping to control household appliances, and even program robots.

Before I get carried away, though, I should point out that JavaScript is far from perfect. It is missing some important programming constructs, such as modules and private functions, which are considered standard in many modern programming languages. Yet it's also an unbelievably flexible language, where many of these gaps can be filled using the tools that it provides. In addition, many libraries have sprung into existence that help to extend JavaScript so that it's now able to reach its full potential.

This book starts off with the basics, assuming no programming or JavaScript knowledge, but quickly gets up to speed covering all the main topics in great depth, such as functions, objects, and DOM manipulation.

More advanced topics, such as error handling and testing, functional programming and OOP, are then introduced after the basics have been covered. There have been some exciting new developments in the world of JavaScript over the last few years, such as Ajax, HTML5 APIs and task runners, and these are covered in the last part of the book. There's also a practical project to build a quiz application that is developed throughout the book towards the end of each chapter. I've written with developing for modern browsers in mind, so I've always tried to use the most up-to-date methods in the examples. Having said that, I've also tried to acknowledge if something might not work in an older browser, or if a workaround is needed.

It's a long way ahead — 16 chapters, to be precise. But remember, every ninja's journey starts with a single page (or something like that, anyway). So, turn the page and let's get started!

Who Should Read This Book

This book is suitable for beginner-level web designers and developers. Some knowledge of HTML and CSS is assumed, but no previous programming experience is necessary.

Conventions Used

You'll notice that we've used certain typographic and layout styles throughout this book to signify different types of information. Look out for the following items.

Code Samples

Code in this book is displayed using a fixed-width font, like so:

```
<h1>A Perfect Summer's Day</h1>
 <p>It was a lovely day for a walk in the park. The
↪ birds were singing.</p>
```

Some lines of code should be entered on one line, but we've had to wrap them because of page constraints. An ↪ indicates a line break that exists for formatting purposes only, and should be ignored:

```
URL.open("http://www.sitepoint.com/responsive-web-design-real
↪ -user-testing/?responsive1");
```

Tips, Notes, and Warnings

Hey, You!

Tips provide helpful little pointers.

Ahem, Excuse Me ...

Notes are useful asides that are related—but not critical—to the topic at hand. Think of them as extra tidbits of information.

Watch Out!

Warnings highlight any gotchas that are likely to trip you up along the way.

Supplementary Materials

- https://github.com/spbooks/jsninja2 contains the book's code archive.
- https://www.sitepoint.com/community/ are SitePoint's forums, for help on any tricky web problems.
- **books@sitepoint.com** is our email address, should you need to contact us to report a problem, or for any other reason.

Chapter **1**

Hello, JavaScript

In this chapter, we're going to introduce the **JavaScript** language, as well as set up a programming environment. We'll also get started with some programming and write a couple of programs in JavaScript!

Here's what this chapter will cover:

- What is programming?

- The history of JavaScript

- The tools that are needed to program in JavaScript

- Installing Node.js

- JavaScript in the console

- Hello, world! Your first JavaScript program

- JavaScript in the web browser

- Graceful degradation and progressive enhancement

- A more complicated JavaScript program

- Project - we'll start a quiz project that will be developed throughout the book

Programming

Programming is about making computers do what you want. A computer program is basically a series of instructions that tell your computer how to perform a task. Unfortunately, though, computers don't speak the same language as us — they only use 1s and 0s. The first computers were programmed using punched cards, with a hole representing a 1 and no hole representing 0.

The first computer programs were written in **machine code** and **assembly language**. These are **low-level programming languages** that are closely associated with a computer's hardware. This means they can be difficult languages to program in because they involve writing abstract code that is heavily tied to a computer's architecture. If speed is very important, however, then writing in machine code or assembly language can be the best option.

High-level programming languages, on the other hand, allow abstractions to be used that make the code easier for humans to read and write. Programs are written in a language such as C, C++ or Java, which is then compiled into machine code and executed. The programs written using these languages are very fast, making high-level languages suited to writing games and professional business software where speed is important. Most native apps are also written in higher-level languages.

Scripting languages are also high-level, but they are interpreted, which means they are translated into machine code at run time. This often makes them slower than compiled languages, although interpreters are becoming ever more sophisticated, and increasingly blurring the lines between compiled and interpreted languages.

JavaScript

The language we'll be learning in this book is JavaScript, often referred to as the language of the web.

Nearly all web browsers can run JavaScript, making it one of the most popular programming languages in the world. It has a low barrier to entry — all you need to program in JavaScript is a text editor and a web browser. Although it is easy to get started, JavaScript can be a tricky language to grasp as it has some unique features and interesting quirks. Once you have mastered it, though, you'll find it is a very flexible and expressive language that can create some powerful applications.

JavaScript is a high-level scripting language that is interpreted and compiled at run time. This means it requires an engine that's responsible for interpreting a program and running it. The most common JavaScript engines are found in browsers such as Firefox, Chrome or Safari, although JavaScript can be run without a browser using an engine such as Google V8. Many modern JavaScript engines use a Just-In-Time (JIT) interpreting process, which considerably speeds up the compilation, making programs run faster.

JavaScript is also a dynamic language, so elements of a program can change while it's running, and it can do lots of things in the background at run time (such as type checking, which we'll cover later) — things that a compiled language like C++ would do at compile time.

The History of JavaScript

The World Wide Web started life as a bunch of pages linked by hyperlinks. Users soon wanted more interaction with these pages, so Netscape (an early browser vendor) asked one of their employees, Brendan Eich, to develop a new language for their Navigator browser. This needed to be done quickly because of the intense competition between Netscape and Microsoft at the time.

Eich managed to create a prototype scripting language in just 10 days. To do this, he borrowed various elements from other languages, including AWK, Java, Perl,

Scheme, HyperTalk and Self. This was an impressive feat, but in the rush to be first to market, a number of quirks and bugs ended up in the language that were never fully addressed.

The new language was originally called Mocha, but it was changed to LiveScript, then hastily rebranded as JavaScript so it could benefit from the publicity that Sun Microsystem's Java language was attracting at the time. This name has often caused some confusion, with JavaScript often considered a lighter version of Java. However, the two languages are unrelated — though JavaScript does have syntactical similarities to Java.

JavaScript made its debut in version 2 of Netscape's Navigator browser in 1995. The following year, Microsoft reverse-engineered JavaScript to create their own version, calling it JScript to avoid copyright issues with Sun Microsystems, who owned the Java trademark. JScript shipped with version 3 of the Internet Explorer browser, and was almost identical to JavaScript — it even included all the same bugs and quirks — but it did have some extra Internet Explorer-only features. Microsoft included another scripting language called VBScript with Internet Explorer at the same time.

JavaScript (and JScript) was immediately popular. It had a low barrier to entry and was relatively easy to learn, which meant an explosion in its usage for making web pages dynamic and more interactive. Unfortunately, its low barrier was also a curse — many people were now writing snippets of code without understanding what they were doing. Code could now be easily copied and pasted, and was often used incorrectly, leading to lots of poor examples appearing all over the web.

JavaScript was also frequently used to create annoying pop-up adverts, as well as for browser sniffing (the process of detecting which browser was being used to view a web page). It had started to gain a negative reputation.

The Browser Wars

By the time Netscape Navigator 4 and Internet Explorer 4 were released, JavaScript had become incredibly popular. Microsoft had started a lot of hype about the term Dynamic HTML, or DHTML for short, to refer to the use of

JavaScript to make HTML more interactive and dynamic. In an attempt to capitalize on this popularity, Netscape and Microsoft tried to add new proprietary features, which lead to different syntaxes being used. This arms race of adding new features became known as the "Browser Wars". The unfortunate downside was that programmers had to write two versions of code to achieve the same results in each browser. Professional programmers often dismissed JavaScript as a toy language, unsuitable for any serious programming, but this was unfair criticism — the language wasn't the problem, it was the way it was being used.

Eventually, Microsoft won the browser wars and Internet Explorer emerged as the dominant browser. Support for standards also increased, helped largely by the efforts of the Web Standards Project (WaSP). Developer and browser vendors started to work together and embrace the standards laid out by the World Wide Web Consortium (W3C) and ECMA.

The open-source web browser, Firefox, debuted in 2002, and Apple launched the Safari browser in 2003. Both had strong standards support, which meant developers were able to produce better web applications using JavaScript that behaved consistently across different browsers.

Web 2.0

In 2005, sites such as Google Maps, Flickr and Gmail started to appear, and demonstrated that JavaScript was capable of creating rich internet applications that looked and behaved like native desktop applications. At around the same time, the term Ajax, short for Asynchronous JavaScript And XML, was coined by Jesse James Garrett. This described a technique of obtaining data from a server in the background and updating only the relevant parts of the web page without the need for a full page reload, enabling users to continue interacting with the rest of the page. This created a more seamless experience for users and was used extensively in many Web 2.0 applications. As a result, professional programmers started to take more notice of JavaScript, and it began to be seen as a powerful and flexible programming language, capable of producing high-quality web applications.

Standards

As JavaScript became used for more sophisticated applications, and browsers embraced standards, the JavaScript landscape changed. A new browser war started, but this time it was about which browser could be the most standards-compliant. There has also been competition to increase the speed of the JavaScript engine that is built into the different browsers. This started in 2008 when engineers at Google developed the V8 engine to run inside the Chrome browser. It was significantly faster than previous JavaScript engines, and signaled another arms race as other browser vendors responded by increasing the speed of their engines. JavaScript now runs significantly faster in modern browsers and the pace of improvement shows no sign of slowing down.

HTML5

HTML5 is the latest HTML specification, though it's actually more of an umbrella term for all the latest technologies that are used on the web. This includes HTML, CSS3 and lots of APIs that use JavaScript to interact with web pages. These will be covered in more detail in [Chapter 10].

HTML5 was finalized in 2014, and the recommendation for the next version, 5.1, was proposed at the end of 2016[1]. It has quickly become the dominant standard for web development. JavaScript is a key feature in how some of its more interesting aspects work.

Node.js

In 2009, Ryan Dahl developed **Node.js** (commonly known as just Node), which allowed server-side applications to be written in JavaScript. Node is based on Google's V8 engine and allows the creation of fast and powerful real-time web applications written exclusively in JavaScript. It also lead to many applications and JavaScript libraries that don't use the browser at all. Node.js has proven to be exceptionally popular, and its usage continues to grow. This has increased the

---

[1.] https://www.w3.org/TR/html/

interest in and use of JavaScript as it starts to appear in many environments outside the web.

The popularity of Node has lead to an interesting development known as Isomorphic JavaScript. This involves having the same JavaScript code that can be run either on the client or server side: if a browser is unable to run the code, it can be run on the server and downloaded, or if the server is unavailable, the code can be run on the client.

JavaScript Versions

In 1996, Netscape and Sun Microsystems decided to standardize the language, along with the help of the European Computer Manufacturers Association, who would host the standard. This standardized language was called ECMAScript to avoid infringing on Sun's Java trademark. This caused even more confusion, but eventually ECMAScript was used to refer to the specification, and JavaScript was (and still is) used to refer to the language itself.

In an ideal world, the ECMAScript standard should mean that all JavaScript engines interpret programs in the same way. But the specification can be difficult to interpret in places, so the implementations of JavaScript can vary from engine to engine. This is why some web browsers behave differently when running JavaScript programs. JavaScript is also a *superset* of ECMAScript as it often contains additional non-standard features such as the `alert()` function.

The working group in charge of maintaining ECMAScript is known as **Technical Committee 39**, or TC-39. It's made up of representatives from all the major browser vendors such as Apple, Google, Microsoft and Mozilla, as well as invited experts and delegates from other companies with an interest in the development of the web. They have regular meetings to decide on how the language will develop.

When JavaScript was standardized by TC-39 in 1997, the specification was known as ECMAScript version 1. Version 2 followed a year later but didn't make any major changes to the language. In 1999, ECMAScript version 3 was published in December 1999 and added a variety of new features.

The development of ECMAScript version 4 was mired by disagreements on TC-39 over the direction the language should take. Some members believed the language needed lots of big changes to make it more robust, while others thought it only needed minor changes. Many new features were proposed, but were often felt to be overly ambitious or too difficult to implement in browsers. After many years without progress, version 4 was eventually abandoned, and the working party skipped over this version and went straight on to developing version 5. It was agreed that this needed be a slimmed down specification that could actually be implemented, and it was finally published in December 2009. ECMAScript version 5 added many new features to the language, but it was far less ambitious than the ill-fated version 4. Despite this, some of these features took a long time to be fully supported by browser JavaScript engines.

After ES5 was published, work started on a new standard that was codenamed "Harmony". The idea with Harmony was to outline all the desirable features for the next versions of JavaScript. It would take another six years, but eventually most of these features made it into ECMAScript version 6, although some of them were put off until version 7 or later.

In 2015, TC-39 decided to adopt a new approach and start publishing a new specification every year, with the version named after the year it was published. This meant that only the features that had been approved would make it into the specification for that year. As a result, ECMAScript version 6 was renamed ECMAScript 2015 when it was published in June 2015 and it added some major new features to the language. The plan is to release a new version in June of each year so the language evolves slowly as new features are added in a more gradual way; rather than making drastic additions every five or so years. This means ES2015 will probably be the last version of JavaScript to have such a large number of new features and make significant changes to the language. In fact, version 7, or ECMAScript 2016, was published in June 2016 and only added two new features to the previous version.

In this book we'll refer to ES2015 as ES6, as this is what it's most commonly called. The code examples will use the most up-to-date syntax, with a note to say which version of ECMAScript introduced a particular feature.

We'll also assume you're using a modern browser (try to update to the latest version of whichever is your favorite).[2]

The Future of JavaScript

These are exciting times for JavaScript as it's used for more and more applications beyond simply making web pages interactive. There's been a huge rise in the use of Single Page Applications (SPAs), which run in the browser and rely heavily on JavaScript. The next iteration of these are Progressive Web Apps (PWAs) that use web technologies to create applications that behave like a native app on a mobile device, but without being installed from an app store. HTML5 games that use JavaScript extensively are also becoming increasingly popular, especially as the graphical ability of browsers continues to improve.

JavaScript and HTML5 technologies can be used to develop browser extensions, Windows desktop widgets and Chrome OS applications. Many non-web-related applications also use JavaScript as their scripting language. It can be used to add interactivity to PDF documents, interact with a database, and even control household appliances!

It certainly seems like JavaScript has a bright future. There are many more exciting new features under discussion that will hopefully make it into future versions of JavaScript and help to make it a more powerful and expressive language. As the web platform continues to evolve and mature, and its usage grows beyond the browser, JavaScript is sure to remain a central part of future developments in technology.

A Ninja Programming Environment

If you're going to be a JavaScript programmer, you're going to need some tools. It is possible to write and run JavaScript programs using just a browser, but in order to get the most out of this book, you'll need a text editor for writing and editing your programs and a JavaScript engine to run them in. This means you'll need a modern, an up-to-date browser, and an installation of the latest version of Node.

[2.] You can see a chart that shows which features have been implemented in different browsers at http://kangax.github.io/compat-table/es2016plus/.

I was a little apprehensive about suggesting that Node be installed at the start of the book when we are still covering the basics of learning JavaScript. But after a lot of consideration, I think it's the best thing to do for the following reasons:

1. A lot of online tutorials require you to have Node installed. I don't think I'll be doing you any favors by leaving you unable to follow these tutorials without a Node installation.
2. Node allows you to use most of the latest features in the language, whereas some of them won't work in browsers.
3. You'll be able to install a huge variety of tools and code libraries using npm (The Node Package Manager), which is currently the largest code repository in the world.
4. Node can be used to install Babel[3], a transpiler that will convert code written in the latest version of JavaScript into code that can will run in most browsers.

If you don't want to install Node at this point (or you are unable to, for whatever reason), then it will still be possible to run most of the code examples in the book. There are also a number of online options that will let you use the latest version of JavaScript.

Installing Node

There are two options for installing Node: The installer or Node Version Manager.

Node Installer

If you use Windows or Mac OS, then you can use the Node Installer[4] to do all the installation for you — all you need to do is download it and follow the instructions.

Node Version Manager

The other option is to use the Node Version Manager (nvm). An advantage of using nvm is that it allows you to install multiple versions of Node and makes it

---

[3.] https://babeljs.io
[4.] https://nodejs.org/en/download/

easy to quickly update your installation to the latest version. Unfortunately, nvm doesn't support Windows, but can be installed on a Mac or Linux. To download and install nvm, just follow the two-step process outlined below:

 The Command Line

If you're not familiar with running apps and tools from the command line, then don't worry, it's not that difficult. It might seem strange at first, but after a while, you'll soon be wondering how you coped without it!

You can find this on Mac OS in *Applications -> Utilities -> Terminal*, or use Spotlight to search for *Terminal*. Type the command into this window and hit *Return* to run it.

On Windows, you access it by entering *cmd* in the *Start* menu.

If you're using Linux, I assume you're already comfortable with opening and using the command line!

Step 1: Install Build Tools

If you have a Mac, you'll need to install the Xcode command line tools by running the following command:

```
xcode-select --install
```

If you're using Linux, you'll need to install the "build-essential" package. This can be done by running the following commands on Debian-based distros (use your package manager of choice with other distros):

```
sudo apt-get update
sudo apt-get install build-essential
```

Step 2: Install nvm

To install nvm, simply run the following command:

```
curl -o-
↪ https://raw.githubusercontent.com/creationix/nvm/v0.31.0/
install.sh
↪ | bash
```

Now that nvm is installed, you'll need to reload your shell, before you can install Node. This can be done using the following command in Mac Os:

```
. ~/.bash_profile
```

Or by using the following command in Linux:

```
. ~/.bashrc
```

Now you can install the latest version of Node with the following command:

```
nvm install node
```

You might have to wait a while for everything to download and install, but once it's finished, you can check everything is working properly by entering the following command:

```
node -v
```

This returns the version number of Node that is installed.

You can use nvm to install multiple different versions of Node, as well as using it to switch from one version to the other. [5].

[5.] You can find out more about it by reading https://www.sitepoint.com/quick-tip-multiple-versions-node-nvm/">https://www.sitepoint.com/quick-tip-multiple-versions-node-nvm/

JavaScript In The Console

A console is a useful tool for experimenting and testing out pieces of code. It allows you to enter code, then it displays the output after you press *Enter*. This is different from a full JavaScript program that contains many lines of code that are interpreted at the same time. A console lets you see the results of each line of code as it is entered and is perfect for trying out small snippets of code. We'll often use the console to demonstrate many of the examples in this book.

There are three options available to use a console:

1. If you installed Node, you can use the REPL, which stands for Read Eval Print Loop. It allows you to write JavaScript in the console then outputs the results. To start the REPL, all you need to do is open up a terminal prompt and enter the command `node`.

This should then display a prompt like the one shown in the screenshot below:

1-1. The REPL

To exit the REPL, simply hold the *ctrl* key and hit *C* twice.

1. Another option is to use the JavaScript console that comes with your browser. You can access the console by opening your browser and pressing F12 (or

Command + Option + I on a Mac) to open the developer tools then clicking on the *Console* tab. It should look similar to the screenshot below:

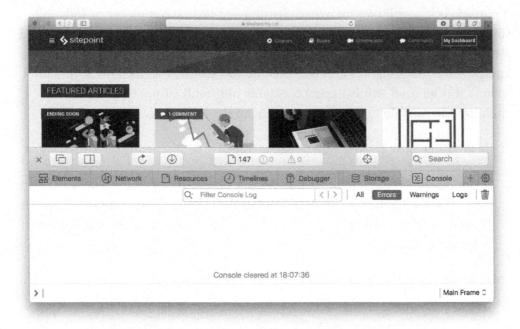

1-2. Browser Console

1. The last option is to use the E66 Console[6] website. This allows you to enter JavaScript commands directly into the browser and see the results. It also lets you write in ES6 and see what it looks like after it has been transpiled into ES5.

[6.] http://es6console.com

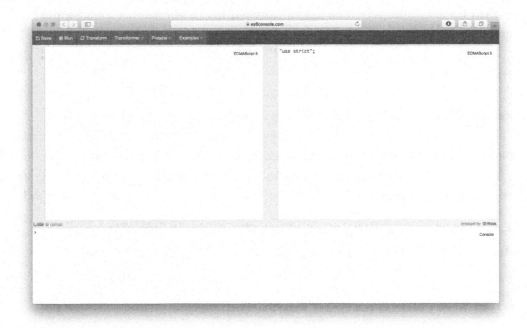

1-3. ES6 Console

Text Editors

One of the best things about programming in JavaScript is that you don't need any fancy and expensive programs to write the code – just a simple text editor.

The default text editor that comes with your operating system (such as Notepad on Windows) will work just fine, although you might want to upgrade to a text editor that is geared towards programming. These offer extra features such as code highlighting, code completion and file browsing without using too much of your system's resources. There are a number of good free options available, including Atom text editor[7] and Brackets[8] (which is actually built using JavaScript!).

Another option is to use an Integrated Development Environment (IDE). These usually have more features than text editors, but they could be considered

---

[7.] https://atom.io/
[8.] http://brackets.io/

overkill for small projects. The community edition of Microsoft Visual Studio[9] is a good option that is also free to use.

Online Options

CodePen[10], JSFiddle[11] and JS Bin[12] are all online services that let you enter HTML, CSS and JavaScript code and view the results. They even allow you to use pre-processors on your JavaScript and CSS. This means you can write your code using the most up-to-date version of JavaScript and it will still work, even if your browser doesn't support it. They also let you save all your creations in the cloud.

Many of the examples in this book have been saved on CodePen, so you can take a look at the code as well as saving your own copy to play around with.

Your First JavaScript Program

That's enough talk about JavaScript! Let's write your first program.

It is a tradition when learning programming languages to start with a "Hello world!" program. This is a simple program that outputs the phrase "Hello world!" to announce your arrival to the world of programming. We're going to stick to this tradition and write a "Hello world" program in JavaScript. It will be a single statement that logs the phrase "Hello world!" to the console.

To get started, you'll need to open up your preferred console (either the Node REPL, browser console, or ES6 Console[13] on the web). Once the console has opened, all you need to do is enter the following code:

```
console.log('Hello world!');
```

---

9. https://www.visualstudio.com
10. http://codepen.io
11. https://jsfiddle.net/
12. https://jsbin.com
13. http://es6console.co

Then press *Enter*. if all went to plan you should see an output of 'Hello world!' displayed; similar to the screenshot below.

1-4. "Hello, world!"

Congratulations, you've just written your first JavaScript program! It might not look like much, but a wise person once said that every ninja programmer's journey begins with a single line of code (or something like that, anyway!).

JavaScript in the Browser

JavaScript is an interpreted language and needs a host environment to run. Because of its origins, the main environment that JavaScript runs in is the browser, although it can be run in other environments; for example, our first program that we just wrote ran in the Node REPL. Node can also be used to run JavaScript on a server. By far the most common use of JavaScript is still to make web pages interactive. Because of this, we should have a look at what makes up a web page before we go any further.

Three Layers of the Web

Nearly all web pages are made up of three key ingredients — HTML, CSS and JavaScript. HTML is used to mark up the content. CSS is the presentation layer, and JavaScript adds the interactivity.

Each layer builds on the last. A web page should be able to function with just the HTML layer — in fact, many websites celebrate "naked day"[14] when they remove the CSS layer from their site. A website using just the HTML layer will be in its purest form and look very old school, but should still be fully functional.

 Keep These Layers Separate

It is widely considered best practice to separate the concerns of each layer, so each layer is only responsible for one thing. Putting them altogether can lead to very complicated pages where all of the code is mixed up together in one file, causing "tag soup" or "code spaghetti". This used to be the standard way of producing a website and there are still plenty of examples on the web that do this.

Unobtrusive JavaScript

When JavaScript was initially used, it was designed to be inserted directly into the HTML code, as can be seen in this example that will display a message when a button is clicked:

```
<button id='button' href='#' onclick='alert("Hello
↳ World")'>Click Me</a>
```

This made it difficult to see what was happening, as the JavaScript code was mixed up with the HTML. It also meant the code was tightly coupled to the HTML, so any changes in the HTML required the JavaScript code to also be changed to stop it breaking.

---

14. https://css-naked-day.github.io/

It's possible to keep the JavaScript code away from the rest of the HTML by placing it inside its own `<script>` tags. The following code will achieve the same result as that above:

```
<script>
const btn = document.getElementById('link')
btn.addEventListener('click', function() {
    alert('Hello World!');
    };
</script>
```

This is better because all the JavaScript is in one place, between the two script tags, instead of mixed with the HTML tags.

We can go one step further and keep the JavaScript code completely separate from the HTML and CSS in its own file. This can be linked to using the `src` attribute in the `script` tag to specify the file to link to:

```
<script src='main.js'></script>
```

The JavaScript code would then be placed in a file called `main.js` inside the same directory as the HTML document. This concept of keeping the JavaScript code completely separate is one of the core principles of *unobtrusive JavaScript*[15].

In a similar way, the CSS should also be kept in a separate file, so the only code in a web page is the actual HTML with links to the CSS and JavaScript files. This is generally considered best practice and is the approach we'll be using in the book.

[15.] https://en.wikipedia.org/wiki/Unobtrusive_JavaScript

Self-Closing Tags

If you've used XML or XHTML, you might have come across self-closing tags such as this script tag:

```
<script src='main.js' />
```

These will fail to work in HTML5, so should be avoided.

You may see some legacy code that uses the language attribute:

```
 <script src='main.js'
↪ language='javascript'></script>
```

This is unnecessary in HTML5, but it will still work.

Graceful Degradation and Progressive Enhancement

Graceful degradation is the process of building a website so it works best in a modern browser that uses JavaScript, but still works to a reasonable standard in older browsers, or if JavaScript or some of its features are unavailable. An example of this are programs that are broadcast in high definition (HD) — they work best on HD televisions but still work on a standard TV; it's just the picture will be of a lesser quality. The programs will even work on a black-and-white television.

Progressive enhancement is the process of building a web page from the ground up with a base level of functionality, then adding extra enhancements if they are available in the browser. This should feel natural if you follow the principle of three layers, with the JavaScript layer enhancing the web page rather than being an essential element that the page cannot exist without. An example might be the phone companies who offer a basic level of phone calls, but provide extra services such as call-waiting and caller ID if your telephone supports it.

Whenever you add JavaScript to a web page, you should always think about the approach you want to take. Do you want to start with lots of amazing effects that push the boundaries, then make sure the experience degrades gracefully for those who might not have the latest and greatest browsers? Or do you want to start off building a functional website that works across most browsers, then enhance the experience using JavaScript? The two approaches are similar, but subtly different.[16]

Your Second JavaScript Program

We're going to finish the chapter with a second JavaScript program that will run in the browser. This example is more complicated than the previous one and includes a lot of concepts that will be covered in later chapters in more depth, so don't worry if you don't understand everything at this stage! The idea is to show you what JavaScript is capable of, and introduce some of the important concepts that will be covered in the upcoming chapters.

We'll follow the practice of unobtrusive JavaScript mentioned earlier and keep our JavaScript code in a separate file. Start by creating a folder called `rainbow`. Inside that folder create a file called `rainbow.html` and another called `main.js`.

Let's start with the HTML. Open up `rainbow.html` and enter the following code:

```html
<head>
<meta charset='utf-8'>
<title>I Can Click A Rainbow</title>
</head>
<body>
<button id='button'>click me</button>
<script src='main.js'></script>
</body>
</html>
```

This file is a fairly standard HTML5 page that contains a button with an ID of `button`. The ID attribute is very useful for JavaScript to use as a hook to access different elements of the page. At the bottom is a `script` tag that links to our JavaScript file.

[16.] http://www.sitepoint.com/progressive-enhancement-graceful-degradation-choice/ might help you to decide which approach to take.

Now for the JavaScript. Open up `main.js` and enter the following code:

```
const btn = document.getElementById('button');

 const rainbow =
↳
['red','orange','yellow','green','blue','rebeccapurple','violet'];

function change() {
 document.body.style.background =
↳ rainbow[Math.floor(7*Math.random())];
}
btn.addEventListener('click', change);
```

Our first task in the JavaScript code is to create a variable called `btn` (we cover variables in Chapter 2).

We then use the `document.getElementById` function to find the HTML element with the ID of `btn` (Finding HTML elements is covered in Chapter 6). This is then assigned to the `btn` variable.

We now create another variable called `rainbow`. An array containing a list of strings of different colors is then assigned to the `rainbow` variable (we cover strings and variables in Chapter 2 and arrays in Chapter 3).

Then we create a function called `change` (we cover functions in Chapter 4). This sets the background color of the body element to one of the colors of the rainbow (changing the style of a page will be covered in Chapter 6). This involves selecting a random number using the built-in `Math` object (covered in Chapter 5) and selecting the corresponding color from the `rainbow` array.

Last of all, we create an *event handler*, which checks for when the button is clicked on. When this happens it calls the `change` function that we just defined (event handlers are covered in Chapter 7).

Open `rainbow.html` in your favorite browser and try clicking on the button a few times. If everything is working correctly, the background should change to every color of the rainbow, such as in the screenshot below.

1-5. I can click a rainbow

If you want to try this out quickly, you can checkout the code on CodePen[17]. For the sake of getting some practice in though, I would recommend you also take the time to create these files, write up the code by hand and try running it in your browser as well. [18]

Don't Break the Web

An important concept in the development of the JavaScript language is that it has to be **backward compatible**. That is, all old code must work the same way when interpreted by an engine running a new specification (it's a bit like saying that PlayStation 4 must still be able to run games created for PlayStation 1, 2 and 3). This is to prevent JavaScript from "breaking the web" by making drastic changes that would mean legacy code on some websites not running as expected in modern browsers.

[17.] http://codepen.io/daz4126/pen/VPRdGa

[18.] rebeccapurple is the official name for the color with a hex code of #663399. It is named after web designer Eric Meyer's daughter, who tragically died, aged just six years old. This was her favorite color, and it was added to the official list of CSS colors as a tribute to her.

So new versions of JavaScript can't do anything that isn't already possible in previous versions of the language. All that changes is the notation used to implement a particular feature to make it easier to write. This is known as *syntactic sugar*, as it allows an existing piece of code to be written in a nicer and more succinct way.

The fact that all versions of JavaScript are backwardly compatible means that we can use **transpilers** to convert code from one version of JavaScript into another. For example, you could write your code using the most up-to-date version of JavaScript and then transpile it into version 5 code, which would work in virtually any browser.

A new version of ECMAScript every year means it's likely that browsers will always be slightly when it comes to implementing the latest features (they're getting faster at doing this, but it's still taken two years for most browsers to support ES6 modules). This means that if you want to use the most up-to-date coding techniques, you'll probably have to rely on using a transpiler, such as Babel[19], at some point.

If you find that some code isn't working in your browser, you can add the following link into your HTML document:

```
<script
↪ src='https://unpkg.com/babel-standalone@6/babel.min.js'></script>
```

Note that this link needs to go *before* any JavaScript that needs to be transpiled.

You also have to change the `type` attribute to `text/babel` in any links to JavaScript files. For example, the link to the JavaScript file in the example above would change to:

```
<script type='text/babel'
↪ src='main.js'></script>
```

[19.] https://babeljs.io

This isn't the best long-term solution as it requires the browser to transpile all the code at run-time, although it's fine for experimenting with code. A better solution is to transpile your code as part of a build process, which is covered in Chapter 15.

A number of online editors such as CodePen[20], Babel REPL[21] and JS Fiddle[22] allow you to transpile code in the browser.[23]

The Project: Quiz Ninja

Throughout this book we will be building an example application called "Quiz Ninja". This is a quiz application where the aim is for the player to answer questions about the real names of super heroes. The quiz application will run in the browser and use many of the concepts covered in the book. At the end of each chapter we'll use the skills we have covered in that chapter to develop the application further.

The application will adhere to the principles of three separate web layers and unobtrusive JavaScript. So we need to keep the HTML, CSS and JavaScript in separate files. Let's create those files now.

Create a folder called `quiz`, and inside that create the following files:

- `index.html`

- `main.js`

- `styles.css`

Add the following code to `index.html`:

[20.] http://codepen.io
[21.] https://babeljs.io/repl
[22.] https://jsfiddle.net
[23.] The ECMAScript 6 compatibility table (http://kangax.github.io/compat-table/es6/) also contains up-to-date information about which features have been implemented in various transpilers.

```
<!doctype html>
<html lang='en'>
<head>
<meta charset='utf-8'>
 <meta name='description' content='A JavaScript Quiz
↪ Game'>
<title>Quiz Ninja</title>
<link rel='stylesheet' href='styles.css'>
</head>
<body>
    <section class='dojo'>
    <div class='quiz-body'>
        <header>
        <h1>Quiz Ninja!</h1>
        </header>
    </div>
    </section>
<script src='main.js'></script>
</body>
</html>
```

This is a standard HTML5 layout with a simple heading at the top of the page.
We'll add more to the page as the application develops in later chapters.

Now it's time to style the page. Add the following code to the **styles.css** file:

```
@import
↪ url('https://fonts.googleapis.com/css?family=Baloo+Da|Roboto');

body{
background: #5F1C1C;
font-family: 'Roboto', sans-serif;
}
.dojo{
 background:
↪ url(https://cdn.rawgit.com/alexmwalker/
6acbe9040d9fe6e5e9fd758a25e1b2a5/raw/
9c8131eb2ccc1e3839a5a5114cb16b5dc74daf04/dojo.svg)
```

```css
↳ no-repeat;
width: 100%;
height: 800px;
background-size: 100% auto;
padding-top: 10px;
}
.quiz-body{
background: rgba(255,255,255,1);
margin: 150px 33%;
padding: 10px 20px 50px 20px;
-webkit-box-shadow: 4px 4px 11px 3px rgba(0,0,0,0.3);
 moz-box-shadow: 4px 4px 11px 3px rgba(0,0,0,0.3);
box-shadow: 4px 4px 11px 3px rgba(0,0,0,0.3);
}
h1{
color: #611BBD;
font-family: 'Baloo Da', cursive;
font-weight: 900;
text-align: center;
font-size: 48px;
margin: 0;
}
button {
color: #ffffff;
background-color: #611BBD;
border-color: #130269;
border-radius: 4px;
margin: 0.2em 0;
display: block;
width: 100%;
font-size: 24px;
}
#question {
font-size: 24px;
}

#result{
color: #fff;
margin: 0.2em 0;
width: 100%;
```

```
text-align: center;
}
.correct {
    background-color: #0c0;
}
.wrong {
color: #fff;
background-color: #c00;
}
```

This file covers all the styles that will be used throughout the project, so quite a few of the styles aren't used at first, but it means we won't need to edit this file again in the book.

And finally we'll add some interactivity using JavaScript. Place the following code inside the `main.js` file:

```
alert('Welcome to Quiz Ninja!');
```

The first line uses the `alert()` function that displays a welcome message to the player in a dialog box in the browser. Although `alert` isn't actually part of the official ECMAScript specification, it's used by all browsers as a way of showing messages.

To give this a try, open the `index.html` file in your favorite browser. You should be greeted by the welcome message alert box, such as in the screenshot below.

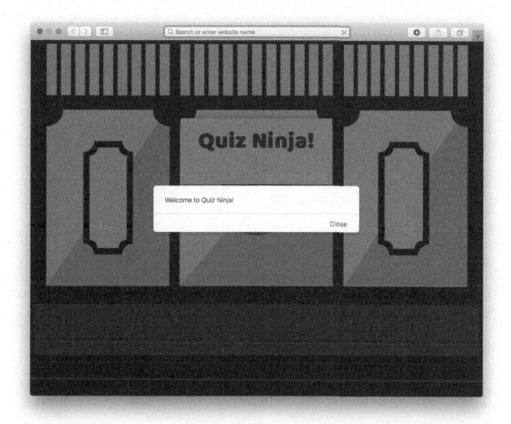

1-6. "Hello, world!"

You can also see a live example on CodePen[24].

This gives us a good solid start to our project that we can build on over the course of the book as our JavaScript knowledge develops.

Chapter Summary

■ JavaScript was created in 1995 by Brendan Eich, an employee of Netscape.

■ It quickly became popular and was soon considered to be the language of the web.

[24.] https://codepen.io/daz4126/pen/YNgvdG

- The browser wars caused many problems for JavaScript and resulted in lots of fragmented code that was hard to maintain.

- The advent of Ajax and its use in Web 2.0 apps, such as Gmail and Google Maps, prompted a resurgence in JavaScript.

- JavaScript's main environment is the browser, but can also be used in other environments.

- You only need a browser to write JavaScript but a good text editor or IDE and Node installation are recommended.

- Graceful degradation and progressive enhancement are the process of ensuring users receive a decent experience even if they lack some of the requirements.

- Unobtrusive JavaScript is when the JavaScript functionality is separated from the HTML content and CSS styling.

- Each new version of JavaScript has to be compatible with older versions.

- A transpiler can be used to convert code from one version of JavaScript into another. They are often used to transpile the latest version of the language into an older version that will work in most browsers.

In the next chapter we're going to start looking at some programming fundamentals — let's get to it, ninja!

Chapter

2

Programming Basics

In the last chapter, we introduced JavaScript, then set up a programming environment. We even got our hands dirty with a few JavaScript programs. In this chapter, we'll delve further and learn how JavaScript works, as well as write some more programs.

This chapter will cover the following topics:

- The importance of well-commented code

- JavaScript grammar — expressions, statements, semicolons and whitespace

- Primitive data types

- Strings — string literals, string properties and methods

- Declaring and assigning constants and variables

- Numbers — decimal, hexadecimal, octal, binary and exponent form, Infinity, and NaN

- Arithmetic operations such as +, -, *, /, and %

- Undefined and null

- Booleans — truthy and falsy values

- Logical operators — AND, OR, and NOT

- Our project — we'll set some question-and-answer variables and use alert boxes to display them

Comments

Our first task on our journey to becoming a JavaScript ninja is learning how to write comments in JavaScript. This may seem a strange place to start, because in programming, a comment is a piece of code that is ignored by the language — it doesn't do anything. Despite this, comments are extremely important: well-commented code is the hallmark of a ninja programmer. It makes it easier for anybody reading your code to understand what's going on, and that includes you! Believe me, you'll be thankful you commented your code when you come back to read it after a few weeks. You don't need to write an essay though, just enough so that it's clear what the code is supposed to do.

In JavaScript there are two types of comment:

- Single line comments starting with // and finishing at the end of the line:

```
// this is a short comment
```

- Multi-line comments starting with /* and finishing with */:

```
/* This is a longer comment
anything here will be ignored
```

```
This is a useful place to put notes
*/
```

It's good practice to write comments in your code. There are even utilities that can take your comments and produce documentation from them such as JSDoc Toolkit[1],Docco[2], and YUIDoc[3]. You'll see lots of comments throughout the code in this book.

JavaScript Grammar

The syntax used by JavaScript is known as a C-style syntax because of its similarities with the C programming language.

A JavaScript program is made up of a series of statements. Each statement ends with a new line or semicolon.

Here is an example of two statements, one on each line:

```
const message = 'Hello World!'
alert(message)
```

This example could also be written as follows, using semicolons at the end of each statement:

```
const message = 'Hello World!';alert(message);
```

There's no need to actually use a semicolon to terminate a statement because JavaScript interpreters use a process called Automatic Semicolon Insertion (ASI). This will attempt to place semicolons at the end of lines for you. However, it can be error-prone and cause a number of automated services such as code minifiers and validators to not work properly.

[1.] http://code.google.com/p/jsdoc-toolkit/
[2.] http://jashkenas.github.io/docco/
[3.] http://yui.github.io/yuidoc/

For this reason, it's considered best practice to combine the two and write each statement on a new line, terminated by a semi-colon, like so:

```
const message = 'Hello World!';
alert(message);
```

A block is a series of statements that are collected together inside curly braces:

```
{
// this is a block containing 2 statements
const message = 'Hello!';
alert(message);
}
```

Blocks do not need to be terminated by a semicolon.

Whitespace (such as spaces, tabs and new lines) is used to separate the different parts of each statement. You can use as much whitespace as required to format your code so it's neat and easy to read. Examples of this include using spaces to indent nested code and multiple lines to separate blocks of code.

Reserved Words

The following words are *reserved* for use by the JavaScript language and cannot be used to name variables (or function parameters and object properties that appear in later chapters):

```
abstract, await, boolean, break, byte, case, catch, char,
class, const, continue, debugger, default, delete, do,
double, else, enum, export, extends, false, final, finally,
float, for, function, goto, if, implements, import, in,
instanceof, int, interface, let, long, native, new, null,
package, private, protected, public, return, short, static,
super, switch, synchronized, this, throw, throws, transient,
```

```
true, try, typeof, var, volatile, void, while, with, yield
```

These words are reserved because many of them are used by the language itself, and you will come across them later in this book.

Some of the reserved words are not used by the language, however; one can only assume they were planned to be used at some point, but never were. There are also a few words *not* reserved but really should have been, as they are an important part of the language:

```
undefined, NaN, Infinity
```

These are covered later in this chapter and should be treated as if they were reserved words and avoided when naming variables, despite the fact that JavaScript may let you do it.

Primitive Data Types

JavaScript has seven different data types. Six of them are *primitive data types* and are listed below:

- String

- Symbol[4]

- Number

- Boolean

- Undefined

- Null

[4.] The symbol primitive data type was only introduced in ES6.

Any value that isn't one of the primitive data types listed above is an **object**. These include arrays, functions and object literals, which will be discussed in later chapters.

JavaScript has a special operator called `typeof` for finding out the type of a value.

Here are some examples of the different value types:

```
typeof 'hello'
<< 'string'

typeof 10
<< 'number'

typeof true
<< 'boolean'

typeof { ninja: 'turtle' }
<< 'object'

typeof [ 1, 2, 3 ]
<< 'object'
```

An operator applies an operation to a value, which is known as the *operand*. A unary operator only requires one operand; for example:

```
typeof 'hello'
```

The operator is `typeof` and the string 'hello' is the operand.

A binary operator requires two operands; for instance:

```
3 + 5
```

The operator is + and the numbers 3 and 5 are the operands.

There is also a ternary operator that requires three operands, which is covered in the next chapter.

Variables

Variables are used in programming languages to refer to a value stored in memory.

Declaring and Assigning

Variables have to be declared before they can be used. From ES6 onwards, JavaScript uses the keywords `const` and `let` to declare variables. The keyword `const` is used when the variable will not be reassigned to another value, whereas `let` is used if the variable might be reassigned later in the program.

To assign a value to a constant or variable, we use the = operator.

This example shows how we would declare a variable called name and assign the string literal 'Alexa' to it:

```
const name = 'Alexa'; // This won't be assigned to another
↪ string
```

This example shows how we would declare the variable score and assign it a value of the number literal 0:

```
let score = 0; // This value may change during the program
```

To see the value of a variable, simply enter it in the console and press enter.

```
name
<< 'Alexa'
```

The constant `name` now has a value of the string literal `Alexa`, so it will behave in exactly the same way. Any reference to `name` will be as if you had entered the string literal:

```
typeof name;
<< 'string'
```

This is a useful way of dealing with long strings or expressions as it saves us from typing them over and over again.

You can even declare and assign multiple variables at the same time if you separate them with commas:

```
let x = 3, y = 4, z = 5;
```

Variables that have been declared using the `let` keyword can be reassigned to another value at some point later in the program. This is done by simply putting them equal to the new value. For example, we would update the `score` variable to have a value of 5, like so:

```
score = 5;
```

In contrast, using `const` means you can't *reassign* the variable to another value. That means that if a variable is assigned to a primitive data type, then the value can't be changed, and will result in an error if you attempt to:

```
const name = 'Alexa';
name = 'Siri';
<< TypeError: Assignment to constant variable.
```

If the variable references a non-primitive data type, such as an array, function or object, then using `const` will not make it **immutable**. This means the underlying data inside the object *can* change (known as **mutating** the object). We can see this in the example below:

```
const name = { value: 'Alexa' }; // an object
name.value = 'Siri'; // change the value
<< 'Siri'
```

Don't worry if you don't quite follow the notation used in this example. We'll cover it in Chapter 5. The important thing to note is that the `value` property of the object referenced by the variable `name` was changed from Alexa to `Siri`.

This highlights an important point. Even if you use `const` to declare a variable, non-primitive data types can still be mutated later in the program.

Using `const` prevents you from reassigning a variable to another object, as it will produce an error, as illustrated below:

```
// declare object
const name = { value: 'Alexa' };

// attempt to reassign to another object
name = { value: 'Siri' }
<< TypeError: Assignment to constant variable.
```

It may seem like a restriction to use `const`, but it actually helps make your programs more predictable if the assignment to variables can't change. For this reason, you should try to use `const` to declare most variables. This helps to avoid any bugs caused by unexpected changes in assignment.

What happened to `var`?

In versions of JavaScript previous to ES6, variables were declared using the keyword `var`. The following code shows how a variable called `number` would be declared and assigned the value of 2:

```
var number = 2;
```

This worked in much the same way as using `let`. The main difference was that variables declared using `let` and `const` have block scope, which is discussed in more detail below. They also prevent you from overwriting any built-in methods by assignment, which is generally frowned upon, whereas using `var` doesn't.

So why was the new word `let` introduced into ES6? Why not just change the behavior of `var`?

Remember that a core tenet of the JavaScript language is that it has to remain backwardly compatible. This means that the behavior of `var` had to remain consistent, so couldn't just be changed in ES6. For that reason, the new keyword `let` was introduced.

You should be aware of `var` though, as you will see it used frequently in older code examples around the web to declare variables.

Scope

Using `const` and `let` to declare variables means they are *block scoped*, so their value only exists inside the block they are declared in.

Scope is an important concept in programming. It refers to where a constant or variable is accessible by the program. There are two common scopes that are often referred to in programs: global scope and local scope.

Global Scope

Any variable declared outside of a block is said to have **global scope**. This means it is accessible everywhere in the program. While this may seem to be a good idea at first, it is not considered good practice. A ninja programmer will try to keep the number of global variables to a minimum, because any variables that share the same name will clash and potentially overwrite each other's values. It might seem unlikely that this would happen, but it is all too common in large programs when you forget which variables you have used. There are also conventions where the same variable name is used in different situations. It can also be a problem when you are writing code in teams, or if you're using code libraries that may use the same variable names as some of your own code.

Local Scope

In ES6, blocks can be used to create a **local scope**. This means that any variables defined inside a block using the `let` or `const` will only be available inside that block and not be accessible outside of that block. This is known as having local scope, as the variable is only visible in the locality of the block.

If `let` or `const` are not used, the variable will have global scope and be available outside the block. This can be demonstrated in the following example, where the variable a can have two different values depending on whether it is defined inside or outside a block:

```
const a = 1;

{ const a = 3; a; }
<< 3
```

Now check the value of a outside the block:

```
a;
<< 1
```

In the example, a is initially defined globally outside the block and is given the value of 1. This means it has global scope and is available inside and outside the block. But then a is defined inside the `local` block using `let`. This gives it local scope inside the block where it has a value of 3, but it retains the value of 1 outside the block. For all intents and purposes, the two a variables are different variables.

Here's another example where we define a global variable and then overwrite it from within the block:

```
let b = 2;

{ b = 4; b; }
<< 4
```

Now check the value of b outside the block:

```
b;
<< 4
```

In this example, b is defined globally outside the block and given the value of 2. Then we reassign the value of b to 4 inside the block, but *without* using `let`. This means that it still refers to the global variable *outside* the block, so the value of b is the same both inside and outside the block and it gets overwritten globally to be a value of 4.

In the next example, we'll create a global variable from within a block that is then still accessible from outside of the block:

```
{ c = 5; c; }
<< 5
```

Now check the value of c outside the block:

```
c;
<< 5
```

In this example, c is defined inside the block, but because this is done without using `let` or `const`, it has global scope and is also available outside the block.

In the last example we'll create a local variable, d, inside a block that is not accessible outside the block:

```
{ const d = 6; d; }
<< 6
```

Now check the value of d outside the block:

```
d;
<< ReferenceError: d is not defined
```

In this example, d is defined inside the block, but by using const so it has local scope and is only accessible inside the block. When we try to log the value of d outside the block, it causes an error because d is not defined globally.

Using let or const to declare variables will ensure they are block scoped, and it is good practice to always use them to declare variables. In general, if a value is unlikely to change in your code then you should declare it using const, and let should only be used for storing values that will need to be reassigned while the program is running.

Naming Constants & Variables

When naming constants and variables, you should try to give them sensible names that describe what the variable represents; hence, answer is a better variable name than x.

Constant and variable names can start with any upper or lower-case letter, an underscore, _, or dollar character, $. They can also contain numbers, but cannot start with them.

Here are some valid examples:

```
$name
_answer
```

```
firstName
last_name
address_line1
```

 Variable Naming

Variables that start with an underscore generally refer to private properties and methods, so it's best to not follow this convention for your own variable names.

The $ character is also used by the popular jQuery library, so using this in your variable names may also cause problems.

Constant and variable names are case sensitive, so `ANSWER` is different to `Answer` and `answer`.

When using multiple words for constant and variable names there are two conventions:

Camel case starts with a lowercase letter and then each new word is capitalized:

```
firstNameAndLastName
```

Underscore separates each new word with an underscore:

```
first_name_and_last_name
```

JavaScript's built-in functions use the camel-case notation and this is probably the best convention to follow when naming the constants and variables in your code. The most important thing is to *be consistent*.

Direct Assignment and Assignment By Reference

When you assign a primitive value to a variable, any changes you make are made directly to that value:

```
const a = 1;
let b = a; // a = 1, b = 1

b = 2; // a = 1, b = 2
```

In the example above, a references the primitive number 1. We then assign b to the same value as a. At this point a and b both have the same value of 1. Then we reassign the value of 2 to b, but the a still has a value of 1.

But if you assign a non-primitive value to a variable, then this is done by *reference*, so any changes that are subsequently made will affect *all* references to that object:

```
const c = { value: 1 };
let d = c; // c.value = 1, d.value = 1
d.value = 2; // c.value = 2, d.value = 2
```

In the example above, the change to the `value` property of d also results in the `value` property of c changing as well. This is because the variables c and d are both referencing the *same* object, so any changes to one of them will also affect the other.

Strings

A string is a collection of characters, such as letters and symbols. We can create a string literal by writing a group of characters inside quote marks like this:

```
'hello'
```

Variables that start with an underscore, generally refer to private properties and methods, so it's best to not follow this convention for your own variable names.

The $ character is also used by the popular jQuery library, so using this in your variable names may also cause problems.

Using a Constructor Function

You can also create a string object using the following constructor function:

```
new String("hello")
<< [String: 'hello']
```

This will create a new string that is the same as the string literal `hello`, although it will be classed as an object rather than a primitive data type. For this reason it is preferable to use the string literal notation, not to mention it requires less typing to use literals!

The same string literal can be created using single quote marks:

```
'hello'
```

If you want to use double quote marks inside a string literal, you need to use single quote marks to enclose the string. And if you want to use an apostrophe in your string, you will need to use double quote marks to enclose the string, otherwise the apostrophe will terminate the string, causing an error:

```
'It's me' // causes an error
"It's me" // this works
```

Another option is to *escape* the quotation mark. You place a backslash before the apostrophe so it appears as an apostrophe inside the string instead of terminating the string:

```
'It\'s me'
```

Backslashes

The backslash is used to escape special characters in strings such as:

- Single quote marks \ '

- Double quote marks \ "

- End of line \n

- Carriage return \r

- Tab \t

If you want to actually write a backslash, you need to escape it with another backslash:

```
"This is a backslash \\"
<< "This is a backslash \"
```

String Properties and Methods

Primitive data types and objects have properties and methods. Properties are information about the object or value, while methods perform an action on the object or value — either to change it or to tell us something about it.

 Wrapper Objects

Technically, only objects have properties and methods. JavaScript overcomes this by creating *wrapper objects* for primitive data types. This all happens in the background, so for all intents and purposes it appears that primitive data types also have properties and methods.

We can access the properties of a string using dot notation. This involves writing a dot followed by the property we are interested in. For example, every string has a `length` property that tells us how many characters are in the string:

```
const name = 'Alexa'; // declare and assign a variable
<< 'Alexa'
```

```
name.length; // retrieve the name variable's length property
<< 5
```

As you can see, this tells us that there are five characters in the string stored in the name constant.

 Good Habits

> You may have noted that we're using the **const** keyword to declare the variable above. We also finished each line with a semicolon. Strictly speaking, this isn't really required for these short examples, but it's good practice and we'll be doing it in all the examples in the book. I would encourage you to do the same so you get yourself into a good habit. Believe me, it will be useful by the time we are writing larger, more complex applications later in the book.

An alternative notation you can use to access a primitive data type's properties are square brackets:

```
name['length']; // note the property name is in quote marks
<< 5
```

It's usually more common to use the dot notation due to it requiring less typing, although there are some occasions, which we'll come across later in the book, when the square bracket notation is preferable.

All properties of primitive data types are immutable, meaning they're unable to be changed. You can try, but your efforts will be futile:

```
name.length;
<< 5

name.length = 7; // try to change the length
<< 7

name.length; // check to see if it's changed
```

```
<< 5
```

A method is an action that a primitive data type or object can perform. To call a method, we use the dot operator (.) followed by the name of the method, followed by parentheses (this is a useful way to distinguish between a property and a method — methods end with parentheses). For example, we can write a string in all capital letters using the toUpperCase() method:

```
name.toUpperCase();
<< 'ALEXA'
```

Or the toLowerCase() method, which will write my name in all lower-case letters:

```
name.toLowerCase();
<< 'alexa'
```

If you want to know which character is at a certain position, you can use the charAt() method:

```
name.charAt(1);
<< 'l'
```

This tells us that the character l is at position 1. If you were thinking that it should be A, this is because the first letter is classed as being at position 0 (you'll find that counting usually starts at zero in programming!).

If you want to find where a certain character or substring appears in a string, we can use the indexOf() method:

```
name.indexOf('A');
<< 0
```

If a character doesn't appear in the string, -1 will be returned:

```
name.indexOf('z');
<< -1
```

If we want the last occurrence of a character or substring, we can use the
lastIndexOf() method:

```
name.lastIndexOf('a');
<< 4
```

If all we want to know if a string contains a certain character, then ES2016
provides the useful includes() method:

```
name.includes('a');
<< true

name.includes('z');
<< false
```

ES6 added a couple of methods to check if a string starts or ends in a particular
character.

To check if a string starts with a certain character, we can use the startsWith()
method. Be careful though, it's case-sensitive:

```
name.startsWith('A');
<< true

name.startsWith('a');
```

```
<< false
```

And we can use the similar endsWith() method to check if a string ends with a particular character:

```
name.endsWith('A');
<< false

name.endsWith('a');
<< true
```

The concat() method can be used to concatenate two or more strings together:

```
'JavaScript'.concat('Ninja');
<< 'JavaScriptNinja'

'Hello'.concat(' ','World','!');
<< 'Hello World!'
```

A shortcut for string concatenation is to use the + operator to add the two strings together:

```
'Java' + 'Script' + ' ' + 'Ninja';
<< 'JavaScript Ninja'
```

The trim() method will remove any whitespace from the beginning and end of a string:

```
'    Hello World    '.trim(); // the space in the middle
↪ will be preserved
<< 'Hello World'

'    \t\t  JavaScript Ninja! \r'.trim(); // escaped tabs and
```

```
↳ carriage returns are also removed
<< 'JavaScript Ninja!'
```

ES6 also introduced the `repeat()` method that will repeat a string the stated number of times:

```
'Hello'.repeat(2);
<< 'HelloHello'
```

Template Literals

Template literals are a special types of string that were introduced in ES6. Template literals use the backtick character, ` , to deliminate the string, as shown in the example below:

```
`Hello!`;
```

This has the advantage of being able to use both types of quote mark within the string:

```
`She said, "It's Me!"`
```

They also allow interpolation of JavaScript code. This means that a JavaScript expression can be inserted inside a string and the result will be displayed, as can be seen in the examples below:

```
const name = `Siri`;
`Hello ${ name }!`;
<< 'Hello Siri!'

const age = 39;
`I will be ${ age + 1 } next year`;
```

```
<< 'I will be 40 next year'
```

The JavaScript expression is placed inside the curly braces with a $ character in front of them. This is then evaluated and the result is returned in the string output.

Template literals can also contain line breaks, which are all converted into a Line Feed (\n):

```
`This is the start ...


.... and this is the end`
<< 'This is the start ...\n\n\n.... and this is the
↪ end'
```

If you want to place a backtick inside a template literal, then it needs to be escaped in the usual way, using a backslash:

```
`This character, \`, is a backtick`
<< 'This character, `, is a backtick'
```

Super-Powered Strings

Template literals can be thought of as super-powered strings as they behave in the same way as normal string literals, but with the extra power of string interpolation. For this reason, it is not uncommon to see backticks used to create *all* strings in ES6 code.

Symbols

Symbols were introduced as a new primitive value in ES6. They can be used to create unique values, which helps to avoid any naming collisions.

Symbols are the only primitives that don't have a literal form. The only way to create them is to use the `Symbol()` function:

```
const uniqueID = Symbol();
```

It is recommended to add a description of the symbol inside the parentheses:

```
const uniqueID = Symbol('this is a unique ID');
```

Because symbols are primitive values, the `typeof` operator should return a type of `symbol`:

```
typeof uniqueID;
<< 'symbol'
```

The description acts as a string representation of the symbol and is used to log the symbol in the console, making it useful for debugging purposes:

```
console.log(uniqueID);
<< Symbol(this is a unique ID)
```

You can manually access the description using the `String()` function:

```
String(uniqueID)
<< 'Symbol(this is a unique ID)'
```

It is possible for two variables to point to the *same* symbol if the `for()` method is used when the symbol is created:

```
const A = Symbol.for('shared symbol');
const B = Symbol.for('shared symbol');
```

The variables A and B now both point to the *same symbol* in memory. In this case the description shared symbol also acts as a shared identifier for the symbol.

The main use-case for symbols is as object property keys, which will be covered in Chapter 5. The uniqueness of symbols, mean that it's impossible for the names of any properties to clash with each other if they are symbols.[5]

Numbers

Numbers can be *integers* (whole numbers, such as 3) or *floating point numbers* (often referred to as just "decimals" or "floats", such as 3.14159). Here are a couple of examples of number literals:

```
typeof 42; // integer
<< 'number'

typeof 3.14159; // floating point decimal
<< 'number'
```

As you can see in the examples above, JavaScript doesn't distinguish between integers and floating point decimals — they are both given the type of number, which is a different approach to most other programming languages. This behavior is set out in the ECMAScript specification, but ES6 provides a handy method called Number.isInteger() that can be used to check if a number is an integer:

```
Number.isInteger(42);
<<< true
```

---

[5] https://www.sitepoint.com/preparing-ecmascript-6-symbols-uses/ contains more information about symbols.

```
Number.isInteger(3.142);
<< false
```

 Constructor Function for Numbers

Just like strings, numbers also have a constructor function:

```
new Number(3)
<< [Number: 3]
```

This is much more verbose than simply writing the number 3, which is known as a number literal, so it is recommended that you stick to using number literals.

Octal and Hexadecimal Numbers

If a number starts with a 0x, it is considered to be in hexadecimal (base 16) notation:

```
0xAF; // A represents 10, F represents 15
<< 175
```

Hexadecimal or "hex" numbers are often used for color codes on the Web.[6].

ES6 now supports octal literals: If a number starts with a zero, followed by the letter o, then it is considered to be in octal (base 8) notation:

```
0o47; // 4 eights and 7 units
<< 39
```

ES6 also supports binary literals: If a number starts with a zero, followed by the letter b then it is considered to be in binary (base 2) notation:

---

[6]. You can read more about them on Wikipedia: http://en.wikipedia.org/wiki/Hexadecimal

```
0b1010; // 1 eight, 0 fours, 1 two and 0 units
<< 10
```

Exponential Notation

Numbers can also be represented in exponential notation, which is shorthand for "multiply by 10 to the power of" (you may have heard this referred to as "scientific notation" or "standard form"). Here are some examples:

```
1e6; // means 1 multiplied by 10 to the power 6 (a million)
<< 1000000

2E3; // 2 multiplied by 10^3 (two thousand)
<< 2000
```

Decimal values can be created by using a negative index value:

```
 2.5e-3; // means 2.5 multiplied by 10 to the power -3
↪ (0.001)
<< 0.0025
```

Number Methods

Numbers also have some built-in methods, although you need to be careful when using the dot notation with number literals that are integers because JavaScript will confuse the dot with a decimal point. Don't worry though, there are a few ways to deal with this, which we'll demonstrate with the toExponential() method; this returns the number as a string in exponential notation.

Use two dots:

```
5..toExponential();
>> "5e+0"
```

Put a space before the dot:

```
5 .toExponential(); >> "5e+0"
```

Always write integers as a decimal:

```
5.0.toExponential(); >> "5e+0"
```

Place the integer in parentheses:

```
(5).toExponential(); >> "5e+0"
```

Assign the number to a constant:

```
const number = 5;
>> 5

number.toExponential();
>> "5e+0"
```

Now let's take a look at a couple of other number methods.

The `toFixed()` method rounds a number to a fixed number of decimal places:

```
const PI = 3.1415926;
<< undefined

 PI.toFixed(3); // only one dot is needed when using
↪ constants or variables
```

```
<< "3.142"
```

Note that the value is returned as a string, rather than a number.

The `toPrecision()` method rounds a number to a fixed number of significant figures that is once again returned as a string (and often using exponential notation):

```
325678..toPrecision(2);
<< "3.3e+5"

2.459.toPrecision(2);
<< "2.5"
```

Arithmetic Operations

All the usual arithmetic operations can be carried out in JavaScript.

Addition:

```
5 + 4.3;
<< 9.3
```

Subtraction:

```
6 - 11;
>> -5
```

Multiplication:

```
6 * 7;
<< 42
```

Division:

```
3/7;
<<0.42857142857142855
```

Exponentiation:

```
2**3; // introduced in ES2017
<< 8
```

You can also calculate the remainder of a division using the % operator:

```
 23%6; // the same as asking "what is the remainder when 13
↳ is divided by 6"
<< 5
```

This is similar to, but not quite the same as, modular arithmetic[7]. That's because the result always has the same sign as the first number:

```
-4%3; // -4 modulo 3 would be 2
<< -1
```

Changing The Value of Variables

If a variable has been assigned a numerical value, it can be increased using the following operation:

```
let points = 0; // initialize points score to zero
<< 0
```

[7.] https://en.wikipedia.org/wiki/Modular_arithmetic

```
points = points + 10;
<< 10
```

This will increase the value held in the `points` variable by 10.

A shorthand for doing this is to use the **compound assignment operator**, +=:

```
points += 10;
<< 20
```

There are equivalent compound assignment operators for all the operators in the previous section:

```
points -= 5; // decreases points by 5
<< 15

points *= 2; // doubles points
<< 30

points /= 3; // divides value of points by 3
<< 10

 points %= 7; // changes the value of points to the remainder
↳ if its current value is divided by 7
<< 3
```

Incrementing Values

If you only want to increment a value by 1, you can use the ++ operator. This goes either directly before or after the variable:

```
let points = 5;
points ++
```

```
<< 6
```

So what's the difference between putting the ++ operator before or after the
variable? The main difference is the value that is returned by the operation. Both
operations increase the value of the points variable by 1, but points++ will
return the original value *then* increase it by 1, whereas ++points will increase the
value by 1, then return the new value:

```
points++; // will return 6, then increase points to 7
<< 6

++points; // will increase points to 8, then return it
<< 8
```

There is also a -- operator that works in the same way:

```
points--; // returns 8, but has decreased points to 7
<< 8

--points; // decreases points to 6, then returns that value
<< 6
```

Infinity

Infinity is a special error value in JavaScript that is used to represent any
number that is too big for the language to deal with. The biggest number that
JavaScript can handle is 1.7976931348623157e+308:

```
1e308; // 1 with 308 zeroes!
<< 1e308

2e308; // too big!
<< Infinity
```

There is also a value -`Infinity`, which is used for negative numbers that go below -1.7976931348623157e+308:

```
-1e309;
<< -Infinity
```

The value of Infinity can also be obtained by dividing by zero:

```
1/0;
<< Infinity
```

The smallest number that JavaScript can deal with is 5e-324. Anything below this evaluates to either 5e-324 or zero:

```
5e-324; zero point (324 zeros) five
<< 5e-324

3e-325;
<< 5e-324

2e-325;
<< 0
```

NaN

`NaN` is an error value that is short for "Not a Number". It is used when an operation is attempted and the result isn't numerical, like if you try to multiply a string by a number, for example:

```
'hello' * 5;
<< NaN
```

The result returned by the `typeof` operator is rather ironic, however:

```
typeof NaN; // when is a number not a number?!?
<< 'number'
```

Checking a Value is a Number

You can check if a value is a number that can be used by using the
Number.isFinite() method. This will return true if the value is a number that
isn't Infinity, -Infinity or NaN:

```
Number.isFinite(1/0);
<< false

Number.isFinite(-Infinity);
<< false

Number.isFinite(NaN);
<< false

Number.isFinite(42);
<< true
```

Type Coercion

Type coercion happens when the operands of an operator are of different types. In
this case, JavaScript will attempt to convert one operand to an equivalent value of
the other operand's type. For example, if you try to multiply a string and a
number together, JavaScript will attempt to coerce the string into a number:

```
'2' * 8;
<< 16
```

This may seem useful, but the process is not always logical or consistent and can
cause a lot of confusion. For example, if you try to *add* a string and a number

together, JavaScript will convert the number to a string and then concatenate the two strings together:

```
'2' + 8;
<< '28'
```

This can make it difficult to spot type errors in your code. The best approach is to try to be very explicit about the types of values you are working with. If you need to change the type, then do it manually, rather than relying on type coercion to do it for you.

 JavaScript Is Weakly Typed

JavaScript is known as a **weakly typed** or **loosely typed** language. This means that you don't need to explicitly specify what data-type a variable is when you declare it. This can lead to unexpected behavior and hard to find bugs in code, particularly when type-coercion takes place in the background.

Strongly typed languages such as Java or Swift require the type of variables to be specified when they are declared. Trying to use the wrong data-type will cause an error.

TypeScript[8] is an open source superset of JavaScript that is maintained by Microsoft. It provides the option to specify the type of variables explicitly when they are declared, effectively making it a strongly typed version of JavaScript. It also adds some extra features and is designed to be make building large-scale applications easier in JavaScript. Programs are written in TypeScript and then transpiled into JavaScript.

Converting Between Strings and Numbers

We can convert numbers to strings and vice versa using a variety of methods.

[8.] http://www.typescriptlang.org

Converting Strings to Numbers

The best way to change a string to a number is to use the `Number` method. This will convert the string form of a number into an actual number:

```
Number('23');
<< 23
```

This is the preferred way to convert strings to numbers as it avoids type coercion in the background. The conversion is also explicit and makes it obvious what is being done.

If the string cannot be converted into a number, then `NaN` is returned:

```
Number('hello');
<<< NaN
```

There are a few tricks that can also be used to convert a string into a number that use type coercion. For example we can multiply a numerical string by 1, which will coerce it into a number:

```
const answer = '5' * 1;
<< 5

typeof answer;
<< "number"
```

Another trick is to simply place a + operator in front of it:

```
const answer = +'5';
<< 5

typeof answer;
```

```
<< 'number'
```

These methods are very hacky and not recommended, but you may see them used every now and then in code examples.

Converting Numbers to Strings

The preferred way of changing a number to a string is to use the `String` function:

```
String(3);
<< '3'
```

You can also use type coercion by "adding" an empty string, although this isn't recommended:

```
3 +'';
<< '3'
```

Another option is to use the `toString()` method:

```
10..toString();
<< '10'
```

This can also be used to change the base of the number. For example, if you want to write the number 10 in binary (base two), you could write:

```
10..toString(2);
<< '1010'
```

You can go up to base 36, although after base 10, letters are used to represent the digits:

```
> 28101..toString(36) // a million in base 36
<< 'lol'
```

Parsing Numbers

There is also a useful function called `parseInt()` that can be used to convert a string representation of a numerical value back into a number. You can specify the base of the number you are trying to convert, for example:

```
parseInt('1010',2); // converts from binary, back to decimal
<< 10

parseInt('omg',36);
<< 31912

parseInt('23',10);
<< 23
```

If a string starts with a number, the `parseInt` function will use this number and ignore any letters that come afterwards:

```
const address = '221B Baker Street';
parseInt(address, 10)
<< 221
```

This is different to the `Number` function, which returns `NaN`:

```
Number(address);
<< NaN
```

And if you use `parseInt` with a decimal, it will remove anything after the decimal point:

```
parseInt('2.4',10);
<< 2
```

Be careful not to think that this is rounding the number to the nearest integer; it simply removes the part after the decimal point, as seen in this example:

```
parseInt('2.9',10);
<< 2
```

There is also a similar function called `parseFloat()` that converts strings into floating point decimal numbers:

```
parseFloat('2.9',10);
<< 2.9
```

Undefined

`Undefined` is the value given to variables that have not been assigned a value. We've already seen it used earlier in this chapter when variables are declared without being assigned a value. It can also occur if an object's property doesn't exist or a function has a missing parameter. It is basically JavaScript's way of saying "I can't find a value for this."

Null

`Null` means "no value". It can be thought of as a placeholder that JavaScript uses to say "there should be a value here, but there isn't at the moment."

If this reminds you a lot of `undefined` then this is because they are both "non-value" values, meaning they are similar, but behave slightly differently. For example, if you try to do sums with them:

```
10 + null; // null behaves like zero
<< 10

10 + undefined; // undefined is not a number
<< NaN
```

null is coerced to be 0, making the sum possible whereas undefined is coerced to NaN, making the sum impossible to perform.

In general, values tend to be set to undefined by JavaScript, whereas values are usually set to null manually by the programmer.

Booleans

There are only two Boolean values: true and false. They are named after George Boole, an English mathematician who worked in the field of algebraic logic. Boolean values are fundamental in the logical statements that make up a computer program. Every value in JavaScript has a Boolean value and most of them are true (these are known as **truthy** values).

To find the Boolean value of something, you can use the Boolean function like so:

```
Boolean('hello');
<< true

Boolean(42);
<< true

Boolean(0);
<< false
```

Only 9 values are always false and these are known as **falsy** values:

```
* "" // double quoted empty string literal
* '' // single quoted empty string literal
```

```
* `` // empty template literal
* 0
* -0 // considered different to 0 by JavaScript!
* NaN
* false
* null
* undefined
```

 Truthy? Falsy?

The fact that empty strings and zero are considered falsy can be problomatic at times, especially since most other programming languages don't behave in the same way. For this reason, a ninja programmer needs to be especially careful when dealing with numbers that might be zero, or strings that are empty.[9]

Logical Operators

A logical operator can be used with any primitive value or object. The results are based on whether the values are considered to be truthy or falsy.

! (Logical NOT)

Placing the ! operator in front of a value will convert it to a Boolean and return the opposite value. So truthy values will return `false`, and falsy values will return `true`. This is known as *negation*:

```
!true; // negating true returns false
<< false

!0; // 0 is falsy, so negating it returns true
<< true
```

[9] For more on truthy and falsy values, see http://www.sitepoint.com/javascript-truthy-falsy/

You can use double negation (!!) to find out if a value is truthy or falsy (it is a shortcut to using the `Boolean` function we employed earlier because you are effectively negating the negation):

```
!!'';
<< false

!!"hello";
<< true

!!3;
<< true

!!NaN;
<< false

!!"false";
<< true

!!'0';
<< true
```

&& (Logical AND)

Imagine a nightclub that only allows people inside if they are wearing shoes AND over 18. This is an example of a logical AND condition: anybody going into the club must satisfy *both* conditions before they are allowed in.

The logical AND operator works on two or more values (the operands) and only evaluates to `true` if *all* the operands are truthy. The value that is returned is the *last* truthy value if they are all true, or the *first* falsy value if at least one of them is false:

```
'shoes' && 18; // both values are truthy
<< 18

'shoes' && 0; // returns 0 because it is falsy
```

```
<< 0
```

|| (Logical OR)

Now imagine that the club relaxes its rules and allows people in if they wear shoes OR they're over 18. This means they only have to satisfy one of the rules to be allowed in. This is an example of a logical OR condition.

The logical OR operator also works on two or more operands, but evaluates to true if *any* of the operands are true, so it only evaluates to false if both operands are falsy. The value that is returned is the *first* truthy value if any of them are true, or the *last* falsy value if all of them are false:

```
'shoes' || 0;
<< 'shoes'

 NaN || undefined;  // both NaN and undefined are falsy, so
↪ undefined will be returned
<< undefined
```

Lazy Evaluation

Remember the rule that people going to the nightclub had to wear shoes *and* be over 21? If a bouncer saw somebody wasn't wearing shoes, there'd be no point in asking them for ID to check their age they wouldn't be allowed in anyway.

When the rules were relaxed, people were allowed in if they were wearing shoes *or* if if they were over 18. If somebody arrived wearing shoes, there would be no need for a bouncer to check their age, since only one of the conditions needed to be met.

These are examples of lazy evaluation — you only check the minimum number of criteria that needs to be met. JavaScript performs a similar task and uses lazy evaluation when processing the logical AND and OR operators. This means it stops evaluating any further operands once the result is clear.

For example, for a logical AND expression to be `true`, all the operands have to be true; if any of them are `false`, there is no point checking any subsequent operands as the result will still be false. Similarly, for a logical OR to be `true`, only one of the operands has to be true; hence, as soon as an operand is evaluated to `true`, the result is returned as `true` and any subsequent operands won't be checked as the result is of no consequence.

An example of this being used is when the operands are used for assignment. You have to be aware that some assignments might not be made because JavaScript will not bother evaluating all of the operands.

This can be seen in the examples below:

```
let a = 0; // declare the variable a and assign the value of
↪ 0
<< 0

false && (a = 1); // (a = 1) is truthy, but it won't
↪ be evaluated, since the first operand is false
<< false

a // the value of a is still 0
<< 0

false || (a = 1); // this will evaluate both operands, so a
↪ will be assigned the value of 1, which is returned
<< 1
```

Bitwise Operators

Bitwise operators work with operands that are 32-bit integers. These are numbers written in binary (base two) that have 32 digits made up of just 0s and 1s. Here are some examples:

```
5 is written as    00000000000000000000000000000101
100 is written as  00000000000000000000000001100100
```

```
15 is written as   00000000000000000000000000001111
```

JavaScript will convert any values used with bitwise operators into a 32-bit integer then carry out the operation. It then changes it back into a base 10 integer to display the return value.

Bitwise operators tend to only be used for low-level programming tasks or applications that require a number of on-off states. They are unlikely to be used often, but are included here for completeness.

Bitwise NOT

The bitwise NOT operator ~ will convert the number to a 32-bit integer, then change all the 1s to 0 and all the 0s to 1s. It then returns the new value as an integer.

For example, 2476 can be represented as:

```
00000000000000000000100110101100
```

Which will change to:

```
11111111111111111111011001010011
```

This is 4294964819, but the result actually uses negative values, as you can see in the code:

```
~2476;
<< -2477
```

This means that in most cases, this operator will return an integer that adds to the original operand to make -1.

Bitwise AND

The bitwise AND operator, &, will convert both numbers into binary, and returns a number that in binary has a 1 in each position for which the corresponding bits of both operands are 1s. Here's an example:

```
12 & 10; // in binary this is 1100 & 1010, so only
↪ the first digit is 1 in both cases. This returns 1000, which
↪ is 8 in binary
<< 8
```

Bitwise OR

There is also the bitwise OR operator, |, which will convert both numbers into binary and return a number that in binary has a 1 in each position for which the corresponding bits of either operands are 1s. Here's an example:

```
12 | 10; // in binary this is 1100 & 1010, so the first
↪ 3 digits contain a 1, returning 1110, which is 14 in binary
<< 14
```

Bitwise XOR

Another operation is the bitwise XOR operator, ^, which stands for "eXclusive OR". This will convert both numbers into binary and return a number that in binary has a 1 in each position for which the corresponding bits of either operands are 1s, but not both 1s. Here's an example:

```
12 ^ 10; // in binary this is 1100 & 1010, so only the
↪ second and third digits are exclusively 1s, so 0110 is
↪ returned, which is 6 in binary
<< 6
```

Don't use ^ to notate exponents

The ^ character is often used as an informal notation for exponents, so be careful not to use this mistakenly when programming in JavaScript. For example 2^3 will *not* return 8. There is a specific `Math` method for doing this that is covered in Chapter 5, and ES2017 introduced the exponent operator **, that allows you to write it as 2**3.

When using non-integer values, this evaluates to 1 if *either* operands are truthy and evaluates to 0 if both operands are truthy or both are falsy:

```
1 ^ 0; // The first operand is truthy
<< 1

 true ^ true; // if both operands are true then the result is
↪ false
<< 0
```

Bitwise Shift Operators

The bitwise shift operators, << and >>, will move the binary representation a given number of places to the right or left, which effectively multiplies or divides the number by powers of two:

```
3 << 1; // multiply by 2
<< 6

16 >> 1; // divide by 2
<< 8

5 << 3; multiply by 2 cubed (8)
<< 40
```

More information about bitwise operators can be found on the Mozilla Developer Network.[10]

Comparison

We often need to compare values when programming. JavaScript has several ways to compare two values.

Equality

Remember earlier, when we assigned a value to a variable? We used the = operator to do this, which would be the logical choice for testing if two values are equal.

Unfortunately, we can't use it because it's used for assigning values to variables. For example, say we had a variable called answer and we wanted to check if it was equal to 5, we might try doing this:

```
const answer = 5;
<< 5
```

What we've actually done is *assign* the value of 5 to the variable answer, effectively overwriting the previous value!

The correct way to check for equality is to use either a double equals operator, ==, known as "soft equality" or the triple equals operator, ===, known as "hard equality".

Soft Equality

We can check if answer is in fact equal to 5 using the soft, or lenient, equality operator ==, like so:

```
answer == 5;
<< true
```

[10.] https://developer.mozilla.org/en/docs/Web/JavaScript/Reference/Operators/Bitwise_Operators

This seems to work fine, but unfortunately there are some slight problems when using soft equality:

```
answer == "5";
<< true
```

As you can see, JavaScript is returning true when we are checking if the variable answer is equal to the *string* "5", when in fact answer is equal to the *number* 5. This is an important difference, but when a soft inequality is used, JavaScript doesn't take into account the data type and will attempt to coerce the two values to the same type when doing the comparison. This can lead to some very strange results:

```
" " == 0;
<< true

" " == "0";
<< false

false == "0";
<< true

"1" == true;
<< true

"2" == true;
<< false

"true" == true;
<< false

null == undefined;
<< true
```

As you can see, some values that are not actually equal to each other have a tendency to be reported as being equal when using the soft equality operator.

Hard Equality

The hard, or strict, equality operator, ===, tests for equality but only returns true if and only if they are of the same data type:

```
answer === 5;
<< true

answer === '5';
<< false

null === undefined;
<< false
```

As you can see, hard equality reports that the variable answer is the number 5, but not the string "5". It also correctly reports that null and undefined are two different values.

Hard Equality's One Quirk

The only strange result produced by hard equality is this:

```
NaN === NaN;
<< false
```

NaN is the only value in JavaScript that is not equal to itself! To deal with this, there is a special Number method called **Number.isNaN()** to test it:

```
Number.isNaN(NaN);
<< true

Number.isNaN(5);
<< false
```

The **Number.isNaN()** method is new to ES6 and replaces the global **isNaN()** method. This old method has the unfortunate property of reporting strings as NaN as well as NaN itself, as can be seen in the example below:

```
isNaN('hello');
<< true
```

This is because of our old nemesis, type coercion! The function first of all tries to convert the string to a number, and strings without numerals are converted to NaN:

```
Number('hello');
<< NaN
```

Because of this, the new **Number.isNaN()** method should always be used to check if a value is NaN.

A JavaScript ninja should always use hard equality when testing if two values are equal. This will avoid the problems caused by JavaScript's type coercion.

If you want to check whether a number represented by a string is equal to a number, you should convert it to a number yourself explicitly rather than relying on type coercion happening in the background:

```
Number('5') === 5
<< true
```

This can come in handy when you're checking values entered in a form as these are usually always submitted as strings.

Inequality

We can check if two values are *not* equal using the inequality operator. There is a soft inequality operator, != and a hard inequality operator, !==. These work in a similar way to the soft and hard equality operators:

```
16 != '16'; // type coercion makes these equal
<< false

16 !== '16';
<< true
```

As with equality, a ninja programmer should use the hard inequality operator as this will give more reliable results unaffected by type coercion.

Greater Than and Less Than

We can check if a value is greater than another using the > operator:

```
8 > 4;
<< true
```

You can also use the "less than" < operator in a similar way:

```
8 < 4;
<< false
```

If you want to check if a value is greater than *or equal* to another value, you can use the >= operator, :

```
8 >= 4;
<< true

8 >= 8;
<< true
```

But be careful; the equality test works in the same way as the soft equality operator:

```
8 >= '8';
<< true
```

As you can see, type coercion means that strings can be confused with numbers. Unfortunately, there are no "hard" greater-than or equal-to operators, so an alternative way to avoid type coercion is to use a combination of the greater-than operator, logical OR, and a hard equality:

```
8 > 8 || 8 === 8;
<< true

8 > '8' || 8 === '8';
<< false
```

There is also a similar "less-than or equal-to" operator:

```
-1 <= 1;
<< true

-1 <= -1;
<< true
```

These operators can also be used with strings, which will be alphabetically ordered to check if one string is "less than" the other:

```
'apples' < 'bananas';
>> true
```

Be careful, though, as the results are case-sensitive, and upper-case letters are considered to be "less than" lower-case letters:

```
'apples' < 'Bananas';
>> false
```

Quiz Ninja Project

Now that we have come to the end of the chapter, it's time to put what we've learned into practice in our Quiz Ninja project.

Since we've been learning all about JavaScript in this chapter, we're going to add some code in the `main.js` file. Open that file and add the following lines:

```
const question = "What is Superman's real name?"
const answer = prompt(question);
alert(`You answered ${answer}`);
```

Now let's go through this code line by line to see what is happening:

```
const question ="What is Superman's real name?";
```

This declares a variable called `question` and assigns the string `What is Superman's real name?` to it.

Next, we need to ask the question stored in the `question` variable, using a prompt dialog:

```
const answer = prompt(question);
```

A prompt dialog allows the player to type in a response, which is then stored in the variable it is assigned to, which is answer in this case.

Finally, we use an alert dialog to display the player's answer using string interpolation to insert the value of answer into the template literal that is displayed in an alert box:

```
alert(`You answered ${answer}`);
```

This shows the player the answer they provided. In the next chapter we'll look at how to check if it's correct.

Have a go at playing the quiz by opening the index.html file in your browser. It should look a little like the screenshot in below.

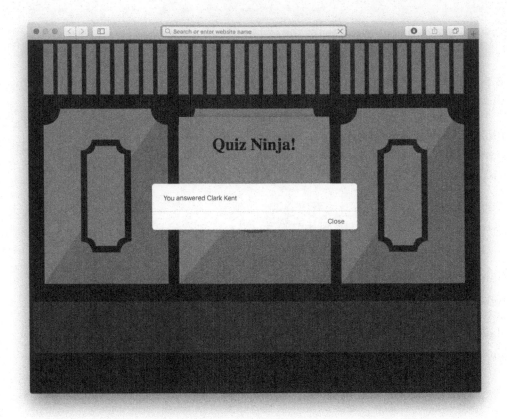

2-1. Let's play Quiz Ninja!

You can also see a live example on CodePen[11].

This is a good example of using the prompt and alert dialogs, along with variables to store the responses in to create some interactivity with the user.

Chapter Summary

- Comments are ignored by the program, but make your program easier to read and understand
- Data types are the basic building blocks of all JavaScript programs.
- There are six primitive data types: strings, symbols, numbers, Booleans, undefined and null.

---

11. https://codepen.io/daz4126/pen/OmapEN

- Non-primitive data types, such as arrays, functions and objects, all have a type of `object`.
- Variables point to values stored in memory and are declared using the `const` or `let` keywords.
- Values are assigned to variables using the = operator.
- Strings and numbers have various properties and methods that provide information about them.
- Symbols are unique, immutable values.
- Boolean values are either `true` or `false`.
- There are only seven values that are `false` in JavaScript and these are known as `falsy` values.
- Data types can be converted into other data types.
- Type coercion is when JavaScript tries to convert a value into another data type in order to perform an operation.
- Logical operators can be used to check if compound statements are true or false.
- Values can be compared to see if they are equal, greater than or less than other values.

In the next chapter, we'll be looking at data structures, logic, and loops.

Chapter

3

Arrays, Logic, and Loops

In this chapter we'll look at some of the data structures used in JavaScript to store lists of values. These are called arrays, sets, and maps. We'll also look at logical statements that allow us to control the flow of a program, as well as loops that allow us to repeat blocks of code over and over again.

This chapter will cover the following topics:

■ Array literals

■ Adding and removing values from arrays

■ Array methods

■ Sets

- Maps

- if and else statements

- switch statements

- while loops

- do … while loops

- for loops

- Iterating over a collection

- Project — we'll use arrays, loops and logic to ask multiple questions in our quiz

Arrays

An array is an ordered list of values. To create an array literal, simply write a pair of square brackets:

```
const myArray = [];
<< []
```

You can also use an array constructor function:

```
const myArray = new Array();
<< []
```

Both of these produce an empty array object, but it's preferable to stick to using array literals because of a variety of reasons[1] ... and they require less typing!

Arrays are not primitive values but a special built-in object, as we can see when we use the typeof operator:

[1.] http://stackoverflow.com/questions/885156/whats-wrong-with-var-x-new-array

```
typeof []
<< 'object'
```

You can read more about creating and manipulating arrays on SitePoint [2].

Initializing an Array

We can create an empty array literal called `heroes` with the following code:

```
const heroes = [];
```

We can find out the value of element 0 in the `heroes` array using the following code:

```
heroes[0]
<< undefined
```

To access a specific value in an array, we write its position in the array in square brackets (this is known as its index). If an element in an array is empty, `undefined` is returned.

Adding Values to Arrays

To place the string `Superman`inside the first element of our `heroes` array, we can assign it to element 0, like so:

```
heroes[0] = 'Superman';
```

Each item in an array can be treated like a variable. You can change the value using the assignment operator =. For example, we can change the value of the first item in the `heroes` array to `Batman`:

[2.] https://www.sitepoint.com/quick-tip-create-manipulate-arrays-in-javascript/

```
heroes[0] = 'Batman';
```

We can add more values to our array by assigning them to other indices:

```
heroes[1] = 'Wonder Woman';
heroes[2] = 'Flash';
```

We can use the index notation to add new items to any position in the `heroes` array:

```
heroes[5] = 'Aquaman';
```

We can look at the `heroes` array by simply typing its name into the console:

```
heroes;
 << ['Batman', 'Wonder Woman', 'Flash', undefined,
 ↪ undefined, 'Aquaman']
```

Here we can see that the sixth item (with an index of 5) has been filled with the string `Aquaman`. This has made the array longer than it was before, so all the other unused slots in the array are filled by the value `undefined`.

Creating Array Literals

We can create an array literal using square brackets that already contain some initial values, so there's no need to add each value one by one. Here's an example:

```
 const avengers = ['Captain America', 'Iron Man', 'Thor',
 ↪ 'Hulk'];
 << ['Captain America', 'Iron Man', 'Thor', 'Hulk']
```

You don't even have to use the same types of items inside an array. This array contains a variety different data types, as well as an empty array object:

```
const mixedArray = [ null, 1, [], 'two', true ];
```

Removing Values from Arrays

The `delete` operator will remove an item from an array:

```
delete avengers[3];
<< true
```

If we look at the `avengers` array, we can see that the fourth entry, 'Hulk' (with an index of 3), has indeed been removed ... but it has been replaced by a value of `undefined`:

```
avengers;
<< ['Captain America', 'Iron Man', 'Thor', undefined]
```

Watch out for this as it can even trip up experienced programmers. The *value* that was in position 3 ('Hulk') has been deleted from the array, but the space that it occupied is still there and contains a value of `undefined`. This means the array still has the same number of elements, and the position can still be referenced as an index, but it will just return `undefined`:

```
avengers[3];
<< undefined
```

Destructuring Arrays

Destructuring an array is the concept of taking values out of an array and presenting them as individual values.

Destructuring allows us to assign multiple values at the same time, using arrays:

```
const [x,y] = [1,2];
```

Even though the assignment is made using arrays, each individual variable exists on its own outside the array. We can see this by checking the value of each variable:

```
x
<< 1

y
<< 2
```

Destructuring also gives us a neat way of swapping the value of two variables over:

```
[x,y] = [y,x];
x
<< 2

y
<< 1
```

Before ES6, a temporary variable would have to be used to achieve the same result:

```
const temp = x;
x = y;
y = temp;
```

You can read more about destructuring on SitePoint[3].

[3.] https://www.sitepoint.com/preparing-ecmascript-6-destructuring-assignment/

Array Properties and Methods

Arrays are a powerful weapon in a JavaScript ninja's toolkit and have some useful methods. To demonstrate these, we're going to use the following `avengers` array that is similar to the one we produced earlier. You'll need to create a reference to it by entering the following into the console:

```
const avengers = ['Captain America', 'Iron Man', 'Thor',
↪ 'Hulk', 'Hawkeye', 'Black Widow'];
```

To find the length of an array, we can use the `length` property:

```
avengers.length;
<< 6
```

The `length` property can be used as part of the index to find the last item in an array:

```
avengers[avengers.length - 1];
<< 'Black Widow'
```

Notice that we have to subtract 1 from the `length` property. This is because the index starts at 0, so the last item in the array will have an index of one less than the array's length.

The `length` property is mutable, meaning you can manually change it:

```
avengers.length = 8;
<< 8

avengers
  << ['Captain America', 'Iron Man', 'Thor', 'Hulk',
↪ 'Hawkeye', 'Black Widow', undefined, undefined]
```

As you can see, if you make the array longer, the extra slots will be filled in with undefined:

```
avengers.length = 3
<< 3

avengers
<< ['Captain America', 'Iron Man', 'Thor']
```

If you make the array shorter than it already is, all the extra elements will be removed completely.

Pop, Push, Shift, and Unshift

To remove the last item from an array, we can use the pop() method:

```
avengers.pop();
<< 'Thor'
```

The method returns the last item of the array, but the array no longer contains that item. If we take a look at the avengers array, we'll see that it no longer contains the string Thor:

```
avengers
<< ['Captain America', 'Iron Man']
```

The shift() method works in a similar way to the pop() method, but this removes the *first* item in the array:

```
avengers.shift();
<< 'Captain America'
```

The push() method appends a new value to the end of the array.

```
avengers.push('Thor');
<< 2
```

The return value is the new length of the array:

The `unshift()` method is similar to the `push()` method, but this appends a new item to the *beginning* of the array:

```
avengers.unshift('Captain America');
<< 3
```

Merging Arrays

The `concat()` method can be used to merge an array with one or more arrays:

```
avengers.concat(['Hulk','Hawkeye', 'Black Widow']);
 << ['Captain America', 'Iron Man', 'Thor', 'Hulk',
 ↪ 'Hawkeye', 'Black Widow']
```

Note that this does not change the `avengers` array, it simply creates another array combining the two arrays. You can use assignment to update the `avengers` array to this new array:

```
 avengers = avengers.concat(['Hulk','Hawkeye', 'Black
 ↪ Widow']);
 << ['Captain America', 'Iron Man', 'Thor', 'Hulk',
 ↪ 'Hawkeye', 'Black Widow']
```

Now if we check the value of the `avengers` array we can see that it now contains the strings "Hulk", "Hawkeye" and "Black Widow":

```
avengers
 << ['Captain America', 'Iron Man', 'Thor', 'Hulk',
↪ 'Hawkeye', 'Black Widow']
```

An alternative is to use the new **spread** operator that was added to ES6. The spread operator is three dots, ... that are placed in front of an array, with the effect of spreading out the elements of that array. This can be used to spread the elements of two arrays and put them together in a new array, like so:

```
 avengers = [ ...avengers, ...['Hulk','Hawkeye', 'Black
↪ Widow'] ];
 << ['Captain America', 'Iron Man', 'Thor', 'Hulk',
↪ 'Hawkeye', 'Black Widow']
```

In the example above, the spread operator is used on the avengers array as well as the new array literal. This has the effect of spreading out all the values in each array, which allows them to be placed inside a new array.

The join() Method

The join() method can be used to turn the array into a string that comprises all the items in the array, separated by commas:

```
avengers.join();
 << 'Captain America, Iron Man, Thor, Hulk, Hawkeye,
↪ Black Widow'
```

You can choose a separator other than a comma by placing it inside the parentheses. Let's try using an ampersand:

```
avengers.join(' & ');
 << 'Captain America & Iron Man & Thor &
```

```
↳ Hulk & Hawkeye & Black Widow'
```

Slicing and Splicing

The slice() method creates a subarray; effectively chopping out a slice of an original array, starting at one position and finishing at another. For example, if we wanted to find the 3rd and 4th item in our array we would use the following code:

```
avengers.slice(2,4) // starts at the third item (index of 2)
↳ and finishes at the fourth (the item with index 4 is not
↳ included)
<< ['Thor', 'Hulk']
```

Note that this operation is non-destructive — no items are actually removed from the array, as we can see if we take a look at the avengers array:

```
avengers
  << ['Captain America', 'Iron Man', 'Thor', 'Hulk',
↳ 'Hawkeye', 'Black Widow']
```

The splice() method removes items from an array then inserts new items in their place. For example, the following code removes the string Hulk and replaces it with Scarlett Witch:

```
avengers.splice(3, 1, 'Scarlet Witch');
<< ['Hulk']
```

This is a destructive operation as it changes the value of the array, as we can see below:

```
avengers
 << ['Captain America', 'Iron Man', 'Thor', 'Scarlet
↳ Witch', 'Hawkeye', 'Black Widow']
```

The first number in the parentheses tells us the index at which to start the splice. In the example we started at index 3, which is the fourth item in the array (Hulk). The second number tells us how many items to remove from the array. In the example, this was just one item. Every value after this is then inserted into the array in the same place the other items were removed. In this case, the string Scarlett Witch is inserted into the array, starting at the fourth item. Notice the splice() method returns the items removed from the array as a subarray. So in the example, it returned the array ['Hulk'].

The splice() method can also be used to insert values into an array at a specific index without removing any items, by indicating that zero items are to be removed:

```
avengers.splice(4,0,'Quicksilver');
<< []
```

Notice that an empty array is returned (because nothing was removed), but the new value of Quicksilver has been inserted at position 4, which we can see if we look at the avengers array:

```
avengers
 << [ 'Captain America','Iron Man', 'Thor', 'Scarlet
↳ Witch', 'Quicksilver', 'Hawkeye', 'Black Widow' ]
```

The splice() method is a particularly flexible method as it can be used to insert or remove values from an array. Be careful, though, as splice() is a destructive method which means it changes the array permanently.

We saw earlier that we can use the delete operator to remove an item from an array. Unfortunately, this leaves a value of undefined in its place. If you want to remove a value completely, you can use the splice() method with a length of 1 and without specifying any values to add:

```
avengers.splice(2,1); // will remove the item at index 2
↳ (i.e. the third item in the array)
<< [ 'Thor' ]
```

As you can see, the value that is removed will be returned as an array containing that value.

If we now look at the avengers array, we can see that the string Thor has been removed completely:

```
avengers;
  << ['Captain America', 'Iron Man', 'Scarlet Witch',
↳ 'Quicksilver', 'Hawkeye', 'Black Widow']
```

Reverse

We can reverse the order of an array using the reverse() method:

```
avengers.reverse();
  << ['Black Widow', 'Hawkeye', 'Quicksilver', 'Scarlet
↳ Witch', 'Iron Man', 'Captain America']
```

Note that this changes the order of the array permanently.

Sort

We can sort the order of an array using the sort() method:

```
avengers.sort();
  << ['Black Widow', 'Captain America', 'Hawkeye', 'Iron
```

```
↳ Man', 'Quicksilver', 'Scarlet Witch']
```

It is alphabetical order by default for String objects. Note that this also changes the order of the array permanently.

 Numbers Get Sorted Alphabetically

Numbers are also sorted alphabetically (that is, by their first digit, rather than numerically), so 9 will come after 10 when you try to sort an array of numbers:

```
[5, 9, 10].sort();
<< [10, 5, 9]
```

This can be fixed using a callback, which is a function that is passed as an argument to the sort() method when it is called.

We'll cover how to do this in Chapter 4

Finding if a Value is in an Array

We can find out if an array contains a particular value using the indexOf() method to find the first occurrence of a value in an array. If the item is in the array, it will return the index of the first occurrence of that item:

```
avengers.indexOf('Iron Man');
<< 3
```

If the item is not in the array, it will return -1:

```
avengers.indexOf('Thor');
<< -1
```

ES6 also introduced the includes() method. This returns a boolean value depending on whether the array contains a particular element or not:

```
avengers.includes('Iron Man');
<< true

avengers.includes('Thor');
<< false
```

You can also add an extra parameter to indicate which index to start the search from:

```
 avengers.includes('Black Widow', 1); // will start the
↪ search from the second element in the array
<< false
```

Multidimensional Arrays

You can even have an array of arrays, known as a multidimensional array. This could be used to create a coordinate system, for example:

```
const coordinates = [[1,3],[4,2]];
<< [[1,3],[4,2]]
```

To access the values in a multidimensional array, we use two indices: one to refer to the item's place in the outer array, and one to refer to its place in the inner array:

```
coordinates[0][0]; // The first value of the first array
<< 1

coordinates[1][0]; // The first value of the second array
<< 4

coordinates[0][1]; // The second value of the first array
<< 3
```

```
coordinates[1][1]; // The second value of the second array
<< 2
```

The spread operator that we met earlier can be used to *flatten* multi-dimensional arrays. Flattening an array involves removing all nested arrays so all the values are on the same level in the array. You can see an example of a flattened array below:

```
const summer = ['Jun', 'Jul', 'Aug'];
const winter = ['Dec', 'Jan', 'Feb'];
const nested = [ summer, winter ];
 << [ [ 'Jun', 'Jul', 'Aug' ], [ 'Dec', 'Jan', 'Feb' ]
 ↪ ]

const flat = [...summer, ...winter];
<< [ 'Jun', 'Jul', 'Aug', 'Dec', 'Jan', 'Feb' ]
```

A summary of creating and manipulating arrays can be found on SitePoint[4].

Sets

Sets were introduced to the specification in ES6. A set is a data structure that represents a collection of unique values, so it cannot include any duplicate values. They are similar in concept to a mathematical set[5], although (for the time being at least) they don't contain mathematical set operations such as union, intersection and product.

Sets offer a useful way to keep track of data without having to check if any values have been duplicated. It's also quick and easy to check if a particular value is in a set, which can be a slow operation if an array is used.

---

4. https://www.sitepoint.com/quick-tip-create-manipulate-arrays-in-javascript/
5. ttps://on.wikipedia.org/wiki/Set_%28mathematics%29

Creating Sets

An empty set is created using the new operator and Set() constructor:

```
const list = new Set();
```

There is, at the time of writing, no literal notation for creating sets.

Adding Values to Sets

Values can be placed into a set using the add method:

```
list.add(1);
<< Set { 1 }
```

Multiple items can be added to the set by repeating the add() method:

```
list.add(2).add(3).add(4);
<< Set { 1, 2, 3, 4 }
```

If you try to add a value that is already contained in the set, then the operation is simply ignored:

```
list.add(1);
<< Set { 1, 2, 3, 4 }
```

Multiple values can be added to a set in one go by placing them inside an array that is provided as an argument:

```
const numbers = new Set([1,2,3]);
```

To see the contents of a set, simply enter the name of the variable that refers to it:

```
numbers
<< Set { 1, 2, 3 }
```

If any values are repeated in the array, then they will only appear once in the set:

```
const moreNumbers = new Set([7,7,7,7,7,8,8,8,9,9]);

moreNumbers
<< Set {7,8,9}
```

This gives a convenient way of eliminating any duplicate values from an array in a single operation.

If a string is used as the argument then each character will be added as a separate element, with any repeated characters ignored:

```
const letters = new Set('hello');
letters
<< Set { 'h', 'e', 'l', 'o' }
```

If you want to add separate words, you need to use the add() method:

```
  const words = new
↳ Set().add('the').add('quick').add('brown').add('fox')

words
<< Set { 'the', 'quick', 'brown', 'fox' }
```

All non-primitive values, such as arrays and objects, are considered unique values, even if they contain the same values. On the face of it, this appears to allow duplicate values appear in a set:

```
const arrays = new Set().add([1]).add([1]);

arrays
<< Set { [ 1 ], [ 1 ] }
```

The two arrays may look the same, but are considered different objects. This can be seen with the following strict equality test:

```
[1] === [1];
<< false
```

Type coercion is not used when values are added to a set, so the string "2" will be added as a new entry, even if the number 2 is already an element of the set:

```
const mixedTypes = new Set().add(2).add('2');

mixedTypes
<< Set { 2, '2' }
```

Set Methods

The number of values in a set can be found using the size() method:

```
const jla = new
↳ Set().add('Superman').add('Batman').add('Wonder Woman');

jla
<< Set { 'Superman', 'Batman', 'Wonder Woman' }

jla.size();
<< 3
```

The `has()` method can be used to check if a value is in a set. This returns a boolean value of `true` or `false`:

```
jla.has('Superman');
<< true

jla.has('Green Lantern');
<< false
```

The `has()` method that sets use is a very efficient operation and much faster than using the `includes()` or `indexOf()` methods to check if a value is in an array.

Sets *do not* have index notation for inspecting individual entries, so you can't find the value of the first element in a set like this:

```
jla[0]
<< undefined
```

Removing Values From Sets

The `delete()` method can be used to remove a value from a set. This returns a boolean value of `true` if the value was removed from the set, or `false` if the value wasn't in the set and couldn't be removed:

```
jla.delete('Superman');
<< true

jla.delete('Flash');
<< false
```

The `clear()` method can be used to remove *all* values from a set:

```
jla.clear();
```

```
jla
<< Set {}

jla.size
<< 0
```

Converting Sets to Arrays

A set can be converted into an array by placing the set, along with the **spread operator** directly inside an array literal.

To demonstrate this, first we'll create a set of three items:

```
const shoppingSet = new
↳ Set().add('Apples').add('Bananas').add('Beans');

shoppingSet
<< Set { 'Apples', 'Bananas', 'Beans' }
```

Then we convert it into an array:

```
const shoppingArray = [...shoppingSet]

shoppingArray
<< [ 'Apples', 'Bananas', 'Beans' ]
```

It's also possible to use the `Array.from()` method to convert a set into an array. The following code would achieve the same result as using the spread operator above:

```
const shoppingSet = new
↳ Set().add('Apples').add('Bananas').add('Beans');
```

```
const shoppingArray = Array.from(shoppingSet);
```

By combining this use of the spread operator with the ability to pass an array to the new Set() constructor, we now have a convenient way to create a copy of an array with any duplicate values removed:

```
const duplicate = [3, 1, 4, 1, 5, 9, 2, 6 ,5,3,5,9];
<< [ 3, 1, 4, 1, 5, 9, 2, 6, 5, 3, 5, 9 ]

const nonDuplicate = [...new Set(repeatedArray)];
<< [ 3, 1, 4, 5, 9, 2, 6 ]
```

Weak Sets

When objects are added to sets, they will be stored there as long as the set exists, even if the original reference to the object is removed. The technical term for this is the object is prevented from being **garbage-collected**, which can cause a **memory leak**. This can be seen in the following example:

```
let array = [1,2,3];
const strong = new Set().add(array);

array = null; // remove reference to the original

strong
<< Set { [ 1, 2, 3 ] }
```

The array still exists inside the set and we can get the original value of array back using the spread operator:

```
array = [...strong][0];

array
```

```
<< [1,2,3]
```

 Memory Leaks

A **memory leak** occurs when a program retains references to values that can no longer be accessed in its memory. This means that memory is being used to store values that are no longer required by the program, effectively wasting system resources.

Memory leaks can cause problems by gradually reducing the overall memory available, which can cause the program, or even the entire system, to run more slowly.

Most modern programming language, including JavaScript, employ various dynamic memory management techniques such as **garbage collection**, which is the process of automatically removing items from memory that are no longer required by the program. Some languages, such as C++, require the programmer to manually manage memory by removing items from memory once they are finished with.

Weak sets avoid this situation by garbage collecting any references to a "dead object" that's had its original reference removed.

To create a weak set, the `new` operator and the `WeakSet()` constructor in the same way that we created a set:

```
const weak = new WeakSet();
```

Only non-primitive data types can be added to weak sets. Trying to add primitive values will throw a type error:

```
weak.add(2)
<< TypeError: Invalid value used in weak set
```

Apart from these restrictions, weak sets behave in the same way as regular sets, and have the `has()`, `add()`, and `delete()` methods that work in the same way.

In the next example we can see what happens if we add an array to a weak set:

```
const array = [1,2,3];
weak.add(array);
<< WeakSet {}
```

Because weak maps use weak references to objects, they don't have access to a list of values they contain. This makes the return value in the example look as though the weak set is empty, when, in fact it isn't.

We can confirm it does indeed contain the array object by using the has() method:

```
weak.has(array);
<< true
```

We can remove the array from the weak set using the delete() method:

```
weak.delete(array);
<< true
```

And check it's been removed using the has() method again:

```
weak.has(array);
<< false
```

Maps

Maps were another data structure introduced in the ES6 specification. They are a convenient way of keeping a list of key and value pairs, and are similar to "hashes", or"hash tables" or "dictionaries" in other programming languages.

At first glance, maps appear to be similar to JavaScript objects (covered in Chapter 5), but they have some noticeable differences:

- Objects are limited to using strings for key values, whereas maps can use any data type as a key.
- There is no efficient way to find the number of key-value pairs an object has, whereas this is easy to do with maps using the `size` property.
- Objects have methods that can be called (see Chapter 5) and prototypes that can be used to create a chain of inheritance (see Chapter 12), whereas maps are solely focused on the storage and retrieval of key-value pairs.
- The value of an object's properties can be accessed directly, whereas maps restrict you to using the `get()` method to retrieve any values.

Creating Maps

An empty map object can be created using the `new` operator and `Map()` constructor:

```
const romanNumerals = new Map();
```

There is, at the time of writing, no literal notation for creating maps.

Adding Entries To Maps

The `set()` method can be used to add a key and value pair to a map. The first value is the key and the second is the value:

```
romanNumerals.set(1,'I');
<< Map { 1 => 'I' }
```

The return value shows the mapping with the key connected to the value using the "hash rocket" symbol (=>).

Multiple items can be added to the set by repeatedly calling the `set()` method in one go:

```
romanNumerals.set(2,'II').set(3,'III').set(4,'IV').set(5,'V')
↳ ; << Map { 1 => 'I', 2 => 'II', 3 => 'III', 4
↳ => 'IV', 5 => 'V' }
```

Map Methods

A map is a bit like a dictionary where you can look up a value based on the key. To look up a value, we can use the `get()` method:

```
romanNumerals.get(4);
<< 'IV'
```

The `has()` method can be used to check if a particular key is in a map. This returns a boolean value of **true** or **false**:

```
romanNumerals.has(5);
<< true

romanNumerals.has(10);
<< false
```

A map can be created with multiple values by using a nested array as a parameter:

```
const heroes = new Map([ ['Clark Kent','Superman'],
['Bruce Wayne', 'Batman']
]);
```

The number of key and value pairs in a map can be found by querying the **size** property:

```
heroes.size
<< 2
```

Removing Entries From Maps

The `delete()` method can be used to remove a key and value pair from a map.
This returns a boolean value of `true` if the value was removed or `false` if it
wasn't in the map. To delete a specific value, you need to specify the key in
parentheses:

```
heroes.delete('Clark Kent');
<< true

heroes.size
<< 1
```

The `clear()` method will remove *all* key and value pairs from a map:

```
heroes.clear();

heroes.size;
<< 0
```

Converting Maps to Arrays

Maps can be converted into a nested array of key-value pairs in a similar way to
sets; using either the spread operator:

```
[...romanNumerals]
  << [ [ 1, 'I' ], [ 2, 'II' ], [ 3, 'III' ], [ 4, 'IV'
↪ ], [ 5, 'V' ] ]
```

... or the `Array.from()` method:

```
Array.from(romanNumerals)
  << [ [ 1, 'I' ], [ 2, 'II' ], [ 3, 'III' ], [ 4, 'IV'
  ↳ ], [ 5, 'V' ] ]
```

Weak Maps

Weak maps work in the same way as weak sets. They are the same as maps, except their keys cannot be primitives, and the garbage collector will automatically remove any dead entries when the reference to the original object is deleted.

To create a weak map, the `new` operator is used along with the `WeakMap()` constructor:

```
const weak = new WeakMap();
```

Weak maps can use the `has()`, `get()`, `set()` and `delete()` methods in the same way as a regular map.

Weak maps and sets are useful for optimizing memory usage and avoiding memory leaks, but they're also limited in that they don't have access to all the methods their regular counterparts have. For example, you cannot use the `size()` method to see how many entries they contain. The choice of which to use will depend on what you plan to use them for.

Logic

In this section, we'll begin to look at logical conditions that allow you to control the flow of a program by running different blocks of code, depending on the results of certain operations.

`if` Statements

An `if` statement has the following structure:

```
if (condition) {
// code to run if condition is true
}
```

The code inside the block will only run if the condition in parentheses is true. If the condition is not a boolean value, it will be converted to a boolean, depending on whether or not it is truthy or falsy (see Chapter 2).

Here is an example that will only display the alert message if the value of the `age` variable is less than 18:

```
const age = 23;
if (age < 18) {
console.log('Sorry, you are not old enough to play');
}
```

Try changing the value of the `age` variable to a value below 18 as it does in this code, and the alert box will show.

```
const age = 12;
if (age < 18) {
console.log('Sorry, you are not old enough to play');
}
```

`else` Statements

The `else` keyword can be used to add an alternative block of code to run if the condition is false. An `if ... else` statement looks like this:

```
if (condition) {
// code to run if condition is true
} else {
// code to run if condition is false
}
```

As an example, we can test if a number is even or odd using the following code:

```
const n = 12;
if (n%2 === 0) {
console.log('n is an even number');
} else {
console.log('n is an odd number');
}
<< 'n is an even number'
```

This uses the % operator that we met in the previous chapter to check the remainder when dividing the variable n by 2. All even numbers leave no remainder when divided by 2, so we can test to see if n%2 is equal to zero; if it is, n must be even. If n is not even, then it must be odd.

Ternary Operator

A shorthand way of writing an if ... else statement is to use the ternary operator, ?, which takes three operands in the following format:

```
condition ? (//code to run if condition is true) : (//code
↪ to run if condition is false)
```

Here's the example for testing if the variable n is odd or even, rewritten to use the ternary operator:

```
const n = 5;
n%2 === 0 ? console.log('n is an even number') :
```

```
↳ console.log('n is an odd number');
<< 'n is an odd number'
```

We could make the example even shorter by placing the ternary operator inside a template string:

```
console.log(`n is a ${(n%2 === 0)? 'even' : 'odd'} number`);
```

This will evaluate the ternary operator and place the result directly inside the template string that is then logged in the console.

The ternary operator can make your code more succinct, but can also make it harder to read, so think carefully before using it.

Switch **Statements**

You can actually string lots of if and else statements together to make a logical decision tree:

```
if (number === 4) {
console.log('You rolled a four');
} else if (number === 5) {
console.log('You rolled a five');
} else if(number === 6){
console.log('You rolled a six');
} else {
console.log('You rolled a number less than four');
}
```

The switch operator can be used to make your code easier to follow when there are lots of conditions to test. The example above can be rewritten using a switch statement like so:

```
switch (number) {
case 4:
console.log('You rolled a four');
break;
case 5:
console.log('You rolled a five');
break;
case 6:
console.log('You rolled a six');
break;
default:
console.log('You rolled a number less than four');
break;
}
```

The value you are comparing goes in parentheses after the `switch` operator. A `case` keyword is then used for each possible value that can occur (4, 5, and 6 in the example above). After each `case` statement is the code that that needs to be run if that case occurs.

It is important to finish each `case` block with the `break` keyword, as this stops any more of the case blocks being executed. Without a `break` statement, the program will "fall through" and continue to evaluate subsequent case blocks. This is sometimes implemented on purpose, but it is a hack and can be confusing. For this reason it should be avoided — a ninja programmer always finishes a `case` block with a `break`!

The `default` keyword is used at the end for any code than needs to be run if none of the cases are true.

Loops

Loops will repeat a piece of code over and over again according to certain conditions.

While **Loops**

We'll start by looking at a while loop. This will repeatedly run a block of code while a certain condition is true, and takes the following structure:

```
while (condition) {
// do something
}
```

Here's an example that will count down from 10, logging a line from the famous song each time:

```
let bottles = 10;
while (bottles > 0){
 console.log(`There were ${bottles} green bottles, hanging on
↪ a wall. And if one green bottle should accidentally fall,
↪ there'd be ${bottles-1} green bottles hanging on the wall`);
bottles--;
}
```

We start by declaring a variable called bottles. Any variables that are used in the loop must be initialized before the loop is run, otherwise there will be an error when they are mentioned.

The loop starts here with the while keyword and is followed by a condition and a block of code. The condition in the example is that the value of the bottles variable has to be greater than zero. This basically means "keep repeating the block of code, as long as the number of bottles is greater than zero".

The block of code uses the alert function to display a message about the number of bottles, then uses the decrement operator to decrease the bottles variable by one.

Here's a more concise way of writing the same loop that moves the increment into the condition:

```
let bottles = 11;
while (--bottles){
  console.log(`There were ${bottles} green bottles, hanging on
↪ a wall. And if one green bottle should accidentally fall,
↪ there'd be ${bottles-1} green bottles hanging on the wall`);
}
```

The reason this code works is because the loop will continue while the `bottles` variable is true, and before each loop, the value of the `bottles` variable decreases by 1. When the `bottles` variable reaches 0, it is not true anymore (remember that 0 is a falsy value) so the loop will stop. Notice that you have to start with one more bottle (11) as it will be decreased by one even before the first block is run.

Infinite Loops

It is important that the condition in a `while` loop will be met at some point, otherwise your code will get stuck in an infinite loop that could possibly crash the program.

Consider the following loop:

```
let n = 1;
while(n>0){
console.log('Hello');
n++;
}
```

This loop will keep running, as the variable n will *always* be above zero. Most browsers will warn you that there is a slow running script when this happens and give you the option to stop it. If not, you can kill the process by closing the tab or restarting the browser. Obviously you want to avoid this happening, though; especially with public-facing code.

do ... while **Loops**

A do ... while loop is similar to a while loop. The only difference is that the condition comes *after* the block of code:

```
do {
do something
} while(condition)
```

This means that the block of code will always be run at least once, regardless of the condition being true or not.

Here's the same example we saw before, rewritten as a do ... while loop:

```
let bottles = 10;
do {
 console.log(`There were ${bottles} green bottles, hanging on
↪ a wall. And if one green bottle should accidentally fall,
↪ there'd be ${bottles-1} green bottles hanging on the wall`);
bottles--;
} while (bottles > 0)
```

For **Loops**

For loops are probably the most commonly type of loop used in JavaScript, and take the following form:

```
for (initialization ; condition ; after) { do something }
```

The *initialization* code is run *before* the loop starts and is usually employed to initialize any variables used in the loop. The *condition* has to be satisfied for the loop to continue. The *after* code is what to do after *each iteration* of the loop, and it is typically used to increment a counter of some sort.

Here's the green bottles example written as a `for` loop:

```
for (let bottles = 10 ; bottles > 0 ; bottles--) {
  console.log(`There were ${bottles} green bottles, hanging on
↪ a wall. And if one green bottle should accidentally fall,
↪ there'd be ${bottles-1} green bottles hanging on the wall`);
}
```

Each part of a `for` loop are optional, and the code could be written as:

```
let bottles = 10; // bottles is initialized here instead
  for ( ; bottles > 0 ; ) { // empty initialization and
↪ increment
  console.log(`There were ${bottles} green bottles, hanging on
↪ a wall. And if one green bottle should accidentally fall,
↪ there'd be ${bottles-1} green bottles hanging on the wall`);
bottles--; // increment moved into code block
}
```

As you can see, it's possible to use a `while` loop, a `do ... while` loop, or a `for` loop to achieve the same results. A `for` loop is considered clearer, as all the details of the loop (the initialization, condition and increment) are shown in one place and kept out of the actual code block.

Nested `for` Loops

You can place a loop inside another loop to create a nested loop. It will have an inner loop that will run all the way through before the next step of the outer loop occurs.

Here's an example that produces a multiplication table up to 12 x 12:

```
for(let i=1 ; j<13 ; i++){
for(let i=1 ; j<13 ; j++){
    console.log(`${j} multiplied by ${i} is ${i*j}`);
```

```
    }
}
```

The outer loop counts up from i=1 to i=12. For every iteration of the outer loop, the inner loop counts up from j=1 to j=12. This means that it starts in the first iteration with i = 1 and j = 1, producing the following output that is logged to the console:

```
<< 1 multiplied by 1 is 1
```

In the next iteration, we are still inside the inner loop, so i remains as 1, but j is incremented to 2, giving:

```
<< 1 multiplied by 2 is 2
```

j continues to increase until it reaches 12. After this, we leave the inner loop and return to the outer loop, where i increases to 2. We then re-enter the inner loop and j is reset back to 1 and begins counting up to 12 again. This continues until the last iteration produces the line:

```
<< 12 multiplied by 12 is 144
```

Looping over Arrays

A for loop can be used to iterate over each value in an array. If we take our avengers array example from earlier, we can create a for loop that outputs each item in the array to the console using the following loop:

```
for(let i=0, max=avengers.length; i < max; i++){
console.log(avengers[i]);
}
<< 'Black Widow'
```

```
<< 'Captain America'
<< 'Hawkeye'
<< 'Iron Man'
<< 'Quicksilver'
<< 'Scarlet Witch'
```

There are a few points to note in this example. Array indices start their numbering at zero, so make sure the value of the initial counter in the `for` loop also starts at zero. We want the loop to continue until it reaches the length of the array; this can be set as the variable `max` in the initialization part of the `for` loop, then the condition becomes `i < max`. This is preferable to using `i < avengers.length` because then the length of the `avengers` array would have to be calculated after every pass through the loop. This might not sound all that important, but it can make a big difference to the speed of the program when using large arrays.

ES6 introduced an improved iterator function for arrays called a `for-of` loop that uses a slightly different syntax:

```
for(const value of avengers){
console.log(value);
}
<< 'Black Widow'
<< 'Captain America'
<< 'Hawkeye'
<< 'Iron Man'
<< 'Quicksilver'
<< 'Scarlet Witch'
```

This replaces all of the setup of a 'for' loop with a variable (`value` in the example above) that represents the value of each element in the array. Note that this variable needs to be declared using `const`.

Looping Over Sets

Sets are **enumerable**, which means they have methods that allow you to loop over each value in the set. The loop will iterate over each value in *the same order they were added to the set*. To demonstrate this, we will use the set of letters that we created earlier:

```
const letters = new Set('hello');
```

We can iterate over each value in the set using a `for-of` loop, like so:

```
for(const letter of letters) {
console.log(letter);
}
<< h
e
l
o
```

Note that weak sets are **non-enumerable**, so it's not possible to loop over them in this way.

Looping Over Maps

Maps are also enumerable, so it's also possible to loop over a map in a similar way to a set. The loop will iterate over each key-value pair in the same order as they were added to the map. For example let's use the `romanNumerals` map that we created earlier:

```
const romanNumerals = new Map();
romanNumerals.set(1,'I').set(2,'II').set(3,'III').set(4,'IV')
↪ .set(5,'V');
romanNumerals
 << Map { 1 => 'I', 2 => 'II', 3 => 'III', 4
```

```
↪ => 'IV', 5 => 'V' }
```

Every map object has a `keys()` method lets us iterate over each key with the following `for-of` loop:

```
for(const key of romanNumerals.keys()) {
console.log(key);
}
<< 1
2
3
4
5
```

There is also a `values()` method that lets us iterate over the values in a similar way:

```
for(const value of RomanNumerals.values()) {
console.log(value);
}
<< I
II
III
IV
V
```

If you want to access both the key and the value, you can use the `entries()` method:

```
for(const [key,value] of RomanNumerals.entries()) {
console.log(`${key} in Roman numerals is ${value}`);
}
<< 1 in Roman numerals is I
2 in Roman numerals is II
3 in Roman numerals is III
```

```
4 in Roman numerals is IV
5 in Roman numerals is V
```

Note that weak maps are also **non-enumerable**, so it isn't possible to loop over them using any of the methods shown above.

Quiz Ninja Project

Now we've reached the end of the chapter, it's time to use what we've learned to add some features to our Quiz Ninja project.

We'll start by creating an array called `quiz` that contains all the questions and answers. Each element in `quiz` will be a nested array that contains the question as its first element and the answer as its second element. Open up `main.js` and add the following code at the top:

```
const quiz = [
    ["What is Superman's real name?","Clark Kent"],
    ["What is Wonder Woman's real name?","Diana Prince"],
    ["What is Batman's real name?","Bruce Wayne"]
];
```

Next, we'll create and initialize a variable called `score` to keep track of how many correct answers the player has given:

```
let score = 0 // initialize score
```

Then we'll loop through the array using a `for-of` loop, assigning the variables `question` and `answer` to each key and value in the map.

The loop starts by asking the question using a prompt dialog that allows the player to enter an answer that is stored in a variable called `response`. We can then compare this to the actual answer stored as `answer`:

```
for(const [question,answer] of quiz){
const response = prompt(question);
if(response === answer){
    alert('Correct!');
    score++;
} else {
    alert(`Wrong! The correct answer was ${answer}`);
}
}
```

An if ... else block is then used to check if the answer is right or wrong. If it's right, an alert dialog is shown saying it is correct and the score is incremented by 1, using score++. Otherwise, if the answer is wrong, an alert dialog informs the player and also lets them know the correct answer.

When the loop has finished iterating through each question in the array, it breaks out of the block and finishes by displaying another alert dialog to inform the player the game is over and telling them how many questions they answered correctly. This uses a template literal to display the score:

```
// At the end of the game, report the player's score
 alert(`Game Over, you scored ${score} point${score !== 1 ?
↪ 's' : ''}`);
```

Notice at the end of this template literal, we use the ternary operator to check if the score is not equal to 1. If this is true, the letter "s" is appended to the end of the word "point" to make it plural. This is a neat trick that can sometimes be overlooked, even on professional websites.

Have a go at playing the quiz in your browser by opening the index.html file. It should look like the screenshot shown below.

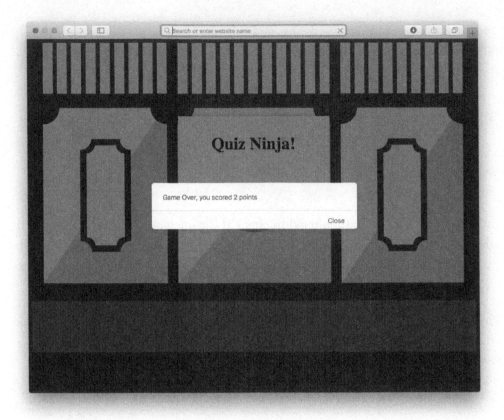

3-1. Quiz Ninja scores

You can also see a live example on CodePen[6].

Our quiz now feels much more like an actual program, and demonstrates the power of concepts such as arrays, logic and loops that we've learned about in this chapter.

Chapter Summary

- Arrays are an ordered list of values

- Multidimensional arrays are arrays that contain other arrays

---

6. http://codepen.io/daz4126/pen/XRyMJe

- Arrays have lots of methods that can be used to manipulate items in the array

- Sets are new in ES6 and are ordered lists of non-duplicate values

- Maps are new in ES6 and are ordered lists of key-value pairs

- We can use an `if` and `else` statement to control the flow of code

- The `switch` statement can be used instead of multiple `if` and `else` statements

- A `while` loop and `do ... while` loop can be used to repeat a block of code while a condition is still true

- A `for` loop works in a similar way to a `while` loop, but has a different syntax

- A `for-of` loop can be used to iterate over an array

- Sets and maps are enumerable, so can also be looped over using a `for-of` loop

In the next chapter, we'll be learning all about functions, a fundamental part of the JavaScript language.

Chapter 4

Functions

A function is a chunk of code that can be referenced by a name, and is almost like a small, self-contained mini program. Functions can help reduce repetition and make code easier to follow.

In this chapter, we'll be covering these topics:

◼ Defining functions—function declarations, function expressions, `Function()` constructors and the new arrow syntax

◼ Invoking a function

◼ Return values

◼ Parameters and arguments

- Hoisting—variables and functions

- Callbacks—functions as a parameter

- Project — we'll be using functions to make the Quiz Ninja code easier to follow

In JavaScript, functions are considered to be first-class objects. This means they behave in the same way as all the other primitive data types and objects in the language. They can be be assigned to variables, stored in arrays and can even be returned by another functions.

This makes functions a very important and powerful part of the JavaScript language with many of its features relying on them. Fully understanding functions is an essential skill of the JavaScript ninja.

Defining a Function

There are a number of ways to define a function in JavaScript. Three of the most common are covered below. ES6 introduced a new way to define functions, using what is known as "arrow" notation. This is covered later in the chapter.

Function Declarations

To define a function literal we can use a `function` declaration:

```
function hello(){
console.log('Hello World!');
}
```

This starts with the `function` keyword and is followed by the name of the function, which in this case is called `'hello'`, followed by parentheses. Following this is a block that contains the code for the function.

This is known as a named function as the function has a name: `'hello'`.

Function Expressions

Another way of defining a function literal is to create a function expression. This assigns an *anonymous function* to a variable:

```
const goodbye = function(){
console.log('Goodbye World!');
};
```

The function in this example is known as an anonymous function because it doesn't have a name; it is simply created, then assigned to the variable `goodbye`. Alternatively, we can create a named function expression instead:

```
const goodbye = function bye(){
console.log('Goodbye World!');
};
```

The name of this function is `bye`, and it has been assigned to the variable `goodbye`.

Notice also that the example ends with a semicolon. This finishes the assignment statement, whereas a normal function declaration ends in a block (there's no need for semicolons at the end of blocks).

Every Function Has a Name

All functions have a read-only property called **name**, which can be accessed like so:

```
hello.name
<< 'hello'
```

The **name** property is not actually part of the ECMAScript standard, although most JavaScript engines support it and use it internally.

Anonymous functions have an empty string as their **name** property in most browsers, although some versions of Internet Explorer use **undefined**.

The **name** property can be useful when debugging code, as the name of a function will be used to indicate which functions are causing a problem.

Function() Constructors

A function can also be declared using the constructor **Function()**. The body of the function is entered as a string, as shown in this example:

```
const hi = new Function('console.log("Hi World!");');
```

It's not recommended to declare functions in this way as there are numerous problems associated with placing the function body inside a string. Even in this simple example, we had to use different quotation marks for the **console.log** method, as those used for defining the function body itself. Functions created this way are also created in the global scope, regardless of where they are actually declared. This can lead to some strange and unexpected behavior.

A ninja programmer should always declare functions using function literals, function declarations or function expressions. These two ways of creating functions are similar, although there are some subtle differences that will be covered later in the chapter. Some people prefer function declarations as they are akin to how functions are declared in other languages. Others prefer function expressions because it is clear that functions are just another value assigned to a variable, rather than a special feature of the language. Whether you use function declarations or function expressions is often a matter of personal taste, but whatever you choose to do, be consistent!

Invoking a Function

Invoking a function is to run the code inside the function's body. To invoke a function, simply enter its name, followed by parentheses. This is how we'd invoke the `hello` function:

```
hello();
<< 'Hello world!'
```

The function can be invoked over and over again just by typing its name followed by parentheses. This is one of the advantages of using functions — there's no need to write repetitive blocks of code. Another advantage is that all the functionality is kept in one place. So if you want to change part of it, you only need to update the one piece of code in the function declaration. This is known as the DRY principle, which stands for Don't Repeat Yourself.

 Keep Your Code DRY

Don't Repeat Yourself,[1] or DRY, is a principle of programming that specifies that every part of a program should only be written once. This avoids duplication and means there's no need to keep multiple pieces of code up to date and in sync.

If you have assigned a function to a variable, you need to place parentheses after the variable to invoke it as a function:

```
goodbye();
<< 'Goodbye World!'
```

---

[1] http://en.wikipedia.org/wiki/Don%27t_repeat_yourself

Remember: you need parentheses to invoke a function — either by name or by reference to the variable it is assigned to. If you skip the parentheses, you are simply referencing the function itself rather than invoking it, as you can see here:

```
goodbye;
<< [Function: goodbye]
```

All that has been returned is the function definition that the variable goodbye is pointing to, rather than running the code. This can be useful if you want to assign the function to another variable, like so:

```
seeya = goodbye;
<< [Function: goodbye]
```

Now the variable seeya also points to the function called bye and can be used to invoke it:

```
seeya();
<< 'Goodbye World!'
```

Return Values

All functions return a value, which can be specified using the return statement, which comes after the return keyword. A function that doesn't explicitly return anything (such as all the examples we have seen so far) will return undefined by default.

The function in this example will return the string 'Howdy World!':

```
function howdy(){
return 'Howdy World!';
}
```

This means we can now assign a function invocation to a variable, and the value of that variable will be the return value of that function:

```
const message = howdy();
<< 'Howdy World!'
```

The variable `message` now points to the return value of the `howdy()` function, which is the string `Howdy World!`. This may seem trivial in this instance (that is, why not just assign the variable to the string directly?), but we can create a more complex function that has different return values depending on certain conditions. This then allows us to assign different values to the `message` variable depending on those conditions.

Parameters and Arguments

Parameters and **arguments** are terms that are often used interchangeably to represent values provided for the function as an input. There is a subtle difference though: any parameters a function needs are set when the function is *defined*. When a function is *invoked*, it is provided with arguments.

To see an example of a function that uses parameters, we'll create a function that squares numbers. In the example that follows, the `square` function takes one parameter, x, which is the number to be squared. In the body of the function, the name of the parameter acts like a variable equal to the value that is provided when the function is invoked. As you can see, it is multiplied by itself and the result is returned by the function:

```
function square(x){
return x*x;
}
```

When we invoke this function, we need to provide an argument, which is the number to be squared:

```
square(4.5);
<< 20.25
```

You can use as many parameters as you like when defining functions. For example, the following function finds the mean of any three numbers:

```
function mean(a,b,c){
return (a+b+c)/3;
}
```

```
mean(1, 3, 6);
<< 3.3333333333333335
```

 ### Rounding Errors

You might have noticed that the answer to the last example was slightly incorrect (it should be just 3.3 recurring, with no 5 on the end). This highlights a problem when doing division in JavaScript (or calculations on any computer, for that matter). The problem stems from the fact that computers use base 2 in the background and therefore struggle to represent any fractions where the denominator is not a power of 2. This means that some division calculations can often have slight rounding errors. This usually doesn't cause a problem, but you should be aware of it.

If a parameter is not provided as an argument when the function is invoked, the function will still be invoked, but the parameter will be given a value of undefined. If we try to invoke the mean function with only two arguments, we can see that it returns NaN because the function cannot do the required operation with undefined:

```
mean(1,2)
<< NaN
```

If too many arguments are provided when a function is invoked, the function will work as normal and the extra arguments will be ignored (although they can be accessed using the `arguments` object that is discussed in the next section):

```
mean(1,2,3,4,5); // will only find the mean of 1,2 and 3
<< 2
```

ES6 also made it possible to create **default parameters** that will use default values for any parameter that isn't provided as an argument. This is covered a little later in the chapter.

Variable Numbers of Arguments

As we have seen in the example above, it's possible to enter as many arguments as you like into a function, even if only some of them are used. There are times when we don't know how many arguments will be entered. For example, we could improve our `mean()` function by allowing a user to calculate the mean of any number of values, rather than restricting them to just 3.

Every function has a special variable called `arguments`. This is an array-like object that contains every argument passed to the function when it is invoked. We can create a simple function called `arguments()` that will return the `arguments` object so we can see what it contains:

```
function arguments(){
return arguments;
}
```

Now let's invoke the `arguments()` function a couple of times to see the results:

```
arguments('hello', NaN);
<< { '0': 'hello', '1': NaN }

arguments(1,2,3,4,5);
```

```
<< { '0': 1, '1': 2, '2': 3, '3': 4, '4': 5 }
```

As you can see, the arguments object that is returned contains every value that was entered. These can then be accessed using an index notation like we did with arrays, so the first argument would be accessed using `arguments[0]`.

The problem is that `arguments` is not an array. It has a `length` property and you can read and write each element using index notation, but it doesn't have array methods such as `slice()`, `join()`, and `forEach()`. There is a way of 'borrowing' methods from arrays, but it is clumsy and unnecessary.

A much better option is to use the `rest` operator. This was introduced in ES6 and can be used to deal with multiple arguments by creating an array of arguments that are available inside the body of the function.

To use the rest operator, simply place three dots in front of the last parameter in a function declaration. This will then collect all the arguments entered into an array. For example, the following function will have access to an array of all the arguments entered:

```
function rest(...args){
return args;
}
```

The `args` parameter is an actual array, and has access to the same methods. For example we can use a `for-of` loop to iterate over each value given as an argument:

```
function rest(...args){
for(arg of args){
    console.log(arg);
}
}

rest(2,4,6,8);
```

```
<< 2
4
6
8
```

Improved Mean Function

We can use a rest parameter to improve our `mean()` function so it accepts any number of values:

```
function mean(...values) {
let total = 0;
for(const value of values) {
    total += value;
    }
return total/values.length;
}
```

This collects all the arguments that are entered into an array called `values`. We can then loop over this array and add up all the values. The variable `total` is used to keep the running total, and the `+=` operator is used to add the next value onto the total. At the end of the function we return the total divide by the number of arguments entered, which we find by calling the `length` property on the `values` array. Let's see if it works:

```
mean(2,8,13,11,4,2);
<< 6.666666666666667
```

Default Parameters

ES6 introduced a convenient way to specify default parameters for a function. These are values that will be used by the function if no arguments are provided when it is invoked. To specify a default parameter, simply assign the default value to it in the function definition:

```
function hello(name='World') {
console.log(`Hello ${name}!);
}
```

Now if we call this function without an argument, it will use `World` as the `name` parameter:

```
hello();
<< 'Hello World!'
```

We can override the default value, by specifying our own argument:

```
hello('Universe');
<< 'Hello Universe!'
```

 Prior to ES6

The way of assigning default values previous to ES6 was to use a line of code similar to the following in the body of the function:

```
name = name || "World";
```

This uses the logical OR operator to check if the `name` parameter has a truthy value. If it does, that means an argument was provided to the function and `name` will stay as that value. If there was no argument provided, the value of `name` will be **undefined**, which is falsy so it will take the value of `World`. This method is still used quite often, but it does have a pitfall in that it relies on **undefined** being falsy. Unfortunately this is not the only falsy value, however. If the `name` argument is meant to be a falsy value, such as 0, for example, it won't be used, and the value will still be set to the default value of `World` instead. For this reason, you should stick to using the ES6 method of declaring default parameters whenever possible.

Default parameters should always come after non-default parameters, otherwise default values will always have to be entered anyway. Consider the following function for calculating a discounted price in a store:

```
function discount(price, amount=10) {
return price*(100-amount)/100;
}
```

This function takes two arguments: the price of an item and the percentage discount to be applied. The store's most common discount is 10%, so this is provided as a default value. This means that the `amount` argument can be omitted in most cases and a 10% discount will still be applied:

```
discount(20) // standard discount of 10%
<< 18
```

If a different discount is applied, the `amount` argument can be provided:

```
discount(15, 20) // discount of 20%
<< 12
```

This will fail to work, however, if the parameters are reversed:

```
function discount(amount=10, price) {
return price*(100-amount)/100;
}
```

Now if we try to use the function with just one argument, the function won't work, because `price` has not been set:

```
 discount(20); // this sets amount = 20, but doesn't provide
↳ a value for price
```

```
<< NaN
```

It will work, however, if both values are entered:

```
discount(10,20);
<< 18
```

This somewhat defeats the object of having default parameters! The golden rule to remember here is to always put default parameters *after* all the other parameters.

Arrow Functions

ES6 introduced a new syntax for declaring functions called the **arrow** syntax. These make declaring functions much more succinct by using less verbose syntax.

Arrow functions can be identified by the arrow symbol, => that gives them their name. The parameters come before the arrow and the main body of the function comes after. Arrow functions are always anonymous, so if you want to refer to them, you must assign them to a variable. For example, the **square** function we wrote earlier can be written like so:

```
const square = x => x*x;
```

Arrow functions have a number of advantages over other ways of declaring functions:

- They are much less verbose than normal function declarations.
- Single parameters don't need putting into parentheses.
- The body of the function doesn't need placing inside a block if it's only one line.
- The **return** keyword isn't required if the return statement is the only statement in the body of the function.

■ They don't bind their own value of this to the function (we'll see why this is a particularly useful property when we cover objects later in the book).

In the square example above parameter, x didn't need to go in parentheses because it's the only parameter. Multiple parameters need to go inside parentheses, for example, the following function adds two numbers together:

```
const add = (x,y) => x + y;
```

If the function doesn't require any parameters, a pair of empty parentheses must go before the arrow:

```
const hello = () => alert('Hello World!');
```

In all the examples, the main body of the function fits onto one line, so there is no need to put it inside a block or explicitly use the return keyword.

Longer functions will still require curly braces to deliminate the body of the function and the return keyword at the end, as can be seen in this (rather simplistic) tax-calculating function:

```
const tax = (salary) => {
const taxable = salary - 8000;
const lowerRate = 0.25 * taxable;
taxable = taxable - 20000;
const higherRate = 0.4 * taxable;
return lowerRate + higherRate;
}
```

As you can see, a number of the benefits are lost, once the function body becomes longer than one line.

Arrow functions make perfect candidates for short, anonymous functions, and you will often see them used later in the book.

Function Hoisting

Hoisting is the JavaScript interpreter's action of moving all variable and function declarations to the top of the current scope, regardless of where they are defined.

Functions that are defined using a function declaration are automatically hoisted, meaning they can be invoked before they have been defined. For example, in the following code the function hoist() can be invoked before it is actually defined:

```
// function is invoked at the start of the code
hoist();

// ...
// ... lots more code here
// ...

// function definition is at the end of the code
function hoist(){
console.log('Hoist Me!');
}
```

This can be quite useful as it means that all function definitions can be placed together, possibly at the end of a program, rather than having to define every function before it is used.

Variable Hoisting

Variable declarations that use the var keyword are automatically moved to the top of the current scope. Variable assignment is not hoisted, however. This means that a variable assigned at the end of a function will have a value of undefined until the assignment is made:

```
 console.log(name); // will return undefined before
↪ assignment

// variable is defined here
var name = 'Alexa';
```

```
console.log(name); // will return 'Alexa' after assignment
```

Variable hoisting can cause quite a bit of confusion and also relies on using var to declare variables. An error will be thrown if you attempt to refer to a variable before it has been declared using const and let. It's better practice to use const and let to declare any variables at the beginning of a block so hoisting is unnecessary.

A function expression (where an anonymous function is assigned to a variable) is hoisted in a similar way to variables. So if it is declared using var then the declaration will be hoisted, but not the actual function. This means the function cannot be invoked until after it appears in the code:

```
// the variable helloExpression has a value of undefined, so
↳ the function cannot be invoked
helloExpression(); // throws an error

// the function declaration can be invoked before it is
↳ declared
helloDeclaration(); // returns 'hello'

// assign function expression to a variable
var helloExpression = function() {
console.log('hello')
}

// declare function declaration
function helloDeclaration() {
console.log('hello')
}

// The function expression can only be invoked after
↳ assignment
helloExpression(); // returns 'hello'
```

This is the major difference between the two ways of defining function literals and it may influence your decision regarding which one to use. Some people like that using function expressions means you're required to define all functions and assign them to variables prior to using them.

Hoisting can be a tricky concept to get your head around initially – you can read more about it on SitePoint[2].

Callbacks

Remember at the start of this chapter when we said that functions in JavaScript are first-class objects, so they behave in just the same way as every other object? This means that functions can also be given as a parameter to another function. A function that is passed as an argument to another is known as a *callback*.

Here's a basic example of a function called `sing()`, which accepts the name of a song:

```
function sing(song) {
console.log(`I'm singing along to ${song}`);
}

sing('Let It Go')
<< 'I'm singing along to Let It Go'
```

We can make the `sing()` function more flexible by adding a `callback` parameter:

```
function sing(song,callback) {
console.log(`I'm singing along to ${song}.`);
callback();
}
```

The callback is provided as a parameter, then invoked inside the body of the function.

[2.] https://www.sitepoint.com/back-to-basics-javascript-hoisting/

But What if the Function Isn't Provided as an Agrument?

There is nothing to actually define a parameter as a callback, so if a function isn't provided as an argument, then this code won't work. It is possible to check if an argument is a function using the following code:

```
if(typeof(callback) === 'function'){
callback();
}
```

This will only attempt to invoke the callback if it is a function.

Now we can create another function called `dance()` that can be used as the callback:

```
function dance() {
 console.log("I'm moving my body to the groove.");↪ class="fn">
We're just logging a simple message to the
↪ console in these examples, but these functions could be used
↪ to do anything in a practical sense.
}
```

Now we can call our `sing` function, but we can also dance as well as sing:

```
sing('Let It Go',dance);
<< 'I'm singing along to Let It Go.'
'I'm moving my body to the groove.'
```

Note that the callback `dance` is passed as an argument without parentheses. This is because the argument is only a reference to the function. The actual callback is invoked in the body of the function, where parentheses are used.

Okay, so in these examples, the `dance()` function doesn't really do anything, except log another message to the console, but hopefully it shows you could do something very different with the `sing()` function depending on the callback function that is provided as an argument, making it a much more flexible function.

A function can also take an anonymous function as a callback. For example, say we want to call the `sing()` function and also want to stand on our head while singing, but we have no `standOnHead()` function. We can write an anonymous function that does it instead:

```
sing('Let It Go',()=>{ console.log("I'm standing on my
↪ head.");});
<< 'I'm singing along to Let It Go.'
'I'm standing on my head.'
```

This is only really useful for one-off tasks. It's often a better idea to keep functions separate and named, so they can be reused. It's also a bad idea to use this method for long function definitions as it can be confusing where the callback starts and ends. Named functions also make it easier to identify the source of bugs in code. In this case, the fact we only needed a one-line anonymous function made it a good candidate for using the arrow notation.

Callbacks are used extensively in many JavaScript functions and we'll see much more of them later in the book. In fact, here's a practical example that solves a problem we encountered in the last chapter:

Sorting Arrays With A Callback

In the last chapter we saw that arrays have a `sort()` method that sorted the items in the array into alphabetical order. This is fine for strings, but you might recall that it didn't work so well for numbers:

```
> [1,3,12,5,23,18,7].sort();
<< [1, 12, 18, 23, 3, 5, 7]
```

The reason for this is that the numbers are converted into strings and then placed in alphabetical order.

So how do you sort an array of numerical values? The answer is to provide a callback function to the `sort()` method that tells it how to compare two values, a and b. The callback function should return the following:

- A negative value if a comes before b

- 0 if a and b are equal

- A positive value if a comes after b

Here's an example of a `numerically` function that can be used as a callback to sort numbers:

```
function numerically(a,b){
return a-b;
}
```

This simply subtracts the two numbers that are being compared, giving a result that is either negative (if b is bigger than a), zero (if a and b are the same value), or positive (if a is bigger than b).

This function can now be used as a callback in the `sort()` method to sort the array of numbers correctly:

```
> [1,3,12,5,23,18,7].sort(numerically);
<< [1, 3, 5, 7, 12, 18, 23]
```

Much better!

Overflow Errors

In some rare instances where an array includes some very large and negative numbers, an overflow error can occur and the result of **a - b** becomes smaller than the smallest number that JavaScript is able to cope with. If this is the case, the following function can be used as a callback instead:

```
function numerically (a,b) {
if (a < b) {
    return -1;
} else if (a> b) {
    return 1;
} else {
    return 0;
}
}
```

Array Iterators

Arrays have a number of methods that utilize callbacks to make them more flexible.

Use of Arrow Functions

You'll notice that arrow functions are frequently used to declare the callbacks in these examples. This because they are short functions, often only taking up one line, making them a good candidate for using the arrow notation.

`forEach()`

In the last chapter, we saw that a `for` loop could be used to loop through each value in an array like so:

```
const colors = ['Red', 'Green', 'Blue']

for(let i = 0, max = colors.length ; i < max ; i++ ) {
console.log(`Color at position ${i} is ${colors[i]}`);
}
```

```
<<  'Color at position 0 is Red'
    'Color at position 1 is Green'
    'Color at position 2 is Blue'
```

An alternative is to use the `forEach()` method. This will loop through the array and invoke a callback function using each value as an argument. The callback function takes three parameters, the first represents the value in the array, the second represents the current index and the third represent the array that the callback is being called on. The example above could be written as:

```
colors.forEach( (color,index) =>
    console.log(`Color at position ${index}  is ${color}`) );
<<  "Color at position 0 is Red"
    "Color at position 1 is Green"
    "Color at position 2 is Blue"
```

map()

The `map()` method is very similar to the `forEach()` method. It also iterates over an array, and takes a callback function as a parameter that is invoked on each item in the array. This is often used to process data returned from databases in array form, such as adding HTML tags to plain text. The difference is that it returns a new array that replaces each value with the return value of the callback function. For example, we can square every number in an array using the `square` function we wrote previously as a callback to the `map()` method:

```
[1,2,3].map( square )
<< [1, 4, 9]
```

An anonymous function can also be used as a callback. This example will double all the numbers in the array:

```
[1,2,3].map( x => 2 * x);
<< [2,4,6]
```

The next example takes each item in the array and places them in uppercase inside paragraph HTML tags:

```
['red','green','blue'].map( color => `<p>
↪ ${color.toUpperCase()}</p>` );
<< ['<p>RED</p>',
↪ '<p>GREEN</p>', '<p>BLUE</p>']
```

Notice in this and the previous example, the anonymous function takes a parameter, `color`, which refers to the item in the array. This callback can also take two more parameters — the second parameter refers to the index number in the array and the third refers to the array itself. It's quite common for callbacks to only used the first, index, parameter, but the next example shows all three parameters being used:

```
['red','green','blue'].map( (color, index, array) =>
↪ `Element ${index} is ${color}. There are ${array.length}
↪ items in total.` );
<< [ 'Element 0 is red. There are 3 items in total.',
'Element 1 is green. There are 3 items in total.',
'Element 2 is blue. There are 3 items in total.' ]
```

Reduce()

The `reduce()` method is another method that iterates over each value in the array, but this time it cumulatively combines each result to return just a single value. The callback function is used to describe how to combine each value of the array with the running total. This is often used to calculate statistics such as averages from data stored in an array. It usually takes two parameters. The first parameter represents the accumulated value of all the calculations so far, and the

second parameter represents the current value in the array. The following
example shows how to sum an array of numbers:

```
[1,2,3,4,5].reduce( (acc,val) => prev + val );
<< 15
```

In the example above, value of `acc` starts as 1 (the first item in the array) then
keeps track of the accumulated total. The next item in the array is then added to
this running total, and so on, until every item in the array has been added
together and the result is returned.

The `reduce()` method also takes a second parameter after the callback, which is
the initial value of the accumulator, `acc`. For example, we could total the
numbers in an array, but starting at 10, instead of zero:

```
[1,2,3,4,5].reduce( (acc,val) => acc + val,10); //
↳ <---- second parameter of 10 here
<< 25
```

Another example could be to calculate the average word length in a sentence:

```
const sentence = 'The quick brown fox jumped over the lazy
↳ dog'
<< 'The quick brown fox jumped over the lazy dog'
```

The sentence can be converted into an array using the `split()` method:

```
<< ['The', 'quick', 'brown', 'fox', 'jumped', 'over',
↳ 'the', 'lazy', 'dog']
```

Now we can use the `reduce()` function to calculate the total number of letters in
the sentence, by starting the count at 0 and adding on the length of each word in
each step:

```
const total = words.reduce( (acc,word) => acc +
↪ word.length,0 );
<< 36
```

And a simple division sum tells us the average word length:

```
const average = total/words.length;
<< 4
```

Filter()

The filter() method returns a new array that only contains items from the
original array that return true when passed to the callback. For example, we can
filter an array of numbers to just the even numbers using the following code:

```
const numbers = [ 2, 7, 6, 5, 11, 23, 12 ]

 numbers.filter(x => x%2 === 0 ); // this returns true if
↪ the number is even

<< [ 2, 6, 12 ]
```

The filter() method provides a useful way of finding all the truthy values from
an array:

```
const array = [ 0, 1, '0', false, true, 'hello' ];
array.filter(Boolean);
<< [ 1, '0', true, 'hello' ]
```

This uses the fact that the Boolean() function will return the boolean
representation of a value, so only truthy values will return true and be returned
by the filter() method.

To find all the falsy values, the following filter can be used:

```
array.filter(x => !x);
[ 0, false ]
```

This uses the not operator, ! to return the compliment of a value's boolean representation. This means that any falsy values will return `true` and be returned by the filter.

There are other array methods that use callbacks that are worth investigating such as `reduceRight()`, `every()`, `find()` and `some()`. More information about them can be found at the Mozilla Developer Network[3].

Chaining Iterators Together

The various iterator functions can be used in combination to create some powerful transformations of data stored in arrays. This is achieved by a process called *chaining* methods together.

Chaining works because the iterator functions return an array, which means that another iterator function can then be chained on to the end and it will be applied to the new array.

For example, we can calculate the sum of square numbers using the `map()` method to square each number in the array and then chain the `reduce()` method on the end to add the results together:

```
[1,2,3].map( x => x*x ).reduce((acc,x) => acc + x );
<< 14
```

Another more complex example could be used to take an array of orders, apply a sales tax to them using `map()` and then use `reduce()` to find the total:

[3.] https://developer.mozilla.org/en-US/docs/Web/JavaScript/Reference/Global_Objects/ Array

```
const sales = [ 100, 230, 55];
 totalAfterTaxSales = sales.map( (amount) => amount * 1.15
↳ ).reduce( (acc,val) => acc + val );
<< 442.75
```

There are some good examples of chaining iterators together on SitePoint[4].

Improving the mean() Function

Earlier in the chapter we created a mean() function that would calculate the mean of any number of arguments. We can improve on this by using the reduce() method to add up all the values provided:

```
function mean(array) {
const total = array.reduce((a, b) => a + b);
return total/array.length;
}
```

Our next improvement will be to add a callback as the last parameter that specifies a function to be applied to all the numbers before the mean is calculated. This will allow us to work out things such as the mean of all numbers if they were doubled or squared.

Here is the code for the improved function that accepts a callback:

```
function mean(array,callback) {
    if (callback) {
    array.map( callback );
    }
const total = array.reduce((a, b) => a + b);
return total/array.length;
}
```

---

4. https://www.sitepoint.com/filtering-and-chaining-in-functional-javascript/

This code is similar to our previous `mean()` function, except in the following `if` block where we check to see if a callback has been provided. If it has, then the callback is applied to each value before being added to the total; otherwise, the total is calculated using just the values from the array given as the first argument:

Let's have a go at using it:

```
mean([2,5,7,11,4]); // this should just calculate the mean
<< 5.8
```

Now let's use an anonymous arrow function to double all the numbers before calculating the mean:

```
mean([2,5,7,11,4],x => 2*x);
<< 11.6
```

This is the equivalent of calculating the mean of `2*2`, `2*5`, `2*7`, `2*11`, and `2*4`.

Last of all, let's use the `square` function we wrote earlier in this chapter as a callback to square all the numbers before calculating the mean:

```
mean([2,5,7,11,4],square);
<< 43
```

This is the equivalent of calculating the mean of `2^2`, `5^2`, `7^2`, `11^2`, and `4^2`.

Hopefully, these examples help to show how using callbacks can make functions more powerful and flexible.

Quiz Ninja Project

Now we have a good understanding of functions, we're going to have a go at refactoring the code for our Quiz Ninja project so it uses functions to describe the main parts of the program. Refactoring is the process of improving the code's structure and maintainability without changing its behavior.

What we're going to do is replace some of the chunks of code with functions. This will make the code easier to follow and maintain because if we want to make a change to the functionality, all we need to do is change the code inside the relevant function.

Open up the `main.js` file and replace all the code with the following:

```
const quiz = [
    ["What is Superman's real name?","Clark Kent"],
    ["What is Wonder Woman's real name?","Diana Prince"],
    ["What is Batman's real name?","Bruce Wayne"]
];

function start(quiz){
let score = 0;

// main game loop
for(const [question,answer] of quiz){
    const response = ask(question);
    check(response,answer);
}
// end of main game loop

gameOver();

// function declarations
function ask(question){
    return prompt(question);
}

function check(response,answer){
```

```
        if(response === answer){
        alert('Correct!');
        score++;
        } else {
        alert(`Wrong! The correct answer was ${answer}`);
        }
}

function gameOver(){
 alert(`Game Over, you scored ${score} point${score !== 1 ?
↪ 's' : ''}`);
}
}
start(quiz);
```

The first part of this code remains the same — we create a map of questions and answers and store it in the `quiz` variable.

Next we create a function called `play()`. This is the main game function that contains all the steps of playing the game. This function also contains a number of functions that help to describe how the game runs. It starts by initializing a variable called `score` to 0.

After this, it iterates over the `quiz` array and invokes the `ask()` function for each question. We then, invoke the `check()` function to check if the player's response is correct. After we have looped through every question in the `quiz` array, the game is over, so the `gameOver()` function is invoked.

This shows how code can be simplified by abstracting it into separate functions that are descriptively named. Another benefit is that it allows us to change the content of the functions at a later time. If we decide that the way to check a question will change, for example, all we need to do is edit the `check()` function.

The `ask()`, `check()` and `gameOver()` functions are defined at the end of the body of the `play()` function. They need to be placed inside the `play()` function as nested functions, as this gives them access to any variables defined inside the `play()` function's scope. Because they are defined using function declarations, they are hoisted, so they can be defined *after* they are invoked.

The ask() function accepts a question parameter. This combination of function name and parameter name is used to make the code very descriptive — it reads almost like an English sentence: "Ask the question". It uses a prompt dialog and returns the text entered by the player, which is then saved in a variable called answer.

The check() function is written after the ask() function and has two parameters: response and answer. This combination of function name and parameter name again make the code read more like an English sentence. Naming functions in this way means we don't need to use comments to explain what the code does — it's self-explanatory.

This function uses the same logic we used in the last chapter to check if the answer entered by the player is the same as the answer stored in the map. If it is, then we increase the score by 1 and if it isn't, we show an alert dialog to tell them what the answer should have been.

When all the questions have been asked, and all the answers have been checked, the loop terminates and the gameOver() function is invoked. This uses an alert dialog to give some feedback about how many questions were answered correctly, using the same code that we used in the previous chapter.

There is an important line at the end of the file:

```
start(quiz);
```

This invokes the start() function with the quiz variable passed to it as an argument. This is required to actually start the quiz!

Once you've made these changes, have a go at playing the quiz by opening the index.html file in your browser.

While you play, you might notice there's been no change to the functionality of the quiz. This is an example of **refactoring** code — the functionality of the application remains the same, but the underlying code has become more flexible and easier to maintain, as well as being more readable and descriptive due to the use of functions. We have abstracted much of the internal game logic out into separate functions, which means we can change the mechanics of different aspects of the quiz by updating the relevant functions.

4-1. Quiz Ninja

You can see a live example on CodePen[5].

I hope this helps to demonstrate how descriptively named functions can make your code more flexible, maintainable, reusable and easier to read.

Chapter Summary

- Functions are first-class objects that behave the same way as other values.

---

5. https://codepen.io/daz4126/pen/QgmVKE

▓ Function literals can be defined using the `function` declaration, or by creating a *function expression* by assigning an anonymous function to a variable.

▓ All functions return a value. If this is not explicitly stated, the function will return `undefined`.

▓ A parameter is a value that is written in the parentheses of a function declaration and can be used like a variable inside the function's body.

▓ An argument is a value that is provided to a function when it is invoked.

▓ The `arguments` variable is an array-like object that allows access to each argument provided to the function using index notation.

▓ The rest operator can be used to access multiple arguments as an array.

▓ Default arguments can be supplied to a function by assigning them to the parameters.

▓ Arrow functions are a new shorthand notation that can used for writing anonymous functions in ES6.

▓ Function declarations can be invoked before they are defined because they are hoisted to the top of the scope, but function expressions cannot be invoked until after they are defined.

▓ A *callback* is a function that is provided as an argument to another function.

Everything that isn't a primitive data type in JavaScript is an object — which is the topic of our next chapter.

Chapter **5**

Objects

Everything in JavaScript is either one of the six primitive data types we met in Chapter 2 (strings, numbers, booleans, symbols, undefined, and null) or an object. We've actually met some objects already; arrays in Chapter 3 and functions in Chapter 4 are both objects, although these are built-in objects that are part of the language. In this chapter we're going to look at user-defined objects, as well as some of the other built-in objects.

In this chapter, we'll cover the following topics:

- Object literals

- Adding properties to objects

- Object methods

- JSON

- The `Math` object

- The `Date` object

- The `RegExp` object

- Project — we'll create quiz and question objects and ask random questions

Object Literals

An object in JavaScript is a self-contained set of related values and functions. They act as a collection of named properties that map to any JavaScript value such as strings, numbers, booleans, arrays and functions. If a property's value is a function, it is known as a **method**.

One way to think about an object is that it's like a dictionary where you look up a property name and see a value. It's like a database of values (in fact, some databases use JavaScript objects to store information). JavaScript objects are similar to a hash or associative array in other programming languages (or even a JavaScript `map`). They are, however, much more flexible, as they can be employed to encapsulate code that can be reused throughout a program. They can also inherit properties from other objects in a similar way to object-oriented languages (we'll cover how to do this in <u>Chapter 11</u>).

Objects are often used to keep any related information and functionality together in the same place. For example, if you wrote functions that found the perimeter and area of a square, you might want to group them together as methods of the same object that also included a `length` property.

A Super Example

An object literal is an object that is created directly in the language by wrapping all its properties and methods in curly braces {}. Object literals are a distinguishing feature of the JavaScript language, as they allow objects to be created quickly without the need for defining a class. They also provide a useful way of organizing your code without polluting the global namespace.

Here is an example of an object literal that describes the Man of Steel:

```
const superman = {
name: 'Superman',
'real name': 'Clark Kent',
height: 75,
weight: 235,
hero: true,
villain: false,
allies: ['Batman','Supergirl','Superboy'],
fly() {
    return 'Up, up and away!';
}
};
```

Each property is a key-value pair, separated by commas. In the example, the first property is called `name` and its value is `Superman`, while the `fly()` property is a method, as its value is a function, signified by the parentheses placed after it. If there were further methods after this, they would be comma-separated as well.

If a property's name doesn't follow the rules for naming variables described in Chapter 2, it needs to be quoted. The property `real name` in the example above needs to be quoted because it contains a space.

 Differing Naming Conventions

It's very uncommon to use property and method names that don't follow the rules for naming variables. In a real-world app, it's likely the `"real name"` property would actually be named `real_name` or `realName`.

All objects are mutable at any time when a program is running. This means that its properties and methods can be changed or removed, and new properties and methods can be added to the object, even if it was declared using `const`.

Creating Objects

To create an object literal, simply enter a pair of curly braces. The following example creates an empty object that is assigned to the variable `spiderman`:

```
const spiderman = {};
```

It's also possible to create an object using a constructor function. This example will also create an empty object:

```
const spiderman = new Object();
```

This method is not recommended, however, and the object literal notation is the preferred way of creating objects. The obvious reason is because it requires less typing and provides a concise way of initializing an object and its properties in one statement.

ES6 provided a shorthand method of creating objects if a property key is the same as a variable name that the property value is assigned to:

```
const name = 'Iron Man';
const realName = 'Tony Stark';

// long way
const ironMan = ( name: name, realName: realName };

// short ES6 way
const ironMan = { name, realName };
```

Accessing Properties

You can access the properties of an object using the dot notation that we've already seen in previous chapters. This will return the value of that property, as can be seen in the example below:

```
superman.name
<< 'Superman'
```

You can also access an object's properties using bracket notation — the property is represented by a string inside square brackets, so needs to be placed inside single or double quotation marks:

```
superman['name']
<< 'Superman'
```

Dot notation is much more common, but bracket notation has a few advantages: it's the only way to access nonstandard property and method names that don't follow the variable naming rules. It also lets you evaluate an expression and use it as the property key:

```
superman["real" + " " + "name"] // the property is built
↪ using string concatenation
<< "Clark Kent"
```

If you try to access a property that doesn't exist, undefined will be returned:

```
superman.city
<< undefined
```

Computed Properties

The ability to create objects with computed property keys was introduced in ES6. This means that JavaScript code can be placed inside square brackets and the property key will be the return value of that code. This can be seen in the example below where the + operator is used to concatenate the strings catch and phrase:

```
const hulk = { name: 'Hulk', ['catch' + 'Phrase']: 'Hulk
↪ Smash!' };
```

If we take a look at the hulk object, we can see the property key is named catchPhrase:

```
<< { name: 'Hulk', catchPhrase: 'Hulk Smash!' }
```

The value of a property has always been allowed to be a JavaScript expression. In the example below a ternary operator is used to return a true or false value for the hero property depending on the value of the bewitched variable:

```
const bewitched = true;
 const captainBritain = { name: 'Captain Britain', hero:
↪ bewitched ? false : true };

captainBritain
<< { name: 'Captain Britain', hero: false }
```

The new Symbol date type can also be used as a computed property key:

```
const name = Symbol('name');

const supergirl = { [name]: 'Supergirl' };
```

You can access the property using the square bracket notation:

```
supergirl[name];
<< 'Supergirl'
```

A new property can be added to an object using a symbol as a key if the square bracket notation is used:

```
const realName = Symbol('real name');

supergirl[realName] = 'Kara Danvers';
<< 'Kara Danvers'
```

The symbols used for property keys are not limited to being used by only one object - they can be reused by any other object:

```
 const daredevil = { [name]: 'Daredevil', [realName]: 'Matt
↳ Murdoch' };
```

Each symbol has a unique value, which means that using them as property keys avoids any naming clashes if you mistakenly use the same value for two different property keys. This might not seem likely in the examples we've seen so far, but it can be a problem if you're working with an object that has a large number of properties or if other developers are also working with the code.

Calling Methods

To call an object's method we can also use dot or bracket notation. Calling a method is the same as invoking a function, so parentheses need to be placed after the method name:

```
superman.fly()
<< 'Up, up and away!'
```

```
superman['fly']()
<< 'Up, up and away!'
```

Checking if Properties or Methods Exist

The in operator can be used to check whether an object has a particular property.
So, for example, we can check if the **superman** object has a property called `city`
using this code:

```
'city' in superman;
<< false
```

Alternatively, you could also check to see if the property or method doesn't
return undefined:

```
superman.city !== undefined;
<< false
```

Another way is to use the hasOwnProperty() method. As mentioned earlier,
objects can inherit properties from other objects, so all objects have a method
called hasOwnProperty(). This can be used to check whether an object has a
property that is its own, rather than one that has been inherited from another
object:

```
superman.hasOwnProperty('city');
<< false

superman.hasOwnProperty('name');
<< true
```

This method will *only* return any properties that belong to that particular object, whereas using in or !== undefined will return true, even if the property has been inherited from another object (inheritance is covered later in Chapter 12).

Finding all the Properties of an Object

We can loop through all of an object's properties and methods by using a for in loop. For example, to log all the properties of the superman object to the console, we could use:

```
for(const key in superman) {
console.log(key + ": " + superman[key]);
}
<< "name: Superman"
<< "real name: Clark Kent"
<< "height: 75"
<< "weight: 235"
<< "hero: true"
<< "villain: false"
<< "allies: Batman,Supergirl,Superboy"
<< "fly: function (){
    console.log(\"Up, up and away!\");
}"
```

In this example, we create a variable called key. We then iterate over the properties of the superman object and use key to log the property name and superman[key] to look up the value of each property.

To make sure that only an object's own properties are returned, a quick check can be implemented beforehand:

```
for(const key in superman) {
if(superman.hasOwnProperty(key)){
    console.log(key + ": " + superman[key]);
}
}
```

The following methods will only iterate over an object's own properties, so a check isn't required to ensure that inherited properties are ignored.

The `Object.keys()` method will return an array of all the keys of any object that is provided as an argument. We can then iterate over this array to access all the keys of an object:

```
for(const key of Object.keys(superman)) {
console.log(key);
}
<<      name
        real name
        height
        weight
        hero
        villain
        allies
        fly
```

ES2017 also adds some the `Object.values()` that works in the same way, but returns an array of all the object's value:

```
for(const value of Object.values(superman)) {
console.log(value);
}
<<      Superman
        Clark Kent
        75
        235
        true
        false
        [ 'Batman','Supergirl','Superboy' ]
        [Function: fly]
```

`Object.entries()` is also part of ES2017 and returns an array of key-value pairs. These key-value pairs are returned in arrays, but they can be destructured and accessed individually using the following notation:

```
for(const [key,value] of Object.entries(superman)) {
console.log(`${key}: ${value}`);
}
<<    name: Superman
    real name: Clark Kent
    height: 75
    weight: 235
    hero: true
    villain: false
    allies: [ 'Batman','Supergirl','Superboy' ]
    fly: [Function: fly]
```

Adding Properties

New properties and methods can be added to objects at any time in a program. This is done by simply assigning a value to the new property. For example, if we wanted to add a new `city` property to our `superman` object, we would do it like so:

```
superman.city = 'Metropolis';
<< 'Metropolis'
```

Now if we take a look at the `superman` object, we can see that it has a city property:

```
superman
<< { name: 'Superman',
    'real name': 'Clark Kent',
    height: 75,
    weight: 235,
    hero: true,
    villain: false,
    allies: [ 'Batman', 'Supergirl', 'Superboy' ],
    fly: [Function: fly]
    city: 'Metropolis' }
```

It's important to note that properties don't always appear in the order they were entered. An object is not an ordered list like an array, set or map, so you should never rely on the properties being in a certain order.

Changing Properties

You can change the value of an object's properties at any time using assignment. For example, we can change the value of the "real name" property like this:

```
superman['real name'] = 'Kal-El';
<< 'Kal-El'
```

We can check the update has taken place by taking a look at the object:

```
superman
 << {'allies': ['Batman', 'Supergirl', 'Superboy'],
 ↪ 'city': 'Metropolis', 'fly': function (){
     console.log('Up, up and away!');
 }, "height": 75, 'hero': true, 'name': 'Superman', 'real
 ↪ name': 'Kal-El", 'villain': false, 'weight': 235}
```

Removing Properties

Any property can be removed from an object using the delete operator. For example, if we wanted to remove the fly method from the superman object, we would enter the following:

```
delete superman.fly
<< true
```

Now if we take a look at the superman object, we can see that the Man of Steel has lost his ability to fly:

```
superman
 << {"allies": ['Batman', 'Supergirl', 'Superboy'],
 ↪ 'city': 'Superman', 'real name': 'Kal-El', 'villain': false,
 ↪ 'weight': 235}
```

Nested Objects

It's even possible for an object to contain other objects. These are known as
nested objects. Here's an example of an object that contains a list of other objects.
It has been assigned to the variable jla:

```
const jla = {
superman: { realName: 'Clark Kent' },
batman: { realName: 'Bruce Wayne' },
wonderWoman: { realName: 'Diana Prince" },
flash: { realName: 'Barry Allen' },
aquaman: { realName: 'Arthur Curry' },
}
```

The values in nested objects can be accessed by referencing each property name
in order using either dot or bracket notation:

```
jla.wonderWoman.realName
<< "Diana Prince"

jla['flash']['realName']
<< "Barry Allen"
```

You can even mix the different notations:

```
jla.aquaman['realName']
<< "Arthur Curry"
```

Objects Are Copied By Reference

An important concept to get your head around is that objects are assigned by *reference*. This means that if a variable is assigned to an object that already exists, it will simply point to the exact same space in memory. So any changes made using *either* reference will affect the same object.

In the example below, we create a new object called `thor` to represent The Mighty Thor and make a copy of it called `cloneThor`:

```
const thor = { name: 'Thor'
// more properties here
};

const cloneThor = thor;
```

The variable `cloneThor` now has all the same properties as the `thor` object. The problem is, we haven't created a new object that is a copy of `thor`; the variables `cloneThor` and `thor` both reference exactly the same object!

We can see this, if we make a change to the `name` property of `cloneThor`:

```
cloneThor.name = 'Clor';
```

Now if we check the value of the name property of the `thor` object, we'll discover a problem:

```
thor.name
<< 'Clor'
```

Changing the `name` property of `cloneThor` has resulted in the `name` property of `thor` changing as well. This happens because the variables `thor` and `cloneThor` both point to the same object in memory. Any changes made to either variable will affect the other.

This doesn't happen when primitive values are used instead of objects, as can be seen in the example below:

```
a = 1;
b = a;
```

At this point, both **a** and **b** will have a value of 1, but if the value of **b** is changed, it won't affect the value of **a**:

```
b = 2;
// check the value of a hasn't changed
a
<< 1
```

Objects as Parameters to Functions

An object literal can be passed as a parameter to a function. This is useful when there are a large number of parameters, as it allows the arguments to be provided by name and in any order. This means you don't have to remember the order to enter them when invoking a function.

The following example shows how this can be done using a function called `greet()`. This accepts three parameters:

```
function greet({greeting,name,age}) {
 return `${greeting}! My name is ${name} and I am ${age}
↪ years old.`;
}
```

Here's an example of how the function can be used. Notice how the order of the properties in the argument object differs from the order they are listed in the object provided as a parameter to the function:

```
 greet({ greeting: `What's up dude`, age: 10, name: `Bart`
↪ });
 << 'What\'s up dude! My name is Bart and I am 10 years
↪ old.'
```

We can provide default values for some of the parameters using assignment, as we saw in the last chapter. In the following example, the `greeting` and `age` parameters now have default values, but the `name` parameter still has to be provided as an argument, otherwise it will be set as `undefined`:

```
function greet({greeting='Hello',name,age=18}) {
  return `${greeting}! My name is ${name} and I am ${age}
↳ years old.`;
}
```

If we leave out the `greeting` argument it will be set to `Hello`, but the default values can also be overridden, as we do with the `age` value in the example below:

```
greet({ name: 'Lisa', age: 8 });
<< 'Hello! My name is Lisa and I am 0 years old.'
```

This technique is referred to as using **named parameters** and is often used when a function has a large amount of optional parameters.

this

The keyword `this` refers to the object that it is within. It can be used inside methods to gain access to the object's properties.

To demonstrate using `this`, we'll create a dice object that has a `sides` property and a `roll()` method that returns a number between 1 and the number of sides.

Here's the code to create our dice object:

```
const dice = {
sides: 6,
roll() {
    return Math.floor(this.sides * Math.random()) + 1;
}
}
```

This object has a `sides` property and a `roll()` method. Inside the `roll()` method we use `this.sides` to refer to the value of the object's `sides` property.

We also use the `random()` and `floor()` methods of the `Math` object to return a number between 1 and the number of sides.

Let's take it for a spin:

```
dice.roll();
<< 5

dice.roll();
<< 3
```

If we want to change the number of sides, all we need to do is modify the `sides` property:

```
dice.sides = 20;
<< 20
```

Now the `roll()` method will return a random number between 1 and 20 instead, without us having to modify it:

```
dice.roll();
<< 12

dice.roll();
<< 18
```

Namespacing

Naming collisions occur when the same variable or function name is used for different purposes by code sharing the same scope. This might not seem likely, but imagine if you have lots of code that has been created over time – you might end up reusing a variable name without realizing. The problem becomes more likely if you use code libraries from other developers or work on code in teams, as you might choose the same name for a function as another member of the team.

A solution to this problem is to use the **object literal pattern** to create a namespace for groups of related functions. This is done by creating an object literal that serves as the namespace, then adding any values as properties of that object, and any functions as methods.

For example, in the last chapter we created some functions for squaring numbers and finding the mean. One of the functions used was called `square()`. This is quite a generic name and it wouldn't be too far fetched to imagine a situation where a `square()` function also existed for drawing squares using the Canvas API (this is covered in Chapter 14). To prevent this happening, we can place all our functions inside an object, thereby creating a namespace for them. In the example below, the namespace is `myMaths`, which is the name of the variable the object that contains the functions has been assigned to:

```
const myMaths = {

square(x) {
    return x * x;
    },
    mean(array,callback) {
        if (callback) {
        array.map( callback );
        }
        const total = array.reduce((a, b) => a + b);
        return total/array.length;
    }
};
```

Now these functions need to be preceded by the namespace to be invoked:

```
myMaths.square(3)
<< 9

myStats.mean([1,2,3])
<< 2
```

This would avoid any clashes with any other functions called `square()` as they would also be defined in their own namespace. For example, a function that draws a square using the canvas API might be `myCanvas.square()`.

Built-in Objects

We've already seen the two main built-in objects included in JavaScript: arrays and functions. JavaScript has a number of other built-in *global* objects that can be accessed from anywhere in a program. They provide a number of useful properties and methods that we'll cover in this section.

JSON

JavaScript Object Notation, or JSON[1], was invented by Douglas Crockford in 2001. It is an extremely popular lightweight data-storage format that is used by a large number of services for data serialization and configuration. It is often used to exchange information between web services, and is employed by sites such as Twitter, Facebook and Trello to share information. The beauty of JSON is that it manages to hit the sweet spot between being both human- and machine-readable.

JSON is a string representation of the object literal notation that we have just seen. There are, however, a couple of key differences:

1. Property names must be double-quoted
2. Permitted values are double-quoted strings, numbers, true, false, null, arrays and objects
3. Functions are not permitted values

A JSON string representation the Caped Crusader is shown below:

```
const batman = '{"name": "Batman","real name": "Bruce
↪ Wayne","height": 74, "weight": 210, "hero": true, "villain":
↪ false, "allies": ["Robin","Batgirl","Superman"]}'
```

---

[1] http://www.json.org

JSON is becoming increasingly popular as a data storage format, and many programming languages now have libraries dedicated to parsing and generating it. Since ECMAScript 5, there has been a global `JSON` object that has methods to allow this to be done in JavaScript.

The `parse()` method takes a string of data in JSON format and returns a JavaScript object:

```
JSON.parse(batman);
<< { name: 'Batman',
'real name': 'Bruce Wayne',
height: 74,
weight: 210,
hero: true,
villain: false,
allies: [ 'Robin', 'Batgirl', 'Superman' ] }
```

The `stringify()` method does the opposite, taking a JavaScript object and returning a string of JSON data, as can be seen in the example:

```
const wonderWoman = {
name: 'Wonder Woman',
'real name': 'Diana Prince',
height: 72,
weight: 165,
hero: true,
villain: false,
allies: ['Wonder Girl','Donna Troy','Superman'],
lasso: function(){
    console.log('You will tell the truth!');
}
}

JSON.stringify(wonderWoman);
  << '{"name":"Wonder Woman","real name":"Diana
↳ Prince","height":72,
  "weight":165,"hero":true,"villain":false,"allies":["Wonder
↳ Girl",
```

```
"Donna Troy","Superman"]}'
```

Note that the `lasso` method is simply ignored by the `stringify()` method.

You can also add a space argument that will add new lines between each key-value pair, which is useful when displaying the results in a browser:

```
JSON.stringify(wonderWoman, null, " ");
 <<  '{\n "name": "Wonder Woman",\n "real name": "Diana
↪ Prince",\n "height": 72,\n "weight": 165,\n "hero": true,\n
↪ "villain": false,\n "allies": [\n  "Wonder Girl",\n  "Donna
↪ Troy",\n  "Superman"\n ]\n}'
```

These methods are particularly useful when it comes to sending data to, and receiving data from, a web server using Ajax requests (see Chapter 13) – or when using localStorage to store data on a user's machine (see Chapter 14). JSON data is easy to exchange between different services, as most languages and protocols are able to interpret data as strings of text – and they only need to be stored as a basic text file.

The Math Object

The `Math` object is a built-in object that has several properties representing mathematical constants, as well as methods that carry out a number of common mathematical operations.

All the properties and methods of the `Math` object are immutable and unable to be changed.

Mathematical Constants

The `Math` object has eight properties that represent a mix of commonly used math constants. Note that they are all named in capital letters, as is the convention for constant values:

```
 Math.PI // The ratio of the circumference and diameter of a
 ↪ circle
<< 3.141592653589793

Math.SQRT2 // The square root of 2
<< 1.4142135623730951

Math.SQRT1_2 // The reciprocal of the square root of 2
<< 0.7071067811865476

Math.E // Euler's constant
<< 2.718281828459045

Math.LN2 // The natural logarithm of 2
<< 0.6931471805599453

Math.LN10 // The natural logarithm of 10
<< 2.302585092994046

Math.LOG2E // Log base 2 of Euler's constant
<< 1.4426950408889634

Math.LOG10E // Log base 10 of Euler's constant
<< 0.4342944819032518
```

Mathematical Methods

The `Math` object also has several methods to carry out a variety of useful mathematical operations.

Absolute Values

The `Math.abs()` method returns the absolute value of a number. So if the number is positive, it will remain the same, and if it's negative, it will become positive:

```
Math.abs(3);
<< 3
```

```
Math.abs(-4.6);
<< 4.6
```

Rounding Methods

The `Math.ceil()` method will round a number *up* to the next integer, or remain the same if it is already an integer:

```
Math.ceil(4.2);
<< 5

Math.ceil(8);
<< 8

Math.ceil(-4.2);
<< -4
```

The `Math.floor()` method will round a number *down* to the next integer, or remain the same if it is already an integer:

```
Math.floor(4.2);
<< 4

Math.floor(8);
<< 8

Math.floor(-4.2);
<< -5
```

The `Math.round()` method will round a number to the *nearest* integer:

```
Math.round(4.5);
<< 5
```

```
Math.round(4.499);
<< 4

Math.round(-4.2);
<< -4
```

ES6 also introduced the `Math.trunc()` method that returns the integer-part of a number – that is, it gets truncated at the decimal point:

```
Math.trunc(4.9);
<< 4

Math.trunc(-4.2);
<< -4
```

Powers and Roots

The `Math.exp()` method will raise a number to the power of Euler's constant:

```
Math.exp(1); // This is Euler's constant
<< 2.718281828459045

Math.exp(0); // Any number to the power of 0 is 1
<< 1

Math.exp(-3);
<< 0.049787068367863944
```

The `Math.pow()` method will raise any number (the first argument) to the power of another number (the second argument):

```
Math.pow(3, 2); // 3 squared
<< 9
```

```
Math.pow(4.5, 0); // Any number to the power of 0 is 1
<< 1

Math.pow(27, 1/3); // A nice way to do cube roots
<< 3
```

The `Math.sqrt()` method returns the positive square root of a number:

```
Math.sqrt(121);
<< 11

Math.sqrt(2); // same as Math.SQRT2
<< 1.4142135623730951

Math.sqrt(-1); // imaginary numbers aren't supported!
<< NaN
```

The `Math.cbrt()` method was introduced in ES6, which returns the cube root of numbers:

```
Math.cbrt(8);
<< 2

Math.cbrt(-1000);
<< -10
```

The `Math.hypot()` method was also introduced in ES6. It returns the square root of the sum of the squares of all its arguments. This can be used to calculate the hypotenuse of a right-angled triangle:

```
 Math.hypot(3,4); // returns the square root of 3 squared + 4
↪ squared
<< 5
```

```
Math.hypot(2,3,6); // more than 2 arguments can be used
<< 7
```

Logarithmic Methods

The `Math.log()` method returns the natural logarithm of a number:

```
 Math.log(Math.E); // Natural logs have a base of Euler's
↪ constant
<< 1

Math.log(1); // log of 1 is zero
<< 0

Math.log(0); // You can't take the log of zero
<< -Infinity

Math.log(-2); // You can't take logs of negative numbers
<< NaN
```

Logarithms in base 2 and 10 were added in ES6:

```
Math.log2(8); // 8 is 2 to the power of 3
<< 3

Math.log10(1000000); // 1 million is 10 to the power 6
<< 6
```

Maximum & Minimum Methods

The `Math.max()` method returns the maximum number from its arguments:

```
Math.max(1,2,3);
<< 3
```

```
Math.max(Math.PI,Math.SQRT2, Math.E);
<< 3.141592653589793
```

And the `Math.min()` method unsurprisingly returns the minimum number from the given arguments:

```
Math.min(1,2,3);
<< 1

Math.min(Math.PI,Math.SQRT2, Math.E);
<< 1.4142135623730951
```

Trigonometric Functions

The `Math` object also has the standard trigonometric functions, which are very useful when working with geometrical objects. All angles are measured in radians for these functions.

 Radians

Radians are a standard unit of angular measurement, equal to the angle of the circle's center corresponding to the arc that subtends it.

Rounding Errors

Be careful if you require exact answers to these calculations, as rounding errors in the background mean the returned value is often slightly inaccurate.

A number of these errors are highlighted in the examples below.

This is to be expected when dealing with floating-point decimal numbers. Computers have lots of trouble dealing with decimal fractions (as they work in binary), and the answers can vary from one platform to another.

Another problem is that the value of π using `Math.PI` is only given correct to 16 significant figures, which will affect the overall accuracy.

These issues are also implementation dependent, which means they rely on the JavaScript engine and operating system they are running on rather than the language itself. So you may get slightly different answers using a different web browser on the same OS or using the same web browser on a different OS!

These rounding errors shouldn't be a big deal for most web applications. Whenever you perform any calculations, make sure your program doesn't rely on exact answers, and has some degree of tolerance instead.

If you find you need more precision, you could consider using the decimal.js library[2].

The `Math.sin()` returns the sine of an angle:

```
 Math.sin(Math.PI/6); // this calculation contains rounding
↪ errors, it should be 0.5
<< 0.49999999999999994
```

The `Math.cos()` returns the cosine of an angle:

```
Math.cos(Math.PI/6);
<< 0.8660254037844387
```

The `Math.tan()` returns the tangent of an angle:

---

2. https://github.com/MikeMcl/decimal.js/

```
Math.tan(Math.PI/4); // another rounding error, this should
↳ be 1
<< 0.9999999999999999

Math.tan(Math.PI/2); // this should be NaN or Infinity
<< 16331778728383844
```

The `Math.asin()` returns the arcsine of a number. The result is an angle:

```
Math.asin(1);
<< 1.5707963267948966
```

The `Math.acos()` returns the arccosine of a number. The result is an angle:

```
Math.acos(0.5);
<< 1.0471975511965976
```

The `Math.atan()` returns the arctangent of a number. The result is an angle:

```
Math.atan(Math.sqrt(3)); // Same as Math.PI/3
<< 1.0471975511965976
```

Methods for the hyperbolic functions[3], `sinh()`, `cosh()` and `tanh()` were also added in ES6, as well as their inverses:

```
Math.sinh(1);
<< 1.1752011936438014

Math.asinh(1.1752011936438014);
<< 1

Math.cosh(0);
```

3. https://en.wikipedia.org/wiki/Hyperbolic_function

```
<< 1

Math.acosh(1);
<< 0

Math.tanh(10);
<< 0.9999999958776927

Math.atanh(0.9999999958776927); // rounding error here
<< 9.999999995520374
```

Random Numbers

The `Math.random()` method is used to create random numbers, which can be very useful when writing programs. Calling the method will generate a number between 0 (inclusive) and 1 (exclusive), like so:

```
Math.random();
<< 0.7881970851344265
```

To generate a random number between 0 and another number, we can multiply the value by that number. The following code generates a random number between 0 and 6:

```
6 * Math.random();
<< 4.580981240354013
```

If we want to generate a random integer, we can use the `Math.floor()` method that we saw earlier to remove the decimal part of the return value. The following code generates a random integer between 0 and 5 (it will never be 6, because it always rounds down):

```
Math.floor(6 * Math.random());
<< 4
```

It's a useful exercise to try and write a function that will generate a random number between two values.

The Date Object

Date objects contain information about dates and times. Each object represents a single moment in time.

Constructor Function

A constructor function is used to create a new date object using the new operator:

```
const today = new Date();
```

The variable today now points to a Date object. To see what the date is, we use the toString() method that all objects have:

```
today.toString();
<< 'Tue Feb 14 2017 16:35:18 GMT+0000 (GMT)'
```

If an argument is not supplied, the date will default to the current date and time. It's possible to create Date objects for any date by supplying it as an argument to the constructor function. This can be written as a string in a variety of forms:

```
const christmas = new Date('2017 12 25');
christmas.toString();
<< 'Mon Dec 25 2017 00:00:00 GMT+0000 (GMT)'

const chanukah = new Date('12 December 2017');
// First day of Chanukah
```

```
chanukah.toString();
<< 'Tue Dec 12 2017 00:00:00 GMT+0000 (GMT)'

const eid = new Date('Sunday, June 25, 2017');
// Eid-al-Fitr
eid.toString();
<< 'Sun Jun 25 2017 00:00:00 GMT+0100 (BST)'
```

As you can see, the string passed to the Date constructor can be in a variety of formats. However, in order to be more consistent, it's better to provide each bit of information about the date as a separate argument. The parameters that can be provided are as follows:

```
new Date(year,month,day,hour,minutes,seconds,milliseconds)
```

Here is an example:

```
const solstice = new Date(2017, 5, 21);
// Summer Solstice
solstice.toString();
<< 'Wed Jun 21 2017 00:00:00 GMT+0100 (BST)'
```

Remember that computer programs start counting at zero, so January is 0, February is 1, and so on up to December, which is 11.

An alternative is to use a timestamp, which is a single integer argument that represents the number of milliseconds since the Epoch (1st January 1970):

```
const diwali = new Date(1508367600000);
diwali.toString();
<< 'Thu Oct 19 2017 00:00:00 GMT+0100 (BST)'
```

The Epoch

The Epoch is 1st January 1970. This is an arbitrary date that is used in programming as a reference point in time from which to measure dates. This allows dates to be expressed as an integer that represents the number of seconds since the Epoch. It results in a very large number and there is a potential problem looming in 2038 when the number of seconds since the Epoch will be greater than 2,147,483,647, which is the maximum value that many computers can deal with as a signed 32-bit integer. Fortunately, this problem will not affect JavaScript dates because it uses floating-point numbers rather than integers, so it can handle bigger values.

Getter Methods

The properties of date objects are unable to be viewed or changed directly. Instead, they have a number of methods known as **getter** methods, which return information about the date object, such as the month and year.

Once you've created a date object it will have access to all the getter methods. There are two versions of most methods – one that returns the information in local time, and the other that uses Coordinated Universal Time (UTC). The `getTime()`, `getTimezoneOffset()` and `getYear()` methods don't have UTC equivalents.

UTC

UTC is the primary time standard by which the world regulates clocks. It was formalized in 1960 and is much the same as Greenwich Mean Time (GMT). The main difference is that UTC is a standard that is defined by the scientific community, unlike GMT.

The `getDay()` and `getUTCDay()` methods are used to find the day of the week that the date object falls on. It returns a number, starting at 0 for Sunday, up to 6 for Saturday:

```
diwali.getDay(); // it's on a Thursday
<< 4
```

The getDate() and getUTCDate()methods return the day of the month for the date object (note that these values start counting from 1, not 0, so they return the actual day of the month):

```
diwali.getDate(); // it's on the 19th
<< 19
```

The getMonth() and getUTCMonth() methods can be used to find the month of the date object. It returns an integer, but remember to count from 0; so January is 0, February is 1, and so on up to December being 11:

```
diwali.getMonth(); // it's in October
<< 9
```

The getFullYear() and getUTCFullYear() methods return the year of the date object. There is also a getYear() method, but it isn't Y2K compliant, so shouldn't be used:

```
diwali.getYear(); // broken for years after 2000
<< 117

diwali.getFullYear(); // use this instead
<< 2017
```

There are also getHours(), getUTCHours(), getMinutes(), getUTCMinutes(), getSeconds(), getUTCSeconds, getMilliseconds(), and getUTCMilliseconds() methods that will return the hours, minutes, seconds and milliseconds since midnight.

The getTime() method returns a timestamp representing the number of milliseconds since the Epoch:

```
diwali.getTime();
<< 1508367600000
```

This can be useful for incrementing dates by a set amount of time. For example, a day can be represented by 1000 * 60 * 60 * 24 milliseconds:

```
 const christmasEve = new Date(christmas.getTime() - 1000 *
 ↳ 60 * 60 * 24) // one day before Christmas
christmasEve.toString();
<< Fri Dec 26 2014 00:00:00 GMT+0000 (GMT)"
```

The getTimezoneOffset() method returns the difference, in minutes, between the local time on the computer and UTC. For example, my timezone is currently the same as UTC, so it returns 0:

```
new Date().getTimezoneOffset();
<< 0
```

Setter Methods

Most of the getter methods covered in the previous section have equivalent **setter** methods. These are methods that can be used to change the value of the date held in a Date object. Each of the methods takes an argument representing the value to which you update the date. The methods return the timestamp of the updated date object.

As an example, we can change the value of the date stored in the diwali variable so that it contains the date of Diwali in 2018, which is on Wednesday, November 7, 2018:

```
diwali.setDate(7);
<< 1507330800000
```

```
diwali.setMonth(10); // November is month 10
<< 1510012800000

diwali.setFullYear(2018);
<< 1541548800000
```

Note that the values returned by these functions is the timestamp representing the number of milliseconds since the Epoch. To see the actual date, we need to use the `toString()` method:

```
diwali.toString();
<< 'Wed Nov 07 2018 00:00:00 GMT+0000 (GMT)'
```

There are also `setHours()`, `setUTCHours()`, `setMinutes()`, `setUTCMinutes()`, `setSeconds()`, `setUTCSeconds`, `setMilliseconds()` and `setUTCMilliseconds()` methods that can be used to edit the time portion of a `Date` object.

Alternatively, if you know the date as a timestamp, you can use the `setTime()` method:

```
diwali.setTime(1447200000000);
<< 1541548800000
```

 Tricky Timezones

Working with dates and timezones can be tricky. The moment.js library[4] gives you a large number of methods that make it easier to work with dates, as well as support for multiple locales.

The `RegExp` Object

A regular expression (or RegExp, for short) is a pattern that can be used to search strings for matches to the pattern. A common use is "find and replace" type

---

[4.] https://momentjs.com

operations. For example, say you were looking for any word ending in "ing", you could use the regular expression /[a-zA-Z]+ing$/.

If that example looks a bit confusing, don't worry, it will become clear as we move through this section. Regular expressions can look a little strange; in fact, they're something of a dark art that could easily fill a whole book! They are certainly useful when manipulating text strings, though, so we'll introduce some of the basics here and recommend that you carry out further reading once you've finished this book.

Here are a couple of resources for the curious:

- Online Regex Tester[5]

- Regular Expressions 101[6]

- Mastering Regular Expressions by Jeffrey Fried[7]

- Regular Expressions Info[8]

Creating Regular Expressions

There are two ways to create a regular expression. The first, and preferred way, is to use the literal notation of writing the regular expression between forward slashes that we've already seen:

```
const pattern = /[a-zA-Z]+ing$/;
```

Alternatively, you can create a new instance of the RegExp object using the new operator and a constructor function:

```
const pattern = new RegExp('[a-zA-Z]+ing');
```

[5.] http://www.regextester.com
[6.] https://regex101.com
[7.] http://www.amazon.com/Mastering-Regular-Expressions-Jeffrey-Friedl/dp/0596528124/
[8.] http://www.regular-expressions.info/

Notice that the backslash character needs to be used twice in the last example.

Using literal regular expressions takes less typing, but there are advantages to using the constructor function as it lets you create regular expressions using strings, which can be useful when the regular expression is provided from user input; in a form, for example. Constructors also have the advantage of letting you create a regular expression using a variable:

```
const language = 'JavaScript';
const pattern = new RegExp(language);
```

RegExp Methods

Once you've created a regular expression object, you can use the `test()` method to see if a string (passed to the method as a parameter) matches the regular expression pattern. It returns `true` if the pattern is in the string, and `false` if it isn't.

We can see an example of the `test()` method used below, using the same pattern we created earlier that tests if a word ends in "ing":

```
pattern.test('joke');
<< false

pattern.test('joking');
<< true

pattern.test('jokingly');
<< false
```

The `exec()` method works in the same way as the `test()` method, but instead of returning `true` or `false`, it returns an array containing the first match found, or `null` if there aren't any matches:

```
pattern.exec('joke');
<< null

pattern.exec('joking');
<< [ 'joking', index: 0, input: 'joking' ]
```

Basic Regular Expressions

At the most basic level, a regular expression will just be a string of characters, so the following will match the string "JavaScript":

```
const pattern = /JavaScript/;
<< /JavaScript/
```

Character Groups

Groups of characters can be placed together inside square brackets. This character group represents any *one* of the characters inside the brackets. For example, the following regular expression matches any vowel:

```
const vowels = /[aeiou]/
<< /[aeiou]/
```

A sequence of characters can also be represented by placing a dash [-] between the first and last characters; for example, all the uppercase letters can be represented as:

```
/[A-Z]/
```

The digits 0-9 can be represented as:

```
/[0-9]/
```

If a \^ character is placed at the start of the sequence of characters with the brackets, it negates the sequence, so the following regular expression represents any character that is *not* a capital letter:

```
/[^A-Z]/
```

These groups can be combined with letters to make a more complex pattern. For example, the following regular expression represents the letter J (lowercase or capital) followed by a vowel, followed by a lowercase v, followed by a vowel:

```
pattern = /[Jj][aeiou]v[aeiou]/;
<< /[Jj][aeiou]v[aeiou]/

pattern.test('JavaScript');
<< true

pattern.test('jive');
<< true

pattern.test('hello');
<< false
```

Regular Expression Properties

Regular expressions are objects, and have the following properties:

- The `global` property makes the pattern return all matches. By default, the pattern only looks for the first occurrence of a match.

- The `ignoreCase` property makes the pattern case-insensitive. By default, they are case sensitive.

■ The `multiline` property makes the pattern multiline. By default, a pattern will stop at the end of a line.

The following flags can be placed after a regular expression literal to change the default properties:

■ g sets the `global` property to true

■ i sets the `ignoreCase` property to true

■ m sets the `multiline` property to true

For example, the following regular expression will match "JavaScript" or "Javaccript" because the `ignoreCase` property is set to `true`:

```
pattern = /java/i
<< /java/i

pattern.test('JavaScript');
<< true
```

These properties can be checked using the dot notation, but cannot be updated once the regular expression has been created, as can be seen in the following example:

```
pattern = /java/i
<< /java/i

pattern.ignoreCase // checking it is true
<< true

pattern.ignoreCase = false // this won't work
<< false

pattern.ignoreCase // has it changed? Nope!
<< true
```

The only way to change the `ignoreCase` property to `false` is to redefine the regular expression:

```
pattern = /java/
<< /java/
```

Special Characters

In a regular expression, there are a number of characters that have a special meaning, commonly known as metacharacters.

- . matches any character, except line breaks

- \w matches any word character, and is equivalent to [A-Za-z0-9_]

- \W matches any non-word character, and is equivalent to [\^A-Za-z0-9_]

- \d matches any digit character, and is equivalent to [0-9]

- \D matches any non-digit character, and is equivalent to [^0-9]

- \s matches any whitespace character, and is equivalent to [\t\r\n\f]

- \S matches any non-whitespace character, and is equivalent to [^ \t\r\n\f]

Modifiers

Modifiers can be placed after a token to deal with multiple occurrences of that token:

- ? makes the preceding token in the regular expression optional

- * matches one or more occurrences of the preceding token

- + matches one or more occurrences of the preceding token

- {n} matches *n* occurrences of the preceding token

- {n,} matches at least *n* occurrences of the pattern

- {,m}matches at most *m* occurrences of the preceding token

- {n,m} matches at least *n* and at most *m* occurrences of the preceding token

- ^ marks the position immediately before the first character in the string

- $ marks the position immediately after the last character in the string

Any special characters or modifiers can be escaped using a backslash. So if you wanted to match a question mark, ?, you would need to use the regular expression /\?/.

For example, the following regular expression will match anything that starts with J followed by one or more vowels, then any letters or numbers ending in ing:

```
pattern = /^J[aeiou]+\w+ing$/
<< /J[aeiou]+\w+ing/
```

As we can see, it now matches the words 'Joking' and 'Jeering':

```
pattern.test('Joking');
<< true

pattern.test('Jeering');
<< true
```

Greedy and Lazy Modifiers

All the modifiers above are **greedy**, which means they will match the longest possible string. They can be made into **lazy** modifiers that match the shortest possible string by adding an extra ? after the modifier.

For example, consider the stringabracadabra:

```
const word = 'abracadabra';
```

The greedy pattern /a.+a/ will return the whole string because it is the longest string that matches the pattern of a, followed by numerous characters and finishing with an a:

```
const greedyPattern = /a.+a/;
greedyPattern.exec(word);
<< [ 'abracadabra', index: 0, input: 'abracadabra' ]
```

The lazy pattern /a.+?a/ changes the + modifier to +?. This will only return the string 'abra' as this is the shortest string that matches the pattern a followed by some characters and ending in an a;.

```
const lazyPattern = /a.+?a/;
lazyPattern.exec(word);
<< [ 'abra', index: 0, input: 'abracadabra' ]
```

A Practical Example

If we were looking for PDF files and had a list of filenames, this regular expression could be used to find them (assuming they have a .pdf extension, of course):

```
const pdf = /.*\.pdf$/;
```

This looks for zero or more occurrences of any character, followed by an escaped period, followed by the letters pdf that must come at the end of the string:

```
pdf.test('chapter5.pdf');
<< true
```

```
pdf.test('report.doc');
<< false
```

String Methods

There are a number of string methods that accept regular expressions as a parameter.

The split() method we saw in Chapter 2 can also accept a regular expression that's used to split a string into the separate elements of an array. The following example uses a regular expression to split a string every time there are one or more occurrences of a whitespace character:

```
'Hello World!'.split(/\s+/) //
<< ['Hello', 'World!']
```

The match() method returns an array of all the matches. By default, only the first is returned:

```
'JavaScript'.match(/[aeiou]/); // return the first vowel
<< ['a']
```

We can use the g flag to return *all* the matches:

```
 'JavaScript'.match(/[aeiou]/g); // return an array of all
↳ the vowels
<< ['a', 'a', 'i']
```

The search() method returns the position of the first match:

```
"I'm learning JavaScript".search(/java/i);
<< 13
```

It returns -1 if there is no match:

```
"I'm learning JavaScript".search(/ruby/i);
<< -1
```

The replace() method replaces any matches with another string. The following example will replace all vowels with a '*' character:

```
'JavaScript'.replace(/[aeiou]/ig,'*');
<< 'J*v*Scr*pt'
```

Matched Groups

Sub-patterns can be created inside a regular expression by placing them inside parentheses. These are known as *capturing groups*. Any matches to these will then be stored in an array of matches.

Each capturing group is numbered according to the position it appears in the pattern. For example, the first capturing group will be numbered 1, and the second 2, etc. The matches will also be stored in special predefined variables $1, $2 etc.

To demonstrate this, here's an example that searches a string and replaces any HTML anchor tags with Markdown[9] notation:

```
const link = "<a href='https://www.sitepoint.com'
↪ title='Oh Yeah!'>Awesome Web Resources</a>"

const mdLink = link.replace(/<a
```

[9.] https://daringfireball.net/projects/markdown/

```
↪ href='(.*?)'.*?>(.*?)<\/a>/g, "[$2]($1)");


mdLink
<< [Awesome Web Resources](https://www.sitepoint.com)
```

The example has two capturing groups – the first captures any text inside the href attribute and stores it in the variable $1 and the second captures the text inside the anchor tags and stores it in the variable $2. These matches can then be used to create the link using Markdown.

Quiz Ninja Project

Now it's time to take another look at our Quiz Ninja project. We're going to store our questions as objects inside an array. Open up `main.js` and enter the following at the top of the file:

```
const quiz = [
          { name: "Superman",realName: "Clark Kent" },
          { name: "Wonder Woman",realName: "Diana Prince" },
          { name: "Batman",realName: "Bruce Wayne" },
          ];
```

Each element in the array contains information about the superheroes used in our quiz. These objects replace the nested arrays we used in the previous chapters, and have properties of `name` and `realName` that will be used to form the questions and answers.

Now we're going to namespace the functions we created in the last chapter. We do this by placing them inside an object called `game` that will be the namespace. This means that any references to the functions need to be replaced with `game.function()` outside the object or `this.function()` inside the object.

Add the following code below the array of questions:

```
const game = {
start(quiz){
    this.questions = [...quiz];
    this.score = 0;
    // main game loop
    for(const question of this.questions){
    this.question = question;
    this.ask();
    }
    // end of main game loop
    this.gameOver();
},
ask(){
 const question = `What is ${this.question.name}'s real
↪ name?`;
    const response =  prompt(question);
    this.check(response);
},
check(response){
    const answer = this.question.realName;
    if(response === answer){
    alert('Correct!');
    this.score++;
    } else {
    alert(`Wrong! The correct answer was ${answer}`);
    }
},
gameOver(){
 alert(`Game Over, you scored ${this.score} point$(this.score
↪ !== 1 ? 's' : ''}`);
 }
}
```

After this, we have to edit the function that starts the game, so it includes the namespace:

```
game.start(quiz);
```

Save these changes then have a go at playing the game again. Once again, we haven't actually added any functionality, but we have made our code more organized by placing all of the functions inside an object. This will make it easier to expand on the functionality in later chapters.

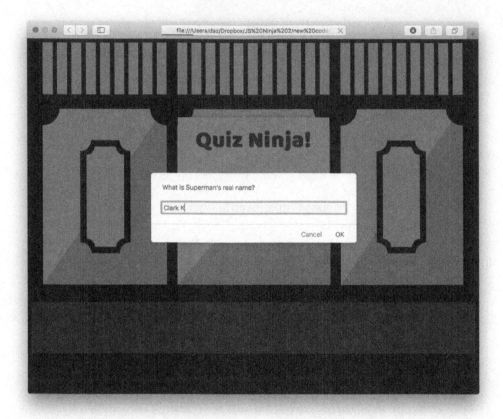

5-1. Quiz Ninja

You can see a live example on CodePen[10].

Chapter Summary

■ Objects are a collection of key-value pairs placed inside curly braces {}.

---

10. https://codepen.io/daz4126/pen/GExXBJ

■ Objects have properties that can be any JavaScript value. If it's a function, it's known as a *method*.

■ An object's properties and methods can be accessed using either dot notation or square bracket notation.

■ Objects are mutable, which means their properties and methods can be changed or removed.

■ Objects can be used as parameters to functions, which allows arguments to be entered in any order, or omitted.

■ Nested objects can be created by placing objects inside objects.

■ JSON is a portable data format that uses JavaScript object literals to exchange information.

■ The `Math` object gives access to a number of mathematical constants.

■ The `Math` object can be used to perform mathematical calculations.

■ The `Date` object can be used to create date objects.

■ Once you've created a `Date` object, you can use the getter methods to access information about that date.

■ Once you've created a `Date` object, setter methods can be used to change information about that date.

■ The `Regex` object can be used to create regular expressions.

Now we've reached the end of the first part of the book, you should have a good grasp of the JavaScript programming language basics. But JavaScript was originally designed to be used in the browser, so in the next chapter we'll look at how to use JavaScript to interact with web pages.

Chapter

6

The Document Object Model

The Document Object Model (DOM) allows you to access elements of a web page and enable interaction with the page by adding and removing elements, changing the order, content and attributes of elements, and even altering how they are styled.

In this chapter, we'll cover the following topics:

- Introduction to the DOM

- Getting elements —`getElementById`, `getElementsByClassName`, `getElementsByTagName`, `querySelector` and `querySelectorAll`

- Navigating the DOM

- Getting and setting an element's attributes

- Updating the DOM by creating dynamic markup

- Changing the CSS of an element

- Our project — we'll dynamically insert each question into the HTML

The Document Object Model

What is the DOM?

The Document Object Model, or DOM for short, represents an HTML document as a network of connected nodes that form a tree-like structure.

The DOM treats everything on a web page as a node. HTML tags, the text inside these tags, even the attributes of a tag are all nodes. The HTML tag is the root node, and every other part of the document is a child node of this.

Take the following piece of HTML as an example:

```
<p class='warning'>Something has gone
↳ <em>very</em> wrong!</p>
```

This can be represented as the tree diagram shown below.

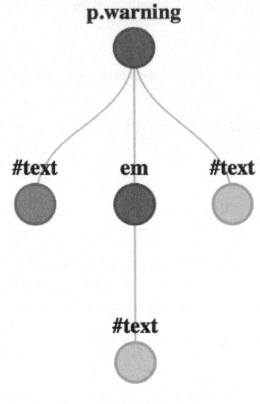

6-1. The DOM tree

The DOM is not actually part of JavaScript because it is *language agnostic* (although JavaScript is, by far, the language most commonly used with it). This means it can be used in any programming language, not just JavaScript. We can use JavaScript to access and modify different parts of a web page using a special built-in object called `document`.

History of the DOM

In the early days of the web, browser vendors such as Netscape and Microsoft developed their own distinct ways of accessing and altering parts of a web page. In the beginning, they tended to focus on common page elements such as images, links and forms – this was known as Dynamic HTML (DHTML). These methods became known as DOM level 0, or legacy DOM. Some of the more common methods, such as those used for selecting images and forms, can still be used in the current DOM.

The World Wide Web Consortium (W3C) started to standardize the process, and created the DOM level 1 in 1998. This introduced a complete model for web pages that allowed every part of them to be navigated.

The DOM level 2 specification was published in 2000 and introduced the popular `getElementById()` method, which made it much easier to access specific elements on a web page. The DOM level 3 specification was published in 2004, and since then the W3C has abandoned using levels. The DOM specification is developed as a living standard[1].

Despite the standardization process, browsers have not always implemented the DOM consistently, so it's been difficult to program for in the past. Fortunately, since Internet Explorer 8, DOM support has been much more consistent, and modern browsers now implement the current DOM level 3. They're also implementing more of the new DOM level 4 features with every update.

An Example Web Page

To illustrate the DOM concepts covered in this chapter, we'll use a basic web page that contains a heading and three paragraph elements. Save the following code in a file called `heroes.html`:

```
<!doctype html>
<html lang="en">
<head>
<meta charset="utf-8">
<title>Justice League</title>
</head>
<body>
    <header>
    <h1 id='title'>Justice League</h1>
    </header>
    <ul id='roster'>
```

---

[1] https://www.w3.org/TR/dom/

```
      <li class='hero'>Superman</li>
      <li class='vigilante hero' id='bats'>Batman</li>
      <li class='hero'>Wonder Woman</li>
      </ul>
  </body>
</html>
```

Below is a node tree diagram for the `<ul>` element with a class of `roster`:

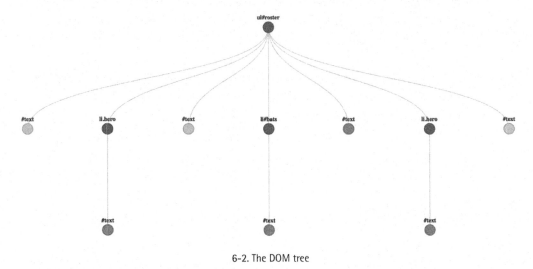

6-2. The DOM tree

 What's With the Extra Text Nodes?

There appear to be some extra #text nodes in this diagram, even in places where there isn't any text. This is because the DOM also stores any whitespace that is in the HTML document as text nodes.

Because we're using the browser, the best way to follow along with the examples in this chapter is to use the console built into the web browser (we discussed how to use this in Chapter 1). This will allow you to enter commands that interact with the elements on the web page and see the results. The screenshot below shows the page with the console open.

6-3. Using the console

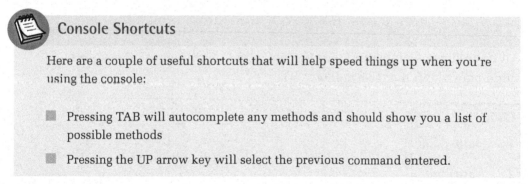

Console Shortcuts

Here are a couple of useful shortcuts that will help speed things up when you're using the console:

- Pressing TAB will autocomplete any methods and should show you a list of possible methods
- Pressing the UP arrow key will select the previous command entered.

Getting Elements

The DOM provides several methods that allow us to access any element on a page. These methods will return a node object or a node list, which is an array-like object. These objects can then be assigned to a variable and be inspected or modified.

For example, we can access the body element of a web page and assign it to the variable body by entering the following code into the browser console:

```
const body = document.body;
```

Now we have a reference to the body element, we can check its type:

```
typeof body;
<< "object";
```

This is a special `Node` object with a number of properties and methods that we can use to find information about, or modify, the `body` element.

For example, we can use the `nodeType` property to find out what type of node it is:

```
body.nodeType;
<< 1
```

All nodes have a numerical code to signify what type they are. These are summmarized in the table below.

Code	Type
1	element
2	attribute
3	text
8	comment
9	body

There are other types not covered in the table, but these aren't used in HTML documents. As we can see from the table, a code of 1 confirms that `body` is an element node.

We can also use the `nodeName` property to find the name of the element:

```
body.nodeName;
<< "BODY"
```

Note that the element name is returned in uppercase letters.

This is a live reference to what is displayed in the browser. You can see this by hovering your cursor over the reference in the console and see it highlighted in the main viewport, as illustrated in the screenshot below:

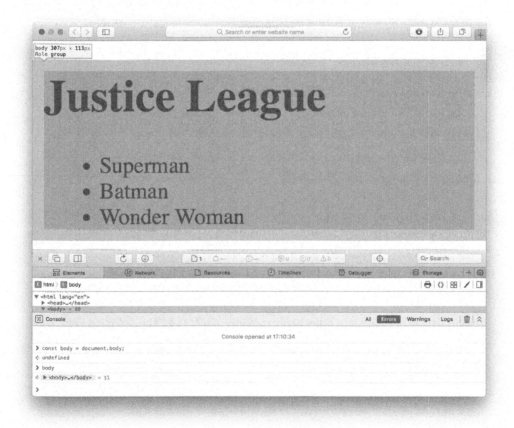

6-4. Highlighting the reference

Legacy DOM Shortcut Methods

There are some methods from DOM Level 0 that can still be employed to access commonly used elements. These include:

▓ `Document.body` returns the body element of a web page.

▓ `Document.images` returns a node list of all the images in the document.

▓ `Document.links` returns a node list of all the `<a>` elements and `<area>` elements that have an `href` attribute.

▓ `Document.anchors` returns a node list of all the `<a>` elements that have a `name` attribute.

▓ `Document.forms` returns a node list of all the forms in the document. This will be used when we cover forms in <u>Chapter 8</u>.

Not Actually Arrays

Node lists are array-like objects, but they are not arrays. You can access each item using index notation. For example, `document.images[0]` will return the first image in the node list of all the images in the document.

They also have a `length` property, which can be used to iterate through every element using a `for` loop, like so:

```
for (let i=0 ; i < document.images.length ; i++) {

// do something with each image using document.images[i]

}
```

Node lists *don't* have any other array methods such as `slice`, `splice` and `join`.

ES6 makes it very easy to turn a node list into an array, however. You can either use the `Array.from()` method:

```
const imageArray = Array.from(document.images);
```

Or you can use the spread operator:

```
const imageArray = [...document.images];
```

Once the node list has been turned into an array, you can use all the array methods on it.

Getting An Element By Its ID

The `getElementById()` method does exactly what it says on the tin. It returns a reference to the element with a unique `id` attribute that is given as an argument. For example, we can get a reference to the `<h1>` heading element with the `id` of `title` in the `heroes.html` page by writing this in the console:

```
const h1 = document.getElementById('title');
```

Every `id` attribute should be unique to just one element (Make sure you follow this rule – it's not enforced by the HTML parser, but odd things can happen in your code if you have more than one element with the same ID). This method will return a reference to the unique element with the ID provided as an argument. For this reason, it's a very quick way of finding elements in a document. It's also supported in all the major browsers, and is probably the most commonly used method of accessing elements on a web page.

If no element exists with the ID provided, `null` is returned.

Get Elements By Their Tag Name

`getElementsByTagName()` will return a live node list of all the elements with the tag name that is provided as an argument. For example, we can get all the list items (HTML tag of `<li>`) in the document using this code:

```
const listItems = document.getElementsByTagName('li');
```

As this is a node list, we can use the index notation to find each individual paragraph in the list:

```
listItems[0];
<< <li class='hero'>Superman</li>

listItems[1];
```

```
<< <li class='vigilante hero'
↳ id='bats'>Batman</li>

listItems[2];
<< <li class='hero'>Wonder Woman</li>
```

If there are no elements in the document with the given tag name, an empty node list is returned.

Get Elements By Their Class Name

getElementsByClassName() will return a live node list of all elements that have the class name that is supplied as an argument. For example, we can return a collection of all elements with the class of hero using the following code:

```
const heroes = document.getElementsByClassName('hero');
```

Note that, in this case, it is exactly the same collection that was returned when we found all of the list items previously.

There are three elements on the page that have the class name of hero, which we can test by querying the length property:

```
heroes.length;
<< 3
```

Note that if there are no elements with the given class, an HTML collection is still returned, but it will have a length of 0:

```
document.getElementsByClassName('villain').length;
<< 0
```

`document.getElementsByClassName` is supported in all the major modern browsers, but was only supported in Internet Explorer 9 and later.

Query Selectors

The `document.querySelector()` method allows you to use CSS notation to find the *first* element in the document that matches that matches a CSS selector provided as an argument. If no elements match, it will return `null`.

The `document.querySelectorAll()` method also uses CSS notation but returns a node list of *all* the elements in the document that match the CSS query selector. If no elements match, it will return an empty node list.

These are both very powerful methods that can emulate all the methods discussed, as well as allowing more fine-grained control over which element nodes are returned.

 Query Selectors

You do have to know a bit about CSS query selectors to be able to use this method! If you don't know, or just need a reminder, you might want check out SitePoint.[2]

For example, the following could be used instead of `document.getElementById()`:

```
document.querySelector('#bats');
  << <li class="vigilante hero"
↪ id="bats">Batman</li>
```

And this could be used instead of `document.getElementsByClassName`:

```
document.querySelectorAll('.hero');
  << NodeList [<li class="hero">, <li
↪ id="bats">, <li class="hero">]
```

---

2. http://www.sitepoint.com/web-foundations/css-selectors/

Note that this is not a *live* node list. See the section later in this chapter for more details about live node lists.

CSS query selectors are a powerful way of specifying very precise items on a page. For example, CSS pseudo-selectors can also be used to pinpoint a particular element. The following code, for example, will return only the last list item in the document:

```
const wonderWoman = document.querySelector('li:last-child');
```

The `querySelector()` method can be called on *any* element, rather than just `document`. For example, we can get a reference to the `<ul>` element, using the following code:

```
const ul = document.querySelector('ul#roster');
```

Now we can use the `querySelector()` method on this element, to find a `<li>` element with an id of 'bats':

```
const batman = ul.querySelector('li#bats')
```

All modern browsers support these methods, and Internet Explorer supported it from version 8 onwards. Version 8 of Internet Explorer only understands CSS2.1 selectors (because that is the highest level of CSS that it supports), so complex CSS3 notations such as `ul ~ p:empty` (which finds any empty `<p>` elements that are also siblings with a `<ul>` element) will fail to work.

jQuery

jQuery is a popular JavaScript framework that makes it very easy to find elements on a page using a CSS-style syntax. It uses `document.querySelectorAll()` in the background whenever it can. For example, the jQuery code `$('ul#roster').find('li#bats');` is basically doing the same as our previous example:

```
const ul = document.querySelector('ul#roster');
ul.querySelector('li#bats')
```

Navigating the DOM Tree

Node objects have a number of properties and methods for navigating around the document tree. Once you have a reference to an element, you can walk along the document tree to find other nodes. Let's focus on a particular part of the document tree in our example. The relationship each node has with the `Batman` node is shown below.

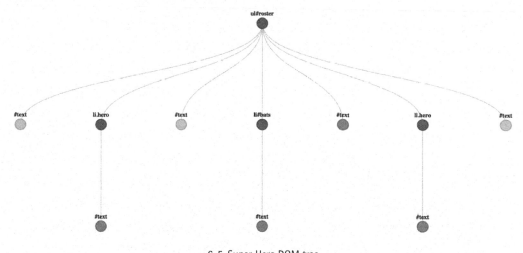

6-5. Super Hero DOM tree

The `childNodes` property is a list of all the nodes that are children of the node concerned. The following example will return all the child nodes of the element with an `id` attribute of `roster`:

```
const heroes = document.getElementById('roster');

heroes.childNodes
<< NodeList [#text "
", <li class="hero">, #text "
", <li id="bats">, #text "
", <li class="hero">, #text "
", <li class="hero">, #text "
```

Note that the `childNodes` property returns *all* the nodes that are children of an element. This will include any text nodes, and since whitespace is treated as a text node, there will often be empty text nodes in this collection.

The `children` property only returns any *element* nodes that are children of that node, so will ignore any text nodes. Note that this is only supported in Internet Explorer from version 9 onwards:

```
heroes.children // this will only contain list items
 << HTMLCollection [<li class="hero">, <li
↪ id="bats">, <li class="hero">, <li
↪ class="hero">] (4)

heroes.children.length
<< 3
```

The `firstChild` property returns the first child of a node:

```
heroes.firstChild
<< #text " "
```

And the `lastChild` property returns the last child of a node:

```
heroes.lastChild
<< #text " "
```

Be careful when using these properties — the first or last child node can often be a text node, even if it's just an empty string generated by some whitespace (this can be seen in both of the examples above).

For example, you might expect the first child node of the `<ul>` element to be a `<li>` element, and the last child to also be a `<li>` element, but they are both in fact text nodes, generated by the whitespace characters in between the `<ul>` and `<li>` tags:

The `parentNode` property returns the parent node of an element. The following code returns the `roster` node because it's the parent of the `wonderWoman` node:

```
const wonderWoman = document.querySelector('ul#roster
↪ li:last-child');
wonderWoman.parentNode
<< <ul id='roster'>…</ul>
```

The `nextSibling` property returns the next adjacent node of the same parent. It will return `null` if the node is the last child node of that parent:

```
wonderWoman.nextSibling
<< #text " "
```

The `previousSibling` property returns the previous adjacent node. It will return `null` if the node is the first child of that parent:

```
wonderWoman.previousSibling
<< #text " "
```

Once again, these methods find the next and previous *node*, not element, so they will often return a blank text node, as in the examples above.

Using these properties allows you to navigate around the whole of the document tree.

Finding the Value of a Node

Finding the text contained within an element is actually trickier than it sounds. For example, the variable wonderWoman has a DOM node that contains the following HTML:

```
<li class='hero'>Wonder Woman</li>
```

It clearly contains the text Wonder Woman, but this is held in a text node, which is the first child of the <li> element node:

```
const textNode = wonderWoman.firstChild;
<< "Wonder Woman"
```

Now we have a reference to the text node, we can find the text contained inside it using the nodeValue method:

```
textNode.nodeValue;
<< "Wonder Woman"
```

We can also find this value using the textContent property. This will return the text content of an element as a string:

```
wonderWoman.textContent
<< "Wonder Woman"
```

Note that Internet Explorer version 8 does not support the `textContent` property, but has the `innerText` property, which works in a similar way.

Getting and Setting Attributes

All HTML elements have a large number of possible attributes such as `class`, `id`, `src`, and `href`. The DOM has numerous getter and setter methods that can be used to view, add, remove or modify the value of any of these attributes.

Getting An Element's Attributes

The `getAttribute()` method returns the value of the attribute provided as an argument:

```
wonderWoman.getAttribute('class');
<< "hero"
```

If an element does not have the given attribute, it returns `null`:

```
wonderWoman.getAttribute('src');
<< null
```

Setting An Element's Attributes

The `setAttribute` can change the value of an element's attributes. It takes two arguments: the attribute that you wish to change, and the new value of that attribute.

For example, if we wanted to change the class of the element in the `wonderWoman` variable to `villain`, we could do so using this code:

```
wonderWoman.setAttribute('class', 'villain');
<< undefined
```

```
wonderWoman.getAttribute('class');
<< "villain"
```

If an element does not have an attribute, the setAttribute method can be used to add it to the element. For example, we can add an id of amazon to the wonderWoman element:

```
wonderWoman.setAttribute('id','amazon');

wonderWoman.getAttribute('id');
<< 'amazon'
```

 Dot Notation

The legacy DOM allows access to attributes using dot notation, like so:

```
wonderWoman.id;
<< 'amazon'
```

Now if we take a look at the wonderWoman variable, we can see that the changes have been made, as this is a live reference to the element:

```
wonderWoman
  << <li class="villain" id="amazon">Wonder
↳ Woman</li>
```

This notation is still supported, although some attribute names such as class and for are reserved keywords in JavaScript, so we need to use className and htmlFor instead.

Classes Of An Element

The className Property

As we've seen, we can modify the class name of an element using the
setAttribute() method. There is also a className property that allows the class
of an element to be set directly. In addition, it can be used to find out the value of
the class attribute:

```
wonderWoman.className;
<< "villain"
```

We can change the class back to hero with the following code:

```
wonderWoman.className = 'hero'
<< "hero"
```

 Be Careful Updating className

Changing the **className** property of an element by assignment will overwrite all
other classes that have already been set on the element.

This problem can be avoided by using the **classList** property instead.

The classList Property

The classList property is a list of all the classes an element has. It has a number
of methods that make it easier to modify the class of an element. It's supported in
all modern browsers and in Internet Explorer from version 10 onwards.

The add method can be used to add a class to an element without overwriting any
classes that already exist. For example, we could add a class of warrior to the
wonderWoman element:

```
wonderWoman.classList.add('warrior');
```

Now we can check that it has been added:

```
wonderWoman.className;
<< "hero warrior"
```

The `remove` method will remove a specific class from an element. For example, we could remove the class of `warrior` with the following code:

```
wonderWoman.classList.remove('warrior');
```

The `toggle` method is a particularly useful method that will *add* a class if an element doesn't have it already, and *remove* the class if it does have it. It returns `true` if the class was added and `false` if it was removed. For example:

```
 wonderWoman.classList.toggle('hero'); // will remove the
↳ 'hero' class
<< false

 wonderWoman.classList.toggle('sport'); // will add the
↳ 'hero' class back
<< true
```

The `contains` method will check to see if an element has a particular class:

```
wonderWoman.classList.contains('hero');
<< true

wonderWoman.classList.contains('villain');
<< false
```

classList and Older Versions of IE

Unfortunately, the **classList** property is only available in Internet Explorer version 10 and above, so if you want to support older versions of Internet Explorer, you could create a function that will add an extra class to an element, rather than just replace the current class. The **addClass** function takes the element and the new class name to be added as parameters. It uses a simple **if** block to check if the value of the element's className property is truthy. If it is, it will append the new class to the end of the current class; otherwise, it will simply set the new class as the element's class:

```
function addClass(element,newClass){
if (element.className) {
    element.className = element.className + ' ' + newClass;
} else {
    element.className = newClass;
}
return element.className;
}
```

Let's test this out on the **wonderWoman** element, which already has a class of **hero**:

```
addClass(wonderWoman,'warrior');
<< "hero warrior"
```

Creating Dynamic Markup

So far we've looked at how to gain access to different elements of a web page and find out information about them. We've also looked at how to change the attributes of elements. In this section, we're going to learn how to create new elements and add them to the page, as well as edit elements that already exist and remove any unwanted elements.

Creating An Element

The document object has a **createElement()** method that takes a tag name as a parameter and returns that element. For example, we could create a new list item as a DOM fragment in memory by writing the following in the console:

```
const flash = document.createElement('li');
```

At the moment, this element is empty. To add some content, we'll need to create a text node.

Creating a Text Node

A text node can be created using the `document.createTextNode()` method. It takes a parameter, which is a string containing the text that goes in the node. Let's create the text to go in our new element:

```
const flashText = document.createTextNode('Flash');
```

Now we have an element node and a text node, but they are not linked together — we need to append the text node to the paragraph node.

Appending Nodes

Every node object has an `appendChild()` method that will add another node (given as an argument) as a child node. We want our newly created text node to be a child node of the list element node. This means that it's the `flash` object that calls the method, with `flashText` as its argument:

```
flash.appendChild(flashText);
```

Now we have a `<li>` element that contains the text we want. So the process to follow each time you want to create a new element with text content is this:

1. Create the element node

2. Create the text node

3. Append the text node to the element node

This can be made simpler by using the `textContent` property that every element object has. This will add a text node to an element without the need to append it, so the code above could have been written as the following:

```
const flash = document.createElement('li');
flash.textContent = 'Flash';
```

While this has cut the number of steps from three down to two, it can still become repetitive, so it's useful to write a function to make this easier. This is what we'll do next.

A Function To Create Elements

When we created our new list item element, all we specified was the type of tag and the text inside it. These will form the parameters of our function. The function will then perform the two steps we used to create the new element, and then return that element:

```
function createElement (tag,text) {
const el = document.createElement(tag);
el.textContent = text;
return el
}
```

Let's try it out by creating another new list item element:

```
const aquaman = createElement('li','Aquaman');
```

We can now create new elements in a single line of code rather than three. It's time to add these new elements to our example page.

Adding Elements to the Page

We have already seen the `appendChild()` method. This can be called on a node to add a new child node. The new node will always be added at the end of any existing child nodes. The following example will add the `flash` element we created above to the end of the `<ul>` element, as shown below:

```
heroes.appendChild(flash);
```

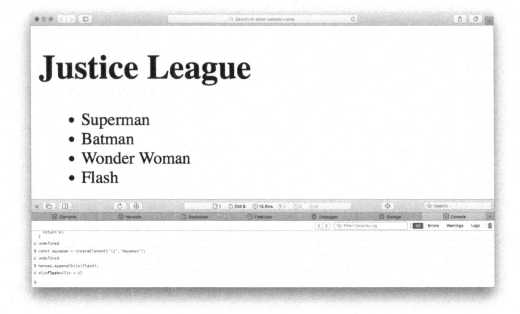

6-6. Append child

The `appendChild` method is useful as you'll often want to add a new element to the bottom of a list. But what if you want to place a new element in between two existing elements?

The `insertBefore()` method will place a new element before another element in the markup. It's important to note that this method is called on the *parent node*. It takes two parameters: the first is the new node to be added, and the second is the node that you want it to go before (it's helpful to think that the order of the parameters is the order they will appear in the markup). For example, we can place the `aquaman` element that we created earlier before the `wonderWoman` element with the following line of code:

```
heroes.insertBefore(aquaman,wonderWoman);
```

This will produce the output shown below.

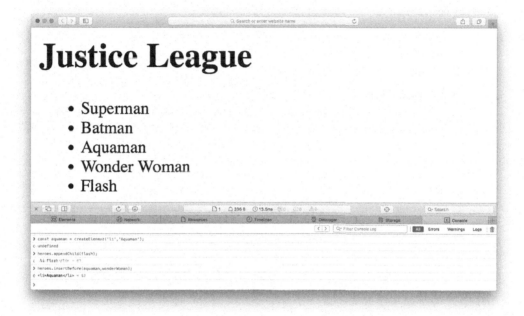

6-7. Insert before

The `appendChild()` and `insertBefore()` methods can be used to move markup that already exists in the DOM as well. This is because a reference to a single DOM element can only exist once in the page, so if you use multiple inserts and appends, only the last one will have an effect. If an element is required to appear in several different places in the document, it would need to be cloned before each insertion.

This can be seen by using the `appendChild()` method on the `wonderWoman` element. Since it already exists, it just moves its position to appear at the end of the `<ul>` element, as shown below:

```
heroes.appendChild(wonderWoman);
```

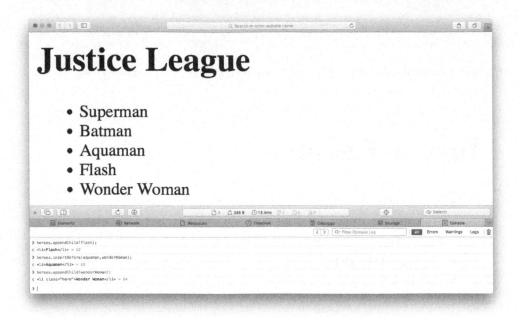

6-8. Moving an existing node

Somewhat annoyingly, there is no `insertAfter()` method, so you need to ensure you have access to the correct elements to place an element exactly where you want it.

Remove Elements From a Page

An element can be removed from a page using the `removeChild()` method. This method is called on the parent node and has a single parameter, which is the node to be removed. It returns a reference to the removed node. For example, if we wanted to remove the `aquaman` element, we would use the following code:

```
heroes.removeChild(aquaman);
<< <li>Aquaman</li>
```

As you can see below, it's been removed.

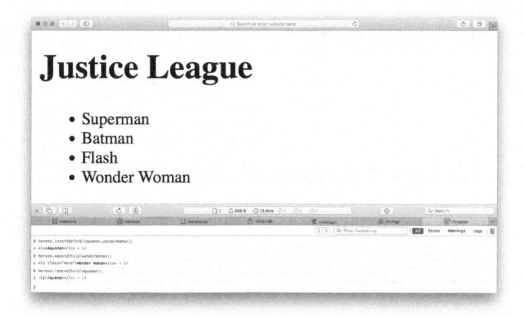

6-9. Remove a child node

Because we have a reference to the element, we can easily put it back into the document if we need to:

```
heroes.appendChild(aquaman);
```

Replacing Elements on a Page

The `replaceChild()` method can be used to replace one node with another. It's called on the parent node and has two parameters: the new node and the node that is to be replaced. For example, if we wanted to change the content of the `<h1>` tag that makes the title of the page, we could replace the text node with a new one, like so:

```
const h1 = document.getElementById('title');
const oldText = h1.firstChild;
 const newText = document.createTextNode('Justice League of
↳ America');
```

```
h1.replaceChild(newText,oldText);
```

the figure below shows that the text has now changed to 'Justice League of America'.

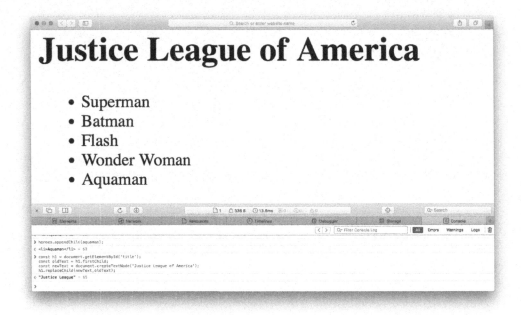

6-10. Replacing an element

innerHTML

The innerHTML element property was standardized as part of the HTML5, although it was already supported by all the major browsers. It returns all the child elements of an element as a string of HTML. If an element contains lots of other elements, all the raw HTML is returned. In the following example, we can see all the HTML that is contained inside the <ul> element with the id of roster:

```
heroes.innerHTML
<<"
    <li class=\"hero\">Superman</li>
 <li class=\"vigilante hero\"
↳ id=\"bats\">Batman</li>
```

```
<li class=\"hero\">Wonder Woman</li>
"
```

The `innerHTML` property is also writable and can be used to place a chunk of HTML inside an element. This will replace all of a node's children with the raw HTML contained in the string. This saves you having to create a new text node as it's done automatically and inserted into the DOM. It's also much quicker than using the standard DOM methods. For example, the heading text that we changed before could be changed in one line:

```
h1.innerHTML = 'Suicide Squad';
```

The power of the `innerHTML` property becomes even more apparent if you want to insert a large amount of HTML into the document. Instead of creating each element and text node individually, you can simply enter the raw HTML as a string. The relevant nodes will then be added to the DOM tree automatically. For example, we could change everything contained within the `<ul>` element:

```
heroes.innerHTML = '<li>Harley
↳ Quinn</li><li>Deadshot</li><li>Killer
↳ Croc</li><li>Enchantress</li><li>Captain
↳ Boomerang</li><li>Katana</li><li>Slipknot</li>';
```

This will now remove all the child elements of the `<ul>` element and replace them with the string of HTML that was provided, as shown in below.

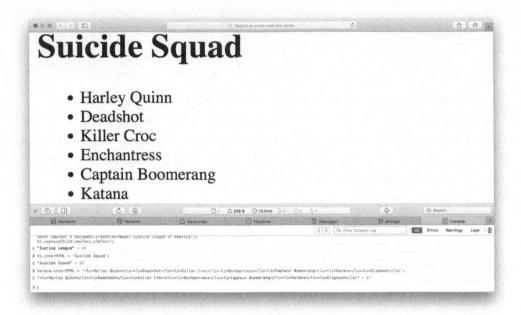

6-11. The `innerHTML` property

 Scripts Inserted Using `innerHTML` Won't Run

To stop any malicious content being added to a page using `innerHTML`, any code contained within `<script>` tags is not executed.

Live Collections

The node lists returned by the `document.getElementsByClassName()` and `document.getElementsByTagName()` methods are *live* collections that will update to reflect any changes on the page. For example, if a new element with the class `hero` is added, or an existing one is removed, the node list updates automatically without having to make another call to the method. Therefore, its use is discouraged for performance reasons, but it can be useful.

To see an example of this, reload the page again to reset the DOM to its original state. Let's take a look at how many elements are in the `<ul>` element:

```
const heroes = document.getElementById('roster');
```

```
const list = heroes.children;

list.length
<< 3
```

Now remove the `batman` element:

```
const batman = document.getElementById('bats');
<< undefined

heroes.removeChild(batman);

list.length;
<< 2
```

You also need to be careful when referring to elements by their index in a collection, as this can change when markup is added or removed. For example, `wonderWoman` element could originally be accessed using this line of code:

```
heroes.children[2];
<< undefined
```

Yet now it refers to `undefined`, as nothing is at the index of 2 in the collection; this is because the `batman` element was dynamically removed from the DOM, which means the index of the remaining elements will now change in the node list.

Updating CSS

Every element node has a `style` property. This can be used to dynamically modify the presentation of any element on a web page.

To see an example of this, reload the page again to reset the DOM. We can add a red border to the `superman` element with the following code:

```
const heroes = document.getElementById('roster');
const superman = heroes.children[0];

superman.style.border = "red 2px solid";
<< "red 2px solid"
```

Camel Case Properties

Any CSS property names that are separated by dashes must be written in camelCase notation, so the dash is removed and the next letter is capitalized because dashes are not legal characters in property names.

For example, the CSS property `background-color` becomes `backgroundColor`. We can change the color of the `superman` background to green using this code:

```
superman.style.backgroundColor = 'blue';
<< "blue"
```

Alternatively, the bracket notation that we saw in chapter 5 can also be used, meaning that CSS properties can be provided as a string and don't need the camelCase notation:

```
superman.style['background color'] = 'blue';
<< "blue"
```

You can see this change below.

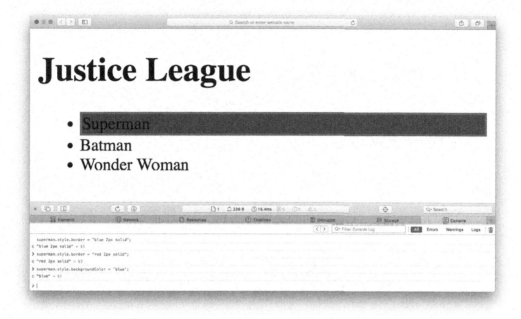

6-12. Changing the style

Disappearing Act

One particularly useful CSS property often employed is the `display` property. This can be used to make elements disappear and reappear on the page as needed:

You can hide the `superman` element with the following code:

```
superman.style.display = 'none';
<< "none"
```

You can see the effect below.

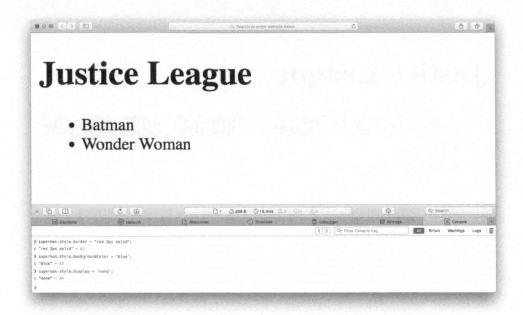

6-13. Hiding the elements

The element can be made to reappear by changing the `display` property back to `block`:

```
superman.style.display = 'block';
<< "block"
```

Checking Style Properties

The `style` property can also be used to see what CSS styles have been set on an element, but unfortunately it applies only to inline styles, and styles set using JavaScript. This means it excludes styles from external stylesheets, which is the most common way of setting styles.

There is a function called `getComputedStyle()` that will retrieve all the style information of an element that is given as a parameter. This is a read-only property, so is only used for finding out information about the style of an element.

For example, if you wanted all the styles applied to the superman element, you could use the following:

```
getComputedStyle(superman);
 << CSSStyleDeclaration {0: "alt", 1:
 ↪ "animation-delay", 2: "animation-direction", 3:
 ↪ "animation-duration", 4: "animation-fill-mode", 5:
 ↪ "animation-iteration-count", 6: "animation-name", 7:
 ↪ "animation-play-state", 8: "animation-timing-function", 9:
 ↪ "background-attachment", …}
```

As you can see, it returns an object (more specifically, it is a CSSStyleDeclaration object) that contains a list of property-value pairs of all the CSS styles that have been applied to the element in question. In this example, there are over 200, although CSSStyleDeclaration objects have some built-in methods to help extract the information. For instance, if I wanted to find out about the element's color property I could use this code in the console:

```
getComputedStyle(superman).getPropertyCSSValue('color').cssTe
 ↪ xt;<< "rgb(0, 0, 0)"
```

This tells us that the color of the text is rgb(0, 0, 0), which is black.

You can read more on the Mozilla Developer Network about the getComputedStyle() function[3] and about CSSStyleDeclaration[4] objects.

This Will Cause An Error in Some Browsers

Some browsers, such as Chrome, do not allow access to the methods of a CSSStyleDeclaration object, such as getPropertyCSSValue(), so attempting to use them will result in an error.

---

3. https://developer.mozilla.org/en/docs/Web/API/window.getComputedStyle
4. https://developer.mozilla.org/en-US/docs/Web/API/CSSStyleDeclaration

Use with Caution

While it may seem useful to be able to edit the styles of elements on the fly like this, it is much better practice to dynamically change the class of an element and keep the relevant styles for each class in a separate stylesheet.

For example, if you wanted to add a red border around the `superman` element (to highlight it for some reason), you could do it in the way we saw earlier:

```
superman.style.border('red 2px solid');
```

A better alternative would be to add a class of `highlighted`:

```
superman.classList.add('highlighted');
```

And then add the following CSS in a separate stylesheet file:

```
.highlighted{
border: red 2px solid;
}
```

This would give more flexibility if it was later decided to change the look of the highlighted elements. It could simply be changed at the CSS level, rather than having to dig around in the JavaScript code. There may be times, however, when you don't have access to a stylesheet or its classes, so in this case you would have to change the CSS dynamically using JavaScript.

Quiz Ninja Project

Now we've learned about the Document Object Model, we can start to add some dynamic markup to display the questions in our quiz. This will mean we won't need as many alert dialogs.

The first thing to do is add some empty `<div>` elements to the HTML by updating `index.html` to the following:

```
<!doctype html>
<html lang='en'>
<head>
<meta charset='utf-8'>
 <meta name='description' content='A JavaScript Quiz
↪ Game'>
<title>Quiz Ninja</title>
<link rel='stylesheet' href='styles.css'>
</head>
<body>
<section class='dojo'>
    <div class='quiz-body'>
    <header>
 <div id='score'>Score:
↪ <strong>0</strong></div>
        <h1>Quiz Ninja!</h1>
    </header>
    <div id='question'></div>
    <div id='result'></div>
    <div id='info'></div>
    </div>
</section>
<script src='main.js'></script>
</body>
```

We've added four `<div>` elements that will be used to show the questions and provide feedback about whether the user has answered a question correctly or not. We've also added a `<div>` element inside the `<header>` that can be used to display the score as the game is being played.

The ID attributes of these elements will act as hooks that allow us to easily gain access to that element using the `document.getElementById()` method. These will be namespaced inside an object called `view`, as they all relate to the view. Add the following code at the start of the `main.js` file, just after the array of questions:

```
// View Object
const view = {
score: document.querySelector('#score strong'),
question: document.getElementById('question'),
result: document.getElementById('result'),
info: document.getElementById('info'),
render(target,content,attributes) {
    for(const key in attributes) {
        target.setAttribute(key, attributes[key]);
    }
    target.innerHTML = content;
}
};
```

This uses the `document.querySelector()` method to access the elements we require and assign them to a variable. So, for example, the `div` with an id of `question` can be accessed in the Javascript code using `view.question`.

We've also added a helper function called `render()` that can be used to update the content of an element on the page. This function has three parameters: the first is the element that displays the content, the second is for the content it's to be updated with, and the last is an object of any HTML attributes that can be added to the element.

The function loops through any attributes provided as the third argument, and uses the `setAttribute()` method to update them to the values provided. It then uses the `innerHTML` property to update the HTML with the content provided.

Now we need to update some of the functions inside the `game` object to use update the HTML.

We will still need to keep using dialogs for the time being, because without them, the JavaScript won't stop running and the game would be unplayable. Don't worry though, we won't need them for much longer.

We're going to update the HTML alongside showing the information. This means that the following methods need updating:

```
  ask(){
 const question = `What is ${this.question.name}'s real
↪ name?`;
    view.render(view.question,question);
    const response =  prompt(question);
    this.check(response);
},
check(response){
    const answer = this.question.realName;
    if(response === answer){
    view.render(view.result,'Correct!',{'class':'correct'});
    alert('Correct!');
    this.score++;
    view.render(view.score,this.score);
    } else {
 view.render(view.result,`Wrong! The correct answer was
↪ ${answer}`,{'class':'wrong'});
    alert(`Wrong! The correct answer was ${answer}`);
    }
},
gameOver(){
 view.render(view.info,`Game Over, you scored ${this.score}
↪ point${this.score !== 1 ? 's' : ''}`);
}
```

In most cases we have placed a call to `view.render()` wherever there is an
`alert()` or `prompt()` dialog that displays the same information in the HTML.
We've also used the `view.render()` method to update the score if a player gains
any points.

Unfortunately, if you have a go at playing the quiz by opening `index.html` in a
browser, you won't notice much difference until right at the end when all the
dialogs have finished displaying. You'll notice that the HTML has also been
updating in the background, as seen in the screenshot below:

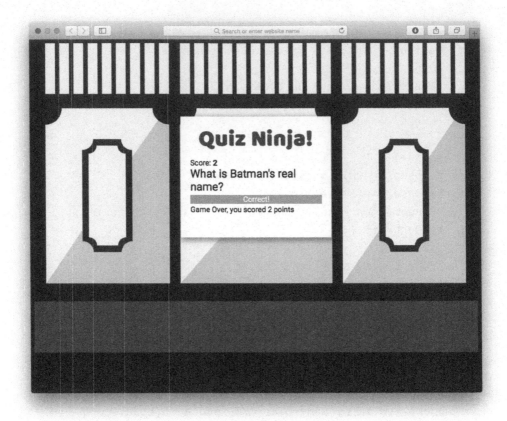

6-14. Current quiz

This is definitely starting to look better, although it would be good if we could see the results of our HTML updates all the way through the game. Don't worry about this, though, because we'll not be using prompts for much longer.

We have used our knowledge of the DOM to dynamically update the markup on the page. We've also continued to keep our code organized by keeping any properties and methods to do with the view in a separate object.

You can see a live example on CodePen[5].

Chapter Summary

[5.] https://codepen.io/daz4126/pen/LLdJww

■ The Document Object Model is a way of representing a page of HTML as a tree of nodes.

■ The `document.getElementById()`, `document.getElementsByClassName()`, `document.getElementsByTagNames()` and `document.querySelector()` can be used to access elements on a page.

■ The `parentNode()`, `previousSibling()`, `nextSibling()`, `childNodes()` and `children()` methods can be used to navigate around the DOM tree.

■ An element's attributes can be accessed using the `getAttribute()` method, and updated using the `setAttribute()` method.

■ The `createElement()` and `createTextNode()` methods can be used to create dynamic markup on the fly.

■ Markup can be added to the page using the `appendChild()` and `insertBefore()` methods.

■ Elements can be replaced using the `replaceChild()` method, and removed using the `removeChild()` method.

■ The `innerHTML` property can be used to insert raw HTML directly into the DOM.

■ The CSS properties of an element can be changed by accessing the `style` property.

Now we've learned how to navigate and dynamically update the markup of a web page, it's time to start interacting with it. In the next chapter we'll be covering a fundamental part of the JavaScript language: events.

Chapter 7

Events

We saw in the last chapter how the DOM is an interface that allows you to use JavaScript to interact with a web page. Events are another part of the DOM and they are what provides the link between the web page and user interactions. Every time a user interacts with a web page, such as clicking on a link, pressing a key, or moving a mouse, an event occurs that our program can detect and then respond to.

In this chapter, we'll cover the following topics:

▨ Introduction to events

▨ Adding event listeners

▨ The event object

- Mouse, keyboard and touch events

- Removing event listeners

- Stopping default behavior

- Event propagation

- Project – we'll add a start button that can be clicked on to start the game

Event Listeners

Imagine you're waiting for a really important email that you need to act upon as soon as it arrives, but you also have some JavaScript programming to do. You could keep checking your email every couple of minutes to see if the message has arrived, but this will cause lots of interruptions to your progress creating the next killer app. Not to mention you might be unable to check your email at the exact moment the message arrives, so it might be too late to act upon. The obvious answer is to set up a notification that will pop up as soon as the email arrives. You can happily program away without the distraction of constantly checking your email, because you'll receive a satisfying ping as soon as the email arrives.

Event listeners in JavaScript work in much the same way. They are like setting a notification to alert you when something happens. Instead of the program having to constantly check to see if an event has occurred, the event listener will let it know when the event happens, and the program can then respond appropriately. This allows the program to continue with other tasks while it waits for the event to happen.

For example, say in your program you want something to happen when a user clicks on the page. The code to check if a user has clicked might look like the example below (JavaScript doesn't actually work like this, so this code would fail to work, although it is the way some programming languages work):

```
if (click) {
doSomething();
} else {
// carry on with rest of the program
```

```
}
```

The problem with this approach is that the program would have to keep returning to this `if` block to check if the click had happened. It's a bit like having to check your email every few minutes. This is known as a *blocking* approach to programming because checking for the click is blocking the rest of the program from running.

JavaScript, on the other hand, uses a *non-blocking* approach that uses *event listeners* to listen out for any clicks on the page. Every time the page is clicked, a callback function will be called. So the program can continue processing the rest of the code while it's waiting for the click event to happen.

The following code can be used to attach an event listener to the document that fires when the user clicks anywhere on the page:

```
document.body.addEventListener("click", doSomething);
```

Event listeners are added to elements on the page and are part of the DOM that we met in the last chapter. In the example above, the event listener has been added to the document's body element. It will call the function `doSomething()` when any part of the page is clicked on. Until that happens, the program will continue to run the rest of the code.

 The `click` Event

The `click` event occurs when a user clicks with the mouse, presses the Enter key, or taps the screen, making it a very useful all-round event covering many types of interaction.

Inline Event Handlers

The original way of dealing with events in the browser was to use inline attributes that were added directly into the markup. Here's an example that adds an `onclick` event handler to a paragraph element:

```
<p onclick="console.log('You Clicked Me!')">Click
↳ Me</p>
```

The JavaScript code inside the quote marks will be run when a user clicks on the paragraph. This method will still work in modern browsers, but it isn't recommended for a number of reasons:

▨ The JavaScript code is mixed up with the HTML markup, breaking the concept of unobtrusive JavaScript, which advocates that JavaScript code should be kept out of the HTML.

▨ Only one event handler for each event-type can be attached to an element.

▨ The code for the event handlers is hidden away in the markup, making it difficult to find where these events have been declared.

▨ The JavaScript code has to be entered in a string, so you need to be careful when using apostrophes and quote marks.

For these reasons, inline event handlers are best avoided, and have only been included here for the sake of completion, and in case you see them in some code examples online.

Older Event Handlers

Another method is to use the event handler properties that all node objects have. These can be assigned to a function that would be invoked when the event occurred. The following example would cause a message to be logged to the console when the page is clicked:

```
document.onclick = function (){ console.log('You clicked on
↳ the page!'); }
```

This method is an improvement on the inline event handlers as it keeps the JavaScript out of the HTML markup. It is also well-supported and will work in almost all browsers. Unfortunately, it still has the restriction that only one function can be used for each event.

Using Event Listeners

The recommended way of dealing with events, and the current standard, is to use event listeners. These were outlined in DOM level 2 and allow multiple functions to be attached independently to different events. They are supported in all modern browsers, although only in Internet Explorer from version 9 onwards.

The addEventListener() method is called on a node object, the node to which the event listener is being applied. For example, this code will attach an event listener to the document's body:

```
document.body.addEventListener('click',doSomething);
```

The addEventListener() method can also be called without a node, in which case it is applied to the global object, usually the whole browser window.

Its first parameter is the type of event, and the second is a callback function that is invoked when the event occurs. There is also a third parameter that we'll cover later in the chapter.

In the next example, we are adding a click event listener to the whole page (because the addEventListener method is called without a node reference preceding it), and using an anonymous function as the callback:

```
addEventListener('click', () => alert('You Clicked!'));
```

Alternatively, a named function could be declared and then referenced in the event listener:

```
function doSomething() {
alert('You Clicked!');
}
```

```
addEventListener('click',doSomething);
```

Note that the parentheses are not placed after the function when it's used as the argument to an event listener; otherwise, the function will actually be called when the event listener is set, instead of when the event happens!

 Support in Old Versions of IE

All modern browsers now support these event listeners. Unfortunately, this has not always been the case, and older versions of Internet Explorer (version 8 and below) use a different syntax. If you need to support these browsers (and if you do, I feel for you!), John Resig has a simple solution for creating cross-browser add and remove event functions.[1]

Example Code

To test the examples in this chapter, create a file called events.html that contains the following HTML code. This includes some paragraph elements to which we'll attach event listeners throughout the chapter:

```
<!doctype html>
<html lang='en'>
<head>
<meta charset='utf-8'>
<title>Events Examples</title>
<style>
    p {
    width: 200px;
    height: 200px;
    margin: 10px;
    background-color: #ccc;
    float: left;
    }
```

[1.] https://johnresig.com/blog/flexible-javascript-events/

```
    .highlight {
    background-color: red;
    }
</style>
</head>
<body>
<p id='click'>Click On Me</p>
<p id='dblclick'>Double Click On Me</p>
<p id='mouse'>Hover On Me</p>
<script src='main.js'></script>
</body>
</html>
```

Now add the following code to a file called main.js that is saved in the same folder as events.html:

```
function doSomething(){
console.log('Something Happened!');
}

addEventListener('click', doSomething);
```

Now try opening events.html in a browser with the console open and click anywhere on the page. You should see this message in the console:

```
<< Something Happened!
```

The Event Object

Whenever an event handler is triggered by an event, the callback function is called. This function is automatically passed an event object as a parameter that contains information about the event.

To see an example of this, change the doSomething() function in the main.js file to this:

```
function doSomething(event){
console.log(event.type);
}
```

Now refresh the events.html page in the browser and try clicking again. You should see the following appear in the console every time you click:

```
<< click
```

In the example, the type property is used to tell us that the type of event logged was a click event.

 Parameter Naming

> The parameter does not have to be called event. It can be given any legal variable name, although calling it event can make it easier to read the code. Many developers often abbreviate it to just e.

Types of Event

The type property returns the type of event that occurred, such as click in the previous example. The different types of events will be discussed in the next section.

The Event Target

The target property returns a reference to the node that fired the event. If you change the doSomething() function to the following, it will show a message in the console telling us the node that was clicked on:

```
function doSomething(event){
console.log(event.target);
}
```

For example, if you click on one of the paragraphs, you should see something similar to the following in the console:

```
<< <p id='click'>Click On Me</p>
```

Coordinates of an Event

There are a variety of ways to find the position of where a mouse event occurs.

The `screenX` and `screenY` properties show the number of pixels from the left and top of the screen respectively where the event took place.

The `clientX` and `clientY` properties show the number of pixels from the left and top of the client that is being used (usually the browser window).

The `pageX` and `pageY` properties show the number of pixels from the left and top, respectively, where the event took place in the *document*. This property takes account of whether the page has been scrolled.

All these event properties are similar, but subtly different. They are useful for finding out the place where a click happened or the position of the mouse cursor. To see the coordinates that are returned for these properties, change the `doSomething()` function to the following:

```
function doSomething(event){
 console.log(`screen: (${event.screenX},${event.screenY}),
↪ page: (${event.pageX},${event.pageY}), client:
↪ (${event.screenX},${event.screenY})`)
}
```

Types of Events

There are several types of events, ranging from when a video has finished playing to when a resource has completed downloading. You can see a full list on the Events page of the Mozilla Developer Network.[2]

In this section, we're going to focus on some of the more common events that occur using the mouse, the keyboard and touch.

Mouse Events

We have already seen the `click` event that occurs when a mouse button is clicked. There are also the `mousedown` and `mouseup` events. These both occur *before* a `click` event is fired.

To see this in action, remove all the code in `main.js` and replace it with the following:

```
const clickParagraph = document.getElementById('click');

 clickParagraph.addEventListener('click',() =>
↪ console.log('click') );
 clickParagraph.addEventListener('mousedown',() =>
↪ console.log('down') );
 clickParagraph.addEventListener('mouseup',() =>
↪ console.log('up') );
```

Try clicking anywhere on the page and you should see all three events fire in the following order:

```
<< mousedown
mouseup
click
```

2. https://developer.mozilla.org/en-US/docs/Web/Events

There is also the `dblclick` event, which occurs when the user doubleclicks on the element to which the event listener is attached. To see an example of this, we'll attach an event listener to the second paragraph in our example (with an ID of `dblclick`). Add the following code to `main.js`:

```
const dblclickParagraph =
↪ document.getElementById('dblclick');
dblclickParagraph.addEventListener('dblclick', highlight);

function highlight(event){
event.target.classList.toggle('highlight');
}
```

Now if you double-click on the second paragraph, it should change color as the class of `highlight` is toggled on and off.

Using `click` and `doubleclick` On The Same Element

You should be very cautious of attaching both a `click` and `doubleclick` event to the same element. This is because it's impossible to tell if a click is the first click of a doubleclick or just a single click. This means that a `doubleclick` event will *always* cause the `click` event to fire.

The `mouseover` event occurs when the mouse pointer is placed over the element to which the event listener is attached, while the `mouseout` event occurs when the mouse pointer moves away from an element. This example uses both the `mouseover` and `mouseout` events to change the color of the third paragraph (with an ID of `mouse`) when the mouse pointer hovers over it, and back again when it moves away from the paragraph:

```
const mouseParagraph = document.getElementById('mouse');
mouseParagraph.addEventListener('mouseover', highlight);
mouseParagraph.addEventListener('mouseout', highlight);
```

The `mousemove` event occurs whenever the mouse moves. It will only occur while the cursor is over the element to which it's applied. The following line of code creates a log in the console whenever the mouse moves over the third paragraph:

```
mouseParagraph.addEventListener('mousemove', () =>
↳ console.log('You Moved!') );
```

Keyboard Events

Three events that occur when a user presses a key are: `keydown`, `keypress` and `keyup`. When a user presses a key, the events occur in that order. They are not tied to any particular key, although the information about which key was pressed is a property of the event object.

1. The `keydown` event occurs when a key is pressed and will *continue to occur* if the key is held down.

2. The `keypress` event occurs after a `keydown` event but before a `keyup` event. The `keypress` event only occurs for keys that produce character input (plus the *Delete* key). This means that it's the most reliable way to find out the character that was pressed on the keyboard.

3. The `keyup` event occurs when a key is released.

To understand the differences in these events, it is important to distinguish between a physical *key* on the keyboard and a *character* that appears on the screen. The `keydown` event is the action of pressing a key, whereas the `keypress` event is the action of a character being typed on the screen.

To see an example of this add the following to `main.js`:

```
addEventListener('keydown',highlight);
```

Now refresh the page and try pressing a key. It should result in the whole document changing color, because event listener was applied to the whole document. If you hold a key down, the event will continue to fire, creating a psychedelic effect on the page.

To see the `keyup` event working, add the code that uses an anonymous arrow function to show the exact time the key was released in the console:

```
addEventListener('keyup', (event) => console.log(`You
↳ stopped pressing the key on ${new Date}`));
```

Each of these keyboard events have an `key` property that returns the printed representation of the key that was pressed, if it has one.

To see this in action, add the following code to `main.js`:

```
addEventListener('keypress', (event) => console.log(`You
↳ pressed the ${event.key} character`));
```

Now when you press a key, you should see a message similar to this in the console:

```
<< You pressed the j character
```

 Supporting Older Browsers

The `key` property has good support in modern browsers, but if you need to support older browsers, then a library such as keycode.js[3] will come in handy as it normalizes the key codes returned. The jQuery library also has a `which` property[4] that does this as well.

---

3. https://github.com/nostrademons/keycode.js/blob/master/keycode.js
4. https://api.jquery.com/event.which/

Modifier Keys

Pressing the modifier keys such as *Shift*, *Ctrl*, *Alt* and *meta* (*Cmd* on Mac) will fire the `keydown` and `keyup` events, but not the `keypress` event as they don't produce any characters on the screen.

The name of the modifier key is still returned by the `key` property. To see this, edit the event listener we just used to listen for a `keydown` event instead:

```
addEventListener('keydown', (event) => console.log(`You
↳ pressed the ${event.key} character`));
```

Now try pressing a modifier key:

```
<< "You pressed the Control character"
```

All event objects also contains information about whether a modifier key was held down when the key event occurred. The `shiftKey`, `ctrlKey`, `altKey`, and `metaKey` are all properties of the event object and return `true` if the relevant key was held down. For example, the following code will check to see if the user pressed the *C* key while holding down the *Ctrl* key:

```
addEventListener('keydown', (event) => {
if (event.key === 'c' && event.ctrlKey) {
    console.log('Action canceled!');
}
});
```

The following code checks to see if the *Shift* key was held down when the mouse was clicked:

```
addEventListener('click', (event) => {
if (event.shiftKey) {
    console.log('A Shifty Click!');
```

```
}
});
```

Modifying Default Behavior

Modifier keys can often already have a purpose assigned in the browser or operating system. And although it's possible to prevent the default behavior in the browser (see later in this chapter), it's not considered best practice to do so.

Touch Events

Many modern devices now support touch events. These are used on smartphones and tablets, as well as touch-screen monitors, satellite navigators and trackpads. Touch events are usually made with a finger, but can also be by stylus or another part of the body. There are a number of touch events that cover many types of touch interactions.

It's important to support mouse events as well as touch events, so non-touch devices are also supported. With so many different devices these days, you can't rely on users using just touch or a mouse. In fact, some devices, such as touchscreen laptops, support both mouse and touch interactions.

The `touchstart` event occurs when a user initially touches the surface.

Using the `touchstart` Event

Be careful when using the `touchstart` event as it fires as soon as a user touches the screen. They may be touching the screen because they want to zoom in or swipe, and a `touchstart` event listener could prevent them from doing this.

The `click` event is often a much safer option as it still fires when the screen is touched, but there's a slight delay of 300ms, allowing the user time to perform another action with the device. The `click` event can be thought of as a "tap" in the context of a touch event.

The `touchend` event occurs when a user stops touching the surface:

```
addEventListener('touchend', () => console.log('Touch
↳ stopped');
```

The `touchmove` event occurs after a user has touched the screen then moves around without leaving. It will continue to occur as long as the user is still touching the screen, even if they leave the element to which the event listener is attached.

The `touchenter` event occurs when a user has already started touching the surface, but then passes over the element to which the event listener is attached.

The `touchleave` event occurs when the user is still touching the surface, but leaves the element to which the event listener is attached.

The `touchcancel` event occurs when a touch event is interrupted, such as a user's finger moving outside the document window, or too many fingers being used at once. A pop-up dialog will also cancel a touch event.

What About Swiping?

There are no "swipe" events. These need to be created by using a combination of `touchstart`, `touchmove`, and `touchleave` events that monitor the distance and direction moved from start to finish of a touch event.

There were proposals for `gesture` events that may be supported in the future, but it seems they are not scheduled to be part of the specification anytime soon.

If you need to implement gestures, it's probably a good idea to use a library such as Hammer.JS[5] or zingtouch[6] that makes events such as swipe, pinch and rotate easy to implement.

Touch Event Properties

Because it's possible to touch a surface many times at once, touch event objects have a property called `touches`. This is a list of touch objects that represents all the touches taking place on that device. It has a `length` property that tells you

---

[5] http://hammerjs.github.io/
[6] https://zingchart.github.io/zingtouch/

how many *touch points* (usually the user's fingers, but could be a stylus) are in contact with the surface. Each touch object in the list can be accessed using index notation. For example, if a user touches the screen with two fingers, `events.touches.length` would return 2. The first touch object can be accessed using `events.touches[0]` and the second using `events.touches[1]`.

Each touch object has a number of properties, many similar to the `event` object, such as `touch.screenX` and `touch.screenY` to find the coordinates of the touch point. They have other properties such as `touch.radiusX` and `touch.radiusY`, which give an indication of the area covered by the touch, and `touch.force`, which returns the amount of pressure being applied by the touch as a value between 0 and 1.

Each touch object has a `touch.identifier` property, a unique ID that can be used to ensure you are dealing with the same touch.

Use Touch Events With Caution

Touch events are complex and difficult to implement. Many of the properties and methods mentioned above are still marked as being experimental and not widely implemented in browsers.

Removing Event Listeners

An event listener can be removed using the `removeEventListener()` method. To see an example, add this line to `events.html`:

```
<p id='once'>A One Time Thing...</p>
```

Now add the following code to `main.js`:

```
const onceParagraph = document.getElementById('once');
onceParagraph.addEventListener('click', remove);

function remove(event) {
console.log('Enjoy this while it lasts!');
```

```
onceParagraph.style.backgroundColor = 'pink';
onceParagraph.removeEventListener('click',remove);
}
```

This adds a `click` event listener to a paragraph element, but then removes it in the callback function named `remove`. This means it will only be called once (try clicking on it again and nothing happens).

 Using Anonymous Functions

Note that you shouldn't use anonymous functions as an argument to `addEventListener()` if you want to remove it later. This is because there needs to be a reference to the same function name in the arguments of `removeEventListener()`.

Stopping Default Behavior

Some elements have default behavior associated with certain events. For example, when a user clicks on a link, the browser redirects to the address in the `href` attribute and a form is submitted when the user clicks on the *Submit* button.

`preventDefault()` is a method of the `event` object that can be used inside the callback function to stop the default behavior happening. To see an example, add the following line to the `events.html` file:

```
<p>
 <a id='broken' href='https://sitepoint.com'>Broken
↪ Link</a>
</p>
```

Then add the following event listener inside the `main.js` file:

```
const brokenLink = document.getElementById('broken');

brokenLink.addEventListener('click',(event) => {
```

```
    event.preventDefault();
    console.log('Broken Link!');
});
```

This will stop the page redirecting to the page specified in the `href#39;` attribute, and show a message in the console instead.

 Think Carefully Before Using `preventDefault()`

Make sure you think carefully before using **preventDefault()** to change default behavior. Users will expect certain behaviors, and preventing them may cause confusion.

Some events do not allow the default behavior to be prevented. This can vary from browser to browser, but each event object has a property called **cancellable** that returns **false** if it cannot be prevented.

You can also see if the default behavior has been prevented by checking the **defaultPrevented** property.

Event Propagation

When you click on an element, you are actually clicking on all the elements it's nested inside of. To illustrate this, add the following piece of HTML to the `events.html` file:

```
<ul id='list'>
<li>one</li>
<li>two</li>
<li>three</li>
</ul>
```

If you click on one of the `<li>` elements, you're also clicking on the `<ul>`, `<body>` and `<html>` elements. An event is said to *propagate* as it moves from one element to another.

Event propagation is the order that the events fire on each element. There are two forms of event propagation: bubbling and capturing.

Bubbling is when the event fires on the element clicked on first, then bubbles up the document tree, firing an event on each parent element until it reaches the root node.

Capturing starts by firing an event on the root element, then propagates downwards, firing an event on each child element until it reaches the target element that was clicked on.

Capturing vs. Bubbling

The capturing model was originally implemented by Netscape, and the bubbling model was implemented in Microsoft browsers back in the bad old days of the Browser Wars. The W3C sensibly came down in the middle and allowed developers to decide which method they prefer to use.

Bubbling

The default behavior is bubbling, which we can see happen if we add the following code to `main.js`:

```
ulElement = document.getElementById('list');
liElement = document.querySelector('#list li');

ulElement.addEventListener('click', (event) =>
console.log('Clicked on ul') );

liElement.addEventListener('click', (event) =>
console.log('Clicked on li') );
```

Now try clicking on the first `<li>` element in the list. There should be a message in the console saying "Clicked on li" because this was the target element. The event then bubbles up to the parent `<ul>` element and displays a message in the console saying "Clicked on ul". The event will continue to bubble all the way to the root HTML element, but nothing will happen because none of the other elements had event listeners attached to them.

If you click on the second or third `<li>` elements in the list you will only see the message "Clicked on ul". This is because, even though these elements don't have an event listener attached to them, the click still bubbles up and is captured by the `<ul>` element that *does* have an event listener attached.

Capturing

The `addEventListener()` method has a third parameter, which is a boolean value that specifies whether capturing should be used or not. It defaults to `false`, which is why bubbling happens by default. There may be instances when you would rather capture the events instead; for example, you might want events on outer elements to fire before any events fire on the element that was actually clicked on.

To implement capturing instead, change the code to the following:

```
ulElement.addEventListener('click', (event) =>
console.log('Clicked on ul'),true);

liElement.addEventListener('click', (event) =>
console.log('Clicked on li'),true);
```

Now if you click on the first list item, "Clicked on ul" will be logged to the console first. The events then propagate downwards to the child `<li>` element, so "Clicked on li" is logged to the console next.

If you want the event to both capture *and* bubble, you must set a separate event handler for both cases, like so:

```
// capturing

ulElement.addEventListener('click', (event) =>
console.log('Clicked on ul'),true);
```

```
liElement.addEventListener('click', (event) =>
console.log('Clicked on li'),true);

// bubbling

ulElement.addEventListener('click', (event) =>
console.log('Clicked on ul'),false );

liElement.addEventListener('click', (event) =>
console.log('Clicked on li'),false );
```

Stopping the Bubbling Phase

The bubble phase can be stopped from occurring by adding the event.stopPropagation() method into the callback function. In the following example, the event will fail to propagate as the third argument is false, which stops capturing, and the event.stopPropagation() method is called, which stops bubbling:

```
liElement.addEventListener('click', (event) => {
console.log('clicked on li');
event.stopPropagation(); }, false);
```

Now clicking on the first <li> element will only log one message, since the click event will not propagate to the <ul> element.

 Be Careful Not to Stop Other Event Listeners Firing

> Be very wary of using the stopPropagation() method to stop the bubble phase occurring. There may be other event listeners attached to elements further up the chain that won't fire as a result.

You can read more about event propagation on SitePoint[7].

[7.] https://www.sitepoint.com/event-bubbling-javascript/

Event Delegation

Event delegation can be used to attach an event listener to a parent element in
order to capture events that are triggered by its child elements.

Let's look at the list items in our example:

```
<ul id='list'>
<li>one</li>
<li>two</li>
<li>three</li>
</ul>
```

If we wanted to attach event listeners to all the `<li>` tags so they were highlighted
when clicked on, it would need more code to add a separate event listener to
each element. In this case, there isn't much difference, but imagine if you had a
list of 100 elements!

A better way is to attach the event listener to the parent `<ul>` element, then use
the `target` property to identify the element that was clicked on. Add the
following to `main.js` to see this in action (remember that the `highlight()`
function used the `target` property):

```
ulElement.addEventListener('click',highlight);
```

Now clicking on any list item will highlight that list item as if it was the target of
the click event.

This is a useful method if you are adding extra list elements to the DOM
dynamically. Any new list elements that are a child of the `<ul>` element will
automatically inherit this event listener, saving you from having to add an event
listener every time a new list item is added.

Quiz Ninja Project

Now that we've reached the end of the chapter, it's time to add some events to our Quiz Ninja Project. We're going to add a button that can be clicked on to start the game.

To start, add this line of code to `index.html`, just before the closing `<body>` tag:

```
<button id='start'>Click to Start</button>
```

This will add a button to the markup. Now we need a reference to it in `main.js`. Add the following line of property to the `view` object:

```
start: document.getElementById('start'),
```

Now we need to attach a 'click' event listener to the button that will start the game when the button is clicked. Add the following code to the end of `main.js`:

```
view.start.addEventListener('click', () =>
↳ game.start(quiz), false);
```

We're also going to add a couple of utility functions that will show and hide elements on a page. These also go in `view` object as they are only concerned with the view:

```
show(element){
element.style.display = 'block';
},
hide(element){
element.style.display = 'none';
}
```

These work by simply changing the `style.display` property to `none` to hide an element, and `block` to display it.

We can use these to make the start button disappear while the game is in progress, then reappear once the game has finished. Add the following line of code to the `game.start()` method:

```
view.hide(view.start);
```

Then add the following line to the `game.gameOver()` method:

```
view.show(view.start);
```

And that's it — hopefully you can see that it wasn't too hard to add a start button with its own event listener attached; especially since the function it invoked was already written. Open `index.html` and have a go at playing the game. It should look similar to the below.

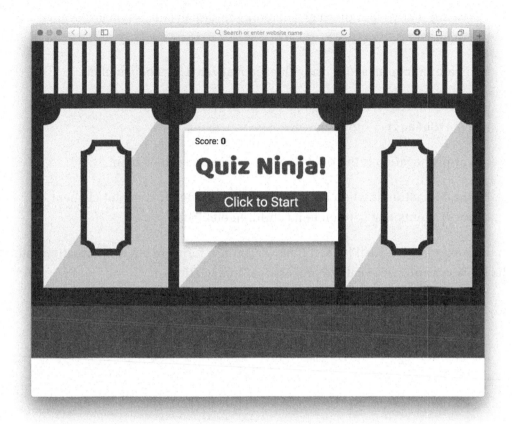

7-1. Our start button

You can see a live example on CodePen[8].

Chapter Summary

- Events occur when a user interacts with a web page.

- An event listener is attached to an element, then invokes a callback function when the event occurs.

- The event object is passed to the callback function as an argument, and contains lots of properties and methods relating to the event.

---

8. https://codepen.io/daz4126/pen/LLdJww

- There are many types of event, including mouse events, keyboard events, and touch events.

- You can remove an event using the `removeEventListener` method.

- The default behavior of elements can be prevented using the `preventDefault()` function.

- Event propagation is the order the events fire on each element.

- Event delegation is when an event listener is added to a parent element to capture events that happen to its children elements.

In the next chapter, we'll look at how we can use forms to enter information into the browser, and use events to process that information.

Chapter

8

Forms

Forms are a very common method of interacting with a web page. A form is the main component of Google's home page, and most of us use forms every day to log in to our favorite sites. In this chapter, we will look at how forms can be used to interact with a JavaScript program.

In this chapter, we'll cover these topics:

▓ Form controls

▓ Accessing form elements

▓ Form properties and methods

▓ Form events

■ Submitting a form

■ Retrieving and changing values from a form

■ Form validation

■ Our project — add a form for answering the questions.

Forms

Forms are made up of a `<form>` element that contains form controls such as input fields, select menus and buttons. These input fields can be populated with information that is processed once the form has been submitted.

Traditionally, when a form was submitted, it would be sent to a server where the information would be processed using a back end language such as PHP or Ruby. It's possible, and becoming more and more common, to process the information in a form on the front end *before* it is sent to the server using JavaScript, which is what we'll be focusing on in this chapter.

Each form control has an initial value that can be specified in the HTML code. This value can be changed by a user entering information or interacting with the form's interface (such as using a slider to increase or decrease a value). The value can also be changed dynamically using JavaScript.

 Forms UX

When it comes to forms, there are plenty of usability and accessibility considerations to keep in mind, such as using correct and semantic markup, making forms keyboard accessible and using WAI-AIRA labels. Most of these fall outside the scope of this book, as we'll be keeping the focus on how to use JavaScript to interact with the forms.

If you'd like to learn more about how to design forms that are accessible and enhance the user experience then *Designing UX: Forms*[1] by Jessica Enders is well worth a read.

[1.] https://www.sitepoint.com/premium/books/designing-ux-forms

A Searching Example

We'll start off with a simple example of a form that contains one input field, and a button to submit a search query, not unlike the one used by Google. This example doesn't use any styles; you just need to create a file called `search.html` that contains the following code:

```
<!doctype html>
<html lang='en'>
<head>
<meta charset='utf-8'>
<title>Search</title>
</head>
<body>
<form name='search' action='/search'>
    <input name='searchInput'>
    <button type='submit'>Search</button>
</form>
<script src='main.js'></script>
</body>
</html>
```

This form has a `name` attribute of `search`, and contains two controls: an input field where a user can enter a search phrase, and a button to submit the form. The form can also be submitted by pressing Enter.

The `action` attribute is the URL that the form will be submitted to so it can be processed on the server side. The input field also has a `name` attribute of `searchInput` that is used to access the information inside it.

You should also create a file called `main.js` to put the JavaScript in. This can be saved in the same directory as `search.html`.

Accessing Form Elements

The legacy DOM had a useful property called `document.forms` that returns an HTML collection of all the forms in the document in the order they appear in the markup. Even though there is only one form in our example, a collection will still be returned, so we have to use index notation to return the first (and only) form object, like so:

```
const form = document.forms[0];
```

This is the equivalent of using the following method that we learned in Chapter 6:

```
const form = document.getElementsByTagname('form')[0];
```

Instead of using a numerical index, we can use the `name` attribute to identify a form:

```
const form = document.forms.search;
```

Be careful referencing elements in this way, however. If the form had the same name as any properties or methods of the `document.forms` object, such as `submit`, for example, that property or method would be referenced instead of the `<form>` element. This is unlikely to happen, as the `document.form` object doesn't have many properties or methods, but it is something to be aware of. To avoid this, square bracket notation can be used (this is also required if the form's name attribute contains any invalid characters, such as spaces or dashes):

```
const form = document.forms['search'];
```

A form object also has a method called `elements` that returns an HTML collection of all the elements contained in the form. In this case the form contains two controls: an input element and a button element:

```
const [input,button] = form.elements;
```

We can also access the form controls using their `name` attributes as if it was a property of the form object. So, for example, the input field has a name attribute of `searchInput` and can be accessed using this code:

```
const input = form.searchInput
```

The square bracket notation can also be used instead (again, this is useful if there are any naming clashes with existing property and method names, or if the name is an invalid variable name):

```
const input = form['searchInput']
```

Form Properties and Methods

Form objects have a number of useful properties and methods that can be used to interact with the form.

The `form.submit()` method will submit the form automatically. Note that submitting a form using this method won't trigger the form `submit` event that's covered in the next section.

A form can be submitted manually by the user employing a button or input element with a type attribute of `submit`, or even an input element with a `type` attribute of `image`:

```
<button type='submit'>Submit</button>
<input type='submit' value='Submit'>
<input type='image' src='button.png'>
```

The `form.reset()` method will reset all the form controls back to their initial values specified in the HTML.

A button with a `type` attribute of `reset` can also be used to do this without the need for additional scripting:

```
<button type='reset'>Reset</button>
```

 Reset Buttons

Reset buttons are generally considered poor for usability, as they are too easy to click and then wipe out all the data that's been entered. So think very carefully before using one in a form.

The `form.action` property can be used to set the `action` attribute of a form, so it's sent to a different URL to be processed on the server:

```
form.action = '/an/other.url'
```

Form Events

Forms trigger a number of events like those discussed in the last chapter. Some of these events are exclusive to forms.

The `focus` event occurs when an element is focused on. In the case of an `<input>` element, this is when the cursor is placed inside the element (either by clicking or tapping on it or navigating to it using the keyboard). To see an example, add the following code to `main.js`:

```
const input = form.elements.searchInput;

 input.addEventListener('focus', () => alert('focused'),
↳ false);
```

Open `search.html` in your browser and place the cursor inside the input field. You should see an alert dialog similar to the one in the screenshot below.

8-1. Our alert dialog

The blur event occurs when the user moves the focus away from the form element. Add the following to main.js, reload the page, and then move the cursor away from the search box:

```
input.addEventListener('blur', () => alert('blurred'),
↪ false);
```

The change event occurs when the user moves the focus away from the form element *after changing it*. So if a user clicks in an input field and makes no changes, and then clicks elsewhere, the change event won't fire, but the blur event will.

Add the following code to main.js and reload the page. You'll notice the alert messagechanged only appears if you actually change the value inside the search box, then move the cursor away from it:

```
input.addEventListener('change', () => alert('changed'),
↪ false);
```

Note that the blur event will also fire, but after the change event.

Submitting a Form

Possibly the most important form event is the submit event, occurring when the form is submitted. Usually this will send the content of the form to the server to be processed, but we can use JavaScript to intercept the form before it's sent by adding a `submit` event listener. Add the following code to the `main.js` file:

```
const form = document.forms['search'];
form.addEventListener ('submit', search, false);

function search() {
alert(' Form Submitted');
}
```

Now reload the page and click on the *Submit* button. You should see an alert dialog saying *Form Submitted*. After you click *OK*, the browser tries to load a nonexistent page (the URL should end in something similar to `.../search?searchInput=hello`). This is because when the event fired, our `search()` function was invoked, displaying the alert dialog. Then the form was submitted to the URL provided in the `action` attribute for processing, but in this case, the URL isn't a real URL, so it doesn't go anywhere. Back-end processing isn't covered in this book, so we'll keep this as a dummy URL and focus on using JavaScript to process the information instead.

We can actually stop the form from being submitted to that URL altogether by using the `preventDefault()` method that we saw in the last chapter. Add the following line to the search function:

```
function search(event) {
alert('Form Submitted');
event.preventDefault();
}
```

Now reload `search.html` and try submitting the form. You'll see that the alert dialog still appears, but after you click *OK*, the form doesn't try to submit itself to the dummy URL.

Retrieving and Changing Values From a Form

Text input element objects have a `value` property that can be used to retrieve the text inside the field.

We can use this to report back what the user has searched for. Edit the `search()` function to the following:

```
function search(event) {
alert(`You Searched for: ${input.value}`);
event.preventDefault();
}
```

Note that in this example, `input` is the variable that we defined at the start of the `main.js` file that points to the input element in our form, but it could have been called anything.

Now refresh the page, enter some text in the search box, and you should see a similar sight to the screenshot shown below:

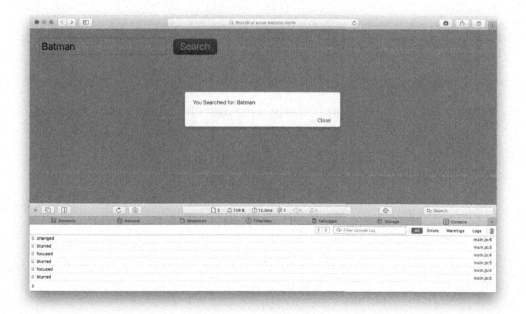

8-2. Reporting what the user searched for

It's also possible to set the value using JavaScript. Add the following line of code to the `main.js` file:

```
input.value = 'Search Here';
```

Now refresh the page and you should see that the string `Search Here` is displayed in the input field.

The problem with this is that the text remains in the field when the user clicks inside it, so it has to be deleted before the user can enter their own text. This is easily remedied using the `focus` and `blur` event handlers. Add the following to `main.js`:

```
input.addEventListener('focus', function(){
if (input.value==='Search Here') {
    input.value = ''
    }
}, false);

input.addEventListener('blur', function(){
if(input.value === '') {
    input.value = 'Search Here';
    } }, false);
```

Now the default text will disappear when the user clicks inside the input field (the focus event) and reappear if the user leaves the field blank and clicks away from it (the blur event).

The placeholder Attribute

Similar functionality can be produced in modern browsers using the **placeholder** attribute in the HTML markup. Simply change the input field to the following in `search.html`:

```
<input type='text' name='search-box' placeholder='Search
↪ Here'>
```

This has slightly different behavior in that the placeholder text is not actually a value of the input field, so it won't be submitted as the field's value if the user fails to fill it in.

Form Controls

In our previous search example, we only used the input and button form controls. But there are others that can help to make our web pages more interactive.

Some common types of form control are:

- `<input>` fields, including text, passwords, check boxes, radio buttons, and file uploads

- `<select>` menus for drop-down lists of options

- `<textarea>` elements for longer text entry

- `<button>` elements for submitting and resetting forms

To demonstrate all these HTML form controls, we'll create another form that contains all these elements. Back in Chapter 5, we created a **superman** object that had lots of properties associated with the Man of Steel. We're going to design a form that allows a user to enter all these details into a browser, so we'll create a similar **hero** object that describes a superhero (or villain).

Create a new project folder that contains the following code in a file called `hero.html`:

```
<!doctype html>
<html lang='en'>
<head>
<meta charset='utf-8'>
<title>Hero Form</title>
</head>
<body>
<form id='hero'>
    <label for='heroName'>Name:
 <input type='text' id='heroName' name='heroName'
↳ autofocus placeholder='Your Super Hero Name' maxlength=32>
    </label>
    <button type='submit'>Submit</button>
</form>
<script src='main.js'></script>
</body>
</html>
```

We'll start with a basic form that's fairly similar to our previous search example, containing a text input field and button to submit the form.

 New Attributes in HTML5

The `input` element includes some of the new attributes introduced in HTML5.

The `autofocus` attribute give focus to this element when a page loads. It is the equivalent to putting the following line of JavaScript in `main.js`:

```
document.forms.hero.heroName.focus();
```

The `placeholder` attribute will insert the value provided in the input field until the user enters some text. This can be useful to place hints about how to fill in the form.

The `maxlength` attribute will limit the number of characters that can be entered in the field to the value given (in this case 32).

There are many new attributes that can be employed to make forms more user-friendly. A good roundup of all the new form elements can be found on SitePoint[2].

We'll also need a file called `main.js` that is saved in the same folder as the `hero.html` file. In this file, let's start off by assigning the form to a variable and then adding an event listener for when the form is submitted:

```
const form = document.forms['hero'];
form.addEventListener('submit', makeHero, false);
```

The event listener will invoke the `makeHero()` function when the form is submitted. This function will return an object based on the information provided in the form. Let's implement that function by adding this code to `main.js`:

```
function makeHero(event) {

 event.preventDefault(); // prevent the form from being
↪ submitted

const hero = {}; // create an empty object

 hero.name = form.heroName.value; // create a name property
↪ based on the input field's value

 alert(JSON.stringify(hero)); // convert object to JSON
↪ string and display in alert dialog
return hero;
}
```

This function uses the `event.preventDefault()` method to stop the form from being submitted. We then create a local variable called `hero` and assign it to an empty object literal. We'll then augment this object with properties from the form, although we only have the `name` property at the moment.

Once the `hero` object is created, it would probably be returned by the function then used elsewhere in the rest of the program. Since this is just for demonstration purposes, we simple use the `JSON.stringify()` method to convert the `hero` object into a JSON string and display it in an alert dialog.

---

2. http://www.sitepoint.com/html5-forms-markup

Open up `hero.html` in a browser and enter the name of a superhero and you should see a screenshot similar the below.

8-3. Entering our hero's name

Now we know our code is working, let's look at some of the other types of form controls.

Input Fields

Input fields are the most common types of form control, but there are several categories of input field as you'll soon see:

Text Input Fields

The default type of input field is `text`, which is used for entering a short piece of text, such as a username. In our example, we use a text input field to enter the name of the superhero. The `type='text'` attribute isn't required (we didn't use it in the search example as `text` is the default), but it is advisable to use it as it makes the intended purpose of the field explicit, helping with maintenance, readability and future-proofing.

The initial value of this field can be set in the HTML using the `value` attribute. For example, you could pre-fill the recommended donation on a charity page like so:

```
<label for='donation-amount'>Enter amount to donate:
 <input type='text' id ='donation-amount'
↳ name='donationAmount' value='10'>
</label>
```

Password Input Fields

`input type='password'` is used to enter passwords or secret information. This works in the same way as an input field with `type='text'`, except the characters are concealed as they are entered so they're unable to be read on the screen.

To see this in action, we will add a `realName` property to our `hero` object. Obviously the real name of a superhero is secret information, so it needs to be hidden from prying eyes when it is being entered. Add the following line to the form in `hero.html` (just before the submit button):

```
<label for='realName'>Real Name:
 <input type='password' name='realName'
↳ id='realName'></label>
```

To process this information, we add the following line to the `makeHero()` function in `main.js`:

```
hero.realName = form.realName.value;
```

As you can see, values from a password input field are accessed in exactly the same way as text input fields using the `value` property.

Checkbox Input Fields

Check boxes are created using input fields with `type='checkbox'`. They are used to select different options that can be checked (true) or left unchecked (false). The user can select *more than one checkbox* from a list.

We'll use checkboxes to add a list of powers that the superhero can have. Add the following lines of code to the form in `hero.html`:

```
<p>Super Powers:</p>
<label for='flight'>Flight:
 <input type='checkbox' id='flight' value='Flight'
↪ name='powers'>
</label>
<label for='strength'>Super Strength:
 <input type='checkbox' id='strength' value='Strength'
↪ name='powers'>
</label>
<label for='speed'>Super Speed:
 <input type='checkbox' id='speed' value='Super Speed'
↪ name='powers'>
</label>
<label for='energy'>Energy Blasts:
 <input type='checkbox' id='energy' value='Energy Blasts'
↪ name='powers'>
    </label>
<label for='telekinesis'>Telekinesis:
 <input type='checkbox' id='telekinesis'
↪ value='Telekinesis' name='powers'>
</label>
```

Notice that all the checkbox elements have the same 'name' property of 'powers'. This means they can be accessed as an HTML collection, like so:

```
form.powers;
```

We can then iterate over this collection using a `for` loop to see if each checkbox was checked. Checkbox objects have a `checked` property that tells us if it has been checked or not. It is a boolean property, so can only have the values `true` or `false`. The value property is used to set the name of the power that can be used if the checkbox has been checked. Add the following code to the `makeHero()` function in `main.js`:

```
hero.powers = [];
for (let i=0; i < form.powers.length; i++) {
if (form.powers[i].checked) {
    hero.powers.push(form.powers[i].value);
}
}
```

This creates a `powers` property for our `hero` object that starts as an empty array. We then iterate over each checkbox to see if it was checked in the form. If it was, we add the `value` property of the checkbox to the `powers` array using the `push` method.

We can refactor this code to be much more succinct by using the array iterators we saw in Chapter 4. The following code will achieve the same result:

```
hero.powers = [...form.powers].filter(box =>
↪ box.checked).map(box => box.value);
```

This uses the spread operator to turn the node list into an array. This then allows us to use the `filter()` method that returns an array containing only the check boxes that were checked (this is because their `checked` property will be truthy). We then chain the `map()` method to the end, which replaces each checkbox in the array with its `value` property. This array is then returned and stored in the `hero.powers` variable.

Note that a checkbox can be set to true using JavaScript by setting its `checked` property to `true`. For example, we could make the first checkbox in the list of powers appear checked with this line of code:

```
document.forms.hero.powers[0].checked = true;
```

Checkboxes can also be checked initially using the `checked` attribute in the HTML:

```
<input type='checkbox' value='Flight' name='powers'
↪ checked>
```

Radio Button Input Fields

Radio buttons are created using input fields with `type='radio'`. Like checkboxes they allow users to check an option as `true`, but they provide an exclusive choice of options, so *only one option* can be selected.

This type of mutually exclusive option could be whether a superhero is a hero or a villain... or even an antihero (you know, those who are unable to decide whether to be good or bad!). Add this line of code to the form in `hero.html`:

```
<p>What type of hero are you?</p>
<label for='hero'>Hero:
 <input type='radio' name='category' value='Hero'
↪ id='hero'>
</label>
<label for='villain'>Villain:
 <input type='radio' name='category' value='Villain'
↪ id='villain'>
</label>
<label for='anti-hero'>Anti-Hero:
 <input type='radio' name='category' value='Antihero'
↪ id='anti-hero'>
</label>
```

All these radio buttons have the same `name` attribute of `category`. This is used to group them together — only one radio button can be checked in a group that has the same name attribute. It also means we can access an HTML collection of all the radio buttons in that group using the property of the same name — as can be seen in this line of code:

```
form.category;
```

If you examine this array after the form has been submitted, it will look similar to the example below:

```
[input, input, input, value: "Antihero"]
```

The value of the radio button that was selected is stored in `form.category.value` (in this case it is `Antithero`). This means we can assign a `category` property to our `hero` object by adding the following code to the `makeHero()` function in `main.js`:

```
hero.category = form.category.value;
```

Each radio button has a `checked` property that returns the boolean values `true` and `false`, depending on if it has been selected or not. It's possible to change the `checked` property to `true` using JavaScript, but because only one radio button can be checked at once, all the others with the same `name` property will change to `false`. So the following line of code would check the`antihero` radio button, but the `hero` and `villian` radio buttons would then be unchecked:

```
form.type[2].checked = true;
```

Radio buttons can also be checked initially using the `checked` attribute in the HTML:

```
<input type='radio' name='type' value='Villain'
↪ checked>
```

Hidden Input Fields

Hidden fields can be created using input fields with `type='hidden'`. These are not displayed by the browser, but have a `value` attribute that can contain information that is submitted with the form. They are often used to send information such as settings or information that the user has already provided. Note that the information in these fields is in no way secret, as it's visible in the HTML, so shouldn't be used for sensitive data. The value of a hidden input field can be changed using JavaScript in the same was as any other input field.

File Input Fields

A file input field can be created using input fields with `type='file'`. These are used to upload files, and most browsers will provide a browse button or similar that lets users select a file from their file system.

Other Input Types

There are lots of new input types included in HTML5, such as `number`, `tel` and `color`. As browsers start to support these, they will implement different user-interface elements depending on the input type. So a number field might use a slider, whereas a date field will show a calendar. They will also validate automatically, so an email input field will show an error message if there's no valid email address.

Let's add an input type of`number` to our form so we can enter the age of our hero. Add the following to `hero.html`:

```
<label for='age'>Age:
 <input type='number' id='age' name='age' min=0
↪ step=1></label>
```

Number input fields also have optional min and max attributes that can be used to limit the input given. The step attribute is used to specify how much the value changes by each click. Most modern browsers will add controls at the side of the input field so the value can be increased or decreased, as shown below.

8-4. Using the number input field to specify our hero's age

We'll also need some JavaScript to process the age information. Add the following line to the makeHero() function in main.js:

```
hero.age = form.age.value;
```

These new input types are yet to be supported, but the good news is that you can start using them now because they will still work; the browser will just display a normal text input field if it doesn't support a particular type.

Select Drop-Down List

Select drop-down lists can be used to select one or more options from a list of values. The multiple attribute is required if more than one option is to be selected. We'll use one in our example to choose the city where our hero operates. Add the following line of code to the form in `hero.html`:

```
<label for='City'>Base of Operations:
<select name='city' id='city'>
<option value='' selected>Choose a City</option>
<option value='Metropolis'>Metropolis</option>
<option value='Gotham City'>Gotham City</option>
 <option value='Keystone City'>Keystone
↪ City</option>
<option value='Coast City'>Coast City</option>
<option value='Star City'>Star City</option>
</select>
</label>
```

Note that the `selected` attribute can be used to set the initial value in the HTML. In this example, the blank option that provides the instructional message 'Choose a City' has this attribute, so it's shown when the page loads.

The `name` attribute of the `select` element is used to access it in JavaScript as a property of the form object:

```
form.city;
```

If only one item was selected, this will return a reference to that selection; otherwise a collection will be returned containing each selection.

Each selection object has a `value` property that's equal to the `value` attribute of the `<option>` tag that was selected. Add the following code to the `makeHero()` function to set the `city` property:

```
hero.city = form.city.value;
```

It is also possible to find out the index of the option that has been selected, using the `selectedIndex` property. For example, if a user selected "Gotham City" from

the menu, `form.city.selectedIndex` would return 2 because it's the third option
in the list. This can then be used to access the actual text contained in the
selected option:

```
form.city.options[form.city.selectedIndex].text
```

From the example above, it should be clear that you can access the text of any
option using index notation. For example, the following code returns the text
from the first option:

```
form.city.options[0].text
<< "Choose a City"
```

Text Areas

A `<textarea>` element is used to enter long pieces of text over multiple lines
such as a comment or blog post. They work in much the same way as input fields.
We access them using the `name` attribute, and use the `value` property to see what
text was entered.

For example, we can add a text area to our form so the origin story of our
superhero can be entered. Add the following lines of code to the form in
`hero.html`:

```
<label for='origin'>Origin Story:
 <textarea id='origin' name='origin' rows='20'
↪ cols='60'></textarea>
</label>
```

The text entered into this text area can now be added as a property of the `hero`
object by placing the following line of code to the `makeHero()` function in
`main.js`:

```
hero.origin = form.origin.value;
```

It is also possible to change the value in the form directly:

```
form.origin.value = 'Born as Kal-El on the planet
↳ Krypton...';
```

The initial value of a text area can be set in the HTML by placing the text between the opening and closing tags:

```
<textarea name='origin' rows='20' cols='60'>Born as
↳ Kal-El on the planet Krypton...</textarea>
```

Buttons

We've already used a button to submit a form, but there are different types of buttons. The default type is `submit`, which is why we didn't have to specify the type in the search example at the start of the chapter. Another type we've already seen is `reset`, which will reset all the form fields to their initial settings. Let's add a reset button to our example by adding the following line to `hero.html`, just before the submit button:

```
<button type='reset'>Reset</button>
```

Now have a go at filling in part of the form and pressing the reset button; all the form fields should clear. Remember: this is *not* recommended good practice for usability reasons!

The other type is simply `button`. This doesn't need to be inside a form element and has no default behavior. It simply creates a clickable button that can have an event listener attached to it:

```
<button type='button'>Click Me</button>
```

There is also a type of 'menu' that can be combined with <menu>, <menuitem> and
<li> tags to create a dropdown menu when it's clicked on, although support for
this is fairly patchy at present.

I Need a Hero!

Now that our example form is complete, have a go at filling it in and pressing the
Submit button. You should see something similar to the screenshot below.

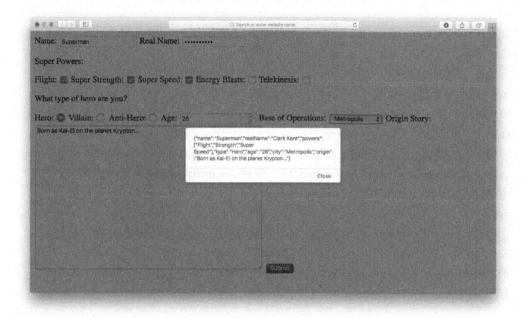

8-5. Hero JSON

We've successfully created a JavaScript object from form inputs that could then
be used in the rest of our program. In this example we've used the
JSON.stringify() method to convert the object into a JSON representation of the
object, which could then be stored in a database or exported to an external web
service.

Form Validation

Form validation is the process of checking whether a user has entered the information into a form correctly. Examples of the types of validation that occur include ensuring that:

- A required field is completed

- An email address is valid

- A number is entered when numerical data is required

- A password is at least a minimum number of characters

Validation can occur on the client side using JavaScript, and on the server side. It is advisable to use both client-side and server-side validation. JavaScript should not be relied upon to validate any data before it's saved to a database. This is because it's possible for a user to modify the JavaScript code and bypass the validation rules. It's also very easy to bypass the front-end completely and send arbitrary data to the application's backend. For these reasons, JavaScript validation should be used to enhance the user experience when filling in a form by giving feedback about any errors before it's submitted. This should then be backed up with more validation performed on the server before the data is eventually saved to a database. Having said that, it's still useful to validate on the client side even if the data will be validated again on the server side. This is because it will ensure that more valid data is sent to the server, which helps to cut down the number of HTTP requests required to send the form back and forward from the server to be corrected.

HTML5 has its own validation API that can be used, although it lacks the full support from all browsers at the moment. The error messages that it produces can look inconsistent across browsers and are difficult to style.

The API works by simply adding relevant attributes to the form fields. For example, if a field is a required field that must be filled in, all you need to do is add a `required` attribute to that field and the browser will take care of the rest.

To see an example of this in action, add a `required` attribute to the `heroName` field in our hero form:

```
<input type='text' id='heroName' name='heroName'
↪ autofocus placeholder='Your Super Hero Name' maxlength=32
↪ required>
```

Now refresh the page and leave the name field blank. As you click in another field, you'll notice that the blank name field is highlighted because it's a required field.

It is also possible to implement custom form validation using JavaScript. For example, say we wanted to exclude any superhero names that begin with an "X". This is not a standard form of validation, so we'd have to write our own. Add this code to `main.js` to see an example of custom validation:

```
form.addEventListener('submit',validate,false);

function validate(event) {
const firstLetter = form.heroName.value[0];
if (firstLetter.toUpperCase() === 'X') {
    event.preventDefault();
    alert('Your name is not allowed to start with X!');

}
}
```

We start by finding the first letter of the value entered in the name field using the index notation (remember that an index of 0 represents the first letter in a string). It then checks to see if the first letter is equal to the string literal X, and alerts the user if this is the case. It also uses the `preventDefault()` method to stop the form from being submitted. Otherwise it returns `true`, which means the form is submitted as normal.

If you refresh the page and enter a name beginning with 'X' in the name field, then try submitting the form, you should receive an error alert dialog as in the screenshot shown below.

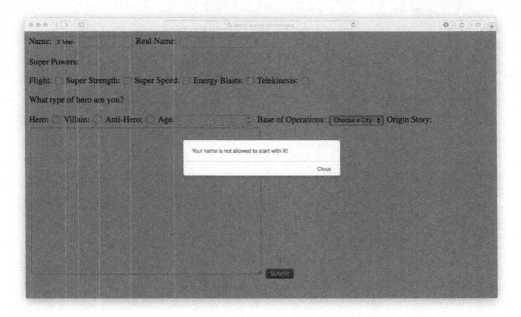

8-6. Validation error alert dialog

We can improve the usability of the form further by giving instant feedback, instead of waiting for the form to be submitted. This can be achieved by adding the event listener directly to the input field that will fire when the user presses a key (using the `keyup` event). The feedback can then be inserted inside the label element of the input field, along with a class of `error` for more direct feedback. Add the following code to `main.js`:

```
const label = form.querySelector('label');
const error = document.createElement('div');
error.classList.add('error');
  error.textContent = '! Your name is not allowed to start
↳ with X.';
label.append(error);

function validateInline() {
    const heroName = this.value.toUpperCase();
```

```
    if(heroName.startsWith('X')){
    error.style.display = 'block';
    } else {
    error.style.display = 'none';
    }
}
```

For this technique to work, we actually add the error message to the HTML in the JavaScript file, regardless of whether the error has been made or not. This is done in the first five lines above, using the DOM to create a `<div>` element that contains the error message and has a class of `error`. It's then added to the `<label>` element using the `append()` method. The trick here is that the element will not be visible as it will start with a style declaration of `display: none;`. This will be updated dynamically as the `keyup` event fires.

The `validateInline()` function is called every time the event is triggered. We start by assigning the variable `heroName` to the value entered in the input field, but we also apply the `toUpperCase()` method to it. This will allow us to check if it begins with an "x" or "X" without having to check both separately.

We then use an `if-else` block to check if the error has been made using the `startsWith()` method, which will return the first letter of a string. If it starts with an "X" then we change the style of the error element to `display: block`, which will make it visible.

The code inside the `else` block is run if there is no error, so it resets the style of the error element to `display: none`, making the error disappear.

To make this technique work, we need to add some custom styling to the error element to make sure it isn't visible initially, and to make the message stand out. Add the following `<style>` block inside the `<head>` section of `hero.html`:

```
<style>
    .error{
        background: #f99;
        border: #900 1px solid;
        display: none;
```

```
    }
</style>
```

 We're Not Using an External CSS File for Simplicity

It would be better to place any styles in an external CSS file, but for the purposes of this example, it's easier to put it straight into the HTML file.

Now if you refresh the page and try to enter a name beginning with "X", you should see an error message above the input field as soon as you try to move to another field. This can be seen in the screenshot below.

8-7. Showing an inline error message

This is a Specific and Perhaps Unrealistic Example

This was a very specific example of inline form validation – checking to see if an input field began with the letter "X", and it was only applied to one element.

In a real application, you might end up having to validate many different elements according to various different rules. If this is the case, it would make sense to write some more generic `addError()` and `removeError()` functions to deal with the different types of validation you might want to apply to the various elements in a form.

Disabling the Submit Button

Another useful technique that can aid usability is to disable the submit button if there are errors on the form. If the submit button is disabled then no action is taken when it's clicked. Most browsers will also display it in a lighter color to indicate that it cannot be clicked on. This prevents users from submitting a form containing any errors.

A submit button can be disable by added the `disabled` attribute to the `<input>` element:

```
<button type='submit' id='submit'
↪ disabled>Submit</button>
```

This can be changed programmatically using the `disabled` property of the `<button>` element. The following function will disable the button if an input field is empty:

```
function disableSubmit(event) {
    if(event.target.value === ''){
    document.getElementById('submit').disabled = true;
    } else {
    document.getElementById('submit').disabled = false;
    }
}
```

We can apply this to the `heroName` field by adding the following event handler that will fire every time a key is pressed:

```
form.heroName.addEventListener('keyup',disableSubmit,false);
```

Quiz Ninja Project

Now we're going to use forms in our Quiz Ninja game so that players can enter their answers without using `prompt` dialogs. Our first task is to add a form element with an ID of `response` in the HTML. This goes in between the `question` and `result` <div> elements in the `index.html` file:

```
<form id='response'>
<input name='answer' type='text'>
<button type='submit'>Submit Answer</button>
</form>
```

Now we add a reference to the form in our JavaScript. Add the following line of code as a property of the `view` object in `main.js`:

```
response: document.querySelector('#response')
```

The next task is to remove the `for-of` loop we've been using to loop through each question. This is because the prompt dialogs pause the execution of the program and wait until the player has entered the answer. This won't happen if we use a form to enter the answers, so the program would just loop through each question without giving the player a chance to answer!

Instead, we're going to use use the `pop()` method to remove each question, one at a time, from the `this.questions` array. Remove the main game loop code from the `game.start()` method in `main.js`, so it looks like this:

```
start(quiz){
    this.score = 0;
    this.questions = [...quiz];
    this.ask();
}
```

This sets up the quiz as it did before, but it also calls the `game.ask()` method, which results in the first question being asked.

Next, we need to change the `game.ask()` method, so it looks like the following:

```
ask(name){
    if(this.questions.length > 0) {
    this.question = this.questions.pop();
 const question = `What is ${this.question.name}'s real
↪ name?`;
    view.render(view.question,question);
    }
    else {
    this.gameOver();
    }
}
```

This checks the `length` property of the `this.questions` array, to see if there are any questions left to ask. If there are, the `pop()` method is used to remove the last element of the array and assign it to `this.question`. We use the same method as before to render the question in the HTML.

Next, we need to add an event handler that fires when the form is submitted. Add the following line of code to the bottom of `main.js`:

```
 view.response.addEventListener('submit', (event) =>
↪ game.check(event), false);
view.hide(view.response);
```

This will call the `game.check()` method that's used to check if the answer submitted by the player is correct. We need to update this method so it has an `event` object as a parameter. We can then use the `event.preventDefault()` method to stop the form from actually being submitted:

```
check(event){
    event.preventDefault();
    const response = view.response.answer.value;
    const answer = this.question.realName;
    if(response === answer){
    view.render(view.result,'Correct!',{'class':'correct'});
    this.score++;
    view.render(view.score,this.score);
    } else {
  view.render(view.result,`Wrong! The correct answer was
↪ ${answer}`,{'class':'wrong'});
    }
    this.ask();
},
```

We can grab the answer that was submitted by querying `view.response.answer.value`, which is the value stored in the `<input>` field. We then assign this to the variable `response` and use exactly the same code as before to deal with the outcome of the player's answer being right or wrong.

We also need to call the `game.ask()` function at the end of the method so the next question is asked after the current question has been answered and checked.

Players can now use the form instead of prompt dialogs to enter their answers, but a lot of the elements are displayed when they are unnecessary. For example, when the page loads, the form is displayed, even though there is no question to answer. To remedy this, we can create a couple of helper functions to update the view at the start and end of the game.

The first helper function is `view.setup()`, which will be used to set up the view when the game starts. Add the following method to the `view` object:

```
setup(){
    this.show(this.question);
    this.show(this.response);
    this.show(this.result);
    this.hide(this.start);
    this.render(this.score,game.score);
    this.render(this.result,'');
    this.render(this.info,'');
    this.resetForm();
}
```

This function makes use of the `view.show()` and `view.hide()` methods we created in the last chapter to make the `question`, `response` and `result` <div> elements visible and hide the `start` button. It also uses the `view.render()` method to reset any HTML content in the `result` and `info` elements back to an empty string. This will stop them displaying any messages from the previous game. It also calls a `view.resetForm()` method. This also needs adding to the `view` object:

```
resetForm(){
    this.response.answer.value = '';
    this.response.answer.focus();
}
```

This method resets the input field to an empty field and gives it focus, which improves usability as it means the player is left to concentrate on just answering the next question.

This will be useful to do after every question, so add a call to this method at the end of the `game.check()` method:

```
check(event){
    event.preventDefault();
    const response = view.response.answer.value;
    const answer = this.question.realName;
    if(response === answer){
```

```
    view.render(view.result,'Correct!',{'class':'correct'});
    this.score++;
    view.render(view.score,this.score);
    } else {
  view.render(view.result,`Wrong! The correct answer was
↳ ${answer}`,{'class':'wrong'});
    }
    view.resetForm();
    this.ask();
}
```

The `view.setup()` method needs calling at the beginning of every game, so it needs adding to the `game.start()` method:

```
start(quiz){
    this.score = 0;
    this.questions = [...quiz];
    view.setup();
    this.ask();
}
```

The other helper method is `view.teardown()`. This is called at the end of the game, and is responsible for hiding any elements that aren't required and making the start button visible again. Add the following method to the `view` object:

```
teardown(){
    this.hide(this.question);
    this.hide(this.response);
    this.show(this.start);
}
```

The method needs calling at the end of the game, so we need to place it in the `game.gameOver()` method:

```
gameOver(){
 view.render(view.info, `Game Over, you scored ${this.score}
↳ point${this.score !== 1 ? 's' : ''}`);
    view.teardown();
}
```

This should make the game look a lot more polished, so only the elements that are required as part of the game are on display at the relevant time. Let's see what it looks like by opening up `index.html` and trying it out. If everything has gone to plan, it should look similar to the screenshot below.

8-8. Playing Quiz ninja-skills

You can see a live example on CodePen[3].

Our quiz is now shaping up nicely, and looking much more professional without all the alert and prompt dialogs.

Chapter Summary

- Forms are the primary method used for entering data into a browser.

- Forms have a variety of controls that are used for entering different types of information.

- HTML5 has a large number of new input types that are beginning to be implemented in modern browsers.

- `document.forms` will return an HTML collection of all the forms on a page.

- `form.elements` will return an HTML collection of all the elements contained within a form.

- Forms have `focus`, `blur`, and `change` events that fire as a user interacts with the form.

- Forms also have a `submit` event that can be used to intercept a form before it's been submitted.

- The information entered into a form can be read or updated using the `value` property of the form controls.

- The HTML5 form validation API can be used to automatically validate a form, but only at a basic level, so a custom validation script may be required.

In the next chapter, we'll be taking a look at the `window` object.

---

3. https://codepen.io/daz4126/pen/ZyoyOz

Chapter

9

The Window Object

Every JavaScript environment has a **global object**. Any variables that are created in the global scope are actually properties of this object, and any functions are methods of it. In a browser environment the global object is the `window` object, which represents the browser window that contains a web page.

In this chapter, we'll cover these topics:

- The Browser Object Model

- Finding out browser information

- Browser history

- Controlling windows

- Cookies

- Timing functions

- Our project — we'll add a countdown timer to our quiz

The Browser Object Model

The Browser Object Model (or BOM for short) is a collection of properties and methods that contain information about the browser and computer screen. For example, we can find out which browser is being used to view a page (though, this method is unreliable). We can also find out the dimensions of the screen it is viewed on, and which pages have been visited before the current page. It can also be used for the rather dubious practice of creating pop-up windows, if you're into annoying your users.

There is no official standard for the BOM, although there are a number of properties and methods that are supported by all the major browsers, making a sort of de facto standard. These properties and methods are made available through the `window` object. Every browser window, tab, popup, frame, and iframe has a `window` object.

 The BOM Only Makes Sense in a Browser Environment

Remember that JavaScript can be run in different environments. The BOM only makes sense in a browser environment. This means that other environments (such as Node.js) probably won't have a `window` object, although they will still have a global object; for example, Node.js has an object called `global`.

If you don't know the name of the global object, you can also refer to it using the keyword `this` in the global scope. The following code provides a quick way of assigning the variable `global` to the global object:

```
// from within the global scope
const global = this;
```

Going Global

All the way back in Chapter 2, we introduced the concept of global variables. These are variables that are created without using the `const`, `let` or `var` keywords. Global variables can be accessed in all parts of the program.

Global variables are actual properties of a global object. In a browser environment, the global object is the `window` object. This means that any global variable created is actually a property of the `window` object, as can be seen in the example below:

```
x = 6;  // global variable created
<< 6

 window.x // same variable can be accessed as a property of
↳ the window object
<< 6

// both variables are exactly the same
window.x === x;
<< true
```

In general, you should refer to global variables without using the `window` object; it's less typing and your code will be more portable between environments. An exception is if you need to check whether a global variable has been defined. For example, the following code will throw a ReferenceError if x has not been defined:

```
if (x) {
// do something
}
```

However, if the variable is accessed as a property of the `window` object, then the code will still work, as `window.x` will simply return `false`, meaning the block of code will not be evaluated:

```
if (window.x) {
// do something
}
```

Some functions we've already met, such as `parseInt()` and `isNaN()`, are actually methods of the global object, which in a browser environment makes them methods of the `window` object:

```
window.parseInt(4.2);
<< 4

window.isNaN(4.2);
<< false
```

Like variables, it's customary to omit accessing them through the `window` object.

 Changes in ES6

ES6 made `parseInt()` and `isNaN()` methods of the `Number` object, so they can be both be called using the following code:

```
Number.parseInt(4.2);
<< 4

Number.isNaN(4.2);
<< false
```

Dialogs

In Chapter 1, we introduced three functions that produced dialogs in the browsers: `alert()`, `confirm()` and `prompt()`. These are not part of the ECMAScript standard, although all major browsers support them as methods of the `window` object.

The `window.alert()` method will pause the execution of the program and display a message in a dialog box. The message is provided as an argument to the method, and `undefined` is always returned:

```
window.alert('Hello');
<< undefined
```

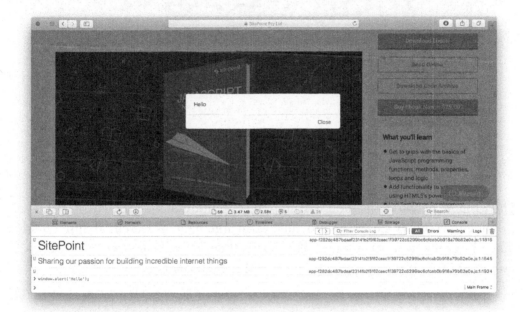

9-1. Alert dialog

The `window.confirm()` method will stop the execution of the program and display a confirmation dialog that shows the message provided as an argument, and giving the options of OK or Cancel. It returns the boolean values of `true` if the user clicks OK, and `false` if the user clicks Cancel:

```
window.confirm('Do you wish to continue?');
<< undefined
```

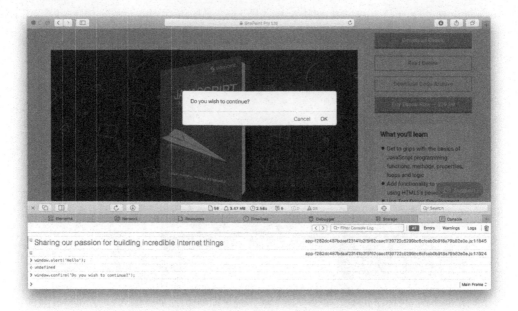

9-2. Confirm dialog

The `window.prompt()` method will stop the execution of the program. It displays a dialog that shows a message provided as an argument, as well as an input field that allows the user to enter text. This text is then returned as a string when the user clicks OK. If the user clicks Cancel, `null` is returned:

```
window.prompt('Please enter your name:');
```

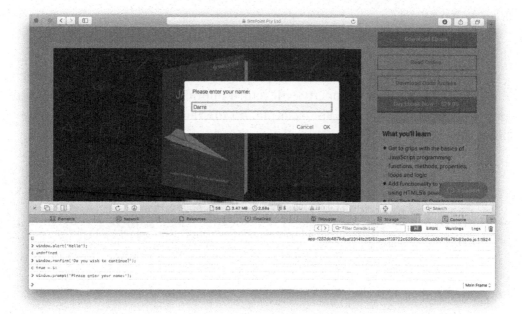

9-3. Prompt dialog

Use With Care

It's worth reiterating again that these methods will stop the execution of a program in its tracks. This means that everything will stop processing at the point the method is called, until the user clicks 'OK' or 'Cancel'. This can cause problems if the program needs to process something else at the same time or the program is waiting for a callback function.

There are some occasions when this functionality can be used as an advantage, for example, a `window.confirm()` dialog can be used as a final check to see if a user wants to delete a resource. This will stop the program from going ahead and deleting the resource while the user decides what to do.

It's also worth keeping in mind that most browsers allow users to disable any dialogs from repeatedly appearing, meaning they are not a feature to be relied upon.

Browser Information

The `window` object has a number of properties and methods that provide information about the user's browser.

Which Browser?

The window object has a navigator property that returns a reference to the Navigator object. The Navigator object contains information about the browser being used. Its userAgent property will return information about the browser and operating system being used. For example, if I run the following line of code, it shows that I am using Safari version 10 on Mac OS:

```
window.navigator.userAgent
  << "Mozilla/5.0 (Macintosh; Intel Mac OS X 10_12_3)
↪ AppleWebKit/602.4.8 (KHTML, like Gecko) Version/10.0.3
↪ Safari/602.4.8"
```

Don't rely on this information though, as it can be modified by a user to masquerade as a different browser. It can also be difficult to make any sense of the string returned, because all browsers pretend to be others to some degree. For example, every browser will include the string 'Mozilla' in its userAgent property, for reasons of legacy Netscape compatibility. The userAgent property has been deprecated from the official specification, but it remains well supported in all major browsers.

Location, Location, Location

The window.location property is an object that contains information about the URL of the current page. It contains a number of properties that provide information about different fragments of the URL.

The href property returns the full URL as a string:

```
window.location.href
  <<
↪ "https://www.sitepoint.com/premium/books/
javascript-novice-to-ninja"
```

This property (as well as most of the others in this section) is a read/write property, which means it can also be changed by assignment. If this is done, the page will be reloaded using the new property. For example, entering the following line into the browser console will redirect the page to the SitePoint JavaScript channel:

```
window.location.href =
↪ 'https://www.sitepoint.com/javascript/'
<< "https://www.sitepoint.com/javascript/"
```

The `protocol` property returns a string describing the protocol used (such as http, https, pop2, ftp etc.). Note that there is a colon (`:`) at the end:

```
window.location.protocol
<< "https:"
```

The `host` property returns a string describing the domain of the current URL *and* the port number (this is often omitted if the default port 80 is used):

```
window.location.host
<< "www.sitepoint.com"
```

The `hostname` property returns a string describing the domain of the current URL:

```
window.location.hostname
<< "www.sitepoint.com"
```

The `port` property returns a string describing the port number, although it will return an empty string if the port is not explicitly stated in the URL:

```
window.location.port
<< ""
```

The `pathname` property returns a string of the path that follows the domain:

```
window.location.pathname
<< "/premium/books/javascript-novice-to-ninja"
```

The `search` property returns a string that starts with a '?' followed by the query string parameters. It returns an empty string if there are no query string parameters. This is what I get when I search for 'JavaScript' on SitePoint:

```
window.location.search
 <<
↪ "?q=javascript&limit=24&offset=0&page=1&
content_types[]=All&slugs[]=all&states[]=available&am
↪ p;order="
```

The `hash` property returns a string that starts with a "#" followed by the fragment identifier. It returns an empty string if there is no fragment identifier:

```
window.location.hash
<< ""
```

The `origin` property returns a string that shows the protocol and domain where the current page originated from. This property is read-only, so cannot be changed:

```
window.location.origin
<< "https://www.sitepoint.com"
```

The `window.location` object also has the following methods:

■ The `reload()` method can be used to force a reload of the current page. If it's given a parameter of `true`, it will force the browser to reload the page from the server, instead of using a cached page.

■ The `assign()` method can be used to load another resource from a URL provided as a parameter, for example:

```
window.location.assign('https://www.sitepoint.com/')
```

■ The `replace()` method is almost the same as the `assign()` method, except the current page will not be stored in the session history, so the user will be unable to navigate back to it using the back button.

■ The `toString()` method returns a string containing the whole URL:

```
window.location.toString();
<< "https://www.sitepoint.com/javascript/"
```

The Browser History

The `window.history` property can be used to access information about any previously visited pages in the current browser session. Avoid confusing this with the new HTML5 History API.[1]

The `window.history.length` property shows how many pages have been visited before arriving at the current page.

The `window.history.go()` method can be used to go to a specific page, where 0 is the current page:

```
window.history.go(1); // goes forward 1 page
window.history.go(0); // reloads the current page
window.history.go(-1); // goes back 1 page
```

---

[1] See http://www.sitepoint.com/javascript-history-pushstate/ post for details.

There are also the `window.history.forward()` and `window.history.back()` methods that can be used to navigate forwards and backwards by one page respectively, just like using the browser's forward and back buttons.

Controlling Windows

A new window can be opened using the `window.open()` method. This takes the URL of the page to be opened as its first parameter, the window title as its second parameter, and a list of attributes as the third parameter. This can also be assigned to a variable, so the window can then be referenced later in the code:

```
const popup = window.open('https://sitepoint.com','
SitePoint','width=400,height=400,resizable=yes');
```

9-4. A popup window

The `close()` method can be used to close a window, assuming you have a reference to it:

```
popup.close();
```

It is also possible to move a window using the `window.moveTo()` method. This takes two parameters that are the X and Y coordinates of the screen that the window is to be moved to:

```
window.moveTo(0,0); // will move the window to the top-left
↪ corner of the screen
```

You can resize a window using the `window.resizeTo()` method. This takes two parameters that specify the width and height of the resized window's dimensions:

```
window.resizeTo(600,400);
```

 Annoying Popups

These methods were largely responsible for giving JavaScript a bad name, as they were used for creating annoying pop-up windows that usually contained intrusive advertisements. It's also a bad idea from a usability standpoint to resize or move a user's window.

Many browsers block pop-up windows and disallow some of these methods to be called in certain cases. For example, you can't resize a window if more than one tab is open. You also can't move or resize a window that wasn't created using `window.open()`.

It's rare that it would be sensible to use any of these methods, so think very carefully before using them. There will almost always be a better alternative, and a ninja programmer will endeavor to find it.

Screen Information

The `window.screen` object contains information about the screen the browser is displayed on. You can find out the height and width of the screen in pixels using the `height` and `width` properties respectively:

```
window.screen.height
<< 1024
```

```
window.screen.width
<< 1280
```

The `availHeight` and `availWidth` can be used to find the height and width of the screen, excluding any operating system menus:

```
window.screen.availWidth
<< 1280

window.screen.availHeight
<< 995
```

The `colorDepth` property can be used to find the color bit depth of the user's monitor, although there are few use cases for doing this other than collecting user statistics:

```
window.screen.colorDepth;
<< 24
```

 ### More Useful on Mobile

The Screen object has more uses for mobile devices. It also allows you to do things like turn off the device's screen, detect a change in its orientation or lock it in a specific orientation.

 ### Use With Care

Many of the methods and properties covered in the previous section were abused in the past for dubious activities such as user-agent sniffing, or detecting screen dimensions to decide whether or not to display certain elements. These practices have (thankfully) now been superseded by better practices, such as media queries and feature detection, which is covered in the next chapter.

The Document Object

Each `window` object contains a `document` object. This object has properties and methods that deal with the page that has been loaded into the window. In Chapter 6, we covered the Document Object Model and the properties and methods used to manipulate items on the page. The `document` object contains a few other methods that are worth looking at.

`document.write()`

The `write()` method simply writes a string of text to the page. If a page has already loaded, it will completely replace the current document:

```
document.write('Hello, world!');
```

This would replace the whole document with the string 'Hello, world!'. It is possible to include HTML in the string and this will become part of the DOM tree. For example, the following piece of code will create an `<h1>` tag node and a child text node:

```
document.write('<h1>Hello, world!</h1>');
```

The `document.write()` method can also be used within a document inside `<script>` tags to inject a string into the markup. This will not overwrite the rest of the HTML on the page. The following example will place the text `"Hello, world!"` inside the `<h1>` tags and the rest of the page will display as normal:

```
<h1>
<script>document.write("Hello, world!")</script>
</h1>
```

The use of `document.write()` is heavily frowned upon as it can only realistically be used by mixing JavaScript within an HTML document. There are still some extremely rare legitimate uses of it, but a ninja programmer will hardly ever need to use it.

Cookies

Cookies are small files that are saved locally on a user's computer. They were invented by Netscape as a way of getting round HTTP being a stateless protocol. This means that a browser does not remember anything from one request to another. So every time a user visits a page, nothing about any previous visits is remembered. Cookies can be used to sidestep this problem by storing information that can then be retrieved between requests.

A restriction of cookies is that they can only be read by a web page from the same domain that set them. This is to stop sites being able to access information about users, such as other sites they have visited. Cookies are also limited to storing up to 4KB of data, although 20 cookies are allowed per domain, which can add up to quite a lot of data.

Cookies can be used for personalizing a user's browsing experience, storing user preferences, keeping track of user choices (such as a shopping cart), authentication and tracking users. The use of cookies for tracking purposes has been much maligned in recent years. Their use for data storage is starting to be replaced in many cases by the new HTML5 localStorage API as it allows more data to be stored. This is covered in <u>Chapter 14.</u>. Cookies are still useful for retaining state information (such as if a user is logged in) because they're passed between the client and server on every HTTP request.

Cookies take the form of a text file that contain a list of name/value pairs separated by semicolons. For example, a cookie file might contain the following information:

```
"name=Superman; hero=true; city=Metropolis"
```

EU Cookie Directive

The EU Cookie Directive is a piece of legislation that requires websites based in an EU country to ask for permission before setting any cookies. It's possible, however, that in the future this requirement may be part of a global browser setting, rather than the onus being on each individual website to ask for permission to set cookies.

Creating Cookies

To create a cookie, you assign it to JavaScript's 'cookie jar', using the `document.cookie` property, like so:

```
document.cookie = 'name=Superman';
<< "name=Superman"
```

The `document.cookie` property acts like a special type of string. Assigning another cookie to it won't overwrite the entire property, it will just append it to the end of the string. So we can add more cookies by assigning them to `document.cookie`:

```
document.cookie = 'hero=true';
<< "hero=true"

document.cookie = 'city=Metropolis';
<< "city=Metropolis"
```

Changing Cookie Values

A cookie's value can be changed by reassigning it to `document.cookie` using the same name but a different value. The following code will update the value of two of the cookies that we set in the previous section:

```
document.cookie = 'name=Batman'
<< "name=Batman"
document.cookie = 'city=Gotham'
```

```
<< "city=Gotham"
```

Reading Cookies

To see the current contents of the cookie jar, simply enter `document.cookie`:

```
document.cookie:
<< "name=Batman; hero=true; city=Gotham"
```

We can use the `split` method to break the string into an array containing each name/value pair, then use a `for of` loop to iterate through the array:

```
const cookies = document.cookie.split("; ");
for (crumb of cookies){
const [key,value] = crumb.split("=");
console.log(`The value of ${key} is ${value}`);
}
<< The value of name is Batman
The value of hero is true
The value of city is Gotham
```

To see an example of cookies used in the wild, you can visit almost any website, open the browser console, and type `document.cookie`.

Cookie Expiry Dates

Cookies are session cookies by default. This means they are deleted once a browser session is finished (when the user closes the browser tab or window). Cookies can be made persistent — that is, lasting beyond the browser session — by adding `"; expires=date"` to the end of the cookie when it's set, where `date` is a date value in the UTC String format `Day, DD-Mon-YYYY HH:MM:SS GMT`. The following example sets a cookie to expire in one day's time:

```
const expiryDate = new Date();
const tomorrow = expiryDate.getTime() + 1000 * 60 * 60 * 24;
expiryDate.setTime(tomorrow);

 document.cookie = `name=Batman; expires=${
↪ expiryDate.toUTCString()}`;
```

An alternative is to set the max-age value. This takes a value in seconds, but it wasn't supported in Internet Explorer before version 10:

```
 document.cookie = 'name=Batman; max-age=86400' // 86400 secs
↪ = 1 day
```

 Don't Rely On Cookie Expiry

Applications that contain sensitive information shouldn't rely on cookies expiring using these methods. Browsers can sometimes hold on to information stored in a cookie that should have expired when the 'session restore' feature is used after a crash.

The Path and Domain of Cookies

By default, cookies can only be read by pages inside the same directory and domain as the file was set. This is for security reasons so that access to the cookie is limited.

The path can be changed so that any page in the root directory can read the cookie. It's done by adding the string '; path=/' to the end of the cookie when it is set:

```
 document.cookie = 'name=Batman; path=/'
```

It's also possible to set the domain by adding "; domain=domainName" to the end of the cookie:

```
document.cookie = 'name=Batman; domain=sitepoint.com';
```

A cookie can only be read by the domain that created it anyway, but doing this will allow all subdomains of sitepoint.com (such as javascript.sitepoint.com and books.sitepoint.com) to read it.

Secure Cookies

Adding the string '; secure' to the end of a cookie will ensure it's only transmitted over a secure HTTPS network:

```
document.cookie = 'name=Batman; secure';
```

Deleting Cookies

To remove a cookie, you need to set it to expire at a time in the past:

```
document.cookie = 'name=Batman; expires=Thu, 01 Jan 1970
↪ 00:00:01 GMT';
```

If a cookie is a session cookie, it will expire when the tab or window is closed.

 Cumbersome Cookies

> JavaScript's cookie handling is quite basic and can also be quite cumbersome. Many developers use a library such as Cookies.js[2] or jsCookie[3]. You could even have a go at developing your own set of functions to make dealing with cookies easier.

Timing Functions

---

2. https://github.com/ScottHamper/Cookies
3. https://github.com/js-cookie/js-cookie

```
setTimeout()
```

The `window` object provides some useful methods for scheduling the execution of a function, and for repeatedly executing functions at regular intervals.

The `window.setTimeout()` method accepts a callback to a function as its first parameter and a number of milliseconds as its second parameter. Try entering the following example into a console. It should show an alert dialog after three seconds (that's 3000 milliseconds):

```
window.setTimeout( () => alert("Time's Up!"), 3000);
<< 4
```

Notice that the method returns an integer. This is an ID used to reference that particular timeout. It can also cancel the timeout using the `window.clearTimeout()` method. Try calling the code again and make a note of the number that is returned:

```
window.setTimeout( () => alert("Time's Up!"), 3000);
<< 5
```

Now quickly enter the following code before the alert pops up, making sure that you enter the number that was returned previously (it might not be 5 in your case!):

```
window.clearTimeout(5);
<< undefined
```

If you were quick enough, and used the correct ID, the alert was prevented from happening.

```
setInterval()
```

The `window.setInterval()` method works in a similar way to `window.setTimeout()`, except that it will repeatedly invoke the callback function after every given number of milliseconds.

The previous example used an anonymous function, but it is also possible to use a named function like so:

```
function chant(){ console.log('Beetlejuice'); }
```

Now we can set up the interval and assign it to a variable:

```
const summon = window.setInterval(chant,1000);
<< 6
```

This should show the message 'Beetlejuice' in the console every second (1,000 milliseconds).

To stop this, we can use the `window.clearInterval()` method and the variable `repeat` as an argument (this is because the `window.setInterval()` method returns its ID, so this will be assigned to the variable `repeat`):

```
window.clearInterval(summon);
```

Using the `this` Keyword

Be careful when using a method that uses the **this** keyword with either of these timing methods. The binding of **this** is set to the **window** object, rather than the method's object, so it can get some unexpected results:

```
const person = {
name: 'Superman',
introduce() {
    console.log(`Hi, I'm ${this.name}`);
}
};

setTimeout(person.introduce, 50);
<< Hi, I'm
```

In the example above, the value of **this.name** is **undefined** because the code is looking for a property of the **window** object called **name**, which doesn't exist.

There are ways to bind **this** to the object instead, and these are discussed in Chapter 12.

Animation

The `setTimeOut()` and `setInterval()` methods can be used to animate elements on a web page. As an example, let's create a web page that shows a colored square, and make it rotate. Create a folder called 'animation' that contains files called `index.html`, `styles.css` and `main.js`. Place the following code inside `index.html`:

```
<!doctype html>
<html lang='en'>
<head>
<meta charset='utf-8'>
<title>Animation Example</title>
<link rel='stylesheet' href='styles.css'>
</head>
<body>
<div id='square'></div>
```

```
<script src='main.js'></script>
</body>
</html>
```

This places a div on the page with an ID of 'square'.

Next, add the following styles.css:

```
#square {
margin: 100px;
width: 100px;
height: 100px;
background: #d16;
}
```

This will set the position, dimensions and color of the div. Now for the animation — add the following code to main.js:

```
const squareElement = document.getElementById('square');
let angle = 0;

setInterval( () => {
angle = (angle + 2) % 360;
squareElement.style.transform = `rotate(${angle}deg)`
}, 1000/60);
```

This code receives a reference to our square div, then sets a variable called `angle` to 0. We then use the `setInterval()` method to increase the value of `angle` by 2 (we also use the `%` operator so that it resets to 0 at 360), then set the `transform` CSS3 property to rotate that number of degrees. The second argument is `1000/60`, which equates to a frame speed of 60 frames per second.

Open `animation.html` in your browser and you should see a rotating square, although it will probably be quite slow and not very smooth. This was the only

way to achieve animation using JavaScript until the
`window.requestAnimationFrame()` method was developed.

`requestAnimationFrame`

This method of the `window` object works in much the same way as the
`window.setInterval()` method, although it has a number of improvements to
optimize its performance. These include making the most of the browser's built-
in graphics-handling capabilities, and not running the animation when the tab is
inactive, resulting in a much smoother performance. It's supported in all major
browsers, including Internet Explorer from version 10 onwards. Change the code
in `main.js` to the following:

```
const squareElement = document.getElementById('square');
let angle = 0;

function rotate() {
angle = (angle + 2)%360;
squareElement.style.transform = `rotate(${angle}deg)`
window.requestAnimationFrame(rotate);
}

const id = requestAnimationFrame(rotate);
```

This is similar to the earlier code, but this time we place the rotation code inside
a function called `rotate`. The last line of this function uses the
`window.requestAnimationFrame()` method and takes the `rotate()` function as
an argument. This will then call the `rotate()` function recursively. The frame
rate cannot be set using `requestAnimationFrame()`; it's usually 60 frames per
second, although it's optimized for the device being used.

To start the animation, we need to call the `requestAnimationFrame()` method,
giving the `rotate()` function as an argument. This will return a unique ID that
can be employed to stop the animation using the
`window.cancelAnimationFrame()` method:

```
cancelAnimationFrame(id);
```

Refresh the `animation.html` page and you should notice that the animation is much faster and smoother than before, as shown below.

9-5. Animation in the browser

Consider Using CSS Instead

The rotation animation example demonstrates how JavaScript can be used to perform animations in the browser. It could also be achieved using pure CSS animation with the following style rules in **styles.css**:

```css
#square {
margin: 100px;
width: 100px;
height: 100px;
background: #cc0;
animation: spin 4s linear infinite;
}

@keyframes spin { from { transform:rotate(0deg); } to {
↳ transform:rotate(3600deg); } }
```

In general, it is typically better to use CSS for any animation effects, although there may be times when JavaScript might be the better solution.

Quiz Ninja Project

We're now going add a timer to give our quiz a `beat the clock` element. We'll do this using the `window` object's `setInterval()` method to add a time limit. First of all, we'll add an element to the HTML for the timer. Update the `<header>` inside the `index.html` file to include an extra `<div>` element with an id of `timer`:

```html
<header>
    <h1>Quiz Ninja!</h1>
 <div id='timer'>Time:
↳ <strong>20</strong></div>
 <div id='score'>Score:
↳ <strong>0</strong></div>
</header>
```

We'll use this ID to add a reference to this element as a property of the `view` object in the `main.js` file:

```
timer: document.querySelector('#timer strong')
```

Next, we need to add the following code to the `game.start()` method:

```
this.secondsRemaining = 20;
this.timer = setInterval( this.countdown , 1000 );
```

This initializes a property of the `game` object called `secondsRemaining` to 20. It is used to measure, in seconds, how the game will last. The next line sets up an interval that calls a method called `countdown()` every second (1,000 milliseconds). This method needs adding to the `game` object:

```
countdown() {
    game.secondsRemaining--;
    view.render(view.timer,game.secondsRemaining);
    if(game.secondsRemaining < 0) {
        game.gameOver();
    }
}
```

This function decreases the `secondsRemaining` variable that we initialized earlier by 1 using the `--` operator, then calls the `view.render()` method so the number of seconds remaining is displayed in the header. Last of all, we check to see if the time has fallen below zero and, if it has, we call the `gameOver()` function as time has run out!

Finally, we have to add a line at the end of the `game.gameOver()` method that will remove the interval when the game has finished, otherwise it will continue to keep counting down past zero! To stop this from happening, we place the following line of code anywhere inside the `gameOver()` function:

```
 gameOver(){
 view.render(view.info,`Game Over, you scored ${this.score}
↪ point${this.score !== 1 ? 's' : ''}`);
```

```
    view.teardown();
    clearInterval(this.timer);
}
```

Try playing the game now by opening `index.html` in a browser and see how you go with the added pressure of beating the clock.

You can see a live example on CodePen[4].

Chapter Summary

- The `window` object is the global object in a browser.

- Global variables are actually properties of the `window` object in a browser environment.

- `alert`, `confirm()`, and `prompt()` are all methods of the `window` object, and open dialogs that halt the execution of the program.

- The `window.navigator` object gives information about the user's browser and operating system, although it can be unreliable.

- The `window.location` object provides information about the URL of the current page.

- The `window.history` object keeps information about the pages that have been visited in the session.

- You can open, close, resize, and move windows (although, this doesn't mean you should!).

- The `window.screen` object provides information about the user's screen.

- `document.write()` is an archaic method of writing text to the document and should be avoided.

---

[4] https://codepen.io/daz4126/pen/YQaoWr

- Cookies can be used to store small pieces of information between requests using the `document.cookie` property.

- The `window.setTimeout()` method can be used to invoke a function after a set amount of time. It can be canceled using the `clearTimeout()` method.

- The `window.setInterval()` method can be used to repeatedly invoke a function. It can be stopped using the `clearInterval()` method.

- The `window.requestAnimationFrame()` method can be used to produce smooth and optimized animation by utilizing the browser's built-in graphics capabilities. It can be canceled using the `cancelAnimationFrame()` method.

In the next chapter, we'll be looking at how to handle errors and write tests in JavaScript.

Chapter **10**

Testing and Debugging

Errors and bugs are a fact of life in programming — they will always be there. A ninja programmer will try to do everything to minimize errors occurring, and find ways to identify and deal with them quickly.

In this chapter, we'll cover the following topics:

- Errors, exceptions, and warnings

- The importance of testing and debugging

- Strict mode

- Debugging in the browser

- Error objects

░ Throwing exceptions

░ Exception handling

░ Testing frameworks

░ Our project — we'll add some log messages and tests to the Quiz Ninja application

Errors, Exceptions, and Warnings

Errors are caused when something goes wrong in a program. They are usually caused by one of the following:

░ System error — there's a problem with the system or external devices with which the program is interacting.

░ Programmer error — the program contains incorrect syntax or faulty logic; it could even be as simple as a typo.

░ User error — the user has entered data incorrectly, which the program is unable to handle.

As programmers, we often have little influence over how external systems work, so it can be difficult to fix the root cause of system errors. Despite this, we should still be aware of them and attempt to reduce their impact by working around any problems they cause. Programmer errors are our responsibility, so we must ensure they are minimized as much as possible and fixed promptly. We also should try to limit user errors by predicting any possible interactions that may throw an error, and ensure they are dealt with in a way that doesn't negatively affect the user experience. It might even be argued that user errors are in fact also programmer errors, because the program should be designed in a way that prevents the user from making the error.

Exceptions

An exception is an error that produces a return value that can then be used by the program to deal with the error. For example, trying to call a method that is nonexistent will result in a reference error that raises an exception, as you can see in the example below when we try to call the mythical `unicorn()` function:

```
unicorn();
<< ReferenceError: unicorn is not defined
```

Stack Traces

An exception will also produce a **stack trace**. This is a sequence of functions or method calls that lead to the point where the error occurred. It's often not just a single function or method call that causes an error. A stack trace will work backwards from the point at which the error occurred to identify the original function or method that started the sequence. The example below shows how a stack trace can help you find where an error originates from:

```
function three(){ unicorn(); }
function two(){ three(); }
function one(){ two(); }
one();

  << index.html:13 Uncaught ReferenceError: unicorn is
↳ not defined
    at three (index.html:13)
    at two (index.html:17)
    at one (index.html:21)
    at index.html:24`
```

In this example, we have three functions: function `one()` invokes function `two()`, which then invokes function `three()`. Function `three()` then invokes the `unicorn()` function that doesn't exist and causes an error. We can use the stack trace to work backwards and see that this error was caused by invoking the function `one()` in the first place.

Warnings

A warning can occur if there's an error in the code that isn't enough to cause the program to crash. This means the program will continue to run after a warning. This might sound good, but it can be problematic, since the issue that produced the warning may cause the program to continue running incorrectly.

An example of a mistake that could cause a warning is assigning a value to a variable that's undeclared:

```
pi = 3.142;
 << JavaScript Warning: assignment to undeclared
↳ variable
```

Note that not all browsers will display a warning for the code in the example above, so you might not see one if you try it out.

Warnings and exceptions are presented differently in various environments. Some browsers will show a small icon in the corner of the browser window to indicate that an exception or warning has occurred. Others require the console to be open to see any warnings or exceptions.

When a runtime error occurs in the browser, the HTML will still appear, but the JavaScript code will stop working in the background, which isn't always obvious at first. If a warning occurs, the JavaScript will continue to run (although possibly incorrectly).

The Importance of Testing and Debugging

JavaScript is a fairly forgiving language when it comes to errors; it didn't implement exceptions at all until ECMAScript version 3. Instead of alerting a user to an error in a program, it just failed silently in the background, and this is sometimes still the case. It might seem like a good idea at first, but the error might give unexpected or incorrect results that nobody spots, or lurk in the background for a long time before causing the program to crash spectacularly. Failing silently makes errors difficult to spot and longer to track down.

For this reason, a ninja programmer should ensure that the code they write fails loudly in development so any errors can be identified and fixed quickly. In production, a ninja programmer should try to make the code fail gracefully (although not completely silently — we still need to know there's an error), so the user experience is not affected, if possible. This is achieved by making sure exceptions are caught and dealt with, and code is tested rigorously.

Strict Mode

ECMAScript 5 introduced a strict mode that produces more exceptions and warnings and prohibits the use of some deprecated features. This is due to the fact that strict mode considers coding practices that were previously accepted as just being "poor style" as actual errors.

Increasing the chance of errors might seem like a bad idea at first, but it's much better to spot errors early on, rather than have them cause problems later. Writing code in strict mode can also help improve its clarity and speed, since it follows conventions and will throw exceptions if any sloppy code practices are used.

Not using strict mode is often referred to as "sloppy mode" as it's forgiving of sloppy programming practices. Strict mode encourages a better quality of JavaScript to be written that befits a ninja programmer, so its use is recommended.

Strict mode simply requires the following string to be added to the first line of a JavaScript file:

```
'use strict';
```

This will be picked up by any JavaScript engine that uses strict mode. If the engine does not support strict mode, this string will simply be ignored.

To see it in action, if you try to assign a value to a variable that is undeclared in strict mode, you'll get an exception, instead of a warning:

```
'use strict';

e = 2.718;
<< ReferenceError: e is not defined
```

You can even use strict mode on a per-function basis by adding the line inside a function. Strict mode will then only be applied to anything inside that function:

```
function strictly(){
'use strict';
// function code goes here
}
```

In fact, the recommended way to invoke strict mode is to place all your code into a self-invoking function (covered in more detail in Chapter 12), like so:

```
(function() {
'use strict';

// All your code would go inside this function

}());
```

Placing 'use strict' at the beginning of a file will enforce strict mode on all the JavaScript in the file. And if you're using anybody else's code, there's no guarantee they've coded in strict mode. This technique will ensure that only your code is forced to use strict mode.

 Modules and 'use strict'

ES6 introduced JavaScript modules (covered later in chapter 15). These are self-contained pieces of code that are in strict mode by default, so the 'use strict' declaration is not required.

Linting Tools

Linting tools such as JS Lint,[1] JS Hint,[2] and ES Lint[3] can be used to test the quality of JavaScript code, beyond simply using strict mode. They are designed to highlight any sloppy programming practices or syntax errors, and will complain if certain style conventions are not followed, such as how code is indented. They can be very unforgiving and use some opinionated coding conventions, such as not using the ++ and -- increment operators (in the case of JS Lint). Linting tools are also useful for enforcing a programming **style guide**. This is particularly useful when you are working in a team, as it ensures everybody follows the same conventions.

It's possible to add a linting tool as a text-editor plugin; this will then highlight any sloppy code as you type. Another option is to use an online linting tool that allows you to simply paste onto a page for feedback. Another option is to install linting software on your computer using npm. This can then be run as part of your workflow.

Passing a lint test is no guarantee that your code is correct, but it will mean it will be more consistent and less likely to have problems.

. Feature Detection

Programming in JavaScript can be something of a moving target as the APIs it uses are in a constant state of flux. And there are new APIs being developed as part of the HTML5 specification all the time (more on these in <u>chapter 14</u>). Browser vendors are constantly adding support for these new features, but they don't always keep up. What's more, some browsers will support certain features and others won't. You can't always rely on users having the most up-to-date browser, either.

The recommended way to determine browser support for a feature is to use feature detection. This is done using an `if` statement to check whether an object

---

[1.] http://jslint.com/
[2.] http://jshint.com/
[3.] http://eslint.org/

or method exists before trying to actually call the method. For example, say we want to use the shiny new `holoDeck` API (as far as I know, this doesn't actually exist ... yet), we would wrap any method calls inside the following `if` block:

```
if (window.holoDeck) {
virtualReality.activate();
}
```

This ensures that no error occurs if the browser doesn't support the method, because referencing a nonexistent object such as `window.virtualReality` will return `undefined`. As it's a falsy value, the `if` block won't run, but calling the method `virtualReality.activate()` outside of the `if` block would cause an exception to be thrown. Feature detection guarantees that the method is only called if it actually exists and fails gracefully, without any exceptions being thrown, if the method doesn't exist.

Modernizr[4] is a library that offers an easy way to implement feature detection and Can I Use?[5] is another useful resource for checking which features are currently supported in different browsers.

The "old-school" way of checking for browser support was known as **browser sniffing**. This involves using the string returned by `window.navigator.userAgent` property that we met in the last chapter to identify the user's browser. The relevant methods can then be used for that browser. This approach is not recommended, however, because the user agent string cannot be relied upon to be accurate. Additionally, given the vast array of features you might be developing for, and the shifting nature of support for them across many browsers, this would extremely difficult to implement and maintain.

Debugging in the Browser

Debugging is the process of finding out where bugs occur in the code and then dealing with them. In many cases, the point at which an error occurs is not

---

[4.] https://modernizr.com/docs
[5.] http://caniuse.com

always where it originated, so you'll need to run through the program to see what's happening at different stages of its execution. When doing this, it can be useful to create what are known as breakpoints, which halt the progress of the code and allow us to view the value of different variables at that point in the program. There are a number of options for debugging JavaScript code in the browser.

The Trusty Alert

The most basic form of debugging is to use the `alert()` method to show a dialog at certain points in the code. Because `alert()` stops a program from running until OK is clicked, it allows us to effectively put breakpoints in the code that let us check the value of variables at that point to see if they're what we expect them to be. Take the following example that checks to see if a person's age is appropriate:

```
function amIOldEnough(age){
if (age = 12) {
    alert(age);
    return 'No, sorry.';
} else if (age < 18) {
    return 'Only if you are accompanied by an adult.';
}
else {
    return 'Yep, come on in!';
}
}
```

The `alert` method inside the `if` block will allow us to see the value of the `age` variable at that point. Once we click on OK, we can then check the function returns the correct message.

If you try the example above, you will find that there is a bug in the code:

```
amIOldEnough(21)
<< 'No, sorry.'
```

Passing an argument of 21 should result in the string Yep, come on in! being returned, but it is returning No, sorry. instead. If you tried running the example, you would have seen the alert message show that the value of the variable age is 12, even though the function was passed an argument of 21. Closer inspection then reveals a classic mistake has been made. Instead of checking if the value of age is equal to 12, we have inadvertently assigned it the value of 12! To check for equality, we should use === instead of = which assigns a value to a variable (even inside an if block).

In actual fact, we want to return the message No, sorry. for all values of age that are *less than* 12, so we could update the code to the following:

```javascript
function amIOldEnough(age){
if (age < 12) {
    alert(age);
    return 'No, sorry.';
} else if (age < 18) {
    return 'Only if you are accompanied by an adult.';
}
else {
    return 'Yep, come on in!';
}
}
```

Try this again and it works as expected:

```javascript
amIOldEnough(21)
<< 'Yep, come on in!'
```

Using alerts for debugging was the only option in the past, but JavaScript development has progressed since then and their use is discouraged for debugging purposes today.

Using the Console

Most modern JavaScript environments have a `console` object that provides a number of methods for logging information and debugging. It's not officially part of the ECMAScript specification, but is well supported in all the major browsers and Node.js.

▪ We've already seen and used the `console.log()` method. This can be used to log the value of variables at different stages of the program, although it will not actually stop the execution of the program in the same way as `alert()` does. For example, we could add some `console.log()` statements in the `amIOldEnough()` function, to log the position in the function as well as the value of the **age** variable:

```
function amIOldEnough(age){
console.log(age);
    if (age < 12) {
    console.log(`In the if with ${age}`);
    return 'No, sorry.';
    } else if (age < 18) {
    console.log(`In the else-if with ${age}`);
    return 'Only if you are accompanied by an adult.';
    } else {
    console.log(`In the else with ${age}`);
    return 'Yep, come on in!';
    }
}
```

▪ The `console.trace()` method will log an interactive stack trace in the console. This will show the functions that were called in the lead up to an exception occurring while the code is running.

Debugging Tools

Most modern browsers also have a debugging tool that allows you to set **breakpoints** in your code that will pause it at certain points. You can then see the values of all the variables at those points and modify them. This can be very useful when trying to track down bugs. Here are the links to the debugger documentation for each of the major browsers:

- Firefox[6]

- Edge[7]

- Chrome[8]

- Safari[9]

One of the most useful commands is the `debugger` keyword. This will create a breakpoint in your code that will pause the execution of the code and allow you to see where the program is currently up to. You can also hover over any variables to see what value they hold at that point. The program can then be restarted by clicking on the play button.

The example below shows how the `debugger` command can be used in the `amIOldEnough()` function. If you try entering the code below into your browser's console, then invoke the `amIOldEnough()` function, the browser's debugging tool will automatically kick in and you'll be able see the value of the `age` variable by hovering over it:

```
function amIOldEnough(age){
debugger;
    if (age < 12) {
    debugger;
    return 'No, sorry.';
    } else if (age < 18) {
    debugger;
    return 'Only if you are accompanied by an adult.';
    } else {
    debugger;
    return 'Yep, come on in!';
```

[6.] https://developer.mozilla.org/en-US/docs/Tools/Debugger

[7.] https://docs.microsoft.com/en-us/microsoft-edge/f12-devtools-guide/debugger

[8.] https://developer.chrome.com/devtools/docs/javascript-debugging

[9.] https://developer.apple.com/library/mac/documentation/AppleApplications/
Conceptual/Safari_Developer_Guide/Debugger/Debugger.html

```
}
}

amIOldEnough(16);
```

```
//# sourceURL=__WebInspectorConsoleEvaluation__
function amIOldEnough(age){
    debugger;
    if (age < 23
        debugger;
        return 'No, sorry.';
    } else if (age < 18) {
        debugger;
        return 'Only if you are accompanied by an adult.';
    } else {
        debugger;
        return 'Yep, come on in!';
    }
}
```

10-1. Using the debugging tool

Remove Debugging Code Prior to Shipping

Remember to remove any references to the **debugger** command before shipping any code, otherwise the program will appear to freeze when people try to use it!

Error Objects

An `error` object can be created by the host environment when an exception occurs, or it can be created in the code using a constructor function, like so:

```
const error = new Error();
```

This constructor function takes a parameter that's used as the error message:

```
const error = new Error('Oops, something went wrong');
```

There are seven more error objects used for specific errors:

■ `EvalError` is not used in the current ECMAScript specification and only retained for backwards compatibility. It was used to identify errors when using the global `eval()` function.

■ `RangeError` is thrown when a number is outside an allowable range of values.

■ `ReferenceError` is thrown when a reference is made to an item that doesn't exist. For example, calling a function that hasn't been defined.

■ `SyntaxError` is thrown when there's an error in the code's syntax.

■ `TypeError` is thrown when there's an error in the type of value used; for example, a string is used when a number is expected.

■ `URIError` is thrown when there's a problem encoding or decoding the URI.

■ `InternalError` is a non-standard error that is thrown when an error occurs in the JavaScript engine. A common cause of this too much recursion.

These error objects can also be used as constructors to create custom error objects:

```
const error = new TypeError('You need to use numbers in this
↪ function');
```

All `error` objects have a number of properties, but they're often used inconsistently across browsers. The only properties that are generally safe to use are:

■ The `name` property returns the name of the error constructor function used as a string, such as "Error" or "ReferenceError".

■ The `message` property returns a description of the error and should be provided as an argument to the `Error` constructor function.

■ The `stack` property will return a stack trace for that error. This is a non-standard property and it's recommended that it is not safe to use in production sites.

Throwing Exceptions

So far we've seen errors that are thrown automatically by the JavaScript engine when an error occurs. It's also possible to throw your own exceptions using the `throw` statement. This will allow for any problems in your code to be highlighted and dealt with, rather than lurk quietly in the background.

The `throw` statement can be applied to any JavaScript expression, causing the execution of the program to stop. For example, all the following lines of code will cause a program to halt:

```
throw 2;
throw 'Up';
throw { toys: 'out of pram' };
```

It is best practice, however, to throw an `error` object. This can then be caught in a `catch` block, which is covered later in the chapter:

```
throw new Error('Something has gone badly wrong!');
```

As an example, let's write a function called `squareRoot()` to find the square root of a number. This can be done using the `Math.sqrt()` method, but it returns `NaN` for negative arguments. This is not strictly correct (the answer should be an imaginary number, but these are unsupported in JavaScript). Our function will throw an error if the user tries to use a negative argument:

```
function squareRoot(number) {
'use strict';
if (number < 0) {
 throw new RangeError('You can't find the square root of
↪ negative numbers')
    }
return Math.sqrt(number);
};
```

Let's test it out:

```
squareRoot(121);
<< 11

squareRoot(-1);
 << RangeError: You can't find the square root of
 ↳ negative numbers
```

Exception Handling

When an exception occurs, the program terminates with an error message. This is ideal in development as it allows us to identify and fix errors. In production, however, it will appear as if the program has crashed, which does not reflect well on a ninja programmer.

It is possible to handle exceptions gracefully by catching the error. Any errors can be hidden from users, but still identified. We can then deal with the error appropriately — perhaps even ignore it — and keep the program running.

try, catch, and finally

If we suspect a piece of code will result in an exception, we can wrap it in a try block. This will run the code inside the block as normal, but if an exception occurs it will pass the error object that is thrown onto a catch block. Here's a simple example using our squareRoot() function from earlier:

```
function imaginarySquareRoot(number) {
            'use strict';
try {
    return String(squareRoot(number));
} catch(error) {
    return squareRoot(-number)+'i';
}
}
```

The code inside the `catch` block will only run if an exception is thrown inside the `try` block. The error object is automatically passed as a parameter to the `catch` block. This allows us to query the error name, message and stack properties, and deal with it appropriately. In this case, we actually return a string representation of an imaginary number:

```
imaginarySquareRoot(-49) // no error message shown
<< '7i'
```

A `finally` block can be added after a `catch` block. This will always be executed after the `try` or `catch` block, regardless of whether an exception occurred or not. It is useful if you want some code to run in both cases. We can use this to modify the `imaginarySquareRoot()` function so that it adds "+ or -" to the answer before returning it:

```
function imaginarySquareRoot(number) {
        'use strict';
let answer;
try {
    answer = String(squareRoot(number));
} catch(error) {
    answer = squareRoot(-number)+"i";
} finally {
    return `+ or - ${answer}`;
}
}
```

Tests

Testing is an important part of programming that can often be overlooked. Writing good tests means your code will be less brittle as it develops, and any errors will be identified early on.

A test can simply be a function that tests a piece of code runs as it should. For example, we could test that the `squareRoot()` function that we wrote earlier returns the correct answer with the following function:

```
function itSquareRoots4() {
return squareRoot(4) === 2;
}
```

Here we're comparing the result of `squareRoot(4)` with the number 2. This will return `true` if our function works as expected, which it does:

```
itSquareRoots4();
<< true
```

This is in no way a thorough test of the function – it might just be a fluke that the function returns 2, and this might be the only value it works for. It does, however, demonstrate how you would start to implement tests for any functions that are written.

Test-driven Development

Test-driven development(TDD) is the process of writing tests before any actual code. Obviously these tests will initially fail, because there is no code to test. The next step is to write some code to make the tests pass. After this, the code is refactored to make it faster, more readable, and remove any repetition. The code is continually tested at each stage to make sure it continues to work. This process should be followed in small piecemeal chunks every time a new feature is implemented, resulting in the following workflow:

1. Write tests (that initially fail)

2. Write code to pass the tests

3. Refactor the code

4. Test refactored code

5. Write more tests for new features

This is often referred to as the "red-green-refactor" cycle of TDD, as failing tests usually show up as red, and tests that pass show as green.

Test-driven development is considered to be best practice, but in reality you'll find most developers tend to be more pragmatic when it comes to writing tests. The TDD mindset can be hard to always use, and at the end of the day, any tests are better than no tests at all. In fact, even the very best coders don't always use TDD[10], and make no apologies for not doing so. We cover an example in this chapter, but won't be using it for the most of the examples in the rest of the book as it would make it far too long!

Testing Frameworks

It is possible to write your own tests, as we saw earlier with the `itSquareRoots4()` test function, but this can be a laborious process. Testing frameworks provide a structure to write meaningful tests and then run them. There are a large number of frameworks available for JavaScript, but we'll be focusing on the Jest framework.

Jest

Jest[11] is a TDD framework, created by Facebook, that has gained a lot of popularity recently. It makes it easy to create and run tests by providing helper methods for common test assertions.

To use Jest, first we need to install it using npm. Enter the following command in a terminal:

```
npm install -g jest
```

This should install Jest globally. To check everything worked okay, try running the following command to check the version number that has been installed:

---

10. http://david.heinemeierhansson.com/2014/tdd-is-dead-long-live-testing.html
11. https://facebook.github.io/jest/

```
jest -v
<< v19.0.2
```

The version number might be different on your install, but if it returns a value, it means Jest is installed correctly.

Next we'll create an example test to see if it works. Let's write a test to see if our squareRoot() function from earlier works. Create a file called squareRoot.test.js and add the following code:

```
function squareRoot(number) {
            'use strict';
if (number < 0) {
 throw new RangeError("You can't find the square root of
↪ negative numbers")
    }
return Math.sqrt(number);
};

test('square root of 4 is 2', () => {
expect(squareRoot(4)).toBe(2);
});
```

This file contains the squareRoot() function that we are testing, as well as a test() function. The first parameter of the test() function is a string that describes what we are testing, in this case that 'square root of 4 is 2'. The second parameter is an anonymous function that contains a function called expect(), which takes the function we're testing as an argument, and returns an **expectation object**. The expectation object has a number of methods called **matchers**. In the example above, the matcher is toBe(), which tests to see if the value returned by our squareRoot() function is the same as the value provided as an argument (2, in this case). These matchers are named so they read like an English sentence, making them easier to understand (even for non-programmers), and the feedback they provide more meaningful. The example above almost reads as 'expect the square root of 4 to be 2'. It's important to recognize that these are just functions at the end of the day, so they behave in exactly the same way as any other function in JavaScript. This means that any valid JavaScript code can be run inside the test function.

To run this test, simply navigate to the folder that contains the file `squareRoot.test.js` and enter the following command:

```
jest -c {}
```

This will run all files that end in "test.js" within that folder. The `-c  {}` flag at the end is shorthand for "configuration". We don't need any extra configuration, so we simply pass it an empty object.

If everything is working okay, it should produce the following output:

```
<< PASS   ./squareRoot.test.js
✓ square root of 4 is 2 (2ms)

Test Suites: 1 passed, 1 total
Tests:       1 passed, 1 total
Snapshots:   0 total
Time:        2.996s
```

Hooray! This tells us that there was 1 test and it passed in a mere 2ms!

Crunching Some Numbers

To demonstrate the TDD process, we'll have a go at creating a small library called "Number Cruncher" that will contain some functions that operate on numbers. The first function we'll try to implement will be called `factorsOf()`. This will take a number as a parameter and return all the factors[12] of that number as an array.

[12.] The factors, or divisors, of a number are any integers that divide exactly into the number without leaving a remainder. For example, the factors of 6 are 1, 2, 3 and 6.

Since we're doing TDD, we need to start by writing the tests first, so create a file called numberCruncher.test.js and add the following code:

```
test('factors of 12', () => {
expect(factorsOf(12)).toEqual([1,2,3,4,6,12]);
});
```

 Use of toEqual()

We have used the toEqual() match in this test. This is because we are testing an array.

This test says our factorsOf() function should return an array containing all the factors of 12 in order, when 12 is provided as an argument. If we run this test, we can see that it fails spectacularly:

```
jest -c {}
<< FAIL   ./numberCruncher.test.js
● factors of 12

    ReferenceError: factorsOf is not defined

 at Object.<anonymous>.test
↪ (numberCruncher.test.js:2:10)
 at process._tickCallback
↪ (internal/process/next_tick.js:103:7)

✕ factors of 12 (6ms)

Test Suites: 1 failed, 1 total
Tests:       1 failed, 1 total
Snapshots:   0 total
Time:        1.424s
```

Well, what did you expect? We haven't written any code yet! Let's have a go at writing the `factorsOf()` function. Add the following to the top of the `numberCruncher.test.js` file:

```
'use strict';

function factorsOf(n) {
const factors = [];
for (let i=1; i < n ; i++) {
    if (n/i === Math.floor(n/i)){
    factors.push(i);
    }
}
return factors;
}
```

This function creates a local variable called `factors` and initializes it as an empty array. It then loops through every integer value from 1 up to n (the number that was given as an argument) and adds it to the array of factors using the `push()` method, if it's a factor. We test if it's a factor by seeing if the answer leaves a whole number with no remainder when n is divided by the integer 1 (the definition of a factor).

 ## This Isn't Totally Realistic

To make things easier in this example, we're putting the code into the same file as the tests, but in reality you'd usually keep them in separate files.

Try running the test again:

```
jest -c {}
<< FAIL   ./numberCruncher.test.js
● factors of 12

    expect(received).toBe(expected)

    Expected value to be (using ===):
```

```
    [1, 2, 3, 4, 6, 12]
    Received:
    [1, 2, 3, 4, 6]

    Difference:

    - Expected
    + Received

    @@ -2,7 +2,6 @@
    1,
    2,
    3,
    4,
    6,
    -  12,
    ]

  at Object.<anonymous>.test
  ↪ (numberCruncher.test.js:14:25)
  at process._tickCallback
  ↪ (internal/process/next_tick.js:103:7)

× factors of 12 (12ms)

Test Suites: 1 failed, 1 total
Tests:       1 failed, 1 total
Snapshots:   0 total
Time:        0.801s, estimated 1s
Ran all test suites.
```

Oh dear, it still failed. This time, the failure message is a bit more specific. It says it was expecting the array [1,2,3,4,6,12] but received the array [1,2,3,4,6]— the last number 12 is missing. Looking at our code, this is because the loop only continues while i < n. We need i to go all the way up to and including n, requiring just a small tweak to our code:

```
function factorsOf(n) {
const factors = [];
for (let i=1; i <= n ; i++) { // change on this line
    if (n/i === Math.floor(n/i)){
    factors.push(i);
    }
}
return factors;
}
```

Now if you run the test again, you should get a nice message confirming that our test has passed:

```
jest -c {}
<< PASS   ./numberCruncher.test.js
✓ factors of 12 (7ms)

Test Suites: 1 passed, 1 total
Tests:       1 passed, 1 total
Snapshots:   0 total
Time:        3.012s
Ran all test suites.
```

Our test passed, but this doesn't mean we can stop there. There is still one more step of the TDD cycle: refactoring.

There are a few places where we can tidy up the code. First of all, we should only really be testing for factors up to the square root of the number, because if i is a factor, then n/i will be a factor as well. For example, if you're trying to find the factors of 36, when we test if 2 is a factor, we see that it divides into 36, 18 times exactly. This means that 2 is a factor, but it also means 18 is as well. So we'll start to find factors in pairs, where one is below the square root of the number, and the other is above the square root. This will have the effect of reducing the number of steps in the for loop dramatically.

Secondly, the test to see if i is a factor of n can be written more succinctly using the % operator. If i is a factor of n, then n%i will equal 0 because there's no remainder.

We'll also need to sort the array at the end of the function, because the factors are not added in order any more. We can do this using the sort() method with a callback that we saw in Chapter 4.

Let's refactor our code in numberCruncher.test.js to the following:

```
function factorsOf(n) {
const factors = [];
for (let i=1 , max = Math.sqrt(n); i <= max ; i++) {
    if (n%i === 0){
    factors.push(i,n/i);
    }
}
return factors.sort((a,b) => a - b);
}
```

Now run the test again to confirm it still passes:

```
jest -c {}
<< PASS  ./numberCruncher.test.js
✓ factors of 12 (8ms)

Test Suites: 1 passed, 1 total
Tests:       1 passed, 1 total
Snapshots:   0 total
Time:        1.615s
Ran all test suites.
```

Now our tests are passing, and our code has been refactored, it's time to add some more functionality. Let's write another function called isPrime() that will return true if a number is prime and false if it isn't. Let's start by writing a couple of new tests for this at the end of numberCruncher.test.js:

```
test('2 is prime', () => {
expect(isPrime(2)).toBe(true);
});

test('10 is not prime', () => {
expect(isPrime(10)).not.toBe(true);
});
```

The first test checks whether true is returned when a prime number (2) is provided as an argument, and another to check that true is not returned if a non-prime number (10) is given as an argument. These tests use the toBe() matcher to check if the result is true. Note the nice use of negation using the not matcher (although we should probably be checking if it's false because this test will pass if anything but true is returned).

 More Matcher Methods

You can see a full list of Jest's matcher methods at the official site[13].

If you run the tests again, you'll see that our new tests are failing, and our factors test is still passing:

```
jest -c {}
<< FAIL   ./numberCruncher.test.js
• 2 is prime

    ReferenceError: isPrime is not defined

 at Object.<anonymous>.test
↳ (numberCruncher.test.js:18:10)
 at process._tickCallback
↳ (internal/process/next_tick.js:103:7)

• 10 is not prime

    ReferenceError: isPrime is not defined
```

13. http://facebook.github.io/jest/docs/expect.html

```
 at Object.<anonymous>.test
↳ (numberCruncher.test.js:22:10)
 at process._tickCallback
↳ (internal/process/next_tick.js:103:7)

✓ factors of 12 (4ms)
✕ 2 is prime (1ms)
✕ 10 is not prime (1ms)

Test Suites: 1 failed, 1 total
Tests:       2 failed, 1 passed, 3 total
Snapshots:   0 total
Time:        0.812s, estimated 1s
Ran all test suites.
```

This is to be expected, since we're yet to write any code for them.

We'd better write the `isPrime()` function. This will use the `factorsOf()` function and check to see if the number of factors in the array returned by the `factorsOf()` function is 2. This is because all prime numbers have precisely two factors. Add the following code to the bottom of the `numberCruncher.test.js` file:

```
function isPrime(n) {
return factorsOf(n).length === 2;
}
```

Now if we run the tests again, we can see that all three of our tests have passed:

```
jest -c {}
<< PASS  ./numberCruncher.test.js
✓ factors of 12 (6ms)
✓ 2 is prime (1ms)
✓ 10 is not prime (1ms)
```

```
Test Suites: 1 passed, 1 total
Tests:       3 passed, 3 total
Snapshots:   0 total
Time:        2.853s
Ran all test suites.
```

Our library of functions is growing! The next step is to again refactor our code. It's a bit brittle at the moment, because both functions accept negative and non-integer values, neither of which are prime. They also allow non-numerical arguments to be provided. It turns out that the `factorsOf()` function fails silently and returns an empty array if any of these are passed to it. It would be better to throw an exception to indicate that an incorrect argument has been used. Let's create some tests to check that this happens. Add the following tests to the `numberCruncher.test.js` file:

```
 it('should throw an exception for non-numerical data', ()
 ↳ => {
     expect(factorsOf('twelve').toThrow();
     });

 it('should throw an exception for negative numbers', ()
 ↳ => {
     expect(() => factorsOf(-2)).toThrow();
     });

 it('should throw an exception for non-integer numbers', ()
 ↳ => {
expect(() => factorsOf(3.14159)).toThrow();
});
```

These tests all use the `toThrow()` method to check that an exception has been thrown if the wrong data is entered as an argument.

While we're at it, we can add some extra tests so the `isPrime()` function also deals with any incorrect arguments. No exceptions are necessary in these cases; non-numerical data, negative numbers and non-integers are simply not prime, so the function should just return `false`. Add the following code to the bottom of the `numberCruncher.test.js` file:

```
test('non-numerical data returns not prime', () => {
expect(isPrime('two')).toBe(false);
});

test('non-integer numbers return not prime', () => {
expect(isPrime(1.2)).toBe(false);
});

test('negative numbers return not prime', () => {
expect(isPrime(-1)).toBe(false);
});
```

If you run the tests again, you'll see that the new tests for the `factorsOf()` function fail as expected, but the new tests for the `isPrime()` function actually pass. This is a happy accident because the `factorsOf()` function is returning an empty array, which is conveniently not of length 2, so `false` is returned by the function anyway.

Let's try and make all the tests pass by throwing some exceptions in the `factorsOf()` function. Change the `factorsOf()` function to the following in `numberCruncher.test.js`:

```
function factorsOf(n) {
if(Number.isNaN(Number(n))) {
 throw new RangeError('Argument Error: Value must be an
↪ integer');
}
if(n < 0) {
 throw new RangeError('Argument Error: Number must be
↪ positive');
}
if(!Number.isInteger(n)) {
 throw new RangeError('Argument Error: Number must be an
↪ integer');
```

```
}
const factors = [];
for (let i=1 , max = Math.sqrt(n); i <= max ; i++) {
    if (n%i === 0){
    factors.push(i,n/i);
    }
}
return factors.sort((a,b) => a - b);
}
```

Now the function checks to see if a negative number or non-integer has been provided as an argument, and throws an exception in both cases. Let's run our tests again:

```
jest -c{}
<< FAIL   ./numberCruncher.test.js
• non-numerical data returns not prime

    RangeError: Argument Error: Value must be an integer

    at factorsOf (numberCruncher.test.js:5:11)
    at isPrime (numberCruncher.test.js:23:10)
 at Object.<anonymous>.test
↳ (numberCruncher.test.js:57:10)


• non-integer numbers return not prime

    RangeError: Argument Error: Number must be an integer

    at factorsOf (numberCruncher.test.js:11:11)
    at isPrime (numberCruncher.test.js:23:10)
 at Object.<anonymous>.test
↳ (numberCruncher.test.js:61:10)


• negative numbers return not prime

    RangeError: Argument Error: Number must be positive
```

```
    at factorsOf (numberCruncher.test.js:8:11)
    at isPrime (numberCruncher.test.js:23:10)
  at Object.<anonymous>.test
↪ (numberCruncher.test.js:65:10)


✓ Returns factors of 12 (4ms)
✓ 2 is prime (1ms)
✓ 10 is not prime
✓ Exception for non-numerical data
✓ Exception for negative numbers (1ms)
✓ Exception for non-integer numbers
✗ Non-numerical data returns not prime (2ms)
✗ Non-integer numbers return not prime
✗ Negative numbers return not prime (1ms)


Test Suites: 1 failed, 1 total
Tests:       3 failed, 6 passed, 9 total
Snapshots:   0 total
Time:        3.516s
Ran all test suites.
```

Oh, no! Our tests for the `factorsOf()` function all pass… but the exceptions have caused the `isPrime()` function to choke and fail the tests. We need to add code that handles any exceptions that might be thrown when the `factorsOf()` function is called from within the `isPrime()` function. This sounds like a job for a `try` and `catch` block! Change the `isPrime()` function in the `numberCruncher.test.js` file to the following:

```
function isPrime(n) {
try{
    return factorsOf(n).length === 2;
} catch(error) {
    return false;
}
}
```

Now we've placed the original code inside a `try` block, so if `factorsOf()` throws an exception, we can pass it on to the `catch` block and handle the error. All we have to do here is simply return `false` if an error is thrown.

Now we'll run our tests again, and hopefully you'll see the following message:

```
jest -c{}
<< PASS  ./numberCruncher.test.js
✓ Returns factors of 12 (4ms)
✓ 2 is prime (1ms)
✓ 10 is not prime
✓ Exception for non-numerical data (1ms)
✓ Exception for negative numbers
✓ Exception for non-integer numbers (1ms)
✓ Non-numerical data returns not prime
✓ Non-integer numbers return not prime (1ms)
✓ Negative numbers return not prime

Test Suites: 1 passed, 1 total
Tests:       9 passed, 9 total
Snapshots:   0 total
Time:        2.381s
Ran all test suites.
```

Hooray! All our tests are now passing. We'll stop there, but hopefully this demonstrates how TDD can be used to keep adding functionality in small increments using the fail, pass and refactor cycle.

Quiz Ninja Project

We're now going to use the `console.log()` method to log when some of the important functions are called. This will help to make our code in the Quiz Ninja project easier to debug. The main functions in the game are all methods of the `game` object: `game.start()`, `game.ask()`, `game.check(event)`, and `game.gameOver()`. Add the following lines of code to the beginning of the relevant functions:

```
console.log('start() invoked');
console.log('ask() invoked');
console.log('check(event) invoked');
console.log('gameOver() invoked');
```

These declarations will log a message in the console when each method is invoked, so we can see where the program is in its runtime. There will be no impact on the player, though, as we're just using the console.

Try playing the game with the console open in the browser. You should see the messages logged in the console as the program runs, as in the screenshot shown below:

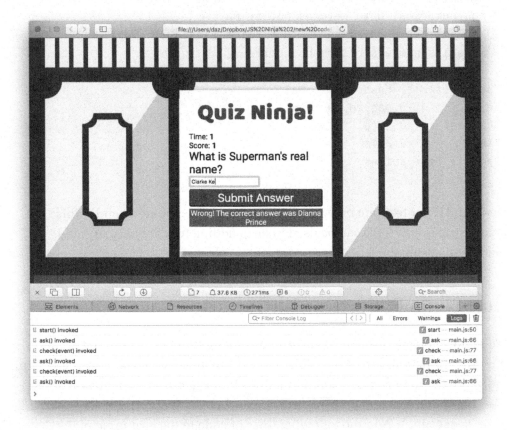

10-2. Playing Quiz Ninja with the console open

You can see a live example on CodePen[14].

Chapter Summary

- Bugs are unavoidable in code, and it's best to find them early rather than later.

- JavaScript can be put into strict mode using the string `"use strict"`. This can be used in a whole file or just a single function.

- Linting tools can be used to ensure your code follows good practice and conventions.

- Feature detection can check whether a method is supported before calling it, helping to avoid an exception being thrown.

- The console and browser's built-in debugging tool can be used to interactively find and fix bugs in code.

- Exceptions can be thrown using the `throw` statement.

- An error object is created when an exception occurs.

- Any code placed inside a `try` block will pass any error objects to a `catch` block when an exception occurs. Any code inside a `finally` block will run if an exception does or does not occur.

- Test-driven development is the practice of writing tests that fail, then writing the code that passes the test, then refactoring the code every time a new feature is implemented.

- The Jest framework can be used to test your code.

In the next chapter, we'll be taking our understanding of functions to the next level and trying out some functional programming techniques in JavaScript.

---

14. https://codepen.io/daz4126/pen/xrWoER

Chapter **11**

Further Functions

We covered functions back in chapter 4, but we were only just beginning to scratch the surface. In JavaScript, functions are **first-class objects**, which means they can be passed around in the same way as every other value. They can have their own properties and methods, as well as accepting other functions as parameters and being returned by other functions. This makes them a very flexible tool to work with in JavaScript, and there are a variety of techniques and patterns that can be used to make code cleaner.

In this chapter, we'll cover the following topics:

▦ Function properties and methods

▦ Immediately Invoked function expressions

- Self-defining functions

- Recursive functions

- Callbacks

- Promises

- Async functions

- Functions that return functions

- Closures

- Introduction to functional programming

- Currying

- Project — improve some of the functions using techniques from this chapter

Function Properties and Methods

The fact that functions are first-class objects means they can have properties and methods themselves. For example, all functions have a `length` property that returns the number of parameters the function has.

Let's use the `square()` function that we wrote in chapter 4 as an example:

```
function square(x) {
    return x*x;
}
```

If we query the `length` property, we can see that it accepts one parameter:

```
square.length
<< 1
```

Call and Apply Methods

The `call()` method can be used to set the value of `this` inside a function to an object that is provided as the first argument.

In the following example, the `sayHello()` function refers to an unspecific object called `this` that has a property called `name`:

```
function sayHello(){
return `Hello, my name is ${ this.name }`;
}
```

We can create some objects that have a `name` property, then use the `call()` method to invoke the `sayHello()` function, providing each object as an argument. This will then take the value of `this` in the function:

```
const clark = { name: 'Clark' };
const bruce = { name: 'Bruce' };

sayHello.call(clark);
<< 'Hello, my name is Clarke'

sayHello.call(bruce);
<< 'Hello, my name is Bruce'
```

If the function that's called requires any parameters, these need to be provided as arguments after the first argument, which is always the value of `this`. For example, let's update the `sayHello()` function to give a more generalized greeting that's provided as an argument:

```
function sayHello(greeting='Hello'){
return `${ greeting }, my name is ${ this.name }`;
}

sayHello.call(clark, 'How do you do');
<< 'How do you do, my name is Clark'
```

```
sayHello.call(bruce);
<< 'Hello, my name is Bruce'
```

If a function doesn't refer to an object as this in its body, it can still be called using the call() method, but you need provide null as its first argument. For example, we could call the square() function using the call() method, like so:

```
square.call(null, 4)
<< 16
```

The apply() method works in the same way, except the arguments of the function are provided as an array, even if there is only one argument:

```
square.apply(null, [4])
<< 16
```

This can be useful if the data you're using as an argument is already in the form of an array, although it's not really needed in ES6, as the spread operator can be used to split an array of values into separate parameters.

These are two powerful methods, as they allow generalized functions to be written that are not tied to specific objects by being methods of that object. This gives flexibility over how the functions can be used.

Custom Properties

There is nothing to stop you adding your own properties to functions in the same way that you can add properties to any object in JavaScript. For example, you could add a description property to a function that describes what it does:

```
square.description = 'Squares a number that is provided as
↳ an argument'
```

```
<< 'Squares a number that is provided as an argument'
```

Memoization

A useful feature of this is that it provides result caching, or **memoization**.

If a function takes some time to compute a return value, we can save the result in a `cache` property. Then if the same argument is used again later, we can return the value from the cache, rather than having to compute the result again. For example, say squaring a number was an expensive computational operation that took a long time. We could rewrite the `square()` function so it saved each result in a `cache` object that is a property of the function:

```
function square(x){
square.cache = square.cache || {};
if (!square.cache[x]) {
    square.cache[x] = x*x;
}
return square.cache[x]
}
```

If we try calling the function a few times, we can see that the `cache` object stores the results:

```
square(3);
<< 9

square(-11);
<< 121

square.cache;
<< {"3": 9, "-11": 121}
```

Immediately Invoked Function Expressions

An **Immediately Invoked Function Expression** – or IIFE (pronounced "iffy") – is an anonymous function that, as the name suggests, is invoked as soon as it's defined. This is easily achieved by placing parentheses at the end of the function definition (remember we use parentheses to invoke a function). The function also has to be made into an expression, which is done by placing the whole declaration inside parentheses, as in this example:

```
(function(){
const temp = 'World';
console.log(`Hello ${temp}`);
})();
<< 'Hello World'
```

IIFEs are a useful way of performing a task while keeping any variables wrapped up within the scope of the function. This means the global namespace is not polluted with lots of variable names.

Temporary Variables

There is no way to remove a variable from a scope once it's been declared. If a variable is only required temporarily, it may cause confusion if it's still available later in the code. Even worse, the name of the variable may clash with another piece of code (an external JavaScript library, for example) resulting in errors. Placing any code that uses the temporary variable inside an IIFE will ensure it's only available while the IIFE is invoked, then it will disappear. The example that follows uses an IIFE to swap the value of two global variables, **a** and **b**. This process requires the use of a temporary variable, called `temp`, which only exists while the IIFE is invoked:

```
let a = 1;
let b = 2;

(()=>{
```

```
const temp = a;
a = b;
b = temp;
})();

a;
<< 2

b;
<< 1

console.log(temp);
<< Error: "temp is not defined"
```

This shows the variable `temp` does not exist after the function has been invoked.

Note that this technique is not needed to swap the values of two variables in ES6, as destructuring can be used, as shown below:

```
let [a,b] = [1,2];
[a,b] = [b,a];

a;
<< 2

b;
<< 1
```

Initialization Code

An IIFE can be used to set up any initialization code that there'll be no need for again. Because the code is only run once, there's no need to create any reusable, named functions, and all the variables will also be temporary. An IIFE will be invoked once, and can set up any variables, objects and event handlers when the page loads. The following example logs a welcome message to the console, then eliminates all the temporary variables used in putting the message together:

```
(function() {
 const name = 'Peter Parker'; // This might be obtained from
↪ a cookie in reality
 const days =
↪ ['Sunday','Monday','Tuesday','Wednesday','Thursday',
↪ 'Friday','Saturday'];
const date = new Date(),today = days[date.getDay()];
console.log(`Welcome back ${name}. Today is ${today}`);

})();
<< 'Welcome back Peter Parker. Today is Tuesday'
```

Note that much of this can be achieved in ES6 by simply placing the code inside a block. This is because variables have block scope when `const` or `let` are used, whereas in previous versions of JavaScript, only functions maintained the scope of variables. The example above would work just as well using the following code:

```
{
 const name = 'Peter Parker'; // This might be obtained from
↪ a cookie in reality
 const days =
↪ ['Sunday','Monday','Tuesday','Wednesday','Thursday',
↪ 'Friday','Saturday'];
const date = new Date(),today = days[date.getDay()];
console.log(`Welcome back ${name}. Today is ${today}`);
}
<< 'Welcome back Peter Parker. Today is Tuesday'
```

Safe Use of Strict Mode

In the last chapter we discussed using strict mode to avoid any sloppy coding practices. One of the problems with simply placing `'use strict'` at the beginning of a file is that it will enforce strict mode on all the JavaScript in the file, and if you're using other people's code, there's no guarantee that they've coded in strict mode.

To avoid this, the recommended way to use strict mode is to place all your code inside an IIFE, like so:

```
(function() {
'use strict';

// All your code would go inside this function

})();
```

This ensures that only your code inside the IIFE is forced to use strict mode.

Creating Self-contained Code Blocks

An IIFE can be used to enclose a block of code inside its own private scope so it doesn't interfere with any other part of the program. Using IIFEs in this way means code can be added or removed separately. The example shows two blocks, A and B, that are able to run code independently of each other:

```
(function() {
// block A
const name = 'Block A';
console.log(`Hello from ${name}`);
}());

(function() {
// block B
const name = 'Block B';
console.log(`Hello from ${name}`);
}());

<<  Hello from Block A
    Hello from Block B
```

Notice that both code blocks include a variable called `name`, but the modules don't interfere with each other. This is a useful approach for separating parts of a program into discrete sections, especially for testing purposes.

Again, this can be achieved in ES6 by simply placing the different parts of code into blocks. ES6 also supports a much more powerful module pattern that is covered in Chapter 15.

Functions that Define and Rewrite Themselves

The dynamic nature of JavaScript means that a function is able to not only call itself, but define itself, and even redefine itself. This is done by assigning an anonymous function to a variable that has *the same name as the function*.

Consider the following function:

```
function party(){
console.log('Wow this is amazing!');
party = function(){
    console.log('Been there, got the T-Shirt');
}
}
```

This logs a message in the console, then redefines itself to log a different message in the console. When the function has been called once, it will be as if it was defined like this:

```
function party() {
console.log('Been there, got the T-Shirt');
}
```

Every time the function is called after the first time, it will log the message "Been there, got the T-Shirt":

```
party();
<< 'Wow this is amazing!'

party();
<< 'Been there, got the T-Shirt'

party();
<< 'Been there, got the T-Shirt'
```

If the function is also assigned to another variable, this variable will maintain the original function definition and not be rewritten. This is because the original function is assigned to a variable, then within the function, a variable with the same name as the function is assigned to a different function. You can see an example of this if we create a variable called beachParty that is assigned to the party() function *before* it is called for the first time and redefined:

```
function party(){
console.log('Wow this is amazing!');
party = function(){
    console.log('Been there, got the T-Shirt');
}
}

 const beachParty = party; // note that the party function
↳ has not been invoked

 beachParty(); // the party() function has now been
↳ redefined, even though it hasn't been called explicitly
<< 'Wow this is amazing!'

party();
<< 'Been there, got the T-Shirt'

beachParty(); // but this function hasn't been redefined
<< 'Wow this is amazing!'

 beachParty(); // no matter how many times this is called it
↳ will remain the same
```

```
<< 'Wow this is amazing!'
```

 Losing Properties

If any properties have previously been set on the function, these will be lost when the function redefines itself. In the previous example, we can set a `music` property, and see that it no longer exists after the function has been invoked and redefined:

```
function party() {
console.log('Wow this is amazing!');
party = function(){
console.log('Been there, got the T-Shirt');
}
}

 party.music = 'Classical Jazz'; // set a property of the
 ↪ function

party();
<< "Wow this is amazing!"

 party.music; // function has now been redefined, so the
 ↪ property doesn't exist
<< undefined
```

This is called the **Lazy Definition Pattern** and is often used when some initialization code is required the first time it's invoked. This means the initialization can be done the first time it's called, then the function can be redefined to what you want it to be for every subsequent invocation.

Init-Time Branching

This technique can be used with the feature detection that we discussed in the last chapter to create functions that rewrite themselves, known as init-time branching. This enables the functions to work more effectively in the browser, and avoid checking for features every time they're invoked.

Let's take the example of our fictional `unicorn` object that's yet to have full
support in all browsers. In the last chapter, we looked at how we can use feature
detection to check if this is supported. Now we can go one step further: we can
define a function based on whether certain methods are supported. This means
we only need to check for support the first time the function is called:

```javascript
function ride(){
    if (window.unicorn) {
        ride = function(){
 // some code that uses the brand new and sparkly unicorn
 ↪ methods
        return 'Riding on a unicorn is the best!';
    }
    } else {
        ride = function(){
        // some code that uses the older pony methods
        return 'Riding on a pony is still pretty good';
    }
    }
    return ride();
}
```

After we've checked whether the `window.unicorn` object exists (by checking to
see if it's truthy), we've rewritten the `ride()` function according to the outcome.
Right at the end of the function, we call it again so that the rewritten function is
now invoked, and the relevant value returned. One thing to be aware of is that the
function is invoked twice the first time, although it becomes more efficient each
subsequent time it's invoked. Let's take a look at how it works:

```javascript
ride(); // the function rewrites itself, then calls itself
<< 'Riding on a pony is still pretty good'
```

Once the function has been invoked, it's rewritten based on the browser's
capabilities. We can check this by inspecting the function without invoking it:

```
ride
<< function ride() {
    return 'Riding on a pony is still pretty good';
    }
```

This can be a useful pattern to initialize functions the first time they're called, optimizing them for the browser being used.

Recursive Functions

A recursive function is one that invokes itself until a certain condition is met. It's a useful tool to use when iterative processes are involved. A common example is a function that calculates the factorial[1] of a number:

```
function factorial(n) {
if (n === 0) {
    return 1;
} else {
    return n * factorial(n - 1);
}
}
```

This function will return 1 if 0 is provided as an argument (0 factorial is 1), otherwise it will multiply the argument by the result of invoking itself with an argument of one less. The function will continue to invoke itself until finally the argument is 0 and 1 is returned. This will result in a multiplication of 1, 2, 3 and all the numbers up to the original argument.

Another example from the world of mathematics is the Collatz Conjecture.[2] This is a problem that is simple to state, but, so far, has not been solved. It involves taking any positive integer and following these rules:

If the number is even, divide it by two

---

[1] http://en.wikipedia.org/wiki/Factorial

[2] http://en.wikipedia.org/wiki/Collatz_conjecture

▪ If the number is odd, multiply it by three and add one

For example, if we start with the number 18, we would have the following sequence:

18, 9, 28, 14, 7, 22, 11, 34, 17, 52, 26, 13, 40, 20, 10, 5, 16, 8, 4, 2, 1, 4, 2, 1, ...

As you can see, the sequence becomes stuck in a loop at the end, cycling through "4,2,1". The Collatz Conjecture states that every positive integer will create a sequence that finishes in this loop. This has been verified for all numbers up to 5 $\times 2^{60}$, but there is no proof it will continue to be true for all the integers higher than this. To test the conjecture, we can write a function that uses recursion to keep invoking the function until it reaches a value of 1 (because we want our function to avoid being stuck in a recursive loop at the end!):

```
function collatz(n, sequence=[n]) {
if (n === 1){
 return `Sequence took ${sequence.length} steps. It was
↪ ${sequence}`;
}

if (n%2 === 0) {
    n = n/2;
} else {
    n = 3*n + 1;
}

return collatz(n,[...sequence,n]);
}
```

This function takes a number as a parameter, as well as another parameter called sequence, which has a default value of an array containing the first parameter. The second parameter is only used when the function calls itself recursively.

The first thing the function does is tests to see if n has a value of 1. If it does, the function returns a message to say how many steps it took. If it hasn't reached 1, it checks if the value of n is even (in which case it divides it by 2), or odd, in which case it multiplies by 3 and then adds 1. The function then calls itself, providing the new value of n and the new sequence as arguments. The new sequence is constructed by placing the old sequence and the value of n inside a new array and applying the spread operator to the old sequence.

Let's see what happens to the number 18:

```
collatz(18);
 << 'Sequence took 21 steps. It was
 ↪ 18,9,28,14,7,22,11,34,17,52,26,13,40,20,10,5,16,8,4,2,1'
```

As you can see, it takes 21 steps, but eventually it ends up at 1.

Have a go at using the function and see if you can find a value above 5×2^{60} that doesn't end at 1 — you'll be famous if you do!

Callbacks

We covered callbacks in Chapter 4. You'll recall that they're functions passed to other functions as arguments and then invoked inside the function they are passed to.

Event-driven Asynchronous Programming

Callbacks can be used to facilitate event-driven asynchronous programming. JavaScript is a single-threaded environment, which means only one piece of code will ever be processed at a time. This may seem like a limitation, but non-blocking techniques can be used to ensure that the program continues to run. Instead of waiting for an event to occur, a callback can be created that's invoked when the event happens. This means that the code is able to run out of order, or *asynchronously*. Events can be DOM events, such as the `click` and `keyPress` that we looked at in Chapter 7, but they can also be events such as the completion of a file download, data returned from a database, or the result of a complex operation. By using callbacks, we ensure that waiting for these tasks to complete doesn't hold up the execution of other parts of the program. Once the task has been completed, the callback will be invoked before returning to the rest of the program.

Here's an example of a function called `wait()` that accepts a callback. To simulate an operation that takes some time to happen, we can use the `setTimeout()` function to call the callback after a given number of seconds:

```
function wait(message, callback, seconds){
setTimeout(callback,seconds * 1000);
console.log(message);
}
```

Now let's create a callback function to use:

```
function selfDestruct(){
console.log('BOOOOM!');
}
```

If we invoke the `wait()` function then log a message to the console, we can see how JavaScript works asynchronously:

```
 wait('This tape will self-destruct in five seconds ... ',
↳ selfDestruct, 5);
 console.log('Hmmm, should I accept this mission or not ...
↳ ?');

<< 'This tape will self-destruct in five seconds ... '
<< 'Hmmm, should I accept this mission or not ... ? '
<< 'BOOOOM!'
```

When the `wait()` function is invoked, any code inside it is run, so the message "This tape will self destruct in five seconds ... " is displayed. The `setTimeout()` function is asynchronous, which means that the callback provided as an argument is placed on top of a stack that gets cleared once the rest of the program has run. This means that control is handed back to the program and the next line in the program is run, which displays the message 'Hmmm, should I accept this mission or not ... ?' Then, after five seconds, the callback is retrieved from the stack and invoked. This demonstrates that the `setTimeout()` function did not block the rest of the program from running. This is known as the JavaScript **event-loop**.

Remember, though, that JavaScript is still single-threaded, so only one task can happen at once. If an event only takes a small amount of time to happen, it will still have to wait until other parts of the program have executed before the callback is invoked. For example, let's see what happens if we set the waiting time to be zero seconds:

```
wait('This tape will self-destruct immediately ... ',
↳ selfDestruct, 0);
console.log('Hmmm, should I accept this mission or not ...
↳ ?');

<< 'This tape will self-destruct immediately ... '
<< 'Hmmm, should I accept this mission or not ... ?'
<< 'BOOOOM!'
```

Notice the callback in the wait() function is still invoked last, despite the wait time being set to zero seconds. We would have expected the callback to have been invoked immediately, but a callback always has to wait for the current execution stack to complete before it's invoked. In this case, the current execution stack is the rest of the function and code already entered in the console. Once these have executed, the callback is invoked before handing control back to the main program.

Callback Hell

The increase in the use of asynchronous programming in JavaScript has meant that more and more callbacks are being used. This can result in messy and confusing "spaghetti code". This is when more than one callback is used in the same function, resulting in a large number of nested blocks that are difficult to comprehend.

Callback hell is the term used to refer to this tangled mess of code. To illustrate this, let's say we had written a game that required the following tasks to be completed:

■ The user logs in and a user object is returned

■ The user ID is then used to fetch player information from the server

■ The game then loads based on the player information

All these operations are asynchronous, so can be written as functions that use callbacks invoked once each task has been completed.

The code might look like the snippet shown below:

```
login(userName, function(error,user) {
    if(error){
        throw error;
    } else {
        getPlayerInfo(user.id, function(error,info){
        if(error){
        throw error;
        } else {
            loadGame(info, function(error,game) {
                if(error){
                        throw error;
                } else {
                // code to run game
                }
        });
    }
    });
}
});
```

You may have noticed there isn't much actual code in the example above. The example only shows the flow from one function to the other, and yet it still manages to look extremely complicated due to the large number of nested `if-else` statements. In reality, there would be lots more code to implement the actual functionality of the `login()`, `getPlayerInfo()` and `loadGame()` functions.

Error-first Callbacks

The code example above uses the *error-first* callback style popularized by Node.js. In this coding pattern, callbacks have two arguments. The first is the error argument, which is an error object provided if something goes wrong when completing the operation. The second argument is any data returned by the operation that can be used in the body of the callback.

Promises

A **promise** represents the future result of an asynchronous operation. Promises don't do anything that can't already be achieved using callbacks, but they help simplify the process, and avoid the convoluted code that can result from using multiple callbacks.

The Promise Life Cycle

When a promise is created, it calls an asynchronous operation and is then said to be *pending*. It remains in this state while the operation is taking place. At this stage, the promise is said to be *unsettled*. Once the operation has completed, the promise is said to have been *settled*. A settled promise can result in two different outcomes:

■ Resolved — the asynchronous operation was completed successfully.

■ Rejected — the asynchronous operation didn't work as expected, wasn't successfully completed or resulted in an error.

Both these outcomes will return any relevant data, and you can take the appropriate action based on the outcome of the promise.

A Super Promise

Imagine if a shady character gave you a red pill, and promised that if you took it, you'd be a superhero. Being an adventurous sort, you swallow the pill and wait to see what happens. You're currently in the pending phase of a promise, waiting to see what the result will be.

Suddenly you find that you have the power to dodge bullets as if time was standing still! The promise has been resolved, and now you need to go off and use your newly acquired powers.

But if nothing happens, you would reject the promise and warn people that a stranger is wandering around giving out red pills and peddling a fanciful story.

This scenario puts a comic-book spin on the phases of a promise. There is a pending phase while you wait on the results of an operation (taking the pill). Then once the promise is settled, you deal with the results in an appropriate way — by using your superpowers if the promise is resolved, or dealing with any problems if it doesn't work out.

The Promise of a Burger Party[3] is a brilliant post by Mariko Kosaka that explains the concept of promises by comparing them to ordering a burger!

Creating A Promise

A promise is created using a constructor function. This takes a function called an **executor** as an argument. The executor initializes the promise and starts the asynchronous operation. It also accepts two functions as arguments: the `resolve()` function is called if the operation is successful, and the `reject()` function is called if the operation fails. The general layout of a promise can be seen in the code below:

```
const promise = new Promise( (resolve, reject) => {
    // initialization code goes here
    if (success) {
        resolve(value);
    } else {
        reject(error);
    }
});
```

---

3. http://kosamari.com/notes/the-promise-of-a-burger-party

A Dicey Example

Let's take a look at an example of a promise that uses the `dice` object we created back in chapter 5:

```
const dice = {
sides: 6,
roll() {
    return Math.floor(this.sides * Math.random()) + 1;
}
}
```

Now let's create a promise that uses the `dice.roll()` method as the asynchronous operation and considers rolling a 1 as a failure, and any other number as a success:

```
const promise = new Promise( (resolve,reject) => {
const n = dice.roll();
setTimeout(() => {
(n > 1) ? resolve(n) : reject(n);
}, n*1000);
});
```

This creates a variable called `promise` that holds a reference to the promise. The promise calls the `roll()` method and stores the return value in a variable called n. Next, we use an `if-else` block to specify the conditions for success (rolling any number higher than 1) and failure (rolling a 1). The `setTimeout()` method we met in Chapter 9 is used to add a short delay based on the number rolled. This is to mimic the time taken for an asynchronous operation to complete.

Notice that both the `resolve()` and `reject()` functions return the value of the n variable. This can be used when dealing with the outcome of the promise once it's been settled.

Dealing With A Settled Promise

Once a promise has been settled, the `then()` method can be used to deal with the outcome. This method accepts two arguments. The first is a *fulfilment function* that's called when the promise is resolved. Any data returned from the `resolve()` function will be passed along to this function. The second argument is a rejection function that's called if the promise is rejected. Similar to the fulfilment function, the rejection function receives any data returned from the `reject()` function.

In the case of our dice example, both functions will receive the value of the number rolled. Let's have a look at how we could deal with that:

```
promise.then( result => console.log(`Yes! I rolled a
↪ ${result}`), result => console.log(`Drat! ... I rolled a
↪ ${result}`) );
```

The first argument is simply a function that logs a celebratory message to the console, stating the number rolled (this is passed to the `then()` method as the variable `result`). The second argument logs an annoyed message and, again, states the number rolled.

Alternatively, the `catch()` method can be used to specify what to do if the operation fails instead:

```
promise.catch( result => console.log(`Drat! ... I rolled
↪ a ${result}`));
```

The `then()` and `catch()` methods can be chained together to form a succinct description of how to deal with the outcome of the promise:

```
promise.then( result => console.log(`I rolled a
↪ ${result}`) )
  .catch( result => console.log(`Drat! ... I rolled a
↪ ${result}`) );
```

To try this code out, paste the following code into your browser console or use JS Bin with ES6/Babel enabled[4]:

```
const dice = {
sides: 6,
roll() {
    return Math.floor(this.sides * Math.random()) + 1;
}
}

console.log('Before the roll');

const roll = new Promise( (resolve,reject) => {
const n = dice.roll();
if(n > 1){
    setTimeout(()=>{resolve(n)},n*200);
} else {
    setTimeout(()=>reject(n),n*200);
}
});

roll.then(result => console.log(`I rolled a ${result}`) )
 .catch(result => console.log(`Drat! ... I rolled a
↪ ${result}`) );

console.log('After the roll');
```

When you press the "Run" button, you should see the following output in the console:

```
before promise
promise pending...
after promise
```

4. https://jsbin.com/lesaxafiya/edit?js,console

Then there should be a pause, while the promise is resolved, followed by the resulting message:

```
Drat! ... I rolled a 1
```

The messages in the console also give an insight into the asynchronous nature of JavaScript. Notice that the last message "after promise" is displayed *before* the result of the settled promise. This shows that the language will continue to process the rest of the code while the promise is being resolved, before coming back and dealing with the result of the promise.

Chaining Multiple Promises

Promises come into their own when multiple asynchronous tasks are required to be carried out one after the other. If each function that performs an asynchronous operation returns a promise, we can chain the `then()` methods together to form a sequential piece of code that's easy to read. Each promise will only begin once the previous promise has been settled.

For example, the player logging in to a game that produced the callback hell earlier, could be written in a much nicer way by using promises:

```
login(userName)
.then(user => getPlayerInfo(user.id))
.then(info => loadGame(info))
.catch( throw error)
```

A number of new additions to the language return promises, and you'll see more examples of them used later in the book.

Async Functions

Async functions were added to the ES2017 specification. These functions are preceded by the `async` keyword and allow you to write asynchronous code as if it was synchronous. This is achieved by using the `await` operator before an asynchronous function. This will wrap the return value of the function in a promise that can then be assigned to a variable. The next line of code is not executed until the promise is resolved.

The example below shows how the `loadGame()` function can be written an `async` function:

```
async function loadGame(userName) {

    try {
    const user = await login(userName);
    const info = await getPlayerInfo (user.id);
    // load the game using the returned info
    }

    catch (error){
    throw error;
    }
}
```

In the example, the loadGame function is preceded by the `async` keyword, meaning the function will run in an asynchronous fashion. We then wrap each step of the process in a `try` block, so any errors are caught. Inside this block, we can write each step in the order it's meant to be processed, so we start by assigning the variable `user` to the return value of the `login()` function. The `await` operator will ensure the next line of code is not executed until the `login()` function returns a `user` object. The `getPlayerInfo()` function is also preceded by the `await` operator. Once this function returns a result, it's assigned to the variable `info`, and this can then be used to load the actual game. A catch block is used to deal with any errors that may occur.

Generalized Functions

Callbacks can be used to build more generalized functions. Instead of having lots of specific functions, one function can be written that accepts a callback. For example, let's create a function that returns a random integer between two values

that are provided as arguments, a and b, or if only 1 argument is provided, it will
return a random integer between 1 and the argument provided:

```
function random(a,b=1) {
 // if only 1 argument is provided, we need to swap the
 ↪ values of a and b
if (b === 1) {
    [a,b] = [b,a];
}
return Math.floor((b-a+1) * Math.random()) + a;
}

random(6);
<< 4

random(10,20);
<< 13
```

This is an example of an abstraction, as it wraps all the logic cleanly away inside
the function.

We could refactor this function to make it more generic by adding a callback
parameter, so a calculation is performed on the random number before it's
returned:

```
function random(a,b,callback) {
 if (b === undefined) b = a, a = 1; // if only one argument
 ↪ is supplied, assume the lower limit is 1
const result = Math.floor((b-a+1) * Math.random()) + a
if(callback) {
    result = callback(result);
}
return result;
}
```

Now we have a function where more flexibility can be added using a callback. For example, we can use the `square()` function from earlier in the chapter to produce a random square number from one to 100:

```
function square(n) {
return n*n;
}

random(1,10,square);
<< 49
```

Or a random even number from two to ten:

```
random(1,5, (n) => 2 * n );
<< 8
```

Notice that in the last example, the callback is an anonymous function that is defined inline as one of the `random()` function's arguments.

Functions That Return Functions

We've just seen that functions can accept another function as an argument (a callback), but they can also return a function.

The example below shows a function called `returnHello()` that returns a "Hello World" message:

```
function returnHello() {
console.log('returnHello() called');
return function() {
    console.log('Hello World!');
}
}
```

When the returnHello() function is invoked, it logs a message to the console then returns another function:

```
returnHello()
<< returnHello() called
```

To make use of the function that is returned, we need to assign it to a variable:

```
const hello = returnHello();
<< returnHello() called
```

Now we can invoke the "Hello World" function by placing parentheses after the variable that it was assigned to:

```
hello()
<< Hello World!
```

This might seem a bit pointless, but let's now take it a step further and use this technique to create a generic "greeter" function that takes a particular greeting as a parameter, then returns a more specific greeting function:

```
function greeter(greeting = 'Hello') {
return function() {
    console.log(greeting);
}
}

const englishGreeter = greeter();
englishGreeter();
<< Hello

const frenchGreeter = greeter('Bonjour');
frenchGreeter();
<< Bonjour
```

```
const germanGreeter = greeter('Guten Tag');
germanGreeter();
<< Guten Tag
```

Closures

Closures are one of JavaScript's most powerful features, but they can be difficult to get your head around initially.

Function Scope

Back in Chapter 2, we saw the value of a variable was only available inside the block it was created inside if the `const` or `let` keywords were used. This also applies to the body of a function if the `var` keyword is used.

In the following example, there are two variables: `outside`, which is available throughout the program, and `inside`, which is only available inside the function:

```
const outside = 'In the global scope';
function fn() {
const inside = 'In the function scope';
}

outside
<< 'In the global scope'

inside
<< ReferenceError: inside is not defined
```

It appears we're unable to access the variable `inside` outside the scope the function.

This is because the variable `inside` is only kept "alive" while the function is active. Once the function has been invoked, any references to variables inside its scope are removed.

It turns out, however, that we can gain access to variables outside the function where it was created, and after the function has been invoked.

A closure is a reference to a variable that was created inside the scope of another function, but is then kept alive and used in another part of the program.

One of the key principles in creating closures is that an "inner" function, which is declared inside another function, has full access to all of the variables declared inside the scope of the function in which it's declared (the "outer" function). This can be seen in the example below:

```
function outer() {
const outside = 'Outside!';
function inner() {
    const inside = 'Inside!';
    console.log(outside);
    console.log(inside);
}
console.log(outside);
inner();
}
```

The `outer()` function only has access to the variable `outside`, which was declared in its scope. The `inner()` function, however, has access to the variable `inside`, declared in its scope, but also the variable `outside`, declared outside its scope, but from within the `outer()` function.

We can see this when we invoke the `outside()` function:

```
outer()
<< Outside!
Inside!
```

```
Outside!
```

This means that whenever a function is defined inside another function, the inner function will have access to any variables that are declared in the outer function's scope.

Returning Functions

As we saw in the example above, functions declared from within another function have access to any variables declared in the outer function's scope.

A **closure** is formed when the inner function is returned by the outer function, maintaining access to any variables declared inside the enclosing function.

```
function outer() {
const outside = 'Outside!';
function inner() {
    const inside = 'Inside!';
    console.log(outside);
    console.log(inside);
}
return inner;
}
```

We can now assign a variable to the return value of the outer() function:

```
const closure = outer();
```

The variable closure now points to the inner() function that is returned by the outer() function.

What makes this a closure is that it now has access to the variables created inside *both* the outer() and inner() functions, as we can see when we invoke it:

```
closure();
<< Outside!
Inside!
```

This is important as the variable `outside` should only exist while the `outer()` function is running. The closure maintains access to this variable, however, even though the `outer()` has been invoked.

A closure doesn't just have access to the value of a variable, it can also change the value of the variable long after the function in which it was originally declared has been invoked.

A Practical Example

A closure is formed when a function returns another function that then maintains access to any variables created in the original function's scope. In the following example, two variables, `a` and `b`, are created in the scope of the `closure()` function. This then returns an anonymous arrow function that maintains access to the variables `a` and `b` even after the `closure()` function has been invoked:

```
function closure() {
const a = 1.8;
const b = 32;
return c => c * a + b;
}
```

Now we can create a new function by invoking the `closure()` function and assigning the return value to a variable called `toFahrenheit`:

```
const toFahrenheit = closure();
```

This new function can then be invoked with its own argument, but the values of `a` and `b` from the original function are still kept "alive":

```
toFahrenheit(30);
<< 86
```

A Counter Example

Closures not only have *access* to variables declared in a parent function's scope, they can also change the value of these variables. This allows us to do things like create a counter() function like the one in the example below:

```
function counter(start){
let i = start;
return function() {
    return i++;
}
}
```

This function starts a count using the variable i. It then returns a function that uses a closure that traps and maintains access to the value of i. This function also has the ability to change the value of i, so it increments i by one every time it's invoked. The reference to the variable i that is defined in the original function is maintained in the new function via a closure.

We can create a counter by assigning the return value of the counter() function to a variable:

```
const count = counter(1);
```

The variable count now points to a function that has full access to the variable i that was created in the scope of the counter() function. Every time we invoke the count() function, it will return the value of i and then increment it by 1:

```
count();
<< 1
```

```
count();
<< 2
```

Generators

ES6 introduced support for generators. These are special functions used to produce iterators that maintain the state of a value.

To define a generator function, an asterisk symbol (*) is placed after the function declaration, like so:

```
function* exampleGenerator() {
// code for the generator goes here
}
```

Calling a generator function doesn't actually run any of the code in the function; it returns a `Generator` object that can be used to create an iterator that implements a `next()` method that returns a value every time the `next()` method is called.

For example, we can create a generator to produce a Fibonacci-style number series (a sequence that starts with two numbers and the next number is obtained by adding the two previous numbers together), using the following code:

```
function* fibonacci(a,b) {
let [ prev,current ] = [ a,b ];
while(true) {
    [prev, current] = [current, prev + current];
    yield current;
}
}
```

The code starts by initializing the first two values of the sequence, which are provided as arguments to the function. A `while` loop is then used, which will continue indefinitely due to the fact that it uses `true` as its condition, which will obviously always be true. Every time the iterator's `next()` method is called, the code inside the loop is run, and the next value is calculated by adding the previous two values together.

Generator functions employ the special `yield` keyword that is used to return a value. The difference between the `yield` and the `return` keywords is that by using `yield`, the state of the value returned is remembered the next time `yield` is called. Hence, the current value in the Fibonacci sequence will be stored for use later. The execution of the loop is paused after every `yield` statement, until the `next()` method is called again.

To create a generator object based on this function, we simply assign a variable to the function, and provide it with two starting numbers as arguments:

```
const sequence = fibonacci(1,1);
```

The generator object is now stored in the `sequence` variable. It inherits a method called `next()`, which is then used to obtain the next value produced by the `yield` command:

```
sequence.next();
<< 2

sequence.next();
<< 3

sequence.next();
<< 5
```

It's also possible to iterate over the generator to invoke it multiple times:

```
for (n of sequence) {
    // stop the sequence after it reaches 100
    if (n > 10) break;
    console.log(n);
```

```
}
<< 8
<< 13
<< 21
<< 34
<< 55
<< 89
```

Note that the sequence continued from the last value produced using the `next()` method. This is because a generator will maintain its state throughout the life of a program.

Functional Programming

Functional programming has gained momentum in recent years, with a dedicated following. The popularity of purely functional languages, such as Clojure, Scala and Erlang, sparked an interest in functional programming techniques that continues to grow. JavaScript has always supported functional-style programming due to functions being first-class objects. The ability to pass functions as arguments, return them from other functions, and use anonymous functions and closures, are all fundamental elements of functional programming that JavaScript excels at.

Functional programming is a programming paradigm. Other examples of programming paradigms include object oriented programming and procedural programming. JavaScript is a multi-paradigm language, meaning that it can be used to program in a variety of paradigms (and sometimes a mash-up of them!). This flexibility is an attractive feature of the language, but it also makes it harder to adopt a particular coding style as the principles are not enforced by the language. A language such as Haskell, which is a purely functional language, is much stricter about adhering to the principles of functional programming.

Pure Functions

A key aspect of functional programming is its use of pure functions. A pure function is a function that adheres to the following rules:

1) The return value of a pure function should only depend on the values provided as arguments. It doesn't rely on values from somewhere else in the program.

2) There are no side-effects. A pure function doesn't change any values or data elsewhere in the program. It only makes non-destructive data transformations and returns new values, rather than altering any of the underlying data.

3) Referential transparency. Given the same arguments, a pure function will always return the same result.

In order to follow these rules, any pure function must have:

- At least one argument; otherwise the return value must depend on something other than the arguments of the function, breaking the first rule
- A return value; otherwise there's no point in the function (unless it has changed something else in the program – in which case, it's broken the "no side-effects" rule).

Pure functions help to make functional programming code more concise and predictable than in other programming styles. Referential transparency makes pure functions easy to test as they can be relied on to return the same values when the same arguments are provided. Another benefit is that any return values can be cached, since they're always the same (see the section on Memoization above). The absence of any side-effects tends to reduce the amounts of bugs that can creep into your code, because there are no surprise dependencies as they only rely on any values provided as arguments.

The following example shows a pure function that writes the string provided as an argument backwards:

```
function reverse(string) {
return string.split('').reverse().join('');
```

```
}
```

The function does not change the actual value of the argument, it just returns another string that happens to be the argument written backwards:

```
const message = 'Hello JavaScript';
reverse(message);
<< 'tpircSavaJ olleH'

message // hasn't changed
<< 'Hello JavaScript'
```

This is an example of a non-destructive data transformation, as the value stored in the variable, `message`, remains the same after it's been passed through the function as an argument.

One point to note is that using `const` to declare variables will help to avoid destructive data transformations. This is because any variables that are assigned to primitive values using `const` cannot be changed (although variables that are assigned to non-primitive objects using `const` can still be mutated, so it's not a complete solution).

Let's take a look at how *not* to write a pure function. The next example shows an impure function that returns the value of adding two values together:

```
let number = 42;
let result = 0;

function impureAdd(x) {
result = number + x;
}

impureAdd(10);
result;
<< 52
```

The function `impureAdd()` is an impure function, as it breaks the rules outlined above. It requires the value, `number`, which is defined outside of the function, it has the side effect of changing the value of result, and it would return a different value if the value of the variable `number` was different.

Here's an example of a pure function that achieves the same result:

```
const number = 42;

function pureAdd(x,y) {
return x + y;
}

result = pureAdd(number,10);
<< 52
```

This function requires the two arguments that it's adding together, so the variable `number` has to be passed to it as an argument. There are no side-effects to this function, it simply returns the result of adding the two numbers together. This return value is then assigned to the variable, `result`, instead of the function updating the value of the variable. This function will also always return the same value given the same inputs.

Functional programming uses pure functions as the building blocks of a program. The functions perform a series of operations without changing the state of any data. Each function forms an abstraction that should perform a single task, while encapsulating the details of its implementation inside the body of the function. This means that a program becomes a sequence of expressions based on the return values of pure functions. The emphasis is placed on using **function composition** to combine pure functions together to complete more complex tasks.

By only performing a single task, pure functions are more flexible, as they can be used as the building blocks for many different situations, rather than be tightly coupled with one particular operation. They also help to make your code more modular, as each function can be improved upon or replaced without interfering with any of the other functions. This makes it easy to replace one function with another to either improve the behavior, modify it slightly, or even change it completely.

As an example, we can use the `square()` function that we created in <u>Chapter 4</u>:

```
function square(x){
return x*x;
}
```

This function can then be used to create a `hypotenuse()` function that returns the length of the hypotenuse of a right-angled triangle,[5] given the lengths of the other two sides as parameters:

```
function hypotenuse(a,b) {
return Math.sqrt(square(a) + square(b));
}

hypotenuse(3,4);
<< 5
```

The `hypotenuse()` function uses the `square()` function to square the numbers, rather than hard coding `a*a` and `b*b` into the function. This means that if we find a more optimal way to square a number, we only have to improve the implementation of the `square()` function. Or if we find an alternative way of calculating the hypotenuse that doesn't rely on squaring numbers (however unlikely that is!), we could just swap the `square()` function for another.

To illustrate the point further, we can create another function called `sum()` that takes an array as an argument as well as a callback. The callback is used to transform the value of each item in the array using the `map()` method. Then the `reduce()` method is used to find the sum of all items in the array:

---

[5] The hypotenuse is the longest side of a right-angled triangle. Its length can be found using the formula $a^2 + b^2 = c^2$, which is commonly known as Pythagoras' Theorem.

```
function sum(array, callback) {
if(callback) {
    array = array.map(callback);
}

    return array.reduce((a,b) => a + b );
}
```

The callback makes the function more flexible as it allows a transformation to be performed on all the numbers in the array before finding the sum. This means it can be used to find the sum of an array of numbers:

```
sum([1,2,3]); // returns 1 + 2 + 3
<< 6
```

Alternatively, we can find the sum after the numbers have been squared by adding the square() function as a callback:

```
sum([1,2,3], square); // returns 1^2 + 2^2 + 3^2
<< 14
```

The sum() function can also be used to create a mean() function that calculates the mean of an array of numbers:

```
function mean(array) {
return sum(array)/array.length;
}

mean([1,2,3];
<< 2
```

We can now use the `sum()`, `square()` and `mean()` functions as the building blocks to build a `variance()` function that calculates the variance[6] of an array of numbers:

```
function variance(array) {
    return sum(array,square)/array.length - square(mean(array))
    }

variance([1,2,3])
<< 0.666666666666667
```

By separating each piece of functionality into individual functions, we're able to compose a more complex function. These functions can also be used to create more functions that require the mean, sum or variance.

Higher-Order Functions

Higher-order functions are functions that accept another function as an argument, or return another function as a result, or both.

Closures are used extensively in higher-order functions as they allow us to create a generic function that can be used to then return more specific functions based on its arguments. This is done by creating a closure around a function's arguments that keeps them "alive" in a return function. For example, consider the following `multiplier()` function:

```
function multiplier(x){
return function(y){
    return x*y;
}
}
```

The `multiplier()` function returns another function that traps the argument x in a closure. This is then available to be used by the returned function.

[6.] The variance is a measure of spread that measures deviation from the mean.

We can now use this generic `multiplier()` function to create more specific functions, as can be seen in the example below:

```
doubler = multiplier(2);
```

This creates a new function called `doubler()`, which multiplies a parameter by the argument that was provided to the `multiplier()` function (which was 2 in this case). The end result is a `doubler()` function that multiplies its argument by two:

```
doubler(10);
<< 20
```

The `multiplier()` function is an example of a higher-order function. This means we can use it to build other, more specific functions by using different arguments. For example, an argument of 3 can be used to create a `tripler()` function that multiplies its arguments by 3:

```
tripler = multiplier(3);

tripler(10);
<< 30
```

This is one of the core tenets of functional programming: it allows generic higher-order functions to be used to return more specific functions based on particular parameters.

Here's another example, where we create a higher-order `power()` function. It returns a second function that calculates values to the power of a given argument. To make this calculation, the second function uses a closure to maintain a reference to the initial argument supplied to the `power()` function:

```
function power(x) {
  return function(power) {
```

```
        return Math.pow(x,power);
    }
}
```

Now we can create some more specific functions that use this higher-order, generic function to build them. For example, we could implement a `twoExp()` function that returns powers of 2, like so:

```
twoExp = power(2);
<< function (power) {
    return Math.pow(x,power);
}

twoExp(5);
<< 32
```

We can also create another function called `tenExp()` that returns powers of 10:

```
tenExp = power(10);
<< function (power) {
    return Math.pow(x,power);
}

tenExp(6);
<< 1000000
```

When a higher-order function returns another function, we can use a neat trick to create an anonymous return function and immediately invoke it with a value instead by using double parentheses. The following example will calculate 3 to the power 5:

```
power(3)(5);
<< 243
```

This works because power(3) returns a function, to which we immediately pass an argument of 5 by adding it in parentheses at the end.

Currying

Currying is a process that involves the partial application of functions. It's named after the logician Haskell Curry[7] — not the spicy food — just like the programming language Haskell is. His work on a paper by Moses Schönfinkel lead to the development of this programming technique.

A function is said to be curried when not all arguments have been supplied to the function, so it returns another function that retains the arguments already provided, and expects the remaining arguments that were omitted when the original function was called. A final result is only returned once all the expected arguments have eventually been provided.

Currying relies on higher-order functions that are able to return partially applied functions. All curried functions are higher-order functions because they return a function, but not all higher-order functions are curried.

The power() function above is an example of a higher-order function that can be curried as it will expects two arguments, but will return another, curried function, if the only one argument is provided.

Currying allows you to turn a single function into a series of functions instead. This is useful if you find that you're frequently calling a function with the same argument. For example, the following multiplier() function is a generic function that returns the product of two numbers that are provided as arguments:

```
function multiplier(x,y) {
    return x * y;
}
```

A basic use of this function could be to calculate a tax rate of 22% on a £400 sale using 0.22 and 400 as arguments:

[7.] http://en.wikipedia.org/wiki/Haskell_Curry

```
const tax = multiplier(0.22,400);
<< 88
```

We could make this function more useful by adding some code at the start that
allows it to be curried so it returns another function if only one argument is
provided:

```
function multiplier(x,y) {
if (y === undefined) {
    return function(z) {
    return x * z;
    }
} else {
    return x * y;
}
}
```

Now, if you found yourself frequently calculating the tax using the same rate of
22%, you could create a new curried function by providing just 0.22 as an
argument:

```
calcTax = multiplier(0.22);
<< function (z){
    return x * z;
}
```

This new function can then be used to calculate the tax, without requiring 0.22
as an argument:

```
calcTax(400);
<< 88
```

By currying the more generic `multiplier()` function, we've created a new, more specific function, `calcTax()`, that is simpler to use.

A General Curry Function

In the last example, we hard-coded the `multiplier()` function so it could be curried. It's possible to use a `curry()` function to take any function and allow it to be partially applied. The curry function is the following:

```
function curry(func,...oldArgs) {
return function(...newArgs) {
    const allArgs = [...oldArgs,...newArgs];
    return func(...allArgs);
}
}
```

This function accepts a function as its first argument, which is stored as `func`. The rest operator is used to collect all the other arguments together as `...oldArgs`. These are the arguments of the function that is the first argument. It then returns a function that accepts some new arguments that are stored in the variable `...newArgs`. These are then lumped together with `...oldArgs` to make `...newArgs` using the spread operator. The return value of this function is obtained by invoking the original function, which is accessed using a closure over `func` and passed the combined arguments `...allArgs`.

Now let's create a generic `divider()` function that returns the result of dividing its two arguments:

```
const divider = (x,y) => x/y;
```

If we test this out, we can see that it does indeed return the quotient [8] of its two arguments:

[8.] The quotient of two numbers is the result obtained by dividing one number by another.

```
divider(10,5);
<< 2
```

We can now use our `curry()` function to create a more specific function that finds the reciprocal[9] of numbers:

```
const reciprocal = curry(divider,1);
```

This creates a new function called `reciprocal()` that is basically the `divider()` function, with the first argument set as 1. If we test it out, we can see that it does indeed find the reciprocal of the argument provided:

```
reciprocal(2);
<< 0.5
```

This example shows how currying uses generic functions as the building blocks for creating more specific functions.

Getting Functional

Advocates of functional programming can be quite partisan about its benefits. But even adopting some of its principles, such as keeping functions as pure as possible, and keeping changes in state to a minimum, will help improve the standard of your programming.

There's a lot more you can learn about functional programming. Find out more by having a look at the numerous articles published on SitePoint[10].

---

9. The reciprocal of a number is the result obtained by dividing one by the number. If you multiply a number by its reciprocal, the answer is always one.
10. https://www.sitepoint.com/tag/functional-js/

Quiz Ninja Project

Our quiz is shaping up nicely, but it's getting a little boring always answering the questions in the same order. Let's use the random() function that we created in this chapter to shake things up a bit. We can use it to make the questions appear at random, rather than just asking them in the order in which they appear in the array. We'll do this by mixing up the array of questions that we select the question from. Because the pop() method always removes the last element in an array, this will mean the question selected will always be selected at random.

Our first task is to add the random() function near the top of main.js:

```
function random(a,b=1) {
 // if only 1 argument is provided, we need to swap the
⮑ values of a and b
if (b === 1) {
    [a,b] = [b,a];
}
return Math.floor((b-a+1) * Math.random()) + a;
}
```

Now we need to create a shuffle() function. This will take an array and change the position of each element. Add the following function declaration underneath the random() function:

```
function shuffle(array) {
for (let i = array.length; i; i--) {
    let j = random(i)-1;
    [array[i - 1], array[j]] = [array[j], array[i - 1]];
}
}
```

This function uses a for loop and iterates *backwards* through the array, selecting a random element to swap each element with. This ensures that the array gets completely shuffled.

Now we have our functions, we can use them to select a question at random. All we need to do is update the `game.ask()` method with an extra line that invokes the `shuffle()` function on the `game.questions` array before we use the `pop()` method to select a question. This can be achieved by updating the `game.ask()` function to the following:

```
ask(name){
    console.log('ask() invoked');
    if(this.questions.length > 0) {
    shuffle(this.questions);
    this.question = this.questions.pop();
  const question = `What is ${this.question.name}'s real
↪ name?`;
    view.render(view.question,question);
}
```

Have a go at playing the game by opening `index.html` in a browser. The `random()` and `shuffle()` functions have made it a bit more interesting to play now that the question appears in a random order:

11-1. Random questions on Quiz Ninja

You can see a live example on CodePen[11].

Chapter Summary

▪ Functions have built-in properties such as `length`, but can have custom properties added.

▪ All functions have `call()` and `apply()` methods that can invoke a function with the value of `this` bound to an object that is provided as an argument.

---

11. https://codepen.io/daz4126/pen/PjRrGB

■ Immediately Invoked Function Expressions or IIFEs are functions that are enclosed in parentheses and followed by double parentheses so they're invoked. They are useful for namespacing variables and setting default values.

■ Functions are able to dynamically redefine themselves in the body of the function, depending on certain conditions.

■ A recursive function will keep invoking itself until a certain condition is met.

■ A callback is a function that's provided as an argument to another function.

■ Callbacks are frequently used in asynchronous programming as part of the event loop. This means that a program can continue to run in a single thread while waiting for another task to be completed.

■ Promises can be used instead of callbacks to deal with multiple asynchronous actions in sequence. They also provide a nicer mechanism for handling errors.

■ Functions that return other functions are known as higher-order functions.

■ A closure is the process of keeping a reference to a variable available outside the scope of the function it was originally defined in.

■ A generator is created by placing an asterisk (*) after the `function` keyword.

■ A generator function will return an iterator object that provides a `next()` method, which returns the next value in a sequence that is defined in the generator function.

■ Functional programming involves breaking processes down into steps that can be applied as a series of functions.

■ Pure functions are functions that don't rely on the state of the code they are called from, have no side-effects, and always give the same result when given the same arguments (referential transparency).

■ Currying or partial application is the process of applying one argument at a time to a function. A new function is returned until all the arguments have been used.

Chapter **12**

Object-Oriented Programming in JavaScript

Object-oriented programming (OOP for short) is a style of programming that involves separating the code into objects that have properties and methods. This approach has the benefit of keeping related pieces of code encapsulated in objects that maintain state throughout the life of the program. The objects can also be reused or easily modified, as required. JavaScript obviously supports objects, as we saw in Chapter 5, so it also supports an object-oriented style of programming. In this chapter, we'll look at what object-oriented programming is and how to implement it in JavaScript.

In this chapter, we'll cover the following topics:

◼ An introduction to OOP

- Constructor functions

- Using classes in JavaScript

- Prototypes

- Public and private methods

- Inheritance

- Creating objects from objects

- Adding methods to built-in objects

- Mixins

- Chaining functions

- This and that

- Borrowing methods from prototypes

- Our project — create questions in an OOP way

Object-Oriented Programming

Object-oriented programming is often used to model representations of objects in the real world. There are three main concepts in OOP: encapsulation, polymorphism and inheritance. I'm going to use my juicer to illustrate how each of these concepts can be applied in a programming environment, since the juicer can be considered an object. It's a wonderful machine that makes fresh juice for me every morning. In many ways, my juicer can be thought of as an object, as it has properties such as speed and capacity, and also has methods or actions it can perform, such as juicing, switching on and switching off.

Encapsulation

When I use my juicer, I put the fruit into the machine, press the "on" button and out comes the juice. I haven't a clue how it does it—only that it makes a very loud noise! This demonstrates the concept of encapsulation: the inner workings are kept hidden inside the object and only the essential functionalities are exposed to the end user, such as the "on" button. In OOP, this involves keeping all the programming logic inside an object and making methods available to implement the functionality, without the outside world needing to know *how* it's done.

Polymorphism

My juicer isn't the only appliance I own that has an "on" button, although the way the on button works is slightly different for each appliance. My juicer also uses the same electrical outlet as other appliances in my kitchen. I can also place various types of fruit into it and it still juices them. These examples demonstrate the concept of polymorphism: the same process can be used for different objects. In OOP, this means various objects can share the same method, but also have the ability to override shared methods with a more specific implementation.

Inheritance

I'd really like the next model up from my juicer, as it can deal with more types of fruit and it's a bit quieter. Even though it has these extra features, I'm sure that inside it uses many of the same parts that my juicer has. This demonstrates the concept of inheritance: taking the features of one object then adding some new features. In OOP, this means we can take an object that already exists and inherit all its properties and methods. We can then improve on its functionality by adding new properties and methods.

Classes

Many object-oriented languages, such as Java and Ruby, are known as **class-based** languages. This is because they use a class to define a blueprint for an object. Objects are then created as an instance of that class, and inherit all the properties and methods of the class. In my juicer example, the `juicer` class would represent the design of the juicer, and each juicer that's made on the production line would be instances of that class.

JavaScript didn't have classes before ES6, and used the concept of using actual objects as the blueprint for creating more objects. This is known as a **prototype-based** language. In the juicer example, this might involve building an actual prototype juicer then using this prototype as the basis for making all the other juicers. The juicers based on the prototype would be able to do everything the prototype could do, with some being able to do even more. Even though ES6 now supports classes, it still uses this prototypal inheritance model in the background.

Constructor Functions

In the objects chapter earlier in the book, we saw it was possible to create new objects using the object literal notation. At the end of the chapter we created a `dice` object:

```
const dice = {
sides: 6,
roll() {
    return Math.floor(this.sides * Math.random() + 1)
}
}
```

An alternative way to create objects is to use a *constructor function*.

This is a function that defines the properties and methods of an object. Here is the `dice` example rewritten as a constructor function:

```
const Dice = function(sides=6){
this.sides = sides;
this.roll = function() {
    return Math.floor(this.sides * Math.random() + 1)
}
}
```

The keyword `this` is used to represent the object that will be returned by the constructor function. In the previous example, we use it to set the `sides` property to the argument that is provided to the constructor function, or 6, if no argument is provided. It also adds a method called `roll()`, which returns a random number from 1 up to the number of sides the dice has.

We can now create an *instance* of the dice constructor function using the `new` operator.

```
const redDice = new Dice();
<< Dice { sides: 6, roll: [Function] }
```

 When Parentheses Aren't Required

The parentheses are not required when instantiating a new object using a constructor function. The following code would also achieve the same result:

```
const redDice = new Dice;
```

The parentheses are required, however, if any default arguments need to be provided.

For example, if we want to create another **Dice** object with four sides, we would have to add 4 as an argument, like so:

```
const whiteDice = new Dice(4);
```

This returns an object that was assigned to the variable `redDice`, which is said to be an instance of the `Dice` constructor function. We can confirm this using the `instanceof` operator:

```
redDice instanceof Dice
<< true
```

Each new object that's created using this function will inherit the properties and methods defined in the function. This means that `redDice` will have a `sides` property and `roll()` method:

```
redDice.sides
<< 6
```

```
redDice.roll()
<< 4
```

Built-In Constructor Functions

JavaScript contains a number of built-in constructor functions such as `Object`, `Array`, and `Function` that can be used to create objects, arrays and functions instead of literals.

The easiest way to create a new object is to use the literal syntax:

```
const literalObject = {};
<< {}
```

It is also possible to use the `Object` constructor function:

```
constructedObject = new Object();
<< {}
```

A literal is still considered to be an instance of the `Object` constructor:

```
literalObject instanceof Object;
<< true
```

Similarly, the easiest way to create an array is to use the literal syntax, like so:

```
const literalArray = [1,2,3];
<< [1, 2, 3]
```

But an alternative is to use the `Array` constructor function:

```
constructedArray = new Array(1,2,3);
<< [1, 2, 3]
```

Array constructor functions exhibit some strange behavior regarding the arguments supplied, however. If only one argument is given, it doesn't create an array with that argument as the first element, as you might expect. It sets the array's `length` property instead, and returns an array full of `undefined`!

```
new Array(5); // you might expect [5]
 << [undefined, undefined, undefined, undefined,
 ↪ undefined]
```

This results in an error being thrown if a floating point decimal number is provided as an argument, because the length of an array must be an integer:

```
new Array(2.5);
<< RangeError: Invalid array length
```

This behavior is another reason why it's recommended to always use literals to create arrays.

ES6 Class Declarations

Before ES6, constructor functions were the only way of achieving class-like behavior in JavaScript.

ES6 introduced the new *class declaration* syntax that does exactly the same thing as a constructor function, but looks much similar to writing a class in a class-based programming language. Here is the dice example again, using a class declaration:

```
class Dice {
    constructor(sides=6) {
    this.sides = sides;
    }

    roll() {
    return Math.floor(this.sides * Math.random() + 1)
    }
}
```

 Capitalizing Constructor Functions

By convention, the names of constructor functions or class declarations are capitalized, which is the convention used for classes in class-based programming languages.

To create an instance of the Dice class, the new operator is again used:

```
const blueDice = new Dice(20);
<< Dice { sides: 20 }
```

The variable `blueDice` now contains an instance of the `Dice` class and behaves in exactly the same way as the `redDice` object:

```
blueDice instanceof Dice
<< true

blueDice.sides
<< 20

blueDice.roll()
<< 13
```

The class declaration syntax works in exactly the same way as the constructor function syntax, because it's actually just syntactic sugar that is implemented in the same way in the background.

The ES6 class declarations are preferable to the constructor function syntax because they are more succinct, easier to read and all code in a class definition is implicitly in strict mode, so doesn't need the `'use strict'` statement. Using ES6 class declarations also avoids a number of pitfalls associated with constructor functions. For example, an error is thrown when trying to call a class constructor without using the `new` operator, whereas doing the same thing with a constructor function can cause a lot of problems that are hard to track down:

```
// Using constructor function - noDice is just set to
↳ undefined without any warning
const noDice = Dice();
noDice
<< undefined

// Using class - an error is thrown
const noDice = Dice();
<< TypeError: Class constructor Dice cannot be invoked
```

```
↪ without 'new'
```

The Constructor Property

All objects have a `constructor` property that returns the constructor function that created it:

```
blueDice.constructor
<< [Function: Dice]
```

When an object literal is used to create a new object, we can see that in the background, the `Object` constructor function is being used:

```
const literalObject = {};
<< {}
literalObject.constructor
<< [Function: Object]
```

We can use the `constructor` property to instantiate a copy of an object, without having to reference the actual constructor function or class declaration directly. For example, if we wanted to make another copy of the `redDice` object, but if the name of its constructor was unknown, we could use the following:

```
const greenDice = new redDice.constructor(10);

greenDice instanceOf Dice
<< true
```

Static Methods

The `static` keyword can be used in class declarations to create a static method. These are sometimes called class methods in other programming languages. A static method is called by the class directly rather than by instances of the class.

For example, the `Dice` class could have a method

```
class Dice {
    constructor(sides=6) {
    this.sides = sides;
    }

    roll() {
    return Math.floor(this.sides * Math.random() + 1)
    }

    static description() {
    return 'A way of choosing random numbers'
    }
}
```

This method is called from the `Dice` class like so:

```
Dice.description()
<< 'A way of choosing random numbers'
```

Static methods are not available to instances of the class. So, in our example, the instances of `Dice` such as `redDice` and `blueDice` cannot call the static `description()` method:

```
redDice.description
<< TypeError: red.description is not a function
```

Prototypal Inheritance

JavaScript uses a prototypal inheritance model. This means that every class has a prototype property that is shared by every instance of the class. So any properties or methods of a class's prototype can be accessed by every object instantiated by that class.

To see how this works, let's create a class for creating ninja turtles:

```
class Turtle {
constructor(name) {
    this.name = name;
    this.weapon = 'hands';
    }
sayHi() {
    return `Hi dude, my name is ${this.name}`;
}
attack(){
return `Feel the power of my ${this.weapon}!`;
}
}
```

This can then be used to create a new turtle instance:

```
const leo = new Turtle('Leonardo');
<< Turtle { name: 'Leonardo' }
```

The variable `leo` points to an instance of the `Turtle` class. It has a `name` property and a `sayHi()` method that references the `name` property:

```
leo.name;
<< 'Leonardo'

leo.sayHi();
```

```
<< 'Hi dude, my name is Leonardo'
```

The Prototype Property

When creating a class, you would normally add any default properties and methods to the class declaration. But what if you want to augment the class with extra methods and properties after it has been created? It turns out that you can still do this using the **prototype** property of the class. This is particularly useful if you don't have access to the class declaration, but still want to add properties and methods to the class.

All classes and constructor functions have a `prototype` property that returns an object:

```
Turtle.prototype;
<< Turtle {}
```

All instances of the the `Turtle` class share all the properties and methods of its prototype. This means they can call any methods of the prototype and access any of its properties. Since the prototype is just an object, we can add new properties by assignment:

```
Turtle.prototype.weapon = 'Hands';
<< 'Hands'
```

We can also add a method to the prototype in a similar way:

```
Turtle.prototype.attack = function(){
return `Feel the power of my ${this.weapon}!`;
}
<< [Function]
```

Now if we create a new `Turtle` instance, we can see that it inherits the `weapon` property and `attack()` method from the `Turtle.prototype` object, as well as receiving the `name` property and `sayHi()` method from the class declaration:

```
const raph = new Turtle('Raphael');

raph.name
<< 'Raphael'

raph.sayHi()
<< 'Hi dude, my name is Raphael'

raph.weapon
<< 'Hands'

raph.attack()
<< 'Feel the power of my Hands!'
```

Notice that there's a reference to `this.weapon` in the prototype `attack()` method, and when the instance calls the `attack()` method, it uses the instance's `weapon` property. This is because `this` in the prototype always refers to the instance that actually calls the method.

Finding Out the Prototype

There are a number of ways to find the prototype of an object. One way is to go via the constructor function's `prototype` property:

```
raph.constructor.prototype;
<< Turtle { attack: [Function], weapon: 'Hands' }
```

Another way is to use the `Object.getPrototypeOf()` method, which takes the object as a parameter:

```
Object.getPrototypeOf(raph);
<< Turtle { attack: [Function], weapon: 'Hands' }
```

Many JavaScript engines also support the non-standard __proto__ property. This is known as dunder proto, which is short for "double underscore proto":

```
raph.__proto__
<< Turtle { attack: [Function], weapon: 'Hands' }
```

The __proto__ property was formalized in ES6 because it was already implemented in most browsers, and many JavaScript libraries already used it. It is not considered part of the official specification, and it's recommended that getPrototypeOf() is used instead.

The __proto__ property can also be used to set the prototype of an object by assignment, but its use has been deprecated in favor of the setPrototypeOf() method.

Every object also has a isPrototypeOf() method that returns a boolean to check if it's the prototype of an instance:

```
Turtle.prototype.isPrototypeOf(raph)
<< true
```

Own Properties and Prototype Properties

In the previous example, the object raph had a name property that it inherited from the class declaration, and a weapon property that it inherited from the prototype property. The object raph has access to both these properties, but the name property is considered to be its *own* property, while the weapon property is inherited from the prototype. Every object has a hasOwnProperty() method that can be used to check if a method is its own property, or is inherited from the prototype:

```
raph.hasOwnProperty('name');
<< true

raph.hasOwnProperty('weapon');
<< false
```

So what's the difference between an object's own properties and prototype properties? Prototype properties are shared by *every* instance of the `Turtle` class. This means they'll all have a `weapon` property, and it will always be the same value. If we create another instance of the `Turtle` class, we'll see that it also inherits a `weapon` property that has the same value of "Hands":

```
const don = new Turtle('Donatello');
<< Turtle { name: 'Donatello' }

don.weapon;
<< 'Hands'
```

Every time an instance of the `Turtle` class queries the `weapon` property, it will return "Hands". This value is the same for all the instances and only exists in one place — as a property of the prototype. This means that it only exists in memory in one place, which is more efficient than each instance having its own value. This is particularly useful for any properties that are the same.

The Prototype Is Live!

The `prototype` object is live, so if a new property or method is added to the prototype, any instances of its class will inherit the new properties and methods automatically, even if that instance has already been created. For example, the `raph` object has a `weapon` property and `attack()` method that are inherited from `Turtle.prototype`. But the `leo` object that was created *before* we added these to the prototype will also have access to them:

```
leo.weapon;
<< 'Hands'
```

```
leo.attack();
<< 'Feel the power of my Hands!'
```

If we now change the value of the prototype's weapon property, this will be reflected in *all* instances of the Turtle class:

```
Turtle.prototype.weapon = 'Feet';
<< 'Feet'

leo.attack();
<< 'Feel the power of my Feet!'

raph.attack();
<< 'Feel the power of my Feet!'

don.attack();
<< 'Feel the power of my Feet!'
```

 Overwriting a Prototype

It is not possible to overwrite the prototype by assigning it to a new object literal if class declarations are used:

```
Turtle.prototype = {}
<< {}
```

Even though it looks like the prototype has been reassigned to an empty object literal, we can see see it hasn't actually changed:

```
Turtle.prototype
<< Turtle { attack: [Function], weapon: 'Feet' }
```

It *is* possible to do this if constructor functions are used, and it can cause a lot of headaches if you accidentally redefine the prototype. This is because any instances that have already been created will retain the properties and methods of the old prototype, but will not receive any of the new properties and methods that are subsequently added to the redefined prototype.

This is another reason why it's recommended to use class declarations instead of constructor functions.

Overwriting Prototype Properties

An object instance can overwrite any properties or methods inherited from its prototype by simply assigning a new value to them. For example, we can give our turtles their own weapon properties:

```
leo.weapon = 'Katana Blades';
<< 'Katana Blades';

raph.weapon = 'Sai';
<< 'Sai'

don.weapon = 'Bo Staff';
<< 'Bo Staff'
```

These properties will now become an "own property" of the instance object:

```
leo
 << Turtle { name: 'Leonardo', weapon: 'Katana Blades'
↪ }
```

Any own properties will take precedence over the same `prototype` property when used in methods:

```
leo.attack();
<< 'Feel the power of my Katana Blades!'
```

When a property or method is called, the JavaScript engine will check to see if an object has its own property or method. If it does, it will use that one; otherwise, it will continue up the prototype chain until it finds a match or reaches the top of the chain.

What Should the Prototype Be Used For?

The prototype can be used to add any new properties and methods after the class has been declared. It should be used to define any properties that will remain the same for every instance of the class. The weapon example was unsuitable because all the turtles use a different weapon (we just used it in the example above to demonstrate overwriting). They do, however, like the same food — pizza! This makes a good candidate for a prototype property, if it wasn't included in the original class declaration:

```
Turtle.prototype.food = 'Pizza';
```

Methods are likely to be the same for all instances of a constructor, so it's fine to add methods to the prototype:

```
Turtle.prototype.eat = function() {
return 'Mmm, this ${this.food} tastes great!';
}
```

 Use With Care When Setting Default Values

Be careful when using the prototype to set default values. They are shallow,[1]

A golden rule to remember is: *Never use arrays or objects as a default value in prototype.*

This is not a problem if arrays or objects are set as default values from within the constructor function in the class declaration.

To summarize, the following points should be considered when using classes and prototypes to create instances:

---

[1] There's more about shallow and deep copies later in the chapter. so any changes to an array or object made by an instance will be reflected in the prototype, and therefore shared between all instances.

■ Create a class declaration that deals with any initialization, shared properties and methods.

■ Any extra methods and properties that need to be augmented to the class declaration after it's been defined can be added to the prototype. These will be added to *all* instances, even those that have already been created.

■ Add any properties or methods that are individual to a particular instance can be augmented using assignment to that object (a mixin could be used to add multiple properties at once, as we'll see later).

■ Be careful when overwriting the prototype completely — the constructor class needs to be reset.

To demonstrate, let's create another `Turtle` instance. Use the class constructor to initialize an instance:

```
const mike = new Turtle('Michelangelo');
```

Verify that the new instance has inherited properties and methods from the prototype:

```
mike.eat();
<< 'Mmm, this Pizza tastes great!'
```

Augment the instance with its own individual `weapon` property:

```
mike.weapon = 'Nunchakus';
<< 'Nunchuks'

mike.attack();
<< 'Feel the power of my Nunchakus!'
```

Totally awesome!

Public and Private Methods

By default, an object's methods are public in JavaScript. Methods and properties are said to be public because they can be queried directly and changed by assignment. The dynamic nature of the language means that an object's properties and methods can be changed after it has been created.

In our Ninja Turtle example, the `name` and `weapon` properties are said to be public, as can be seen if we query their value:

```
raph.weapon
<< 'Sai'
```

This means they can also be changed to any value, using assignment:

```
raph.weapon = 3;
<< 3
```

This is something you may want to avoid if your objects are public facing — giving users or external services too much access to properties and methods could be a recipe for disaster!

Fortunately, we can use the concept of variable scope to keep some properties and methods private inside of a class declaration. This will prevent them from being accessed or changed. Instead, we will provide a getter method to return the values of any private properties.

In the example that follows, the `Turtle()` class has been modified to include a private `_color` property (some of the other properties and methods have also been removed for clarity):

```
class Turtle {
    constructor(name,color) {
    this.name = name;
```

```
    let _color = color;
    this.setColor = color => { return _color = color; }
    this.getColor = () => _color;
    }
}
```

The `_color` property is created as a variable inside the scope of the constructor function inside the class declaration. This makes it impossible to access outside of this scope. The getColor() and setColor() methods are known as *getter and setter methods* and they form a closure over this variable and provide controlled access to the property instead:

```
raph = new Turtle('Raphael','Red');
 << Turtle { name: 'Raphael', setColor: [Function],
↪ getColor: [Function] }

raph.getColor();
<< 'Red'

raph.setColor(4);
<< 4
```

In this example, things don't work much differently than before, except functions are now being used to access and change the private properties. The big change, however, is that now we have full control over the getter and setter methods. This means that any private properties can only be changed in a *controlled* way, so we can stop certain assignments from being made by screening the data before any changes are made to a private property. For example, we could insist that the `color` property is a string:

```
this.setColor = (color) => {
if(typeof color === 'string'){
    return _color = color;
    } else {
    throw new Error('Color must be a string');
```

```
    }
}

raph.setColor(4);
<< Error: Color must be a string
```

Inheritance

The examples we've seen so far have all demonstrated inheritance by inheriting properties and methods from the prototype. But the prototype is just another object, so it also has its own prototype, which in turn has its own prototype... and so on, creating a chain of inheritance.

The Prototype Chain

We can see an example of a prototype chain by looking at the prototype of the raph instance of the Turtle class that we created in the last section, using the Object.getPrototypeOf() method:

```
Object.getPrototypeOf(raph)
<< Turtle {}
```

We can peer further down the prototype chain, but calling the Object.getPrototypeOf() method recursively. This shows us that the prototype of the prototype is an apparently empty object literal, although it's actually an instance of the built-in Object() constructor function (more about this in the next section):

```
Object.getPrototypeOf(Object.getPrototypeOf(raph))
<< {}
```

If we try find the next prototype, we receive null:

```
Object.getPrototypeOf(Object.getPrototypeOf(Object.getPrototy
↳ peOf(raph)))<< null
```

This is the end of the prototype chain for our Turtle instance, and shows that all prototype chains end at the `Object()` constructor function. This can be seen in the diagram below:

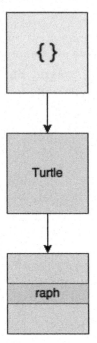

12-1. The prototype chain

The Object Constructor

As we saw in the last example, all objects ultimately inherit from the prototype of the `Object()` constructor function.

When an object calls a method, the JavaScript engine will check to see if the object has that method. If it doesn't, it will check if the object's prototype has the method. If not, it will check whether the prototype's prototype has it. This continues all the way up the prototype chain, until it reaches the prototype of the `Object()` constructor function, from which all objects in JavaScript inherit. If the prototype of `Object()` is without the method, an error will be returned saying the object doesn't exist:

```
raph.makePizza();
<< TypeError: raph.makePizza is not a function
```

But in the prototype chain example, `Object.prototype` was displayed as an empty object, so it has no methods — right? Er, actually, that's not the case.

The prototype of the `Object` constructor function has a large number of methods that are inherited by all objects. The reason why the prototype appears as an empty object literal is because all of its methods are not enumerable.

Enumerable Properties

Properties of objects in JavaScript are said to be *enumerable* or *non-enumerable*. If they aren't enumerable, this means they will not show up when a `for-in` loop is used to loop through an object's properties and methods.

There is a method called `propertyIsEnumerable()` that every object has (because it's a method of `Object.prototype`) that can be used to check if a property is enumerable. We can see in the following example that the `eat()` method we created earlier is enumerable (in fact, all properties and methods that are created by assignment are enumerable):

```
Turtle.prototype.propertyIsEnumerable('eat');
<< true
```

All objects inherit a `toString()` method from `Object.prototype`, but it's not enumerable, so it won't show up in any objects:

```
Object.prototype.propertyIsEnumerable('toString');
<< false
```

In fact, the `propertyIsEnumerable()` method can be used to show that it isn't, itself, enumerable:

```
Object.prototype.propertyIsEnumerable('propertyIsEnumerable')
↪ ;<< false
```

Good practice is for all built-in methods to be non-enumerable, and any user-defined methods to be made enumerable. This is so all the built-in methods don't keep showing up when looking at an object's methods, but user-defined methods are easy to find.

Inheritance Using extends

A class can inherit from another class using the `extends` keyword in a class declaration.

For example, say we decided to start again with our `Turtle` class as:

```
class Turtle {
constructor(name) {
    this.name = name;
    }
sayHi() {
    return `Hi dude, my name is ${this.name}`;
}

swim() {
    return `${this.name} paddles in the water`;
}
}
```

This class declaration is similar to before, and defines properties and methods for a *normal* turtle. In our previous example, we then started adding more specific properties such as weapons that don't really apply to normal turtles, they are for *ninja turtles*. Instead of polluting the Turtle class with these properties, it would be a good idea to create a *sub-class* or *child class* of the Turtle class called ninjaTurtle. This is created in a similar fashion, using a class declaration, but notice the use of the **extends** keyword:

```
class NinjaTurtle extends Turtle {
constructor(name) {
    super(name);
    this.weapon = 'hands';
}
attack() { return `Feel the power of my ${this.weapon}!` }
}
```

Inside the child class declaration, the keyword **super** refers to the parent class, and can be used to access any properties and call any methods of the parent class. In the example above we use it to call the constructor function of the **Turtle** class.

Polymorphism

The concept of polymorphism means that different objects can have the same method, but implement it in different ways. The **Object.prototype** object has a **toString()** method that is shared by all objects. This means every object created in JavaScript will have a **toString()** method. Polymorphism means that objects are able to override this method with a more specific implementation. So although every object has a **toString()** method, the way it's implemented can vary between different objects. For example, calling it on an array object will return each value in a comma-separated string:

```
[1,2,3].toString()
<< '1,2,3'
```

Calling it on a primitive number will return a string containing that number:

```
2..toString; // remember 2 dot operators for integers!
<< '2'
```

Numbers, Strings, and Booleans

The number, string, and boolean primitive types that we met way back in <u>Chapter 2</u> have their own corresponding constructor functions: `Number`, `String`, and `Boolean` respectively.

Rather bizarrely, though, these constructors don't produce primitive values:

```
new Number(2); // the return value looks like a primitive
<< 2;

typeof Number(2); // but it's actually an object!
<< "object"
```

Similarly, primitive values are not instances of these constructor functions:

```
2 instanceof Number;
<< false
```

In fact, the two things are not strictly equal:

```
Number(2) === 2;
<< false
```

Primitives are actually without their own methods. The primitive wrapper objects `Number`, `String`, and `Boolean` are used in the background to provide primitive values with methods. When a method is called on a primitive value, JavaScript creates a wrapper object for the primitive, which converts it into an object and then calls the method on the object. This means it's possible to call methods on primitives, as we saw in Chapter 2:

```
2..toExponential();
<< '2e+0'
```

In the background, something similar to this is happening:

```
new Number(2).toExponential();
<< '2e+0'
```

Even custom objects, such as the Turtle objects we created earlier, have a `toString()` method:

```
raph.toString();
<< '[object Object]'
```

It may convey little information, but it does return a string representation of the object.

The `toString()` method is used by a number of built-in functions in the background. It can be used without fear of causing an error because *every* object has the method, as it's inherited from `Object.prototype`.

One example of a function that uses the `toString()` method is the `console.log()` method. If an object is given as an argument to this method that isn't a string, it will call `toString()` on that object in the background and display the return value in the console. For example, the code:

```
console.log([1,2,3]);
<< [ 1, 2, 3 ]
```

It's often a useful exercise to override the `toString()` method using the prototype, so something more meaningful is displayed. For example, we could edit the `Turtle()` class declaration so it includes a more descriptive `toString()` method:

```
class Turtle {
// other turtle methods here

toString() {
    return `A turtle called ${this.name}`;
}
}

raph.toString();
<< 'A turtle called Raphael'
```

The toString() method is a good demonstration of polymorphism, since different objects have the same method but implement it differently. The advantage of this is that higher-level functions are able to call a single method, even though it may be implemented in various ways.

Adding Methods to Built-in Objects

It is possible to add more methods to the prototype of JavaScript's built-in objects — such as Number, String, and Array — to add more functionality. This practice is known as **monkey-patching**, but it's mostly frowned upon in the JavaScript community, despite it being an incredibly powerful technique[2].

As an example, we can add isOdd() and isEven() methods to the Number wrapper object's prototype. These methods will then be available to number primitives:

```
Number.prototype.isEven = function() {
return this%2 === 0;
}

Number.prototype.isOdd = function() {
return this%2 === 1;
}
```

We can try a few more examples to check that these work:

```
42.isEven();
<< true

765234.isOdd();
<< false
```

[2.] The Ruby programming community, on the other hand, generally embrace monkey-patching, so it is quite common in Ruby code examples.

Arrays are powerful objects, but seem to have some basic methods missing in JavaScript that are found in other languages. We can add a `first()` and `last()` methods that return the first and last items in the array:

```
Array.prototype.first = function() {
return this[0];
}

Array.prototype.last = function() {
return this[this.length -1];
}
```

Again, we can check that these work with a couple of examples:

```
const turtles = ['Leonardo', 'Donatello', 'Michaelangelo',
↪ 'Raphael'];

turtles.first();
<< 'Leonardo'

turtles.last();
<< 'Raphael'
```

Another useful method that arrays lack is a decent `delete()` method. There is the `delete` operator that we met in Chapter 3, but the way this works is not very intuitive as it leaves a value of `null` in place of the item that's removed. In that chapter, we saw that it's possible to remove an item completely from an array using the `splice()` method. We can use this to create a new method called `delete()` that removes an item from the array at the index provided:

```
Array.prototype.delete = function(i) {
return self.splice(i,1);
}
```

A useful example of monkey-patching is to add support for methods that are part of the specification, but not supported natively in some browsers. An example is the `trim()` method, which is a method of `String.prototype`, so all strings should inherit it. It removes all whitespace from the beginning and the end of strings, but unfortunately this method is not implemented in Internet Explorer version 8 or below. This can be rectified using this polyfill code that will use the built in `String.prototype.trim` if it exists, and if it doesn't, it monkey-patches the `String` prototype with the function provided (this is because of lazy evaluation when using the || operator):

```
String.prototype.trim = String.prototype.trim || function()
↳ {
return this.replace(/^\s+|\s+$/,'');
}


' hello '.trim();
<< 'hello'
```

While monkey-patching built-in objects can seem a good way to add extra or missing functionality, it can also add unexpected behavior. The current consensus in the JS community is that this shouldn't be done, so you should avoid monkey-patching any of the built-in object constructor prototypes, unless you have a very good reason. Further problems could occur if the method you've added is then implemented natively in the language.

If you do decide to do it, the suggested way is to check for built-in methods first then try to mimic the built-in functionality from the specification, like in the `trim()` polyfill shown above. This can still be problematic, though, if the specification changes and is different from your implementation. Remember also that you can never guarantee a method won't be implemented at some point in the future.

You can read more about monkey-patching on SitePoint[3].

[3.] https://www.sitepoint.com/pragmatic-monkey-patching/

An alternative way to avoid causing problems is to use extends to subclass a built class and create your own class. For example, you could create your own array class by extending the built in array class, like so:

```
class myArray extends Array {
constructor(...args){
    super(...args);
    }
delete(i) {
    return this.splice(i,1);
    }
}
```

To create one of your new array objects, use the new keyword:

```
const list = new myArray(1,2,3);
            << myArray [ 1,2,3 ]
```

Now we can check that our delete() method works:

```
list.delete(1);
myArray [ 2 ]

list
<< myArray [ 1, 3 ]
```

An obvious problem with this is that you would have to use this more unwieldy syntax instead of array literals, although it has the advantage of not interfering with the built-in array class at all.

Property Attributes and Descriptors

We've already seen that all objects are collections of key-value paired properties. It turns out that each property has a number of attributes that provide information about the property. These attributes are stored in a property descriptor, which is an object that contains values of each attribute.

All object properties have the following attributes stored in a property descriptor:

- `value` — This is the value of the property and is `undefined` by default

- `writable` — This boolean value shows whether a property can be changed or not, and is false by default

- `enumerable` — this boolean value shows whether a property will show up when the object is displayed in a `for in` loop, and is `false` by default

- `configurable` — this boolean value shows whether you can delete a property or change any of its attributes, and is `false` by default.

So far, we've just set properties by assignment, which only allows you to set the `value` attribute of the property. It's also possible to set each of the property attributes by using a property descriptor. For example, consider the following object, which has the single property of `name`:

```
const me = { name: 'DAZ' };
```

The property descriptor for the `name` property might look like this:

```
{ value: 'DAZ', writable: true, enumerable: true,
↳ configurable: true }
```

We've already seen how to add more properties by assignment:

```
me.age = 21;
<< 21
```

The disadvantage with this is that it can only be used to set the `value` attribute of the property. In this case the `value` attribute of the `age` property has been set (rather optimistically) as 21. But it's not possible to set the `writable`, `enumerable`, and `configurable` attributes in this manner. These will be set as `true` when an assignment is made. Note that these are the exact opposite of the default values for those attributes.

Getting and Setting Property Descriptors

The `Object()` constructor function has a number of methods for getting and defining property descriptors. We can see these values using the `Object.getOwnPropertyDescriptor()` method:

```
Object.getOwnPropertyDescriptor(me,'name');
<< { value: 'DAZ',
writable: true,
enumerable: true,
configurable: true }
```

Instead of using assignment, we can add properties to an object using the `Object.defineProperty()` method. This provides more fine-grained control when adding new properties, as it allows each attribute to be set. The first argument is the object to which you want to add the property, followed by a property descriptor containing the attributes you want to set. Any attributes left out will take the default values:

```
 Object.defineProperty(me, 'eyeColor', { value: 'blue',
↳ writable: false, enumerable: true });
<< { name: 'DAZ', age: 21, eyeColor: 'blue' }
```

As you can see, the object is returned with the new property added. The example above has created a property called **eyeColor** that is effectively read-only (because the`writable`> attribute was set to false). If we try to change it by assignment, it will look as if it has changed:

```
me.eyeColor = 'purple'
<< 'purple'
```

But in reality, it hasn't:

```
me.eyeColor
<< 'blue'
```

Getters and Setters

An object property descriptor can have `get()` and `set()` methods instead of a value attribute. All objects must have one or the other, they can't have both. The `get()` and `set()` methods can be used to control how a property is set using assignment and the value that is returned when a property is queried.

They are particularly useful if a property relies on the value of another property.

For example, if we add `age` and `retirementAge` properties to the `me` object, we can then create a `yearsToRetirement` property that depends on these properties:

```
me.age = 21;
me.retirementAge = 65;

Object.defineProperty(me, 'yearsToRetirement',{
get() {
if(this.age > this.retirementAge) { return 0; }
else { return this.retirementAge - this.age; }
},
set(value) {
this.age = this.retirementAge - value;
return value;
}
});
```

The getter bases the `yearsToRetirement` property on the `age` and `retirementAge` properties, so returns the relevant value when queried:

```
me.yearsToRetirement
<< 44
```

The setter also allows the age to be changed by setting the `yearsToRetirement` property:

```
me.yearsToRetirement = 10;
<< 10

me.age
<< 55
```

These getter and setter methods allow much more fine-grained control over how assignment works. It also means we can change the way assignment works, and use the `get()` method to return anything we like, regardless of what value was set using assignment. For example, we could change the property to the following in a bid to stay forever young:

```
Object.defineProperty(me, 'age', {
    get() {
    return 21;
    },
    set(value) {
    return value;
    }
});
```

If we test this out, we can see that querying the property always returns 21, despite it appearing to be assigned to different values:

```
me.age = 30;
<< 30

me.age
<< 21
```

The **get** and **set** property descriptors are particularly useful for controlling the getting and setting of properties in classes.

The next example shows how we can create a `Dice` class that uses a **get** function that will return a description of the number of sides, rather than just the actual number, and a **set** function that prohibits a non-positive number of sides to be set:

```
class Dice {
constructor(sides=6){
    Object.defineProperty(this, 'sides', {
        get() {
        return `This dice has ${sides} sides`;
        },
        set(value) {
        if(value > 0) {
            sides = value;
            return sides;
        } else {
            throw new Error('The number of sides must be
positive');
        }
        }
    });

    this.roll = function() {
        return Math.floor(sides * Math.random() + 1)
    }
    }
}
```

The number of sides can now be assigned in the usual way, but it will act a little differently:

```
const yellowDice = new Dice;

yellowDice.sides
<< "This dice has 6 sides"

yellowDice.sides = 10;
<< 10

yellowDice.sides
<< "This dice has 10 sides"

yellowDice.sides = 0;
<< Error: "The number of sides must be positive"
```

These getter and setter methods give you much more power in controlling the way property assignment works. However, they should be used sparingly and with care, as changing the expected behavior of an assignment has the potential to cause a lot of confusion.

Creating Objects from Other Objects

It's possible to avoid using classes altogether, and create new objects based on another object that acts as a blueprint or prototype instead.

The Object() constructor function has a method called create that can be used to create a new object that is an exact copy of the object that is provided as an argument. The object that is provided as the argument acts as the prototype for the new object.

For example, we can create a Human object that will form the basis for other Human objects. This is simply created as an object literal:

```
const Human = {
arms: 2,
legs: 2,
walk() { console.log('Walking'); }
}
```

This will act as the prototype for all other Human objects. Its name is capitalized as it acts in a similar way to a class in class-based programming languages, and it's only used to create Human objects. It should follow the same rules for prototypes that we saw earlier — it will contain all the methods that Human objects have, as well as any properties that won't change very often. In this case, the properties are arms and legs, and the method is walk().

We can create an instance of Human using the Object.create() method:

```
const lois = Object.create(Human);
```

This will create a new object that inherits all the properties and methods from the Human object:

```
lois.arms
<< 2

lois.legs
<< 2

lois.walk()
<< Walking
```

This is because the Human object is the prototype of the lois object:

```
Human.isPrototypeOf(lois);
<< true
```

Extra properties can then be added to each instance using assignment:

```
lois.name = 'Lois Lane';
<< 'Lois Lane'

lois.job = 'Reporter';
<< 'Reporter'
```

An alternative way is to add a second argument to the `Object.create()` method containing properties that are to be added to the new object:

```
const jimmy = Object.create(Human, { name: { value: 'Jimmy
↪ Olsen', enumerable: true }, job: { value: 'Photographer',
↪ enumerable: true } });
```

This method is a little unwieldy as the properties have to be added using property descriptors, making the syntax awkward and overly verbose. It's often easier to create the object, then add each new property one by one. This can be made quicker using the `mixin()` function that is covered later.

The Human Object Is a Prototype

The `Human` object will be the prototype for any objects created using it as an argument and remember that prototypes are live. This means that any changes made to the `Human` object will be reflected in all the objects created this way.

Object-Based Inheritance

The `Human` object can also act like a 'super-class', and become the prototype of another object called `Superhuman`. This will have all the properties and methods that the `Human` object has, but with some extra methods:

```
const Superhuman = Object.create(Human);

Superhuman.change = function() {
```

```
 return `${this.realName} goes into a phone box and comes out
↳ as ${this.name}!`;
};
```

This method relies on the `name` and `realName` properties. It can be a good idea to create default values in the prototype so the method will still work. In this case, we can use names that prompt some real data to be added:

```
Superhuman.name = 'Name Needed';
<< 'Name Needed'

Superhuman.realName = 'Real Name Needed';
<< 'Real Name Needed'
```

Now we can use the `Superhuman` object as a prototype to create more objects based on it:

```
const superman = Object.create(Superhuman);
```

Once a `Superhuman` object has been created, we can overwrite the default properties by assignment:

```
superman.name = 'Superman';
superman.realName = 'Clark Kent';
```

Now we can see that it has inherited the `change()` method from the `Superhuman` object:

```
superman.change()
  << Clark Kent goes into a phone box and comes out as
↳ Superman!
```

This method of adding custom properties is certainly more long-winded than using a constructor function, where the initial values are passed as an argument to the constructor function. This can be fixed by adding a `init()` method to the `Superhuman` object that accepts initialization properties:

```
Superhuman.init = function(name,realName){
this.name = name;
this.realName = realName;
  this.init = undefined; // this line removes the init
↪ function, so it can only be called once
return this;
}
```

Now a new object can easily be created and initialized:

```
const batman = Object.create(Superhuman);
batman.init('Batman','Bruce Wayne');

batman.change();
 << 'Bruce Wayne goes into a phone box and comes out as
↪ Batman!'
```

A new object can also be created and initialized in a single line by adding the call to the `init()` method at the end of the line that creates the object. This is an example of *chaining* (a technique that will be explained in more detail later in the chapter):

```
 const aquaman = Object.create(Superhuman).init('Aquaman',
↪ 'Arthur Curry');

aquaman.change();
 << 'Arthur Curry goes into a phone box and comes out
↪ as Aquaman!'
```

Object Prototype Chain

Creating objects from objects will create a prototype chain.

Every time a new object is created using the `Object.create()` method, the new object inherits all the properties and methods from the parent object, which becomes the new object's prototype. For example, we can see that the prototype of the `superman` object is the `Superhuman` object using this code:

```
Superhuman.isPrototypeOf(superman);
<< true
```

And we can also see that the prototype of the `Superhuman` object is the `Human` object:

```
Human.isPrototypeOf(Superhuman);
<< true
```

Additionally, we can verify that the `Superhuman` object is the prototype of any other objects created using it:

```
Superhuman.isPrototypeOf(batman);
<< true
```

 The `instanceof` Operator Won't Work Here

The **instanceof** operator will not work when objects have been created this way. It only works when using constructor functions to create objects.

This produces the chain of inheritance shown in the diagram below:

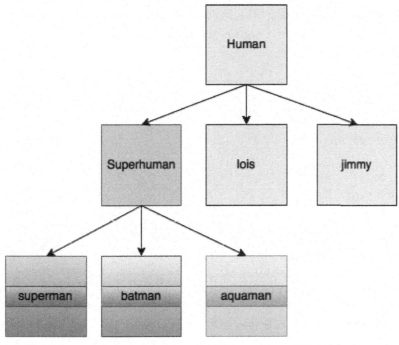

12-2. The prototype chain

Because of this chain, the superman object has all the properties and methods of the Human and Superhuman objects:

```
superman.walk();
<< Walking

superman.change();
 << 'Clark Kent goes into a phone box and comes out as
↳ Superman!'
```

Mixins

A mixin is a way of adding properties and methods of some objects to another object without using inheritance. It allows more complex objects to be created by 'mixing' basic objects together.

Basic mixin functionality is provided by the `Object.assign()` method. This will assign to the object provided as the first argument all of the properties from any objects provided as further arguments:

```
const a = {};

const b = { name: 'JavaScript' };

Object.assign(a,b);
<< { name: 'JavaScript' }

a.name
<< 'JavaScript'
```

There is a problem with this method, however. If any of the properties being mixed in are arrays or nested objects, only a shallow copy is made, which can cause a variety of issues (see note).

Copying By Reference

When objects are copied by assignment, they are only copied by reference. This means that another object is not actually created in memory; the new reference will just point to the old object. Any changes that are made to either objects will affect both of them. Arrays and functions are objects, so whenever they're copied by assignment they will just point to the same object. And when one changes, they all change. This is known as making a shallow copy of an object. A deep or hard copy will create a completely new object that has all the same properties as the old object. The difference is that when a hard copy is changed, the original remains the same. But when a shallow copy is changed, the original changes too.

This affects our mixin function when we try to copy a property that is an array or object, as can be seen in this example:

```
const a = {};
const b = { numbers: [1,2,3] };

Object.assign(a,b);
<< { numbers: [1,2,3] }
```

a now has a reference to the numbers property in the b object, rather than its own copy. Any changes made to either object will affect them both:

```
b.numbers.push(4);
<< 4

b.numbers
<< [1,2,3,4]

a.numbers // This has also changed
<< [1,2,3,4]
```

To avoid only a shallow copy, we're going to create our own mixin() function that will assign all properties of an object to another object as a *deep* copy.

This means that *every* object will inherit this method and be able to use it to augment itself with the properties and methods from other objects.

```
function mixin(target,...objects) {
    for (const object of objects) {
    if(typeof object === 'object') {
        for (const key of Object.keys(object)) {
            if (typeof object[key] === 'object') {
            target[key] = Array.isArray(object[key]) ? [] : {};
            mixin(target[key],object[key]);
            } else {
            Object.assign(target,object);
            }
        }
        }
    }
    return target;
}
```

This code looks very complicated at first glance, so let's dive into it and see what's happening.

The first parameter is the object that we are applying the mixin to. The second parameter uses the rest parameter `...objects` to allow multiple objects to be "mixed in" at once. These will be available in the function as an array called `objects`.

We then use a `for-of` loop to iterate through each object in this array.

Next we iterate through each property in the object using the `Object.keys()` iterable.

The next line is the important part that ensures a deep copy. The problematic properties that are not deep copied are arrays and objects. Both of these return `object` when the `typeof` operator is used. If that is the case, we need to do something different than just use `Object.assign()` to copy the property.

If the property is an object, we use a ternary operator to check whether it is an array or an object using the `Array.isArray()` method. If it is an array, then its constructor function will be `Array`. We create a new array literal, otherwise we create a new object literal.

Then we apply the `mixin` method recursively to add each property one at a time to the literal that was just created, instead of just using assignment.

And finally, the `else` statement states that `Object.assign` should still be used for any properties that are not arrays or objects because a shallow copy will work fine for those.

Let's test this to see if it makes a deep copy:

```
const a = {}, b = { foo: 'bar' }, c = { numbers: [1,2,3] };

mixin(a,b,c);
<< { foo: 'bar', numbers: [ 1, 2, 3 ] }

c.numbers.push(4);
<< 4

a.numbers
<< [ 1, 2, 3 ]

c.numbers
<< [ 1, 2, 3, 4]
```

It works as expected — all the properties from the objects b and c are mixed into the object a, and the array numbers is not copied by reference — any changes to it only affect the object they are acted on.

The `mixin()` function is a particularly powerful way of dealing with objects, and has a number of uses.

Using Mixins to Add Properties

One use for the `mixin()` function is to add a large number of properties to an object all at once. For example, we can instantiate a new `Superhuman` object, then add all its individual properties in one go, instead of one at a time, as we did earlier, while avoiding having to use the more verbose property descriptor notation:

```
const wonderWoman = Object.create(Superhuman);
```

Instead of assigning each property, one at a time:

```
wonderWoman.name = 'Wonder Woman';
<< 'Wonder Woman'

wonderWoman.realName = 'Diana Prince';
<< 'Diana Prince'
```

We can just mix in an object literal and add both properties at once:

```
 mixin(wonderWoman,{ name: 'Wonder Woman', realName: 'Diana
↪ Prince' });

wonderWoman.change()
 << 'Diana Prince goes into a phone box and comes out
↪ as Wonder Woman'
```

Using Mixins to Create a copy() Function

Another use of the `mixin()` function is to create a `copy()` method that can be used to make an exact, deep copy of an object:

```
function copy(target) {
 const object =
↪ Object.create(Object.getPrototypeOf(target));
    mixin(object,target);
    return object;
}
```

The copy function also takes a parameter called `target`, which is the object to be copied. The first thing we do is create a new object based on the prototype of the object that we are copying.

The `mixin()` function is then used to add all the properties and methods of the object to this new object, effectively making an exact copy of itself.

We can now use this function to make exact copies of objects, as demonstrated below with a clone of the `superman` object:

```
const bizarro = copy(superman);

bizarro.name = 'Bizarro';
<< 'Bizarro';

bizarro.realName = 'Subject B-0';
<< 'Subject B-0'

bizarro.change()
  << 'Subject B-0 goes into a phone box and comes out as
↪ Bizzaro!'
```

Note that this is a deep copy and isn't copied by reference, so any subsequent changes to the `superman` or `bizarro` objects will not affect the other.

Factory Functions

Our `copy()` function can now be used to create a *factory function* for superheroes. A factory function is a function that can be used to return an object.

Our factory function will be based on the `Superhuman` object:

```
function createSuperhuman(...mixins) {
const object = copy(Superhuman);
return mixin(object,...mixins);
}
```

This uses our `copy()` function to make a copy of the `Superhuman` object, then uses the `mixin()` function to augment any properties and methods of any objects that are provided as arguments. These properties and methods overwrite any default properties of the `superHuman` object. This allows us to provide an initialization object literal as an argument:

```
const hulk = createSuperhuman({name: 'Hulk', realName:
↳ 'Bruce Banner'});

hulk.change()
<< 'Bruce Banner goes into a phone box and comes out
↳ as Hulk!'
```

The `createSuperhuman()` function is an example of a factory function that can now be used to create as many superhuman objects as required.

Using the Mixin Function to Add Modular Functionality

Inheritance allows us to add functionality to objects by inheriting properties and methods from other objects. While this is useful, it can be undesirable to create a chain of inheritance — sometimes we just want to add properties and methods without linking the two objects together. The `mixin()` function lets us encapsulate properties and methods in an object, then add them to other objects without the overhead of an inheritance chain being created.

One way to think about the difference between prototypal inheritance and inheritance from mixin objects is to consider whether an object *is* something or whether it *has* something. For example, a tank *is a* vehicle, so it might inherit from a `Vehicle` prototype. The tank also *has a* gun, so this functionality could be added using a `gun` mixin object. This gives us extra flexibility, since other objects might also use a gun, but not be a vehicle, such as a `soldier` object, for example. The `soldier` object might inherit from a `Human` prototype and also have the `gun` mixin.

We can use this idea to add superpowers to our superhero objects used earlier. All the superheroes are super human, so they inherited any common traits from a

Superhuman prototype. But they also have superpowers, and each superhero has a different mix of powers. This is a perfect use case for mixin objects: we can create some superpower mixin objects that can then be added to any of our superhero objects as required.

Here are some examples of superpowered mixin objects:

```
const flight = {
fly() {
 console.log(`Up, up and away! ${this.name} soars through the
↳ air!`);
    return this;
}
}

const superSpeed = {
move() {
 console.log(`${this.name} can move faster than a speeding
↳ bullet!`);
    return this;
}
}

const xRayVision = {
xray() {
    console.log(`${this.name} can see right through you!`);
    return this;
}
}
```

 Returning this

Each of the mixins above has a return value of **this** — you'll see why a littler later
in the chapter!

Now we can add the relevant superpowers to each object in a modular fashion
using the `mixin()` function:

```
mixin(superman,flight,superSpeed,xRayVision);

mixin(wonderwoman,flight,superSpeed);
```

Now we can see they have gained some extra methods:

```
superman.xray();
<< 'Superman can see right through you!'

wonderWoman.fly();
 << 'Up, up and away! Wonder Woman soars through the
↳ air!'
```

We can also add the mixins as an argument to the `createSuperhero()` factory function that we made earlier to create a superhero object with all the relevant methods from the start:

```
 const flash = createSuperhuman({ name: 'Flash', realName:
↳ 'Barry Allen' }, superSpeed);
```

In one assignment we have created a superhero object that's inherited all the default properties from the `Superhuman` object, has the correct name details and any relevant powers:

```
flash.change()
 << 'Barry Allen goes into a phone box and comes out as
↳ Flash!'

flash.move()
<< Flash can move faster than a speeding bullet!
```

Chaining Functions

If a method returns `this`, its methods can be chained together to form a sequence of method calls that are called one after the other. For example, the `superman` object can call all three of the superpower methods at once:

```
superman.fly().move().xray();
<<  Up, up and away! Superman soars through the air!
    Superman can move faster than a speeding bullet!
    Superman can see right through you!
```

This is a technique that is commonly used by a number of JavaScript libraries, most notably jQuery. It helps to make code more concise by keeping multiple method calls on the same line, and with some clever method naming it can make the calls read almost like a sentence; the Jest testing library that we used in Chapter 10 makes use of this.

A big drawback with this technique is that it can make code more difficult to debug. If an error is reported as occurring on a particular line, there is no way of knowing which method caused the error, since there are multiple method calls on that line.

It's worth keeping in mind that if a method lacks a meaningful return value, it might as well return `this` so that chaining is possible.

Binding `this`

We saw earlier that the value of `this` points to the object calling a method. It allows us to create generalized methods that refer to properties specific to a particular object. Be aware of a certain problem when a function is nested inside another function, which can often happen when using methods in objects, especially ones that accept callback functions. The problem is that the value of `this` loses its scope, and points to the global object inside a nested function, as can be seen in this example:

```
superman.friends = [batman,wonderWoman,aquaman]

superman.findFriends = function(){
this.friends.forEach(function(friend) {
    console.log(`${friend.name} is friends with ${this.name}`);
}
);
}

superman.findFriends()
<<  Batman is friends with undefined
    Wonder Woman is friends with undefined
    Aquaman is friends with undefined
```

The `findFriends()` method fails to produce the expected output because `this.name` is actually referencing the `name` property of the global `window` object, which has the value of `undefined`.

There are a couple of solutions to this problem.

Use `that = this`

A common solution is to set the variable `that` to equal `this` *before* the nested function, and refer to `that` in the nested function instead of `this`. Here is the example again, using `that`:

```
superman.findFriends = function(){
const that = this;
this.friends.forEach(function(friend) {
    console.log(`${friend.name} is friends with ${that.name}`);
}
);
}

superman.findFriends();
<<  Batman is friends with Superman
    Wonder Woman is friends with Superman
```

```
    Aquaman is friends with Superman
```

You might also see `self` or `_this` used to maintain scope in the same way.

Use `bind(this)`

The `bind()` method is a method for all functions and is used to set the value of `this` in the function. If `this` is provided as an argument to `bind()` while it's still in scope, any reference to `this` inside the nested function will be bound to the object calling the original method:

```
superman.findFriends = function() {
this.friends.forEach(function(friend) {
    console.log(`${friend.name} is friends with ${this.name}`);
}.bind(this);)
}

superman.findFriends();
<<  Batman is friends with Superman
    Wonder Woman is friends with Superman
    Aquaman is friends with Superman
```

Use `for-of` Instead Of `forEach()`

ES6 introduced the `for-of` syntax for arrays and this does not require a nested function to be used, so `this` remains bound to the `superman` object:

```
superman.findFriends = function() {
for(const friend of this.friends) {
    console.log(`${friend.name} is friends with ${this.name}`);
};
}

superman.findFriends();
<<  Batman is friends with Superman
```

```
    Wonder Woman is friends with Superman
    Aquaman is friends with Superman
```

Use Arrow Functions

Arrow functions were introduced in ES6, and one of the advantages of using them is that they don't have their own `this` context, so `this` remains bound to the original object making the function call:

```
superman.findFriends = function() {
this.friends.forEach((friend) => {
    console.log(`${friend.name} is friends with ${this.name}`);
}
);
}

superman.findFriends();
<<  Batman is friends with Superman
    Wonder Woman is friends with Superman
    Aquaman is friends with Superman
```

For this reason, arrow functions should be used when anonymous functions are required in callbacks (and they require less typing as well!)

Borrowing Methods from Prototypes

It's possible to borrow methods from objects without having to inherit all their properties and methods. This is done by making a reference to the function that you want to borrow (that is, without parentheses so that it isn't invoked).

For example, the `batman` object doesn't have any of the superpower methods that the `superman` object has, but we can create a reference to them that can then be used by another object. For example, we can create a `fly()` function by referencing the `superman` object's `fly` method:

```
const fly = superman.fly;
<<
```

This method can now be called on another object using the `call` method that all functions have, and that we learned about in Chapter 11:

```
fly.call(batman);
<< Up, up and away! Batman soars through the air!
```

Borrowing Array Methods

One of the most common uses of borrowing methods was to borrow methods from arrays in ES5. There are many *array-like* objects in JavaScript, such as the `arguments` object that's available in functions, and the node lists that many of the DOM methods return. These act like arrays but are missing a lot of the methods arrays have — often it would be convenient if they had them.

For example, the `arguments` object can use the `slice()` method from the `Array` constructor's prototype by assigning a variable that points to it:

```
const slice = Array.prototype.slice;
```

This method can then be called on the `arguments` object using the `call()` method:

```
slice.call(arguments, 1, 3);
```

The `call()` method takes the object that the function is to be applied to as its first argument, then the usual arguments come afterwards.

The method can also be borrowed directly from an array literal, like so:

```
[].slice.call(arguments, 1, 3)
```

An array-like object can effectively be turned into an array using the `slice()` method with no arguments:

```
const argumentsArray =
↳ Array.prototype.slice.call(arguments);
```

This will return the `arguments` object as an array (since the `slice()` method returns an array).

Most of these techniques are not needed from ES6 onwards as the `Array.from()` method can be used to turn an array-like object into an array:

```
const argumentsArray = Array.from(arguments);
```

Alternatively, the spread operator can be used to easily turn an array-like object into an array like so:

```
const argumentsArray = [...arguments];
```

You will still see a lot of the "array method borrowing" techniques used in the wild, and transpilers also use these techniques to replicate ES6 functionality.

Composition Over Inheritance

There are a number of benefits to object-oriented programming, but there are also some problems that come with inheritance.

Earlier in the chapter we created a `Turtle` class, then extended that class to create a child class called `ninjaTurtle`. But should the `ninjaTurtle` class be a child of a `Turtle` class or a `Ninja` class? Some languages use multiple inheritance (although JavaScript is not one of them), but this can cause more problems than it solves.

The "Gorilla Banana" problem occurs when you need a method from an object, so you inherit from that object. The name comes from a quote by Joe Armstrong, the creator of the Erlang programming language:

> You wanted a banana but what you got was a gorilla holding the banana and the entire jungle.

The problem he describes is that if an object requires a `banana()` method that belongs to the `Gorilla` class, you have to inherit the whole class to gain access to that method. But as well as the method you wanted, the object also inherits a lot of other properties and methods that are not needed, causing it to become unnecessarily bloated.

A design pattern that seeks to solve these problems is to use "composition over inheritance". This approach advocates creating small objects that describe single tasks or behaviors and using them as the building blocks for more complex objects. This is similar to the idea of pure functions that we discussed in the last chapter. These single-task objects are easier to test and maintain and can be combined together, using a mixin function, to create more complex objects. Composition over inheritance sees objects as building blocks that go together to make other objects rather than classes that are monolithic structures layered on top of each other.

If you do decide to use classes, it's recommended to make them "skinny" — meaning they don't have too many properties and methods. Another good practice when creating classes is to keep inheritance chains short. If you have long lines of inheritance, the objects at the end of these chains will usually end up being bloated with properties and methods they don't need. It also causes problems if any of the objects in the chain need to change, as these changes will also affect other objects in the chain. A good rule of thumb is to only inherit once, keeping the inheritance chain to just two objects makes unpicking any issues far easier.

If you want to use a particular method from a class, but it has lots of properties and methods you don't need, then it would be preferable to just borrow the method instead, as we saw in the last section. So, borrow the banana method from the Gorilla class instead of inheriting the whole Gorilla!

```
banana = Gorilla.prototype.banana;
```

An even better approach would be to move the banana() method into a separate object then add it as a mixin to the Gorilla class, and any other objects that required it.

The author (and general all-round JavaScript genius) Eric Elliot has a lot to say about this[4] that is worth reading.

Quiz Ninja Project

We're going to make a big change to the user interface of the quiz game in this chapter. Instead of using a text input to answer the question, we're going to provide three options that the player can choose from by simply clicking on the answer. This involves making the most changes to our code so far, so let's get started.

The first thing we have to do is update the index.html file to replace the form with an empty <div> element. This will still have an ID of response as it will be where we place the buttons that contain the answers for the player to click on:

```
<div id='response'></div>
```

Then we have to remove the form helper methods in the view object. The view.resetForm() method can be deleted, as well as the call made to it in the view.setup() method. The following code needs removing:

```
resetForm(){
    this.response.answer.value = '';
    this.response.answer.focus();
```

---

4. https://medium.com/javascript-scene/the-two-pillars-of-javascript-ee6f3281e7f3

```
}

// .... inside setup()

this.resetForm();
```

We can also remove this line from the end of main.js as we don't need to hide the form at the start of the game anymore:

```
view.hide(view.response);
```

Next we need to update the ask() function to the following:

```
ask(name){
    console.log('ask() invoked');
    if(this.questions.length > 2) {
    shuffle(this.questions);
    this.question = this.questions.pop();
 const options = [this.questions[0].realName,
↪ this.questions[1].realName, this.question.realName];
    shuffle(options);
 const question = `What is ${this.question.name}'s real
↪ name?`;
    view.render(view.question,question);
    view.render(view.response,view.buttons(options));
    }
    else {
    this.gameOver();
    }
}
```

First of all, this needs to check if the quiz.questions.length property is greater than 2, rather than 0, as we need at least three options in our array of questions in order to ask a question and present three possible answers. Then we shuffle the array of questions and select a question as before.

The next section involves selecting the three options that we will present to the player. These are placed inside an array called `options`. Obviously one of the options has to be the correct answer, which is `this.question.realName`. The other two options are simply the first and second elements in the shuffled array. The fact that we shuffled the array in order to choose a question at random means that the first two elements will also be different every time we select the options. These options now need displaying, so we need to use the `view.render()` method, although we need to use a helper method called `view.buttons()` to create the HTML to be rendered. Add the following code to the `view` object:

```
buttons(array){
 return array.map(value =>
↪ `<button>${value}</button>`).join('');
}
```

This method accepts an array as an argument, then uses the `map()` method to surround each value in the array with an HTML `<button>` tag. It then joins each element of the array together to produce a string of HTML. For example, if the array [`'Clark Kent'` , `'Bruce Wayne'` , `'Diana Prince'`] was provided as an argument to the function, it would return the following string of HTML:

```
 <button>Clark Kent</button> <button>Bruce
↪ Wayne</button> <button>Dianna
↪ Prince</button>
```

This can then be used as an argument for the `view.render()` method to display a list of buttons inside the response `<div>`.

The answer will be submitted when the player clicks on one of these buttons. This means we need to change the event listener to fire on `click` events instead of the `submit` event. Change the code at the bottom of `main.js` to the following:

```
 view.response.addEventListener('click', (event) =>
↪ game.check(event), false);
```

It still calls the `game.check()` method, but only when the player clicks on a button inside the "response' `<div>`.

We'll also have to update the `game.check()` method to take into account that the response from the player comes from clicking on a button rather than submitting a form. Update the function definition so that it looks like the following:

```
check(event){
    console.log('check(event) invoked');
    const response = event.target.textContent;
    const answer = this.question.realName;
    if(response === answer){
    view.render(view.result,'Correct!',{'class':'correct'});
    this.score++;
    view.render(view.score,this.score);
    } else {
  view.render(view.result,`Wrong! The correct answer was
↳ ${answer}`,{'class':'wrong'});
    }
    this.ask();
}
```

We have removed the `event.preventDefault()` line, as this is no longer needed as we are not using a form to submit the answer. We also need to remove the call to `view.resetForm()` at the end of the method. Since we're not using a form, we don't need to reset it. The `response` variable needs to updated to point to the text contained inside the button element, which is stored in `event.target.textContent`. We can then use this to compare the player's response with the actual answer.

Finally, we should probably update the `quiz` object that contains the questions so it includes more questions, as with only three, we can only ask one round before the game ends:

```
const quiz = [
    { name: "Superman",realName: "Clark Kent" },
    { name: "Wonder Woman",realName: "Diana Prince" },
```

```
  { name: "Batman",realName: "Bruce Wayne" },
  { name: "The Hulk",realName: "Bruce Banner" },
  { name: "Spider-man",realName: "Peter Parker" },
  { name: "Cyclops",realName: "Scott Summers" }
    ];
```

You might like to add some extra questions of your own, as it will make the game more interesting to have more than three options!

Have a go at playing the quiz by opening `index.html` in your browser. Providing options that the player can choose from makes the game much easier to play by not requiring any typing:

12-3. Multiple-choice options in the quiz

You can see a live example on CodePen[5].

---

5. https://codepen.io/daz4126/pen/Kqojgj

Chapter Summary

- Object-oriented programming (OOP) is a way of programming that uses objects that encapsulate their own properties and methods.

- The main concepts of OOP are encapsulation, polymorphism and inheritance.

- Constructor functions can be used to create instances of objects.

- ES6 introduced class declarations that use the `class` keyword. These can be used in place of constructor functions.

- Inside a constructor function or class declaration, the keyword `this` refers to the object returned by the function.

- All instances of a class or constructor function inherit all the properties and methods of its prototype.

- The prototype is live, so new properties and methods can be added to existing instances.

- The prototype chain is used to find an available method. If an object lacks a method, JavaScript will check whether its prototype has the method. If not, it will check that function's prototype until it finds the method or reaches the `Object` constructor function.

- Private properties and methods can be created by defining variables using `const` and defining a function inside a constructor function. These can be made public using getter and setter functions.

- Monkey-patching is the process of adding methods to built-in objects by augmenting their prototypes. This should be done with caution as it can cause unexpected behavior in the way built-in objects work.

- A mixin method can be used to add properties and methods from other objects without creating an inheritance chain.

- Methods can be chained together and called in sequence if they return a reference to `this`.

- Polymorphism allows objects to override shared methods with a more specific implementation.

- The value of `this` is not retained inside nested functions, which can cause errors. This can be worked around by using `that = this`, using the `bind(this)` method and using arrow functions.

- Methods can be borrowed from other objects.

- Composition over inheritance is a design pattern where objects are composed from "building-block" objects, rather than inheriting all their properties and methods from a parent class.

In the next chapter, we'll be looking at how to send and receive data using JavaScript.

Chapter **13**

Ajax

Ajax is a technique that allows web pages to communicate asynchronously with a server, and it dynamically updates web pages without reloading. This enables data to be sent and received in the background, as well as portions of a page to be updated in response to user events, while the rest of the program continues to run.

The use of Ajax revolutionized how websites worked, and ushered in a new age of web applications. Web pages were no longer static, but dynamic applications.

In this chapter, we'll cover the following topics:

- Clients and servers

- A brief history of Ajax

■ Communicating with the server using the Fetch API

■ Receiving data with Ajax

■ Sending data with Ajax

■ Form data

■ Our project — obtain questions using Ajax

Clients and Servers

The web of computers known as the internet can be separated into two parts: clients and servers. A client, such as a web browser, will request a resource (usually a web page) from a server, which processes the request and sends back a response to the client.

JavaScript was originally designed as a client-side scripting language, meaning that it ran locally in the browser, adding dynamic features to the web page that was returned from the server. Ajax allows JavaScript to request resources from a server on behalf of the client. The resources requested are usually JSON data or small fragments of text or HTML rather than a whole web page.

Consequently, a server is required when requesting resources using Ajax. Typically this involves using a server-side language, such as PHP, Ruby, Node.js, or .NET to serve the data response following an Ajax request (usually from a back-end database). To practice using Ajax, you can either set up a local development server on your own computer, or request the files from an external website that uses cross-origin resource sharing (CORS) in order to avoid the same-origin policy that browsers enforce. All the examples in this chapter can be run without having to set up a local development server, although it may be worth looking into if you wish to do a lot of Ajax or server-side development.

Same-Origin Policy

The same-origin policy in browsers blocks all requests from a domain that is different from the page making the request. This policy is enforced by all modern browsers and is to stop any malicious JavaScript being run from an external source. The problem is that the APIs of many websites rely on data being transferred across domains.

Cross-origin resource sharing (CORS)[1] is a solution to this problem as it allows resources to be requested from another website outside the original domain. The CORS standard works by using HTTP headers to indicate which domains can receive data. A website can have the necessary information in its headers to allow external sites access to its API data. Most modern browsers support this method and respect the restrictions specified in the headers.

A Brief History of Ajax

When the World Wide Web started, web pages contained static content. Any changes to the content on the page required a full page reload, often resulting in the screen going blank while the new page loaded. Remember, this was back in the 1990s, when dial-up modems were the norm.

In 1999, Microsoft implemented the XMLHTTP ActiveX control in Internet Explorer 5. It was developed initially for the Outlook web client, and allowed data to be sent asynchronously in the background using JavaScript. Other browsers implemented this technique, although it remained a relatively unknown feature, and was rarely used.

Asynchronous loading techniques started to be noticed when Google launched Gmail and Google Maps in 2004 and 2005 respectively. Those web applications used asynchronous loading techniques to enhance the user experience by changing the parts of the page without a full refresh. This gave them a much snappier and responsive quality that felt more like a desktop application.

The term "Ajax" was coined by Jesse James Garrett in 2005 in the article "Ajax: A New Approach to Web Applications,"[2] where he referred to techniques being used by Google in its recent web applications. Ajax was a neat acronym that

---

[1] http://en.wikipedia.org/wiki/Cross-origin_resource_sharing

referred to the different parts of the process being used: Asynchronous JavaScript and XML:

Asynchronous   When a request for data is sent, the program doesn't have to stop and wait for the response. It can carry on running, waiting for an event to fire when a response is received. By using callbacks to manage this, programs are able to run in an efficient way, avoiding lag as data is transferred back and forth.

JavaScript   JavaScript was always considered a front-end language, not used to communicate with the server. Ajax enabled JavaScript to send requests and receive responses from a server, allowing content to be updated in real time.

XML   When the term Ajax was originally coined, XML documents were often used to return data. Many different types of data can be sent, but by far the most commonly used in Ajax nowadays is JSON, which is more lightweight and easier to parse than XML. (Although it has never really taken off, the termAjaj is sometimes used to describe the technique.) JSON also has the advantage of being natively supported in JavaScript, so you can deal with JavaScript objects rather than having to parse XML files using DOM methods.

After the publication of Garrett's article, Ajax use really started to take off. Now users could see new content on web pages without having to refresh the page. Shopping baskets could be updated in the background, partial page content could be loaded seamlessly, and photo galleries could dynamically load images.

Today, it's unusual for Ajax not to be used when a partial web page update is required. The explosion in the use of public APIs also means that Ajax is used more than ever to transport data back and forth between sites.

[2.] https://web.archive.org/web/20080702075113/http://www.adaptivepath.com/ideas/essays/archives/000385.php

APIs

An application programming interface (API) is a collection of methods that allows external access to another program or service. Many websites allow controlled access to their data via public APIs. This means that developers are able to interact with the data and create mashups of third-party services. A weather site, for example, might have an API that provides methods that return information about the weather in a given location, such as temperature, wind speed, and so on. This can then be used to display local weather data on a web page. The information that's returned by APIs is often serialized as JSON. Since the data is being provided by an external site, CORS will have to be enabled in order to access information from an API. Some services may also require authentication in order to access their APIs.

The Fetch API

The XMLHttpRequest object was finally standardized by the WHATWG and W3C as part of the HTML5 specification, despite it originally being implemented by Microsoft many years earlier, and already available in most browsers.

It has since been superseded by the *Fetch API*, which is currently a living standard for requesting and sending data asynchronously across a network. The Fetch API uses promises to avoid callback hell, and also streamlines a number of concepts that had become cumbersome when using the XMLHttpRequest object.

We're going to start by taking a look at how the Fetch API works and the different interfaces that it uses. After this we'll build a page that demonstrates the ideas we've looked at.

Basic Usage

The Fetch API provides a global `fetch()` method that only has one mandatory argument, which is the URL of the resource you wish to fetch. A very basic example would look something like the following piece of code:

```
fetch('https://example.com/data')
.then( // code that handles the response )
```

```
.catch( // code that runs if the server returns an error )
```

As you can see, the `fetch()` method returns a promise that resolves to the response returned from the URL that was provided as an argument. In the example above, the promise will be resolved when a response is received from the URL `https:example.com/data`. Because it's a promise, we can also use a `catch` statement at the end to deal with any errors that may occur.

Response Interface

The Fetch API introduced the Response interface that deals with the object that's returned when the promise is fulfilled. Response objects have a number of properties and methods that allow us to process the response effectively.

For example, each response object has an `ok` property that checks to see if the response is successful. This is based on the HTTP status code[3], which can be accessed using the `status` property. This will usually be 200 if the response was successful, 201 if a resource was created, or 204 when the request is successful but no content is returned. The `ok` property will return `true` if the `status` property is between 200 and 299. We need to manually check if this happens because the promise will only be rejected in the case of a network error, rather than something like a "404 page not found error", which is still considered a successful request in terms of the promise.

This means that we can use an `if` block to check if the request was successful, and throw an error otherwise:

```
const url = 'https:example.com/data';

fetch(url)
.then((response) => {
if(response.ok) {
return response;
}
```

---

[3]. http://en.wikipedia.org/wiki/List_of_HTTP_status_codes

```
throw Error(response.statusText);
})
.then( response => // do something with response )
.catch( error => console.log('There was an error!') )
```

Notice that the error thrown refers to the **statusText** property of the response object and specifies the status message that corresponds to the code returned, for example it might be "Forbidden" for a status code of 403.

Some other properties of the Response object are:

- **headers** – A Headers object (see later section) containing any headers associated with the response
- **url** – A string containing the URL of response
- **redirected** – A boolean value that specifies if the response is the result of a redirect
- **type** – A string value of "basic", "cors", "error" or "opaque". A value of "basic" is used for a response from the same domain. A value of "cors" means the data was received from a valid cross-origin request from a different domain. A value of "opaque" is used for a response received from "no-cors" request from another domain, which means access to the data will be severely restricted. A value of "error" is used when a network error occurs.

The response object also contains a number of methods that return promises that can then be chained together.

Redirects

The **redirect()** method can be used to redirect to another URL. It creates a new promise that resolves to the response from the redirected URL.

Here is an example of how a redirect response promise would be resolved:

```
fetch(url)
  .then( response => response.redirect(newURL)); //
↪ redirects to another URL
```

```
.then( // do something else )
 .catch( error => console.log('There was an error: ',
↪ error))
```

At the present time, there is no support for the `redirect()` method in any browser.

Text Responses

The `text()` method takes a stream of text from the response, reads it to completion and then returns a promise that resolves to a USVSting object that can be treated as a string in JavaScript.

Here is an example of how a text response promise would be resolved:

```
fetch(url)
 .then( response => response.text() ); // transforms the
↪ text stream into a JavaScript string
.then( text => console.log(text) )
 .catch( error => console.log('There was an error: ',
↪ error))
```

In this example, once the promise has been resolved, we use the `string()` method to return a promise that resolves with a string representation of the text that was returned. In the next statement, we take the result of the promise and use `console.log()` to display the text in the console.

File Responses

The `blob()` method is used to read a file of raw data, such as an image or a spreadsheet. Once it has read the whole file, it returns a promise that resolves with a `blob` object.

Here is an example of how a file response promise would be resolved:

```
fetch(url)
  .then( response => response.blob() ); // transforms the
↳ data into a blob object
.then( blob => console.log(blob.type) )
  .catch( error => console.log('There was an error: ',
↳ error))
```

This example is similar to the text example above, but we use the `blob()` method to return a blob object. We then use the `type` property to log the MIME-type to log what type of file we have received.

JSON Responses

JSON is probably the most common format for AJAX responses. The `json()` method is used to deal with these by transforming a stream of JSON data into a promise that resolves to a JavaScript object.

Here is an example of how a JSON response promise would be resolved:

```
fetch(url)
  .then( response => response.json() ); // transforms the
↳ JSON data into a JavaScript object
.then( data => console.log(Object.entries(data)) )
  .catch( error => console.log('There was an error: ',
↳ error))
```

Again, this is very similar to the earlier examples, except this response returns some JSON data that is then resolved as a JavaScript object. This means we can manipulate the object using JavaScript. In the example below, the `Object.entries()` method is used to view the key and value pairs in the returned object.

Creating Response Objects

Although most of the time you will be dealing with a response object that is returned from a request you make, you can also create your own response objects using a constructor function:

```
const response = new Response( 'Hello!', {
ok: true,
status: 200,
statusText: 'OK',
type: 'cors',
url: '/api'
});
```

The first argument is the data that is to be returned (for example a text stream, file or JSON data). The second argument is an object that can be used to provide values for any of the properties listed above.

These can be useful to use if you are creating an API that needs to send a response, or if you need to send a dummy response for testing purposes.

Request Interface

We can get more fine-grained control over the request being made by providing a `Request` object as an argument. This allows a number of options to be set about the request.

Request objects are created using the `Request()` constructor, and include the following properties:

- `url` – The URL of the requested resource (the only property that is required).
- `method` – a string that specifies which HTTP method should be used for the request. By default, this is GET.
- `headers` – This is a `Headers` object (see later section) that provides details of the request's headers.
- `mode` – Allows you to specify if CORS is used or not. CORS is enabled by default.

- **cache** – Allows you to specify how the request will use the browser's cache. For example, you can force it to request a resource and update the cache with the result, or you can force it to only look in the cache for the resource.
- **credentials** – Lets you specify if cookies should be allowed with the request.
- **redirect** – Specifies what to do if the response returns a redirect. There's a choice of three values: "follow" (the redirect is followed), "error" (an error is thrown) or "manual" (the user has to click on a link to follow the redirect).

Hypertext Transfer Protocol

The Web is built upon the Hypertext Transfer Protocol, or HTTP. When a client (usually a browser) makes a request to a server, it contains information about which HTTP verb to use. HTTP verbs, also known as HTTP methods[4] are the what HTTP uses to tell the server what type of request is being made, which then determines the server will deal with the request.

The five most commonly used verbs when dealing with resources on the web are:

- GET requests to retrieve resources

- POST requests, usually used to create a resource but can actually perform any task

- PUT requests to *upsert*, which means insert a resource or update it entirely

- PATCH requests to make partial updates to a resource

- DELETE requests to delete a resources.

By default, a link in a web page will make a GET request. Forms are also submitted using a GET request by default, but they will often use a POST request.

Thre is an excellent blog post[5] by Rob Miller explains each of these verbs in more depth if you're interested in learning more about them.

A constructor function is used to create a new Request object. An example is shown below:

```
const request = new Request('https://example.com/data', {
method: 'GET',
```

[4.] https://developer.mozilla.org/en-US/docs/Web/HTTP/Methods
[5.] https://robm.me.uk/web-development/2013/09/20/http-verbs.html

```
mode: 'cors',
redirect: 'follow',
cache: 'no-cache'
});
```

The `url` property is the first argument, and is required. The second argument is an object made up of any of the other properties listed above.

Once the Request object is assigned to a variable, it can then be used as the parameter of the `fetch()` method:

```
fetch(request)
.then( // do something with the response )
.catch( // handle any errors)
```

Alternatively, you can enter the URL and object directly as arguments of the `fetch()` method, without having to create a Request object:

```
fetch('https://example.com/data', {
    method: 'GET',
    mode: 'cors',
    redirect: 'follow',
    cache: 'no-cache'
})
.then( // do something with the response )
.catch( // handle any errors)
```

Headers Interface

HTTP **headers** are used to pass on any additional information about a request or response. Typical information contained in headers includes the file-type of the resource, cookie information, authentication information and when the resource was last modified.

The Fetch API introduced a `Headers` interface, which can be used to create a Headers object, which can then be added as a property of Request and Response objects.

A new Headers instance is created using a constructor function, as seen in the example below:

```
const headers = new Headers();
```

The constructor function can be provided with an optional argument containing any initial header values:

```
const headers = new Headers({ 'Content-Type': 'text/plain',
↳ 'Accept-Charset' : 'utf-8', 'Accept-Encoding':'gzip,deflate'
↳ })
```

A `Headers` object includes the following properties and methods that can be used to access information about the headers, as well as edit the header information.

`has()` – Can be used to check if the headers object contains the header provided as an argument.

For example:

```
headers.has('Content-Type');
<< true
```

`get()` - Returns the value of the header provided as an argument

For example:

```
headers.get('Content-Type');
<< 'text/plain'
```

set() – Can be used to set a value of an already existing header, or create a new header with the value provided as an argument if it does not already exist.

For example:

```
headers.set('Content-Type', 'application/json');
```

append() – Adds a new header to the headers object.

For example:

```
headers.append('Accept-Encoding','gzip,deflate');
```

delete() – Removes the header provided as an argument.

For example:

```
headers.delete('Accept-Encoding')
```

keys(), values() and entries() – Iterators that can be used to iterate over the headers key, values or entries (key and value pairs).

For example:

```
for(const entry of headers.entries(){
console.log(entry);
}
<< [ 'Content-Type', 'application/json' ]
```

Putting It All Together

We can use the Headers, Request and Response objects to put together a typical example that sets up the URL, Request and Headers before calling the `fetch()` method:

```
const url = 'https:example.com/data';
 const headers = new Headers({ 'Content-Type': 'text/plain',
↪ 'Accept-Charset' : 'utf-8', 'Accept-Encoding':'gzip,deflate'
↪ })

const request = (url,{
headers: headers
})

fetch(request)
.then( function(response) {
if(response.ok) {
return response;
}
throw Error(response.statusText);
})
.then( response => // do something with response )
.catch( error => console.log('There was an error!') )
```

Receiving Information

To demonstrate how to update a web page using Ajax, we'll need to set up a demonstration page. Create a file called `ajax.html` that contains the following code:

```
<!doctype html>
<html lang='en'>
<head>
<meta charset='utf-8'>
<title>Ajax Example</title>
```

```
</head>
<body>
<button id='number'>Number Fact</button>
<button id='chuck'>Chuck Norris Fact</button>
<div id='output'>
    Ajax response will appear here
</div>
<script src='main.js'></script>
</body>
```

This is a standard HTML5 web page that contains two buttons and a `<div>` element. Each button will be used to make a different type of Ajax request. One will request plain text and the other will request a JSON string from an external API. The div with an id of `output` will be where we'll insert the response we receive from the Ajax request.

For our Ajax requests, we'll be using a couple of online APIs. The first is NumbersAPI[6], which returns facts about random numbers as a text string. The second is chucknorris.io[7], which returns a JSON string, containing a random satirical factoid about everybody's favorite hard man, Chuck Norris.

 Not All These "Facts" Are Safe For Work

Some of the "facts" returned by chucknorris.io can be mildly offensive and use inappropriate language, so proceed with caution!

Now we need a JavaScript file. This should be called `main.js` and can be saved in the same directory as the other files. Add the following code to start with:

```
const textButton = document.getElementById('number');
const apiButton = document.getElementById('chuck');
const outputDiv = document.getElementById('output');
```

[6.] http://numbersapi.com/
[7.] https://api.chucknorris.io

This assigns each of the buttons in the HTML file to a variable, so we can refer to them later in the file.

Next, we'll assign some URLs to variables:

```
const textURL = 'http://numbersapi.com/random';
const apiURL = 'https://api.chucknorris.io/jokes/random';
```

And finally, we'll assign an event handler to each button. Let's start with the Number Fact button:

```
textButton.addEventListener('click', () => {
fetch(textURL)
.then( response => {
outputDiv.innerHTML = 'Waiting for response...';
if(response.ok) {
return response;
}
throw Error(response.statusText);
})
.then( response => response.text() )
.then( text => outputDiv.innerText = text )
  .catch( error => console.log('There was an error:',
↪ error))
},false);
```

This uses the format we saw earlier to construct a fetch request. This returns a promise that resolves to a string. We can then place that string inside the <div> with an id of output by assigning it its innerText property.

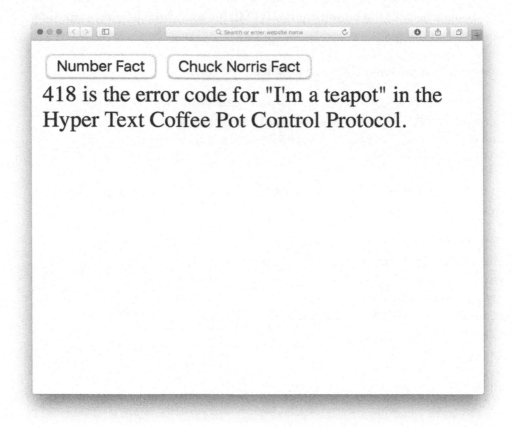

13-1. A number fact

And now for the Chuck Norris Fact button:

```
apiButton.addEventListener('click', () => {
fetch(apiURL)
.then( response => {
outputDiv.innerHTML = 'Waiting for response...';
if(response.ok) {
return response;
}
throw Error(response.statusText);
})
.then( response => response.json() )
.then( data => outputDiv.innerText = data.value )
 .catch( error => console.log('There was an error:',
```

```
↪ error))
},false);
```

This is almost identical to the Number example, except the response returns JSON, so we use the `json()` method to return a promise that resolves as a JavaScript object. This object has a `value` property that contains the Chuck Norris fact, so we insert it into the `<div>` with an id of `output` using `innerText` again.

This example shows how easy it is to request data from a server, then insert it into a web page, although there are some subtle differences depending on what type of data is returned.

Spinners

In the previous example we displayed a message to say we were waiting for a response. It is common for sites to use spinners (or egg timers in the old days!) to indicate that the site is waiting for something to happen. Ajax Load[8] and Preloaders.net[9] are both good resources for creating a spinner graphic for your site.

Let's try this out. Open `ajax.html` in a browser and try pressing each button. You should see a similar sight to the screenshot below:

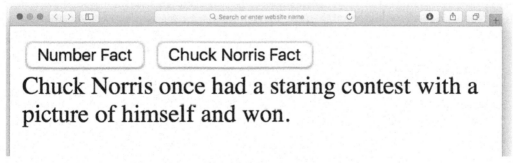

13-2. A Chuck Norris "Fact"

[8.] http://www.ajaxload.info/
[9.] http://preloaders.net/

Sending Information

We can also use Ajax to send information. This can be a variety of formats, but is usually a JSON string.

To illustrate this, we're going to create a very simple To Do list application that sends information about a task to a server in JSON format, then receives a response to confirm that the task has been saved on a server.

Unfortunately, we don't have a database to save our tasks to, so we're going to have to use a dummy site called JSONPlaceholder[10]. This spoofs the process of sending JSON data to a server, then receiving JSON data in response. It has a number of fake APIs that can be used to create fake examples of posts, comments, albums, photos, todos and users. We'll be using the fake todo API.

To get started, create an HTML document called `todo.html` that contains the following code:

```html
<!doctype html>
<html lang='en'>
<head>
<meta charset='utf-8'>
<title>To Do List</title>
</head>
<body>
 <form id='todo'
↪ action='https://jsonplaceholder.typicode.com/todos'
↪ method='POST'>
 <input type='text' name='task'  placeholder='Add Task'
↪ autofocus required>
    <button type='submit'>Add Task</button>
</form>
<script src='main.js'></script>
</body>
</html>
```

[10.] https://jsonplaceholder.typicode.com

This is a simple HTML page that contains a form with a text input element for adding a task, and a button to submit it.

13-3. A simple To-Do List

Next, we need to create a JavaScript file called `main.js` and add the following code:

```
const form = document.forms['todo'];
form.addEventListener('submit', addTask, false);

function addTask(event) {
event.preventDefault();
const number = form.task.value;
const task = {
    userId: 1,
    title: form.task.value,
    completed: false
}
const data = JSON.stringify(task);
const url = 'https://jsonplaceholder.typicode.com/todos';

const headers = new Headers({
    'Accept': 'application/json',
    'Content-Type': 'application/json'
});
const request = new Request(url,
{
method: 'POST',
header: headers,
body: data
}
)
```

```
fetch(request)
.then( response => response.json() )
 .then( task => console.log(`Task saved with an id of
↳ ${task.id}`) )
 .catch( error => console.log('There was an error:',
↳ error))


}
```

This code creates an event listener that first of all prevents the default behavior of the form, so it doesn't get submitted when the Add Task button is clicked. Next it creates a task object with a `title` property that is taken from what was entered in the form. It also has a `completed` property that has a default value of `false`. This object is then transformed into a JSON string using the `JSON.stringify` method and assigned to the variable `data`.

After this, we build the Headers and Request objects. Because we are sending JSON, we need to add headers of `"Accept": 'application/json'` and `'Content-Type': 'application/json'`. Because we are *sending* data, we need to ensure that the `method` property of the request object is `POST` so that a POST request is used to send the data. The most important property of the request object is `body` – this is where the data we want to send is placed. We use the `data` variable here, so that JSON is sent to the server.

Then we use the `fetch()` method to send the request and deal with the response. This creates a promise that resolves to a JSON object, so we use the `json()` method to create another promise that resolves to a JavaScript object. This object has a single property of `id` to mimic successfully saving the task to a database (as this would result in it being assigned an ID by the database).

We can use this to log a message to the console that refers to the `id` property that was returned.

If you open up the `todo.html` file, add a task in the form and then submit it, you should see a message in the console similar to the one below.

```
<< Task saved with an id of 201
```

This fakes the fact that the task has been saved to a database and the relevant data has been returned. In reality, the data hasn't been saved, and the ID property has just been randomly generated for demonstration purposes.

 Not Quite A Realistic Example

If this was a real live site that was saving to an actual database, you would probably expect more data to be returned than just the id, including more information about the task itself, such as a timestamp of when it was created.

Most forms will have an `action` attribute that specifies the URL to use if the form is sent without using Ajax. It will also have a `method` attribute that will specify the HTTP verb to use. These methods are available as properties of the `form` object, so we could use these properties to create a more generalized request object, as follows:

```
const request = new Request(form.action,
{
method: form.method,
header: headers,
body: data
}
)
```

FormData

The Fetch API includes the `FormData` interface, which makes it much easier to submit information in forms using Ajax.

A `FormData` instance is created using a constructor function:

```
const data = new FormData();
```

If a form is passed to this constructor function as an argument, the form data instance will serialize all the data automatically, ready to be sent using Ajax. In our last example, we created the task manually based on the data provided in the form. The `FormData` interface helps to reduce the amount of code needed when submitting forms.

We can use this to cut down the amount of code in `main.js` by changing it to the following:

```
const form = document.forms['todo'];

form.addEventListener('submit', addTask, false);

function addTask(event) {
event.preventDefault();
const task = new FormData(form);
 const url =
↳ `http://echo.jsontest.com/id/1/title/${form.task.value}`;
const headers = new Headers({
    'Accept': 'application/json',
    'Content-Type': 'application/json'
});
const request = new Request(url,
{
method: 'POST',
mode: 'cors',
header: headers,
body: JSON.stringify(task)
}
)

fetch(request)
.then( response => response.json() )
 .then( data => console.log(`${data.title} saved with an
↳ id of ${data.id}`) )
 .catch( error => console.log('There was an error:',
```

```
↪ error))


}
```

In this function, we create a new `FormData` instance using the `FormData()` constructor function and provide the form as an argument. This does all the hard work of creating the task object for us.

It's also possible to add data to the form data instance as key-value pairs using the `append()` method:

```
data = new FormData(); // no form provided as an argument
↪ creates an empty form data instance

data.append('height', 75);
```

The `FormData` interface really comes into its own when a form contains files to upload. This was a notoriously difficult task in the past, often requiring the use of Flash or another third-party browser plugin to handle the upload process. The `FormData` instance will automatically create the necessary settings required, and take care of all the hard work if any file uploads are present in the form.

A Living Standard

The Fetch API is, at the time of writing, what is known as a "living standard", which means that the specification is being developed in the wild . This means that, despite it being available to use, it's still subject to change as developers, browser vendors and end-users provide feedback about how it works. It's an experimental technology, and new features might get added, or the syntax and behavior of some properties and methods might change in the future. Don't let this put you off though – living standards often stay relatively stable, especially once they are implemented in browser engines. The latest versions of most browsers already support it (all, except Internet Explorer, anyway), but you should check the level of support before using it in production. By using it you are helping to develop future standards. Just make sure you keep up-to-date with the current specification.

If you don't want to live on the edge, you could consider using a library to take care of Ajax requests. The advantage of this approach is that the library will take care of any implementation details behind the scenes – it will use the most up-to-date methods, such as the `fetch` API, if it's supported, and fallback on using older methods, if required.

The jQuery library is a good option for this – it has the generic `ajax()` method that can be used in a very similar way to the `fetch()` method. For example, if you want to get the data from the number API, you would use the following code:

```
$.ajax('http://numbersapi.com/random')
.done(text => outputDiv.innerHTML = text );
```

Quiz Ninja Project

We can use Ajax to fetch the questions from a server, instead of keeping them in an object inside our JavaScript file. First of all, we need to remove the array of objects stored in the `quiz` variable at the start of the `main.js` file, and transfer the information into a separate file. This information has been saved in the JSON format on SitePoint's S3 account, and can be found at the following URL (it also contains lots more questions than the three we've been using so far): http://spbooks.github.io/questions.json

To access this JSON data, use the Fetch API. Add the following code to the top of file:

```
const url = 'http://spbooks.github.io/questions.json';

fetch(url)
.then(res => res.json())
.then(quiz => {
 view.start.addEventListener('click', () =>
↳ game.start(quiz.questions), false);
```

```
view.response.addEventListener('click', (event) =>
↳ game.check(event), false);
});
```

First of all we create a variable called `url` to store a reference to the URL. Then we use the Fetch API, which returns a promise. If this is successful, then we use the `json()` method, which returns the data as a JavaScript object. If this is successful, then we register the two event handlers that were initially at the end of the file (those need removing from the end of the file). This means the start button won't work until the data has finished loading.

Everything else in the file stays the same. Keeping the quiz data in a separate file and loading it using Ajax is beneficial as it keeps the question data separate from the actual application logic. It means it's much easier to edit all in one place. It also means we could potentially create lots of different JSON quiz files that could be linked to, enabling a variety of different quizzes to be played.

13-4. Ajaxed Quiz Ninja

You can see a live example on CodePen[11].

Chapter Summary

- Ajax is a technique for sending and receiving data asynchronously in the background.

- The data can be sent in many forms, but it is usually in JSON.

- Ajax can be used for making partial page updates without having to do a full page reload.

[11.] https://codepen.io/daz4126/pen/LLdKby

- Ajax can be used for communicating with external APIs.

- Ajax requests can be made using the Fetch API.

- The Response interface allows you to control the response received from a request or to create your own response objects.

- The Request interface allows you to create a request object that contains information about the request being made, such as the URL and headers.

- The Headers interface allows you to create HTTP headers that can be added to a request or response object.

- Requests can retrieve data using a GET request, or send data using a POST request.

- The FormData interface makes it easier to send data from forms.

In the next chapter, we'll look at some APIs that comprise part of the HTML5 specification, then learn how to implement them.

Chapter **14**

HTML5 APIs

HTML5 is the latest version of the Hypertext Markup Language used to create web pages. The latest iteration is HTML 5.1, which finally became a W3C recommendation in November 2016.

HTML5 was for HTML what ES6 was for JavaScript – it added a large number of new features to the specification. It also went beyond the actual markup language and brought together a number of related technologies such as CSS and JavaScript. We've already seen in Chapter 8 some of the new form elements as well as the validation API that has been introduced. In this chapter, we'll be looking at some of the other APIs that were made available in HTML5 and beyond.

In this chapter, we'll cover the following topics:

- The development of HTML5 and the JavaScript APIs

- The `data-` attribute

- HTML5 APIs—local storage, geolocation, web workers, and multimedia

- Drawing shapes with canvas

- Shims and polyfills — how to make the most of HTML5 APIs, even when they're without browser support

HTML5

The W3C plans to develop future versions of HTML5 much more frequently than previously, using smaller version increments. HTML 5.1 has already become the latest standard, and HTML 5.2 is in development. You can read more about the new features in HTML5.1 and what to expect in HTML 5.2 on SitePoint[1].

The HTML5 specification is separated into modules that allow different features to be developed at different paces then implemented without having to wait for other features to be completed. It also means that when a previously unforeseen development occurs, a new module can be created to cater for it. Modules can be at different stages of maturity, from ideas to full implementation. A useful site that checks to see if a specific feature can be used is Can I Use[2].

You can find out more about the HTML5 standard by reading *Jump Start HTML5* by Tiffany Brown, Kerry Butters, and Sandeep Panda[3].

The `data-` Attribute

The `data-` attribute is a way of embedding data in a web page using custom attributes that are ignored by the browser. They're also private to a page, so are not intended to be used by an external service – their sole purpose is to be used

---

[1.] https://www.sitepoint.com/whats-new-in-html-5-1/

[2.] http://caniuse.com/

[3.] https://www.sitepoint.com/premium/books/jump-start-html5>

by a JavaScript program. This means they're perfect for adding data that can be used as a hook that the program utilizes to access information about a particular element on the page.

The names of these attributes can be decided by the developer, but they must use the following format:

▨ Start with `data-`.

▨ Contain only lowercase letters, numbers, hyphens, dots, colons or underscores.

▨ Include an optional string value.

Examples could be:

```
data-powers = 'flight superSpeed'
data-rating = '5'
data-dropdown
data-user = 'DAZ'
data-max-length = '32'
```

The information contained in the attributes can be used to identify particular elements. For example, all the elements with an attribute of `data-dropdown` could be identified as dropdown menu. The values of the attributes can also be used to filter different elements. For example, we could find all the elements that have a `data-rating` value of 3 or more.

Each element has a `dataset` property that can be used to access any `data-` attributes it contains. Here's an example of some markup:

```
<div id='hero' data-powers='flight superSpeed'>
Superman
</div>
```

The `data-powers` attribute can be accessed using the following code:

```
const superman = document.getElementById('hero');
const powers = superman.dataset.powers;
<< 'flight superSpeed'
```

Notice that the `data-` prefix is dropped. To access the attribute, `powers` is used as if it's a property of the `dataset` object. If a `data-` attribute's name contains hyphens, they are replaced with camel-case notation, so `data-max-length` would be accessed using `dataset.maxLength`.

 Browser Support

The support for the `data-` attribute is generally very good in modern browsers. Even Internet Explorer 8 has partial support! Some older browsers are unable to understand the `dataset` property, however, but any `data-` attribute can be found using the standard `getAttribute` method. So the previous code could be replaced with the following if you still need to support older browsers:

```
const powers = superman.getAttribute('data-powers');
```

The restriction of only using a string value can be overcome by encoding any JavaScript object or value as a JSON string, then performing type-conversion later, as required. For example, the value of `data-max-length` will return a string, but can easily be converted into a number using the following code:

```
const maxLength = Number(element.dataset.maxLength);
```

Data attributes provide a convenient way of adding data directly into the HTML markup, enabling a richer user experience.

HTML5 APIs

The HTML5 specification contains a number of APIs that help to gain access to hardware, such as cameras, batteries, geolocation, and the graphics card.

Hardware evolves quickly, and APIs are frequently introduced to give developers access, and control new features that appear in the latest devices.

In this section, we'll look at some of the more popular APIs that are already supported in most modern browsers. However, due to the ever-changing nature of most APIs, it's still best practice to use feature detection before using any of the API methods.

HTML5 Web Storage

The Web Storage API provides a key-value store on the client's computer that is similar to using cookies but has fewer restrictions, more storage capacity, and is generally easier to use. This makes it perfect for storing information about users, as well as storing application-specific information that can then be used during future sessions.

The Web Storage API has some crucial differences with cookies:

▓ Information stored is *not* shared with the server on every request.

▓ Information is available in multiple windows of the browser (but only if the domain is the same).

▓ Storage capacity limit is much larger than the 4KB limit for cookies[4].

▓ Any data stored does not automatically expire as it does with cookies. This potentially makes cookies a better choice for something like showing a popup once a day.

If a browser supports the Web Storage API, the `window` object will have a property called `localStorage`, which is a native object with a number of properties and methods used to store data. The information is saved in the form of key-value pairs, and the values can only be strings. There is also a `sessionStorage` object that works in the same way, although the data is only saved for the current session.

[4.] There is no actual limit in the specification, but most browsers have a limit set at 5GB per domain.

Here is a basic example of storing information. To save a value locally, use:

```
localStorage.setItem('name', 'Walter White');
```

To illustrate that it's being saved locally, try completely closing your browser, reopening it, and entering the following code in the console:

```
localStorage.getItem('name');
<< "Walter White"
```

Rather than using the getItem() and setItem() methods, assignment can be used instead. In the next example, we simply reference localStorage.name as if it was a variable to change its value:

```
localStorage.name = 'Heisenberg';

console.log(localStorage.name);
<< "Heisenberg";
```

To remove an entry from local storage, use the removeItem method:

```
localStorage.removeItem('name');
```

Alternatively, this can be done using the delete operator:

```
delete localStorage.name;
```

To completely remove everything stored in local storage, use the clear() method:

```
localStorage.clear();
```

Every time a value is saved to local storage, a `storage` event is fired. Note that this event is only fired on any *other* windows or tabs from the same domain, and only if the value of the item being saved changes. The event object sent by the event listener to the callback has a number of properties that provide information about the updated item:

- `key` tells us the key of the item that changed

- `newValue` tells us the new value to which it has been changed

- `oldValue` tells us the previous value before it was changed

- `storageArea` tells us if it is stored in local or session storage.

The code following will add an event listener that logs information about any changes to the Web Storage (note that this example won't work locally as it needs to be running on a server):

```
addEventListener('storage', (event) => {
  console.log(`The ${event.key} was updated from
↪ ${event.oldValue} to ${event.newValue} and saved in
${event.storageArea}`) }, false);
```

The fact that only strings can be saved might seem like a restriction at first, but by using JSON, we can store any JavaScript object in local storage. For example, we could save the `hero` object that we created using a form in Chapter 8 by adding the following line of code to the end of the `makeHero()` function:

```
localStorage.setItem('superman', JSON.stringify(hero);
```

This will save the `hero` object as a JSON string using the string 'superman' as the key. To retrieve the superhero as a JavaScript object:

```
superman = JSON.parse(localStorage.getItem('superman'));
```

The Web Storage API provides a useful way of storing various types of information on a user's computer without the restriction of cookies.

Geolocation

The Geolocation API is used to obtain the geographical position of the device. This means it can be used to find the user's exact location, then link to nearby places or measure the speed at which the user is moving. This information can then be used to filter data based on the user's location or speed and direction of travel. An example of this might be a search function that returns results based on your location. Because of privacy concerns, permission to use this has to be granted by the user first.

If geolocation is available, it will be a property of the `navigator` object that we met in Chapter 9. This property has a method called `getCurrentPosition()` that will return a `position` object to a specified callback function, called `youAreHere()` in the example:

```
navigator.geolocation.getCurrentPosition(youAreHere);
```

The `position` object passed to the `youAreHere()` function has a `coords` property with a `latitude` and `longitude` property, which together give the coordinates of the device. These coordinates can then be used in conjunction with other applications or web services (such as a mapping service) to obtain the user's exact location. In this example, we simply show an alert dialog that displays the user's coordinates:

```
function youAreHere(position) {
  console.log(`Latitude: ${position.coords.latitude},
↪ Longitude: ${position.coords.longitude}`);
}
```

The `position` object has several other properties that can be used to find out information about the location and movement of the device:

- `position.speed` property returns the ground speed of the device in meters per second.

- `position.altitude` property returns an estimate of the device's altitude in meters above the WGS84[5] ellipsoid, which is a standard measurement for the center of the Earth.

- `position.heading` property returns the direction the device is moving in. This is measured as a bearing in degrees, clockwise from North.

- `position.timestamp` property returns the time that the position information was recorded.

The `position` object also has properties that calculate the accuracy of the measurements. These can be useful, as sometimes you only need to know the town or city users are in, while at other times you may need their exact position. `position.accuracy` property returns the accuracy of the `latitude` and `longitude` properties in meters. The lower the returned value, the more accurate the measurements are, as is the case for the `position.altitudeAccuracy` property, which returns the accuracy of the `altitude` property in meters.

In addition, the `geolocation` object has a `watchPosition()` method that will call a callback function every time the position of the device is updated. This method returns an ID that can be used to reference the position being watched:

```
const id = navigator.geolocation.watchPosition(youAreHere);
```

The `clearWatch()` method can be used to stop the callback being called, using the ID of the watch as an argument:

```
navigator.geolocation.clearWatch(id);
```

[5.] http://en.wikipedia.org/wiki/World_Geodetic_System

The Geolocation API provides a useful interface for adding location-based information to a website or application.

Web Workers

We saw in earlier chapters that JavaScript is a single-threaded language, meaning that only one process can run at one time. Web workers allow processes to be run in the background, adding support for concurrency in JavaScript. The idea is that any processes that could take a long time are carried out in the background, so a website will continue to function without fear of the dreaded "script has become unresponsive" message that occurs when a script runs for too long, shown below.

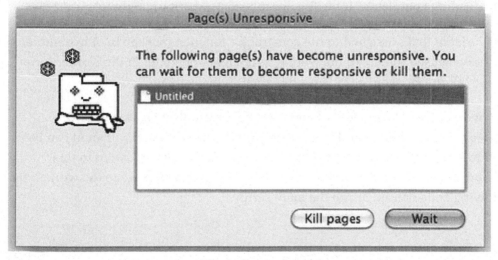

14-1. An unresponsive script

To get started, use the Worker() constructor function to create a new worker:

```
const worker = new Worker('task.js');
```

Chrome Support

At the time of writing, the Chrome browser won't let you run workers from local files like this. A workaround is start Chrome using the `--allow-file-access-from-files` flag, or simply use a different browser for this example.

If you decide to use the `--allow-file-access-from-files` flag, make sure you only use this for development, rather than for regular browsing.

This function takes the name of another JavaScript file as an argument. In the example, this is a file called `task.js`. If this file exists, it will be downloaded asynchronously. The worker will only start once the file has finished downloading completely. If the file doesn't exist, an error is thrown.

The variable that's assigned to the constructor function (`worker` in our example) can now be used to refer to the worker in the main program. In the worker script (`task.js`), the keyword `self` is used to refer to the worker.

Web workers use the concept of messages to communicate back and forth between the main script and worker script. The `postMessage()` method can be used to send a message *and* start the worker working. The argument to this method can send any data to the web worker. To post a message *to* the worker, the following code is used inside the main script:

```
worker.postMessage('Hello');
```

To post a message *from* the worker, the following is used in the worker script:

```
self.postMessage('Finished');
```

When a message is posted, a `message` event is fired, so they can be dealt with using an event listener. The data sent with the message as an argument is stored in the `data` property of the `event` object that's passed to the callback function. The following example would log any data returned from the worker to the console:

```
worker.addEventListener('message', (event) => {
console.log(event.data);
}, false);
```

When a worker has completed its task, it can be stopped using the `terminate()` method from within the main script:

```
worker.terminate();
```

Or using the `close()` method from inside the worker script:

```
self.close();
```

A Factorizing Example

Back in Chapter 10, we created a function that found the factors of a given number. This works well, but can take a long time to find the factors of large numbers. If it was used in a website, it would stop any other code from running while it calculated the factors. To demonstrate this, save the following code in a file called `factors.html`:

```
<!doctype html>
<html lang='en'>
<head>
<meta charset='utf-8'>
<title>Factorizor</title>
</head>
<body>
<button id='rainbow'>Change Color</button>
<form>
 <label for='number'>Enter a Number to
↪ Factorize:</label>
 <input id='number' type='number' name='number' min=1
↪ value='20'>
```

```
    <button type='submit'>Submit</button>
</form>
<div id='output'></div>
<script src='main.js'></script>
</body>
</html>
```

This web page has a button that will change the background color of the page, and an input field where a number can be entered. The factors will be displayed inside the `output` div. To get this working, create a file called `main.js` in the same directory as `factors.html` that contains the following code:

```
const btn = document.getElementById('rainbow');

 const rainbow =
↳
['red','orange','yellow','green','blue','rebeccapurple','violet'];

function change() {
document.body.style.background = rainbow[Math.floor(7*
Math.random())];
}
btn.addEventListener('click', change);
```

This first piece of code was covered way back in Chapter 1 and uses an event listener to change the background color if the button is clicked. We also need to factorize the number entered in the form, so add this code to the end of `main.js`:

```
const form = document.forms[0];
form.addEventListener('submit', factorize, false);

function factorize(event) {
// prevent the form from being submitted
event.preventDefault();

const number = Number(form.number.value);
```

```
document.getElementById('output').innerText =
↳ factorsOf(number);
}


function factorsOf(n) {
if(Number.isNaN(Number(n))) {
 throw new RangeError('Argument Error: Value must be an
↳ integer');
}
if(n < 0) {
 throw new RangeError('Argument Error: Number must be
↳ positive');
}
if(!Number.isInteger(n)) {
 throw new RangeError('Argument Error: Number must be an
↳ integer');
}
const factors = [];
for (let i=1 , max = Math.sqrt(n); i <= max ; i++) {
    if (n%i === 0){
    factors.push(i,n/i);
    }
}
return factors.sort((a,b) =>  a - b);
}
```

This uses the same `factorsof()` function from <u>Chapter 10</u> and adds a `submit` event listener to the form. When the form is submitted, it will find the factors of the number in the input field, then place the result inside the `output` div.

This works well, even coping with some large numbers, as can be seen in the screenshot below.

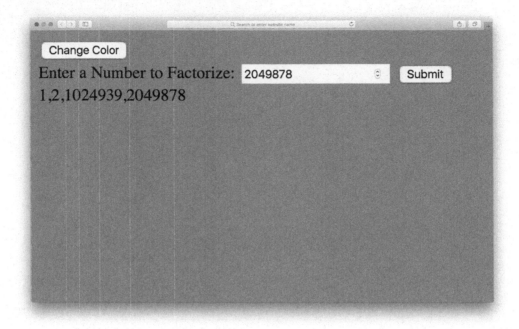

14-2. Our Factorizor in action

But if you enter a sizable number (around 18–20 digits), it takes longer to process the answer, and the browser will display a warning that means something is taking a long time.

To make matters worse, it's impossible to click on the *Change Color* button while the factors are being calculated — the whole program freezes until the operation is complete. (If you recklessly decided to try a huge number and now have an unresponsive web page on your hands, you can simply close the tab and reopen it, or use the Chrome Task Manager to kill the process.)

The good news is that we can use web workers to solve this problem.

Running This Example

The file containing the worker code is expected to be hosted on a server. This is the best option, but if you want to run an example locally you need to turn off the *same origin policy*[6] setting in the browser.

[6.] *https://developer.mozilla.org/en-US/docs/Same-origin_policy_for_file:_URIs*

Firstly, we create a new file called `factors.js;` and save it in the same folder as `main.js`. Then we remove the `factorsOf()` function from the `main.js` file and add it into our new `factors.js;` file. We'll be adding more to this file later, but first we need to edit the `factorize()` function in the `main.js` file so it looks like the following:

```
function factorize(event) {
// prevent the form from being submitted
event.preventDefault();
 document.getElementById('output').innerHTML = '<p>This
↪ could take a while ...</p>';
const number = Number(form.number.value);

if(window.Worker) {
    const worker = new Worker('factors.js');
    worker.postMessage(number);
    worker.addEventListener('message', (event) => {
    document.getElementById('output').innerHTML = event.data;
    }, false);
}
}
```

We start by preventing the form from being submitted, then display a message that says "This could take a while ...". This message is displayed until the worker returns a result, so in the cases of small numbers, this will hardly be seen.

After checking whether web workers are supported, it adds a new web worker. It then uses the `postMessage()` method to send a message to the worker, which is the number we want to factorize. When the number has been factorized, the worker will send a message back to say it has finished.

To deal with this, we set up an event listener that will fire when a message is received back from the worker. The information sent from the worker is stored in the `data` property of the `event` object, so we use `innerHTML` to insert the data into the `output` div.

Now we go back to the `factors.js;` file and add this event listener code to the end of the file:

```
self.addEventListener('message', (event) => {

const factors = String(factorsOf(Number(event.data)));
self.postMessage(factors);
self.close();

}, false);
```

This will fire when the worker receives a message, occurring when the form is submitted. The number to be factorized is stored in the `event.data` property. We use the `factorsOf()` function to find the factors of the number, then convert it into a string and send a message back containing the answer. We then use the `close()` method to terminate the worker, since its work is done.

Now if we test the code, it will still take a long time to factorize a long number, but the page will not freeze. You can also continue to change the background color while the factors are being calculated in the background.

Shared Web Workers

The examples we have seen so far are known as dedicated web workers. These are linked to the script that loaded the worker, and are unable to be used by another script. You can also create shared web workers that allow lots of different scripts on the same domain to access the same worker object.

Web workers allow computationally complex operations to be performed in a separate thread, meaning that the flow of a program won't suffer interruptions, and an application will not freeze or hang. They are a useful feature that help to keep sites responsive, even when complicated operations are being carried out.

Service Workers

The Service Worker API allows a worker script to run in the background with the added benefit of being able to intercept network requests. This allows you to take alternative action if the network is offline, and effectively create app-like offline experiences. Service workers also allow access to push notifications and background syncing. Service workers require a secure network to run on HTTPS to avoid any malicious code hijacking network requests.

There are a large number of different examples of using the Service Worker API in The Service Worker Cookbook[7], which is maintained by Mozilla.

Websockets

As we saw in the last chapter, the main form of communication on the web has always been the HTTP protocol. This uses a system of request and response to send data back and forth. A problem with this method of communication is when you only get a response when a request is sent. But what if the response comes later? For example, imagine a chat application. You send a message to somebody then wait for a reply, but you can't get a reply unless you send them another request... and you'll only get the reply if they have sent the response when you send your request. How long do you wait until you send the next request? This was partially solved using Ajax and a method called 'polling' where a request was periodically sent to see if there had been a response.

Websocket is a new protocol that allows two-way communication with a server – also known as push messaging. This means that a connection is kept open and responses are 'pushed' to the client as soon as they are received.

To see this in action, we'll create a mini-messaging application that uses the websocket protocol to communicate with an Echo server. This sends a response that is exactly the same as the message it receives.

Create a file called `websocket.html` and add the following HTML code:

```
<!doctype html>
<html lang='en'>
<head>
<meta charset='utf-8'>
<title>Websocket Example</title>
</head>
<body>
```

[7.] https://serviceworke.rs

```html
<form>
    <label for='message'>Enter a Message:</label>
    <input type='text' name='message'>
    <button type='submit'>Submit</button>
</form>
<div id='output'></div>
<script src='main.js'></script>
</body>
</html>
```

Apart from the usual standard HTML elements, this has a form for entering and submitting a short message and an empty output `<div>` element, where the message and responses will be displayed.

Next we need to place our JavaScript code inside a file called `main.js`:

```js
const URL = 'wss://echo.websocket.org/';
const outputDiv = document.getElementById('output');
const form = document.forms[0];
const connection = new WebSocket(URL);
```

This sets up some variables to store information. The first is `URL`, which is the URL we'll be using to connect to the websocket. Notice that it starts `wss://` instead of `https://` This is the secure protocol used by websockets instead of HTTP. The site is the Echo server hosted at websocket.org. This accepts messages then returns the same message (like an echo).

The next variable is `outputDiv` and it's used to store a reference to the `<div>` element where we will be displaying the messages. The `form` variable is also used to store a reference to the form element.

Last of all, we create a variable called `connection` that stores a reference to our websocket object. This is created using a constructor function, and takes the URL as a parameter. We will use the variable `connection` to refer to the websocket connection throughout the program.

When the code new WebSocket(URL) runs, it creates an instance of a WebSocket object and tries to connect to the URL. When this is successful, it fires an event called "open". This is one of a number of events that a WebSocket object can emit. To deal with it, we can add an event handler to main.js:

```
connection.addEventListener('open', () => {
    output('CONNECTED');
}, false);
```

This works in the same way as the event handlers we've seen previously, and is called on the connection object. In this case, we call a function called output() with the string "CONNECTED" provided as an argument. The output() is used to output messages to the screen. We need to add that function next:

```
function output(message) {
const para = document.createElement('p');
para.innerHTML = message;
outputDiv.appendChild(para);
}
```

This function takes a string as an argument then appends a new paragraph element to the <div> with an ID of output. The message is then placed inside this paragraph. This has the effect of producing a constant stream of messages inside this <div>.

Now we need to add some code to allow us to add some messages. We'll start by adding an event listener to deal with when the form is submitted:

```
form.addEventListener('submit', message, false);
```

This invokes a function called message(), so let's write that now:

```
function message(event) {
event.preventDefault();
```

```
const text = form.message.value;
output(`SENT: ${text}`);
connection.send(text);
}
```

First of all we stop the default behavior, so the form doesn't actually get submitted. Then we grab the value of the text input and store it in a local variable called `text`. We then use the `output()` function again to add the message to the "output" `<div>`, with the phrase "SENT:" at the start.

The last line is an important one. This calls a method of the `connection` object called `send()`. This sends the message to the URL that the websocket is connected to. When this message is received, the server will process it and send a response. The `connection` object waits for the response, and when it receives one, a "message" event is fired. The "echo.websocket.org" server simply responds with the same message, but any message could be processed in a variety of ways before sending a response.

Let's create an event handler to deal with the response:

```
connection.addEventListener('message', (event) => {
output(`RESPONSE: ${event.data}`);
}, false);
```

This uses the `event` object that is provided as an argument to the event, and we can use the `data` property to access the data that was returned. It's then a simple case of using the `output()` function again to add this message to the growing stream of messages in the "output" `<div>`, but this time with the phrase "RESPONSE:" added to the beginning.

If you open `websocket.html` in a browser, you should see something similar to in the screenshot below:

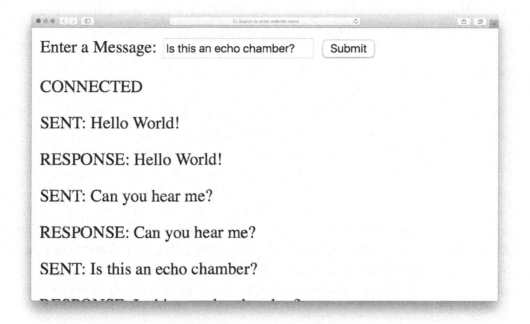

14-3. Websocket messages

There are a couple of other events that the `connection` object responds to that are worth knowing about: The `close` event occurs when the connection is closed, which can be done using the `close()` method. The `error` event is fired when any sort of error occurs with the connection. The information about the error can be accessed in the `data` property of the `event` object.

Typical event listeners for these events might looks like the ones below:

```
connection.addEventListener('close', () => {
    output('DISCONNECTED');
}, false);

connection.addEventListener('error', (event) => {
 output(`<span style='color: red;'>ERROR:
↳ ${event.data}</span>`);
}, false);
```

Websockets are an exciting technology, and you can see lots of examples of how they can be used, as well as finding out more about them at websocket.org[8].

Notifications

The Notification API allows you to show messages using the system's notifications. This is usually a popup in the corner of the screen, but it changes depending on the operating system. An advantage of using the system notification is that they will still be displayed even if the web page that calls them isn't the current tab.

Before you can send notifications, you need to get permission granted by the user. This can be achieved using the `requestPermission()` method of a `Notification` global object. To try this out, visit any website in your browser (https://sitepoint.com for example), and enter the following code in the console:

```
if(window.Notification) {
    Notification.requestPermission();
}
```

This will ask for permission, similar to in the screenshot below:

14-4. Permission for notifications

This returns a promise with the `permission` property of the `Notification` object set to either "granted" or "denied". If it's set to granted, you can create a new notification using a constructor function, like so:

---

8. https://www.websocket.org/demos.html

```
if(window.Notification) {
Notification.requestPermission()
.then((permission) => {
    if(Notification.permission === 'granted') {
    new Notification('Hello JavaScript!');
    }
});
}
```

This will produce a system notification with the title "Hello JavaScript!".

The constructor function's first parameter is the title of the notification, and is required. The function also accepts a second parameter, which is an object of options. These include body that specifies any text that you want to appear below the title, and icon where you can specify a link to an image that will be displayed as part of the notification:

```
 const notification = new Notification('JavaScript: Novice to
↪ Ninja',{
    body: 'The new book from SitePoint',
    icon: 'sitepointlogo.png'
});
```

Depending on your browser and operating system, some notifications close automatically after a short period of time, and some will stay on the screen until the user clicks on them. You can close the notification programmatically using the close() method:

```
notification.close();
```

The notification instance has a number of events that it can react to, including click (when a user clicks on it), show (when the notification appears) and close (when the notification is closed).

For example, you could open a new window when the user clicked on the notification using the following code:

```
notification.addEventListener('click', () => {
window.open('https://sitepoint.com')
}, false);
```

Multimedia

Before HTML5, it was notoriously difficult to display audio and video in browsers, and plugins such as Flash often had to be used. HTML5 introduced the `<audio>` and `<video>` tags used to insert audio and video clips into a web page. It also introduced a Media API for controlling the playback of the clips using JavaScript.

An audio clip can be inserted into a page with the `<audio>` tag, using the `src` attribute to point to the audio file:

```
<audio src='/song.mp3' controls>
Your browser does not support the audio element.
</audio>
```

A video clip can be inserted with the `<video>` tag, using the `src` attribute to point to the movie file:

```
<video src='http://movie.mp4' controls>
Your browser does not support the video element.
</video>
```

Any content inside the `<audio>` or `<video>` tags will only display if the browser does not support them; hence, it can be used to display a message to users of older browsers without support for these features. The `controls` attribute can be added (without any value) and will display the browser's native controls, such as play, pause, and volume control, as can be seen in the screenshot below.

14-5. Browser video controls

The audio or video element can be referenced by a variable using one of the DOM methods we saw in Chapter 6:

```
const video = document.getElementsByTagName('video')[0];
```

Audio and video elements have a number of properties and methods to control the playback of the clip.

The play() method will start the clip playing from its current position:

```
video.play();
```

The pause() method will pause the clip at its current position:

```
video.pause();
```

The volume property is a number that can be used to set the audio volume:

```
video.volume = 0.9;
```

The `muted` property is a boolean value that can be used to mute the audio:

```
video.muted = true;
```

The `currentTime` property is a number value that can be used to jump to another part of the clip:

```
video.currentTime += 10; // jumps forward 10 seconds
```

The `playbackRate` property is used to fast-forward or rewind the clip by changing its value. A value of 1 is playback at normal speed:

```
video.playbackRate = 8; // fast-forward at 8 times as fast
```

The `loop` property is a boolean value that can be set to `true` to make the clip repeat in a loop:

```
video.loop = true;
```

The `duration` property can be used to see how long the clip lasts:

```
video.duration;
<< 52.209
```

Checking Properties Are Available

Some of the properties are only available once the browser has received all the metadata associated with the video. This means that, in order to ensure a value is returned, you should use an event listener that fires once the metadata has loaded, like the one shown below:

```
video.addEventListener('loadedmetadata', () => {
↳ console.log(video.duration); });
```

Audio and video clips also have a number of events that will fire when they occur, including:

- The `play` event, which fires when the clip starts and when it resumes after a pause.

- The `pause` event, which fires when the clip is paused.

- The `volumechange` event, which fires when the volume is changed.

- The `loadedmetadata` event, which we saw in the note above, and which fires when all the video's metadata has loaded.

These events allow you to respond to any interactions the user has with the video. For example, the following event listener can be added to check whether the user has paused the video:

```
video.addEventListener('pause', () => {
console.log('The video has been paused'); }, false)
```

The audio and video elements bring native support for multimedia into the browser, and the API gives developers full control of the playback of audio tracks and video clips.

The W3C has a full list of all the properties, methods and events that are available for video elements[9].

[9.] https://www.w3.org/2010/05/video/mediaevents.html

Other APIs

The list of APIs is constantly growing, and includes APIs for accessing a device's camera, uploading files, accessing the battery status, handling push notifications, building drag-and-drop functionality, creating 3D effects with WebGL, and many more! A comprehensive list of HTML5 APIs can be found at the Mozilla Developer Network[10].

 Privacy Concerns

There are some security and privacy considerations to keep in mind when considering some HTML5 APIs – especially those on the cutting edge that haven't been used in the wild for long. For example, there are concerns that the ambient light API might make it possible to steal data[11] and the battery API has been dropped by Apple and Mozilla due to concerns over user profiling[12].

Drawing with Canvas

The `canvas` element was introduced to allow graphics to be drawn onto a web page in real time using JavaScript. A `canvas` element is a rectangular element on the web page. It has a coordinate system that starts at (0,0) in the top-left corner. To add a `canvas` element to a page, the `<canvas>` tag is used specifying a `height` and `width`. Anything placed inside the tag will only display if the `canvas` element is unsupported:

```
<canvas id='canvas' width='400' height='400'>Sorry,
↪ but your browser does not support the canvas
↪ element</canvas>
```

---

10. https://developer.mozilla.org/en-US/docs/WebAPI
11. https://www.theregister.co.uk/2017/04/20/
ambient_light_sensors_can_steal_data_says_security_researcher/
12. http://www.theregister.co.uk/2016/11/07/
apple_mozilla_kill_api_to_batter_battery_snitching/

This canvas can now be accessed in a JavaScript program using the
`document.getElementById()` method:

```
const canvasElement = document.getElementById('canvas');
```

The next step is to access the context of the canvas. This is an object that contains
all the methods used to draw onto the canvas. We'll be using a 2-D context, but
it's also possible to render in 3-D using WebGL.

The `getContext()` method is used to access the context:

```
const context = canvasElement.getContext('2d');
```

Now we have a reference to the context, we can access its methods and draw onto
the canvas. The fill and stroke colors can be changed by assigning a CSS color to
the `fillStyle` and `strokeStyle` properties respectively:

```
context.fillStyle = "#0000cc"; // a blue fill color
context.strokeStyle = "#ccc"; // a gray stroke color
```

These colors will be utilized for everything that's drawn onto the canvas until
they're changed.

The `lineWidth` property can be used to set the width of any line strokes drawn
onto the canvas. It defaults to one pixel and remains the same until it's changed:

```
context.lineWidth = 4;
```

The `fillRect()` method can draw a filled-in rectangle. The first two parameters
are the coordinates of the top-left corner, the third parameter is the width, and the
last parameter is the height. The following produces a filled-in blue rectangle in
the top-left corner of the canvas at coordinates (10,10) that is 100 pixels wide and
50 pixels high:

```
context.fillRect(10,10,100,50);
```

The `strokeRect()` method works in the same way, but produces a rectangle that is not filled in. This will draw the outline of a rectangle underneath the last one:

```
context.strokeRect(10,100,100,50);
```

Straight lines can be drawn employing the `moveTo()` and `lineTo()` methods. These methods can be used together to produce a path. Nothing will actually be drawn onto the canvas until the `stroke()` method is called. The following example will draw a thick red T shape onto the canvas by moving to the coordinates (150,50), then drawing a horizontal line 30 pixels long, and finally moving to the middle of that line and drawing a vertical line 40 pixels long:

```
context.beginPath();
context.moveTo(130, 50);
context.lineTo(180, 50);
context.moveTo(155, 50);
context.lineTo(155, 90);
context.strokeStyle = '#c00';
context.lineWidth = 15;
context.stroke();
```

The `arc()` method can be used to draw an arc of a given radius from a particular point. The first two parameters are the coordinates of the center of the arc; the next parameter is the radius, followed by the start angle, then the finish angle (note that these are measured in radians). The last parameter is a boolean value that says whether the arc should be drawn counter-clockwise. The following example will draw a yellow circle of radius 30 pixels at center (200,200), since `Math.PI * 2` represents a full turn:

```
context.beginPath();
context.arc(200, 200, 30, 0, Math.PI * 2, false);
context.strokeStyle = '#ff0';
```

```
context.lineWidth = 4;
context.stroke();
```

The `fillText()` method is used to write text onto the canvas. The first parameter is the text to be displayed, while the next two parameters are the x and y coordinates, respectively. The `font` property can be used to set the font style used, otherwise the style is inherited from the `canvas` element's CSS setting (note that it needs to be changed *before* the `fillText()` method is used to draw the text). The following example will draw the text "Hello" in green at coordinates (20,50), as shown below.

```
context.fillStyle = '#0c0'; // a blue fill color
context.font = 'bold 26px sans-serif';
context.fillText('Hello', 20, 200);
```

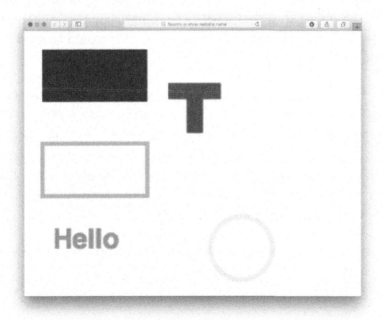

14-6. Drawing on a canvas

This is only a short introduction to what the `canvas` element can do. It is being used more and more in websites to draw data charts that are updated in real-time, as well as to animate HTML5 games.

Shims and Polyfills

HTML5 APIs progress at a rapid rate — new APIs are constantly being introduced, and existing APIs often change. Modern browsers are very quick to update and implement many of the changes, but you can't always guarantee that users will have the most up-to-date browser. This is where a shim or a polyfill comes in handy. These are libraries of code that allow you to use the APIs as usual. They then fill in the necessary code that's not provided natively by the user's browser.

The terms shim and polyfill are often used interchangeably. The main difference between them is that a shim is a piece of code that adds some missing functionality to a browser, although the implementation method may differ slightly from the standard API. A polyfill is a shim that achieves the same functionality, while also using the API commands that would be used if the feature was supported natively.

This means that your code can use the APIs as normal and it should work as expected in older browsers. The advantage here is that the same set of standard API commands can be used — you don't need to write additional code to deal with different levels of support. And when users update their browsers, the transition will be seamless, as their experience will remain the same. Once you are confident that enough users have up-to-date browsers, you can remove the polyfill code without having to update any actual JavaScript code.

A comprehensive list of shims and polyfills is maintained by the Modernizr team.[13]

[13.] https://github.com/Modernizr/Modernizr/wiki/HTML5-Cross-Browser-Polyfills

Quiz Ninja Project

We're going to use the Web Storage API to store the high score of the game. This will be stored locally even after the browser has been closed, so players can keep a record of their best attempt and try to beat it. To do this, we first add an extra `<div>` element to the header to show the high score. Change the `<header>` element in `index.html` to the following:

```
<header>
 <div id='timer'>Time:
 ↳ <strong>20</strong></div>
 <div id='score'>Score:
 ↳ <strong>0</strong></div>
 <div id='hiScore'>High Score:
 ↳ <strong></strong></div>
<h1>Quiz Ninja!</h1>
</header>
```

Now we need to add a method to the `game` object updates, and return the high score. Add the following to the end of the `game` object:

```
hiScore(){
    const hi = localStorage.getItem('highScore') || 0;
    if(this.score > hi || hi === 0) {
    localStorage.setItem('highScore',this.score);
    ** NEW HIGH SCORE! **');
    }
    return localStorage.getItem('highScore');
}
```

This method sets a local variable called `hi` to the value that's stored inside the object under the key `highScore`. If a high score is yet to be set already, it will be `null`, so we'll initialize it to `0` in this case using lazy evaluation. Next, we check to see if value of `this.score` (which will be the player's final score) is bigger than the current high score that we just retrieved. If it is, we show a message to congratulate the player, and also update the value stored in `localStorage` using the `setItem()` method.

Have a go at playing it by opening up `index.html`, as shown below, and try to get a new high score.

14-7. high scores in action

You can see a live example on CodePen[14].

Chapter Summary

---

14. https://codepen.io/daz4126/pen/ZyxdLY

- HTML5.1 is the latest incarnation of the Hypertext Markup Language. It covers a variety of technologies, including several APIs that are accessible using JavaScript.

- `data-` attributes help to embed custom data into a web page that can then be used to enhance the user experience with JavaScript.

- The Web Storage API allows key-value pairs to be stored on the user's device in a similar way to cookies, but without the same storage restrictions.

- The Geolocation API allows you to access the geographic coordinates of the user's device, as long as the user gives permission.

- The Web Worker API can be used to perform computationally intensive tasks in the background, which helps to avoid websites becoming unresponsive.

- Websockets are a new protocol for communicating over the internet, and allow real-time, two-way communication.

- The Notification API allows you to display notifications on the user's system.

- The `<audio>` and `<video>` elements can be employed to embed audio tracks and video clips in a web page. They also have a Media API that can help control the playback using JavaScript.

- The `canvas` element can be used to dynamically draw geometric shapes, text, and images on a web page in real-time using JavaScript.

- A shim or polyfill is a piece of code that adds support of missing features to older browsers.

In the next chapter, we'll cover how to organize and optimize your code.

Chapter **15**

Modern JavaScript Development

As you build more and more complex JavaScript projects, you'll find the amount of code you're using increases into hundreds and then thousands of lines. This can be difficult to manage without some sort of organizing. The first step is to break the code into separate files, but this presents its own problems, such as how to include all the files on a web page, and which code to put in which files. Indeed, how do you ensure that a file has access to the code in another file?

Just as real-life ninjas have lots of nifty weapons such as nunchakus and shuriken stars, there are lots of cool tools that a JavaScript ninja can use to help organize code and make it run more efficiently. In this chapter, we'll look at the various frameworks and tools that can be employed to improve the quality of your code. In turn, it will make it more organized and easier to maintain, promoting reuse. We'll also look at how to make your applications ready for production.

In this chapter, we'll cover the following topics:

- Libraries

- Modular JavaScript

- MVC frameworks

- Package managers

- Optimizing your code with minification

- Build processes using Webpack

- Our project — we'll separato our code into a modular architecture and prepare for it for deployment.

Libraries

A JavaScript library is a piece of code that provides several methods that make it easier to achieve common tasks. JavaScript is an extremely flexible language that can accomplish most programming tasks – but not all undertakings are as easy to do as they should be. A library will abstract functionality into easier-to-use functions and methods. These can then be used to complete common tasks without having to use lots of repetitive code.

DOM Manipulation Example

A good example of how librarios can help save time is in DOM manipulation. The DOM API provides all the tools required to manipulate the DOM, but some can be verbose and take several lines of code to attain even the most basic of tasks.

For example, if we wanted to add a class to a paragraph element referenced by the variable para, then append another paragraph on the end, we could do it using the following:

```
para.classList.add('important');
const newPara = document.createElement('p');
```

```
newPara.textContent = 'Another Paragraph';
para.appendChild(newPara);
```

Yet by using the jQuery library, we can achieve the same result using a single line of code:

```
$(para).addClass('important').append('<p>Another
↪ Paragraph</p>');
```

This shows how using a library can reduce the amount of code you have to write, as well as making common tasks easier to implement. Popular libraries such as jQuery are often well-tested, and help to iron out edge cases and bugs in older browsers that would be difficult to do with your own code. They also unify a number of implementations of the same feature that are different across different browsers. For example, adding event listeners uses a different syntax in some older browsers, but you can use a single method in jQuery that will select the implementation depending on the browser.

jQuery

jQuery is the most popular of all the JavaScript libraries used today. It is used in a huge number of commercial websites and has a plugin system that makes it easy to extend and use to build common web page elements, such as a lightbox or carousel widget.

jQuery was released in 2006, originally as a DOM manipulation library. It has since grown much bigger, and now provides hundreds of methods for selecting nodes, as well as traversing the DOM, animation effects, Ajax and events. It also has its own testing library:QUnit[1].

A big advantage of using jQuery is its support for older browsers, particularly Internet Explorer. If you find yourself having to support these browsers then jQuery could save you a huge amount of time and headache. For example,

---

[1.] http://qunitjs.com/

`classList` isn't supported in older versions of Internet Explorer, so you'd have to write your own polyfill code to fix it. But if you used jQuery, you'd just have to use the `addClass()` method and it would make sure the code worked in most browsers.

jQuery is a very powerful and polished library that provides a considerable number of useful methods. It has become so popular that many online tutorials assume you're using jQuery rather than just JavaScript. You can learn more about jQuery by reading the excellent *jQuery: Novice to Ninja: New Kicks and Tricks by Earle Castledine and Craig Sharkie*[2].

 Dollar Symbols

The jQuery library uses the $ symbol as a convenient alias for the the global `jQuery` object that contains all of jQuery's methods. This prevents the global scope from being polluted with any of jQuery's methods. The $ symbol has become synonymous with jQuery, and you can confidently expect that any mention of it implies that jQuery is being used.

Underscore & Lodash

Underscore[3] and Lodash[4] are very similar libraries of functions that provide additional functionality to the language. They both provide a large number of utility functions under the namespace _ (this is where these libraries get their name from as the _ character is often referred to as an underscore or a lodash). A number of JavaScript libraries list one of these as a core dependency.

It's worth considering using one of these libraries in your projects as it will give you access to a large number of well-tested utility functions that are often required in projects, and particularly geared towards a functional style of programming that was discussed in <u>Chapter 11</u>. Some of these functions have been added in recent versions of ECMAScript, but there are still a large number that will help save you the time of writing your own implementation and effectively reinventing the wheel. A good example can be seen by looking at some

[2] https://www.sitepoint.com/premium/books/jquery-novice-to-ninja-new-kicks-and-tricks
[3] http://underscorejs.org/
[4] https://lodash.com

of the functions that act on arrays. These provide some very useful functionality that is often required and, some may argue, criminally missing from language itself:

```
// flatten an array
_.flatten([1, [2, [3, [4]], 5]]);
<< [1, 2, [3, [4]], 5]

// return the last element in an array
_.last([1, 2, 3]);
<< 3

// randomly shuffle an array
_.shuffle([1, 2, 3, 4]);
// => [4, 1, 3, 2]
```

Both of these libraries are very similar. In fact, Lodash started life as a fork of Underscore. Since then, they have diverged a little, but still have many similarities. The underlying code, however, has become quite different. Lodash can be thought of as a "superset" of Underscore as it does everything Underscore does, but also adds some extra features. Lodash also has a modular architecture that allows you to selectively use only the functions that you require in your projects, rather than having to include the whole library.

Advantages and Disadvantages of Libraries

A big advantage of utilizing a popular library is that it will be used by lots of people and thoroughly tested. It will most likely have been optimized and battle-tested for nearly every eventuality. Using a library means you can be confident that your code will be as bullet-proof as possible in many browsers. In addition, there will usually be lots of online documentation and a strong community ready to help out if you become stuck. The popularity of libraries often means that others will have encountered the same problem as you, often making it easy to find a solution by searching on the internet.

There are some disadvantages to using libraries, however. You need to include the code for the library as well as your own code. This increases the amount of code that needs to be downloaded by a website, which in some cases can cause performance issues. Thankfully, most modern libraries are relatively small once server-side optimizations are made (such as gzip compression), minimizing any latency issues. Another problem with libraries is that they might fail to implement the functionality in the precise way that you want it to perform. This might not be a problem, but sometimes you'll have to get your hands dirty and write your own functions in order to achieve the functionality for which you are looking. Using a library can also make your code slower than using plain vanilla JavaScript. This is because there are often more lines of code in using the abstracted functions in a library rather than writing a direct implementation in just JavaScript, which is "closer to the metal", so to speak. These speed differences can be barely noticeable, although there are occasions when using a library is a poor choice for some operations. Using plain JavaScript can be significantly faster than a library[5].

The debate about whether to use a library or not is a big one that stretches back to the start of programming, and refuses to go away. Indeed, there has been a movement towards using plain JavaScript in recent years. Additionally, the Vanilla JS[6] website showcases plain JavaScript as if it were a library, highlighting that many tasks can be accomplished with a similar amount of code but much better performance. This is now truer than ever since ES6, as a lot of problems that some libraries addressed have been fixed in the vanilla flavor of JavaScript. The relatively fast uptake and adoption of ES6 means there are less reasons to use a library for some functionality. Having said that, the native implementation of some functions and APIs can often be awkward and difficult to use as well as lacking support in older browsers. This means that libraries will continue to be used by developers as an aid to productivity and consistency.

You only need to look at any professionally produced website to see that some sort of library has been used in its production. Libraries are often the pragmatic choice to complete a project in a realistic time frame, especially when working in a large team. They can also be useful in supporting older browsers and ironing out any browser-specific bugs or quirks, or if performance isn't the most important factor (when prototyping sites, for example).

[5.] http://www.sitepoint.com/jquery-vs-raw-javascript-1-dom-forms/
[6.] http://vanilla-js.com/

When to Use a Library

It can be helpful to use a library, but you should certainly question whether it's worth the extra work. You have to learn the library's notation, which can either be similar or very different to standard JavaScript. Every library you use will add to the total file size that's downloaded so you need to assess whether the extra overhead is worth it. Having said that, browsers will cache it after the first download, and if you use a CDN, the chances are it will already be in the browser's cache.

It's also advisable to consider that the popularity of a particular library can be here today, gone tomorrow. Some of the most popular libraries of the past have fallen out of favor and even discontinued, almost overnight. This can potentially cause problems if you've relied on one particular library in most of your projects.

Many libraries have become monolithic, with a plethora of methods that try to do everything. An example of this is jQuery. While it contains a large number of useful methods, it also provides many features that are often unnecessary. jQuery's modular structure means that you can include only the parts you need on a module-by-module basis. But if you find that you're not using many of the methods a library offers, you should consider using a lighter alternative that only focuses on solving one problem (some suggestions are given below). And if you're only using a handful of methods, maybe avoid using a library altogether and try using plain old JavaScript. You could even package together useful functions you've created in a module that serves as your own personal library.

Finding Libraries

It is certainly worth considering using a library to make some common tasks easier. There's a large number of JavaScript libraries in this list on Wikipedia[7], while MicroJS[8] is a high-quality repository of small JavaScript libraries that focus on specific tasks, and Just[9] is a library of functions that just do one task without depending on any other functions or libraries.

[7.] https://en.wikipedia.org/wiki/List_of_JavaScript_libraries
[8.] http://microjs.com/
[9.] http://anguscroll.com/just/

Be careful not to rely on a library and find that you're learning how to use the library's methods, rather than the language itself. A library should not be used because of a lack of understanding of JavaScript. Instead, it should be used to speed up JavaScript development by making it easier to complete common tasks. Using a library can sometimes make your code more sloppy. It's easy, for example, to write short jQuery expressions that look concise but are spectacularly inefficient. And even if you do choose to use a library, remember that a ninja should always be inquisitive as to how things work. In fact, reading a library's source code is a great way of learning some powerful JavaScript programming techniques.

Modular JavaScript

A module is a self-contained piece of code that provides functions and methods that can then be used in other files and by other modules. This helps to keep code organized in separate, reusable files, which improves code maintainability. The code in a module should have a single purpose, and group together functions with distinct functionality. For example, you might keep any functions used for Ajax in their own module. This could then be used in any projects where Ajax was required. Keeping code modular helps to make it more *loosely coupled* and interchangeable, meaning you can easily swap one module for another without affecting other parts of a project. Indeed, small single-purpose modules are the exact opposite of large monolithic libraries as they enable developers to use only the modules that are needed, avoiding any wasted code. Modules also allow a public API to be exposed, while keeping the implementation hidden away inside the module.

Coupling

The coupling of code refers to how dependent certain elements or modules of code are on each other. Two pieces of code are said to be tightly coupled if one relies on the other to run. This often occurs if a piece of code makes hard-coded references to another piece of code, requiring it to be used. This will often mean that changes to one piece of code will necessitate changes in the other. On the other hand, two pieces of code are said to loosely coupled if one piece of code can be easily substituted by another without affecting the final outcome. This is often achieved by referring to common methods that are shared by the alternative modules. For example, you might have a choice of two modules that simplify the process of connecting to a websocket. Both of these modules would likely implement a `connect()` method, so your code could simply refer to `connect()` rather than having to explicitly refer to a particular module. This would then allow you change between the two modules without having to change any of the underlying code. It is considered good design to keep code as loosely coupled as possible as this allows for the most flexibility in developing systems of code, as different modules can be used independently and in a variety of different applications, rather than being restricted to a single use-case.

ES6 Modules

For a long time, JavaScript didn't support modules, but native support for them was finally added in ES6. They allow you to keep parts of code in self-contained files.

There are a few important points about modules that are worth keeping in mind:

- All code in modules is always in strict mode without the need for `'use strict'` and there is no way to opt out of this.
- A module has its own global scope, so any variables created in the top-level of a module can only be accessed within that module.
- The value of `this` in the top level of a module is `undefined`, rather than the global object.
- You can't use HTML-style comments in modules (although this isn't very common in any JavaScript program these days).

A ES6 module file is just a normal JavaScript file, but uses the keyword `export` to specify any values or functions that are to be made available from the module.

This highlights another important fact about modules – not everything in the module needs to be used.

Browser Support

At the time of writing, most major browsers are on the cusp of supporting ES6 modules, so you should be able to run these examples straight in your browser. If they don't work, however, you can use a build process that packages all the modules together into one file. We explain how to do this later in this chapter.

For example, a very simple Pi module would have the following code saved in a file called `pi.js`:

```
export const PI = 3.1415926;
```

This would then be imported into your main JavaScript file, `main.js` using the following code:

```
import { PI } from './pi.js';
```

This would then allow you to use the variable `PI` inside the `main.js` file.

Functions can also be exported from a module. For example, we could create a library for our stats functions that we used earlier:

```
function square(x) {
return x * x;
}

function sum(array, callback) {
if(callback) {
    array = array.map(callback);
}
return array.reduce((a,b) => a + b );
}
```

```
function variance(array) {
return sum(array,square)/array.length - square(mean(array))
}

function mean(array) {
return sum(array) / array.length;
}

export {
variance,
mean
}
```

Notice that an alternative to using `export` when the function is defined is to add the export directive after the function definition, as seen in the example above with the `variance()` function.

To import these functions into the `main.js` file, you'd add this line of code:

```
import { mean, variance } from './stats.js';
```

Now the `mean()` and `variance()` functions can be used in the `main.js` file. Notice that the `square()` and `sum()` functions are not available because they were not exported in the module. This effectively makes them private functions of the stats module.

You can be selective in which values or functions to import from the module. For example, if you only wanted to use the `mean()` function, you could use the following line of code instead:

```
import { mean } from './stats.js';
```

If there are lots of values and functions that need to be imported, then everything in a module file can be imported using the wildcard symbol * along with a namespace for the imported values and functions using the following notation:

```
import * as stats from './stats.js';
```

This will then import all the functions from the `stats.js` module and they'll be given a namespace of `stats`. So, the `mean` function could be used as follows:

```
stats.mean([2,6,10]);
```

Default Exports

Default exports refer to *a single* variable, function or class in a module that can be imported without having to be explicitly named. The syntax for default exports is purposely easier to read because this is how modules were designed to be used.

The following example demonstrates how this would be done for a variable:

```
const PI = 3.145926;

export default PI;
```

The next example demonstrates exporting a single default function:

```
function square(x) {
    return x * x;
}

export default square;
```

The last example shows how to export an object as the default value:

```
const stats = {

square(x) {
```

```
    return x * x;
},

    sum(array, callback) {
    if(callback) {
        array = array.map(callback);
    }
        return array.reduce((a,b) => a + b );
    },

mean(array) {
    return this.sum(array) / array.length;
},

variance(array) {
 return this.sum(array,this.square)/array.length -
↪ this.square(this.mean(array))
}
}

export default stats;
```

 Don't Use More Than One Default Export

Having more than one default export will result in a syntax error.

To import these default values, you would use the following code:

```
import PI from './pi.js';
import square from './square.js';
import stats from './stats.js';
```

The big difference with default exports is that you don't need to use curly braces or make any mention of the value that is being imported, making the statement read more elegantly.

Aliases

The alias that is assigned to the imported module does not have to match its name in the actual module. For example, you could import the **square** function in the following way:

```
import sq from './square.js';
```

The function would then be called using **sq()** rather than **square()**:

```
sq(8)
<< 64
```

Node.js Modules

Node.js had already implemented modules before they were introduced in ES6, and used a slightly different notation called Common JS modules[10]. At the time of writing it is proving difficult to merge the two notations in an elegant way, although it is expected that Node.js will support ES6 modules in some way in the future. Despite this, I expect you will continue to see the Common JS module pattern used by Node.js tutorials for a long time to come.

A Common JS module is created in a separate file, and the **module.exports** method is used to make any functions available to other files, in a similar way to ES6 modules. For example, we could create a module for squaring numbers using the following code inside a file called squareFunction.js:

```
module.exports = x => x * x;
```

This is simply the **square()** function we saw earlier in the chapter written as an anonymous function that's assigned to **module.exports** as if it was a variable.

---

[10] http://wiki.commonjs.org/wiki/Modules/1.1

To use the module, it needs to then be required inside the another JS file (or from within the Node REPL). This is done using the `require()` method. This takes the file that contains the module as an argument and returns the function that was exported:

```
const square = require('./squareFunction');
```

The function that was exported in the module is now assigned to the variable `square`, which is then used to call the function in the usual way:

```
square(6);
<< 36
```

MVC Frameworks

Model-View-Controller (MVC) is a design pattern that's been used for a long time in server-side languages. It's a common way of designing software, and used by server-side frameworks such as Ruby On Rails and Django. In recent years it has been used in JavaScript code to make it easier to organize large-scale web applications.

MVC separates an application into three distinct, independent components that interact with each other:

■ **Models** are objects that implement the functionality for creating, reading, updating and deleting (known as CRUD tasks) specific pieces of information about the application, as well as any other associated logic and behavior. In a to-do list application, for example, there would be a task model providing methods to access all the information about the tasks such as names, due dates and completed tasks. This data will often be stored in a database or some other container.

■ **Views** provide a visual representation of the model showing all the relevant information. In a web application, this would be the HTML displayed on a web page. Views also provide a way for users to interact with an application, usually via forms. In a to-do list application, the views would display the tasks as an HTML list with checkboxes that a user could tick to say a task had been completed.

- **Controllers** link models and views together by communicating between them. They respond to events, which are usually inputs from a user (entering some data into a form, for example), process the information, then update the model and view accordingly. In a to-do list application, the controller functions would respond to the event of a user clicking on a check box and then inform the model that a task had been completed. The model would then update the information about that task.

 MV*

It is quite common to see the acronym MV* used to describe JavaScript frameworks, rather than MVC. This is because many JavaScript implementations do not strictly follow the controller pattern. Sometimes controller code is mixed into the views, and sometimes other patterns are used, such as Model-View-Presenter (MVP), Model-View-ViewModel (MVVM), and AngularJS, which calls itself a Model-View-Whatever (MVW) framework. These tend to be only slight variations on the MVC pattern, but for simplicity, MV* is used as a catch-all term. There has been a recent trend for many of these frameworks to embrace a more component-based architecture, which can be found in Angular (from version 2 onwards) and Ember 2.

A Quick List Example

Here's an example of how the MVC architecture can be implemented using JavaScript. It will be a simple list creator that allows the user to add items to a list by entering them into a form field.

To start, create a folder called MVC and save the following as list.html:

```
<!doctype html>
<html lang='en'>
<head>
<meta charset='utf-8'>
<title>MVC List</title>
```

```
</head>
<body>
<form id="input">
    <label for='name'>Name:</label>
    <input type='text' name='name' autofocus required >
    <button type='submit'>Submit</button>
</form>
<ul id='list'></ul>
<script src='main.js'></script>
</body>
</html>
```

This is a basic HTML web page containing a form with a single input field for entering a list item. It also contains an empty <ul> element in which to place the list items. Now we need to create the JavaScript file. Create a file called main.js saved in the same folder.

In JavaScript, a model is often represented by a class that can create new instances of an object. This will keep track of any properties the list item has, as well as any methods. In this example, we'll create an Item class, and use the constructor function to instantiate an Item object with a name property provided as an argument to the constructor function. We also assign a reference to the form to a variable called form. Add this code to main.js:

```
'use strict'

const form = document.forms[0];

class Item {
constructor(name) {
    this.name = name;
    }
}
```

Each new list item that is created will be an instance of the Item class.

Next we'll create a `controller` object. This will be responsible for adding an event listener to the form to see when the user adds information. When this happens, it will create a new instance of the model and then render the updated view. Add the following code to `main.js`:

```
const controller = {
watch(form) {
    form.addEventListener('submit', (event) => {
 event.preventDefault(); // prevent the form from being
↳ submitted
    this.add(form.name.value);
    }, false);
},

add(name) {
    const item = new Item(name);
    view.render(item);
}
};
```

After this, we create a view object with a `render()` method. This is used to produce an HTML fragment that shows the instance's name (from the `name` property stored in the model). It is dynamically inserted into the list using DOM API methods. Add the following code to the `main.js` file:

```
const view = {
render(item) {
    const list = document.getElementById('list');
    const li = document.createElement('li');
    li.innerHTML = item.name;
    list.appendChild(li);
    // reset the input field
    form.name.value = '';
}
};
```

Finally, we have to call the `watch()` method of the controller. This keeps an eye on the form and checks when it is submitted. Add the following line to the end of the `main.js` file:

```
controller.watch(form);
```

Open up `list.html` in your browser and have a go at adding some items to the list. It should look a little like the screenshot shown below.

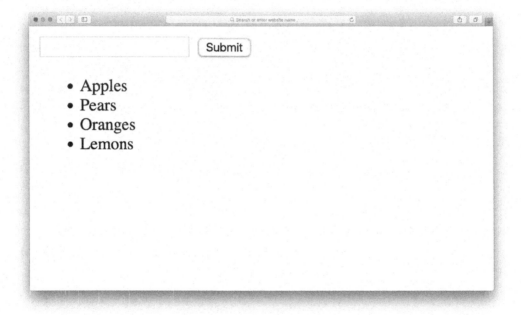

15-1. An MVC to-do list

This is just a small and simple example of the MVC pattern to give an idea of how it works. In reality, the model would contain many more properties and methods. The controller would also contain more methods for editing and deleting instances of the model. There's also likely to be more views to display the different states of the model, and there would need to be more robust code used in order for the controller to monitor the changes that may happen in the views. Most MVC implementations also tend to be more generalized in their implementation and avoid hard-coding details about which elements are being updated on the page (such as the reference to the `list` id in the example). Despite this, I hope the example demonstrates how to separate code into the three distinct components of MVC.

Persistence

Most web applications will need some form of persistence to save the information held in the models in order to maintain state. This could be done using the Web Storage API that we covered in the last chapter. Another option that's often used in real-world applications is to send a JSON representation of the model to a back-end database using Ajax whenever a model changes.

MV* Frameworks

An MVC architecture can take a lot of code to implement, and many frameworks have emerged that take care of much of the setup code for you. One of the main features of MVC frameworks is data binding, which is the process of linking the model and view together. As a result, a large amount of boilerplate controller code is not needed as the framework takes care of it all in the background for you. One-way data binding is when a change in the model will automatically result in the view being updated. And two-way data binding is when a change in the view automatically updates the model.

The views are simply web pages written in HTML, although it is common to use templating languages so dynamic data can be inserted into the page (more about these in the section that follows):

■ Aurelia[11] is a modern framework that uses ES6, and focuses on letting you write dynamic web applications while keeping the implementation details in the background.

■ Angular[12] is a powerful framework by Google to make creating dynamic web applications easier. This is done by extending the HTML language using custom ng- attributes.

[11.] http://aurelia.io

[12.] https://angular.io/

■ Ember[13] is a framework designed to make building large web applications easier. It does this by using common conventions that avoid the need for lots of set-up code, though it can become more difficult if you don't follow these conventions.

Templates

Many MVC frameworks use templating languages to insert dynamic data into the page. Templates can be written in HTML or another language, such as markdown, which compiles into HTML. They can be whole web pages, but are often just partials — parts of a page. This means that the application can update part of the page without having to make a request to the server, saving an HTTP request. This is usually done by dynamically inserting the fragment of HTML into the DOM.

Templating languages allow HTML to be separated from the JavaScript program, making maintenance easier because they're no longer tightly coupled. The templates are often stored in separate files or inside their own script tags, so they can be reused and quickly edited in one place if changes need to be made. It also means that inserting large strings of HTML into a document (which can have adverse effects on performance) is avoided. All that's needed is a reference to the relevant file that contains the template.

Templating languages often have a mechanism for inserting dynamic data into the HTML. These tend to fall into two camps: placing dynamic code inside curly braces (the "mustache" symbol) or inside the special <% %> tags made popular by Embedded Ruby (ERB).

For example, Mustache, Pug and Handlebars would use this to insert the value of the variable `name` into a heading tag:

```
<h1>Hello {{ name }}</h1>
```

EJS, on the other hand, would use the following to achieve the same result:

[13.] http://emberjs.com/

```
<h1>Hello <%= name %></h1>
```

Templating languages also enable you to insert basic programming logic into views, allowing you to conditionally show different messages or use loops to show multiple pieces of similar code.

For example, say we wanted to display the following array of to-do objects:

```
const tasks = [
    { name: 'Get Milk' },
    { name: 'Go for a run' },
    { name: 'Finish writing last chapter' },
    { name: 'Phone bank' },
    { name: 'Email Craig' }
    ]
```

Mustache implements logic-less templates that don't require any lines of logic to be explicitly written in JavaScript; instead, it is inferred from the context. This is how it would iterate over the `task` array to display a list of tasks:

```
<ul>
{{#tasks}}
<li>{{name}}</li>
{{/task}}
</ul>
```

EJS uses more explicit JavaScript coding to achieve the same result. Each line of JavaScript code is placed inside the special <% %> tags. If any values need to be evaluated, they are placed inside <%= %> instead:

```
<ul>
    <% tasks.forEach(function(task) { %>
    <li><%= task.name %></li>
    <% }); %>
```

```
    </ul>
    <% } %>>
```

Both of these templates would return this HTML code:

```
<ul>
    <li>Get Milk</li>
    <li>Go for a run</li>
    <li>Finish writing last chapter</li>
    <li>Phone bank</li>
    <li>Email Craig</li>
    </ul>
```

There are a number of popular templating languages to choose from, a selection of some of the most popular are shown in the list below:

- Handlebars[14]

- Pug[15]

- EJS[16]

- Mustache[17]

- Nunjucks[18]

Web Components

The W3C are working on developing a standard called Web Components[19] that attempts to extend HTML and introduce new features such as templates, custom

---

[14.] http://handlebarsjs.com/

[15.] https://github.com/pugjs/pug

[16.] http://www.embeddedjs.com/

[17.] https://github.com/janl/mustache.js

[18.] http://mozilla.github.io/nunjucks/

[19.] https://www.webcomponents.org/introduction

tags, the ability to import HTML partials, and a shadow DOM. The idea is to use it to develop modular and self-contained components that can be reused in different applications. The proposal is currently a living standard. The Polymer Project[20] is a JavaScript library that attempts to implement web components.

View Libraries

Over the past few years, a number of libraries have sprung up that deal with just the view layer of MVC. They have the single goal of making it easier to update the user interface while also keeping what is displayed synchronized with underlying data that it's representing. This means they can be integrated into a project and used either on their own or alongside other libraries that deal with other aspects of the application. The two view libraries that have emerged as the most popular so far are React and Vue.js.

React[21] is developed by Facebook and it has been hugely successful; quickly becoming one of the most popular JavaScript libraries that's used by a large number of popular websites such as the BBC, PayPal and Netflix. Vue.js[22] was developed by Evan You after he worked on AngularJS at Google. His idea was to design a lightweight view library that built on all the good things about AngularJS. It has become a very popular library (second only to React in terms of GitHub stars) and is starting to be adopted by a number of large websites.

Both React and Vue.js have changed the way developers think about the way user interfaces are built; particularly the way in which JavaScript is used. They have a number of similarities, but also solve the problems in very different ways.

React and Vue.js both use the concept of a *virtual DOM* to speed up the process of updating HTML pages. Instead of directly changing the DOM, as we did in Chapter 6, a virtual DOM is updated in memory. The real DOM is only updated when it needs to be and this is done by comparing any differences between the virtual DOM and actual DOM and only updating those elements that have actually changed. This is a process known as *reconciliation* and it's what makes React and Vue extremely fast at rendering web pages.

---

20. https://www.polymer-project.org
21. https://facebook.github.io/react/
22. https://vuejs.org

They also use the concept of components to represent visual elements. This means you can create multiple components that can then be reused in other projects as well as being combined to make larger components. Each component is entirely self-contained, with all the HTML, CSS and JavaScript being defined inside the component itself.

The main differences between React and Vue.js are to do with their respective implementations. React uses its own language called JSX. This allows HTML and JavaScript to be mixed together in an elegant and concise way. The result is transformed into JavaScript that is then used to produce the HTML views. Vue.js uses HTML-like templates that can contain logic and directives along with JavaScript objects to store any data.

There has been a certain amount of controversy created by view libraries such as React and Vue.js regarding the mixing of HTML and JavaScript and the use of inline JS and CSS in HTML files. This directly contradicts the "Three Layers of the Web" separation of concerns principle that was discussed all the way back in Chapter 1, and for a long time represented the gold-standard, best practice of web development. Many people have now started to feel that this is an outdated belief that worked for *web pages* that are just documents that use JavaScript to add extra functionality to the top. React and Vue.js were designed primarily for building dynamic *web applications* where the line between presentation and logic becomes much more blurred, since you're dealing with interactive elements. The stance that many React and Vue.js developers take is that everything to do with those interactive components should be encapsulated together in the component: presentation, markup and logic. This is an argument that looks like it will rage on for a long time though!

React and Vue.js aren't the only view libraries available. There are a number of alternatives that have a similar goal of managing the view layer and keeping data synchronized, but go about it in a slightly different way. Some focus on improving the rendering speed, while others use different notations.

View libraries are worth considering if you find your user interface is starting to become more complicated or has to react quickly to changes in data. They also make it easier to build more modular user interfaces with reusable components that can be combined together in different ways. There are a number of options available, and it's worth experimenting with a few of them in order to find one that fits your needs.

Package Managers

As modules have become more widely used in JavaScript, there's been a need for tools to manage them. Package managers allow developers to download modules from a central repository. A **package** is just a directory with one or more files of code, as well as a `package.json` file that contains information about the code in the package. Developers can also share any modules they create by uploading them to the central repository for others to use. A package manager makes it easy to install, upgrade and remove any packages that are used in a project. They also allow you to manage different versions of packages.

When you start to use more modules, you'll find that some of them depend on other modules to work. These are known as *dependencies*. Dependency management is the process of ensuring that all the dependencies a module requires are met. This can be difficult to do manually once a project becomes large, so package managers can also help with dependency management.

npm

The Node Package Manager was developed soon after Node.js was introduced to allow JavaScript code to be shared by developers. It has since grown into the largest repository of code libraries available.

npm allows you to install JavaScript packages onto your machine. Some packages rely on other packages, so npm acts as a *dependency manager*. For example, if you use npm to install a package, it will also install all the packages that the original package depends on as well.

If you followed the instructions to install Node.js all the way back in chapter 1 then you'll already have npm installed. If you didn't, you'll need to go back and do that before moving on, if you want to follow the examples in this section.

Searching for Packages

The npm repository is huge — it contains almost half a million different packages, ranging from popular libraries, such as jQuery and Lodash, to tiny modules that are literally a single line of code.

To find a package, you can use the `search` command. For example, if you wanted to find a package for testing, you could use the command `npm search test`. This will return a list of packages, including a description, the author and the date they were last updated.

You can also search for a package on the npm website[23].

npm init

The `npm init` command is used when you start a project. It walks you through creating a `package.json` file. This is a file that contains information about a JavaScript project in JSON format. This includes meta-information, such as the name and version number. It also includes information about any dependencies the project has, and can be used to specify how tests will be run.

To try it out, create a new directory called `project-x` and navigate to it in a terminal. Then enter the following command:

```
npm init
```

You'll then be walked through a number of questions about the project. Enter "project-x" as the name, then you can just accept the default suggestions for all the other questions by simply pressing ENTER. This should result in a file called `package.json` saved in the root of the directory, with contents similar to those shown below:

```
{
"name": "project-x",
```

---

23. https://www.npmjs.com

```
"version": "1.0.0",
"description": "",
"main": "index.js",
"scripts": {
  "test": "echo \"Error: no test specified\" && exit
↪ 1"
},
"author": "",
"license": "ISC"
}
```

This file will be updated by npm when you use it to install packages, so it keeps track of any packages used by the project and which dependencies it has. You can also edit it manually to specify any information about the project that might be required by other tools.

Installing Packages Locally

By default, any packages that are installed by npm are only installed in the current directory. They are all saved in a folder called `node_modules` in the root of the project directory. Any files in here can then be imported into your main JavaScript file and used.

To install a package locally, the `install` command is used. Adding the `--save` flag will ensure the `package.json` file is updated with the relevant information about the package.

For example, if we wanted to install the Lodash library we met in <u>Chapter 11</u>, we'd use the following command, from inside our project directory:

```
npm install --save lodash
```

Now, if you take a look inside the `package.json` file, you'll see that the following properties have been added:

```
  "dependencies": {
    "lodash": "^4.17.4"
}
```

This states that the lodash package is now a dependency of this project. The value of "^4.14.4" refers to the version of Lodash that has been installed. This uses semantic versioning where the first number refers to the major version number, the second is the minor version number, and the third number is for patches. The caret symbol (^) means that when npm is installing the package, it install the latest version that matches the major version number only.

Dependencies

When you install a package using npm it will become a **dependency** of your project by default. This will get listed under "dependencies" in the `package.json` file as we saw in the example above. If a package is a dependency, it means the application requires it to run.

Alternatively you can install a package as a `devDependency`. These are packages that aren't required by the application itself but are used in development to complete tasks to do with the application. Examples of these could be running tests or transpiling the code. Any packages installed as a `devDependency` will not be packaged in the final build of an application that is deployed.

To install a package as a `devDependency`, you need to add the `--save-dev` flag, like so:

```
npm install --save-dev jest
```

This will install the Jest testing framework that we met in Chapter 10 and add the following lines to the package.json file:

```
  "devDependencies": {
    "jest": "^20.0.4"
```

```
}
```

You can also install a specific version of a package by placing the @ symbol after the package name, followed by the version you require. For example, you could install version 18.1.0 of Jest, using the following command:

```
npm install --save-dev jest@18.1.0
```

 Which Version?

It is usually best to just install the latest version of a package, although there may be times when you need to install a specific version of a package so it's compatible with other packages.

The package.json File

The `package.json` file is used to manage any packages that are installed locally. It keeps track on which packages are installed, and what dependencies they rely on. It also allows you to specify specific versions of packages to use.

All `package.json` require the following pieces of information:

■ "name" – This must be all in lowercase and contain no spaces.
■ "version" – This uses semantic versioning of the form major.minor.patch.

You can create a `package.json` file inside a directory by running the `npm init` command. This will ask you some questions that will be used to populate the file. If you don't want to go through the process of answering all the questions, you can use the `--yes` or `-y` flag to bypass the questions and use the default options:

```
npm install --yes
```

You can also set most of the default options using `npm set` command:

```
npm set init.author.email "daz@sitepoint.com"
npm set init.author.name "DAZ"
npm set init.license "MIT"
```

 README

> Most projects will have a file in the root directory called README. This files serves as the application's documentation and contains information about it. If you leave the description field blank, then npm will use the first line of the README file as the description.

One of the most powerful features of the `package.json` file is that it contains all the information about a project's dependencies. So if you clone somebody else's project, all the information about the packages it requires are contained inside the `package.json` file. npm also makes it trivially easy to then install all the packages that are required to run the application by simply entering the following command from inside the root directory of the project:

```
npm install
```

This will then download and install all the necessary packages, as well as any dependencies.

Version 5 of npm introduced the `package-lock.json` file, which is automatically created when any changes are made to the `node_modules` directory or the `package.json` file. This acts as an exact snapshot of the packages used in a project at any single point in time, and helps avoid problems that were caused when a package updated and conflicted with the latest versions of some of its dependencies.

Installing Globally

It is also possible to install packages globally so they're available system-wide from any directory on your machine. While this might sound like a good idea at first, it isn't usually recommended, as the package files are not saved with the project (they are installed in the system folders on your machine) and there will be no reference to the package as a dependency in the `package.json` file.

There are some cases, however, when it makes sense to install a package globally. This is usually when the package is to be used on a system-wide basis, rather than just for a specific project.

To install a package globally, the `global` flag needs to be added to the `install` command:

```
npm install --global lodash
```

There are also some cases where it makes sense to have a global install as well as a local install. Lodash is a good example of this. You might want it available on your system so you can have quick access to the library when you're experimenting with code in the Node REPL, but you might also want it as a specific dependency in a web application you build. If you didn't install it locally, this would mean the code would work fine on your machine (because you have a global install), but it wouldn't work on a machine that didn't have a global install of Lodash. The easiest solution to this is to install the package both globally and locally. There is nothing wrong with this, it just means the files exist in two (or more) different places on your machine.

 Permissions

You need to be careful about permissions when installing packages globally. When you install locally, you are installing packages to a directory that the current user owns and has permission to alter. When you install globally you are sometimes required to install the package into a system directory that you don't have permission to access. This means you often need to sign in as a "super user" to install them. There are some security issues with doing this, and there can also be permission issues if packages try to alter or write to any files.

Three ways to fix this problem are explained on the npm website[24].

Listing Installed Packages

You can list all the packages that have been installed locally using the `list` command:

```
npm list
```

This will often produce a much longer list than expected, as it also lists the packages that have also been installed as dependencies. The list is presented as a tree that shows the dependency hierarchy.

If you only want to see the packages that you have installed directly, you can use the `depth` flag, with a value of 0:

```
npm list --depth=0
```

This will only list the direct dependencies of the application (including `devDependencies`).

You can find out which packages have been installed globally by adding the `--global` or `-g` flag:

```
npm list --global
```

Updating A Package

You can find out if any of the packages you have installed have been updated by running the following command:

```
npm outdated
```

This will display a list of any packages that are listed in `package.json` and have a more recent version available than what's currently installed.

It's worth using this command every now and then to check if any updates are available, as it is often beneficial to keep the packages up to date.

npm makes it easy to update a package to the latest version using the `update` command. For example, you can update to the latest version of Jest using the following command:

```
npm update jest
```

You can update *all* the packages in the directory by simply entering the following command:

```
npm update
```

To find out if any packages that have been installed globally are out of date, run the following command:

```
npm outdated -g
```

If any global packages need updating, this is done using the `update` command, but you need to add the `--global` or `-g` flag:

```
npm update --global
```

Uninstalling Packages

You can use npm to uninstall a package using the `uninstall` command:

```
npm uninstall lodash
```

This will remove the package from the `node_modules` directory.

Use npm To Remove Packages

You can easily remove a package that has been installed locally by simply deleting its directory from the `node_modules` directory, but it is preferable to use npm as this will also take care of removing any redundant dependencies as well as updating the `package.json` file to reflect the changes.

To remove it from the dependencies in package.json, you will need to use the save flag:

```
npm uninstall --save lodash
```

If it was installed as a `devDependency`, you will need to add the `--save-dev` flag to remove it from the `package.json` file:

```
npm uninstall --save-dev jest
```

Global packages can be uninstalled by adding the `--global` or `-g` to the uninstall command:

```
npm uninstall --global lodash
```

Aliases

npm uses a number of aliases for common commands that can be used to cut down on a few keystrokes.

i is an alias for `install` un is an alias for `uninstall` up is an alias for `update` ls is an alias for `list`

Yarn

Yarn[25] has emerged recently as a popular alternative to npm. It was developed to try and get around some problems that npm had with the speed and consistency of installing packages, as well as some security concerns to do with npm allowing packages to run on installation.

Yarn generally installs packages much faster than npm due to the fact that it caches packages. It has a slightly different set of commands, but generally works in the same way as npm.

Content Delivery Networks

Content delivery networks (CDNs) are systems of distributed servers that can deliver web resources, such as JavaScript, CSS or image files to a user based on their geographic location. This means they're able to deliver the content quickly and efficiently with a high degree of availability. These resources also get cached on the user's machine, meaning that less requests need to be made to download the resource. This is particularly beneficial when using a CDN for a popular library such as jQuery. This is because once the user has downloaded the file from a site, it will be cached, and can then be used again by other sites without the need for another network request.

unpkg[26] is a global *content delivery network* (or CDN) that allows you to include any package from npm in a web page without having to install it on your own machine. Using a CDN, such as unpkg, is a good way to quickly add a npm package to your project, especially if you just want to test it out. But using this approach has some drawbacks. Some libraries, such as React, put the burden of processing onto the browser, rather than when the code is transpiled. This is fine when experimenting, but in a production environment, this would take too much toll on the browser, and result in a sub-optimal experience for the user. For this reason, you will eventually need to consider using a build tool such as Webpack to take care of managing any external libraries that you use, and for that reason, this is covered later in the chapter.

[25.] https://github.com/yarnpkg/yarn
[26.] https://unpkg.com

Deploying JavaScript

When it comes to deploying your JavaScript program, it's time to think about optimizing the code. If you've used multiple external libraries and lots of modules, you might have a large number of files that need to be included in your HTML file. One way of doing this is to simply include a different `<script>` tag for each JavaScript file. However, this is not optimal for a number of reasons:

■ The scripts must be included in the correct order.

■ Each file represents a separate request to the server.

■ The files will be large.

The solution is to combine all the scripts into a single minified and compressed file. This file is often named `bundle.min.js` to signify that it's a number of files bundled together and has also been minified. Once you've combined all the files into a single file, and minified and compressed it, the next step is to add it to the HTML file. The optimal position for the `<script>` tag is right at the end of the page, just before the closing `<body>` tag, which we have used in all our examples:

```
<!doctype html>
<html lang='en'>
<head>
    <meta charset='utf-8'>
    <title>Ninja JavaScript</title>
</head>
<body>

    ...

    <script src='bundle.min.js'></script>
</body>
</html>
```

This will ensure the page has finished loading before the JavaScript code is processed.

Transpiling Code

Code transpilers take JavaScript code and turn it into JavaScript code! That might sound strange but it's all to do with the fact that browsers struggle to keep up with the fast-moving pace of ECMAScript versions. A code transpiler allows you to write your code in the latest version of ECMAScript, using all the latest features, then convert it into an older variant of JavaScript that is compatible with most browsers.

The most common use of transpilers recently has been to allow developers to write in ES6 code then transpile it into ECMAScript 5, which was widely supported by most browsers. This has helped to facilitate the swift adoption of ES6 code, and meant it could be used in production code and tutorials. This, in turn, probably contributed to browser vendors implementing ES6 features into their browser engines quickly.

Most ES6 features have now been implemented in the most up-to-date browsers, but this probably won't make transpilers redundant. Developers will always want to use the most up-to-date language features, and browser engines will always be slightly behind the curve (although browser vendors are getting *much* faster at implementing features these days). It also means you can ensure your deployed code will still work on any older browsers that some of your audience might still be using.

Babel[27] is the most popular transpiler for converting the most up-to-date version of ECMAScript into an older flavor of JavaScript.

Minification

Minification is the process of removing any unnecessary characters from your code to reduce the file size. This includes all comments, whitespace, and other characters that are superfluous.

Tools are available to do this, known as *minifiers*. Some popular choices include:

- YUI Compressor[28]

---

[27]. https://babeljs.io

■ Google's Closure[29]

■ UglifyJS[30]

These tools can also change variable and function names to single letters. This is often referred to as code obfuscation as it can make the code more difficult to read. They will also try to employ optimizations to make the code run faster. For example, here is the myMaths object that we created at the start of this chapter after it has been converted to ES5 and then minified using UglifyJS:

```
var myMaths={square:function(n){return
  n*n},sum:function(n,t){return
  t&&(n=n.map(t)),n.reduce(function(n,t){return
  n+t})},mean:function(n){return
  this.sum(n)/n.length},variance:function(n){return
  this.sum(n,this.square)/n.length-this.square(this.mean(n))}};
```

As you can see, it is significantly smaller in size, but much more difficult to read and make sense of!

Minifying your code can have a major effect on the overall size of your files, making them download and run faster. It also means that your code can use descriptive naming conventions and be well-commented, as these will be stripped away by the minifier tools. As a general rule, you should aim to use well-commented and descriptive code in development and minified code in production (since there's no need for end users to read comments).

Files can also be compressed on the server using a file-compression tool such as gzip, which can have a dramatic effect reducing the file size. Using both minification and compression in production means that JavaScript files are a mere fraction of their original size, making them much quicker to download.

---

28. https://www.npmjs.org/package/yui
29. https://developers.google.com/closure/compiler/
30. https://github.com/mishoo/UglifyJS

Folder Structure

As you application gets larger, you will need to start thinking about having a more structured approach to organizing your files. You can organize your files in any way you like, but there are some conventions that are often used for directory names that are worth knowing about.

Root Files

In the root of any folder structure you will find a file called `index.html`. This is traditionally the page that a web browser will load by default, although it is possible to instruct it to load *any* file by programming how the server responds to requests.

For small projects, such as most of the examples in this book, it is usually okay to put *all* the JavaScript into a single file in the root directory. It is usually called `main.js`, `index.js`, `app.js` or something similar. As a project gets bigger, you'll find that it helps to separate different parts of functionality into different modules then use this file as an *entry-point* for loading any modules. You might also want to move all of your JavaScript into a separate folder, called `js`, `scripts` or something similar.

In a similar way, it is customary to have a single CSS file in the root directory or keep multiple CSS files saved in a folder called `CSS`, `stylesheets` or similar.

src folder

Code that needs to be transpiled is often placed inside a folder called `src` (short for "source"). The transpiler can then compile the JavaScript code into a single file in a different location (usually this is either the root directory or the `dist` folder).

dist folder

The output of any transpiled code from the `src` folder is usually placed inside a folder called `dist` (short for "distribution"). This is the only part of the application code that is actually distributed when it is deployed. Even though there might be many different files inside the `src` folder, the result of transpilation means there is usually only a single JavaScript file inside the `dist` folder, usually called `budle.js` or `bundle.min.js` if it has also been minified.

lib folder

Any modules are usually stored in a folder called `lib` (short for "library") that is usually placed inside the `src` folder. Third-party libraries are often placed inside a folder called `vendor`, although they are sometimes also placed inside the `lib` folder.

Third-Party Code

Any third-party code installed using npm will be installed into a directory called `node_modules`. This can be configured to use a different folder name, but for consistency it is best to stick to this convention.

If you only use a small number of modules, you can just keep them all in the root of the `lib` directory, but as the size of your application grows, you might need to start thinking about how to organize the modules into separate folders.

Organization By Type

This structure has folders for the different types of file that will be used in your project such as Javascript, CSS, Images and Tests. All your JavaScript files then go in the `JS` folder, all your stylesheet files go in the CSS folder, all your HTML files go in the `views` folder etc.

A typical folder structure based on type might look like the following:

- src
    - CSS
    - JS
    - views
    - tests
- dist
    - index.html
    - bundle.min.js

- package.json
- node_modules
- README

Modular Organization

This structure groups files by *feature* rather than *type*. So instead of placing all the JavaScript files in one place (based on type), we would put all the files associated with a certain feature together in a single folder. So all the JavaScript files, stylesheets, views and tests associated with feature X would go in a folder called `featureX`, for example.

There are a number of advantages to this approach, particularly in big projects:

- It keeps all the code related to that particular feature all in one place, making it easy to find.
- It's extensible – modules can grow to incorporate their own file structure and sub-directories as required.
- It allows developers to work on a specific feature without affecting another feature. This is particular useful when you're working in teams.
- The modular nature of this approach makes it easy to switch one feature for another, without affecting the rest of the project.
- Each module is self-contained, making them easy to test.

A typical modular folder structure might look like the following:

- src
  - index.html
  - lib
    - app
      - app.js
      - app.css
      - app.test.js
        - moduleA
      - moduleA.html
      - moduleA.js
      - moduleA.css
      - moduleA.test.js

- moduleB
  - moduleB.html
  - moduleB.js
  - moduleB.css
  - moduleB.test.js
- dist
  - index.html
  - bundle.min.js
- package.json
- node_modules
- README

Note that the **app** folder is for *shared* resources that are used by the main application itself.

Note also that inside each module's directory, you might begin to have sub-directories for JavaScript, CSS and tests rather than single files, if the modules start to become large themselves.

Start Small

Personally I would recommend that you start any project with just the root files: `index.html`, `main.js` and `main.css`.

As the project starts to grow, you could progress using an `application` folder to place the application specific JavaScript and CSS code, as well as any tests and HTML views.

If you start to transpile your code, you should consider keeping your original code in a `src` directory and transpiling the code into a `dist` directory.

If the project grows further still, you might begin to separate the code into separate modules that require their own folders, particularly if the project is being worked on by a team of developers.

The important thing when choosing a directory structure is that it works for you and remains consistent. Also remember that your code structure will have to fit in with any third-party tools that you choose to use. Most tools will allow you to configure the directory structure to suit your needs, although sometimes it's easier to stick to the conventions that they used.

Webpack

Webpack is a module bundler that takes all the JavaScript files used in your project and bundles them altogether in one file.

Webpack also uses the concept of "loaders", which allows you to perform tasks such as:

- Transpiling code

- Minifying code

- Linting code

- Testing code

- Compiling CSS preprocessor files (such as Sass, Less or Stylus) into standard CSS files.

Webpack's loaders also let you compile multiple CSS and image files into a single destination folder. It's also possible to write your own loader file to automate a specific task.

Webpack is an important tool for managing a modern JavaScript project and getting it ready for deployment. We're going to have a look at how to install Webpack, as well as a few examples of how to use it. We'll only be focusing on bundling JavaScript files in these examples, but you can see how to do the same with your CSS by checking out the documentation.

A Webpack Example

To get started, we need to create a new folder called `webpack-example`, then navigate to that folder in the terminal and create a `package.json` file:

```
npm init -y
```

Next, we use npm to install Webpack. Since it's only used as part of the development process, we use the `--save-dev` flag:

```
npm install --save-dev webpack
```

Webpack should now be added to the `devdependencies` property in the `package.json` file.

Webpack basically bundles files together into an output file. To test it out, we're going to try and use our installation of Lodash. If you didn't install Lodash earlier, do it now, using the following command:

```
npm install lodash --save
```

Now create a simple HTML file called `webpack.html` that includes the following code:

```
<!doctype html>
<html lang='en'>
<head>
<meta charset='utf-8'>
<title>Webpack Example</title>
</head>
<body>
<script src='bundle.js'></script>
</body>
</html>
```

This page doesn't really do anything, although it refers to a file called `budle.js`. This is going to be created by Webpack. It is convention to call the output file `budle.js` as it's all the JavaScript files bundled together as a single file.

Next we need to create a JavaScript file called `main.js` that contains the following code:

```
import _ from 'lodash';
console.log(_.now());
```

This uses the ES6 module syntax to import the Lodash library, and assigns it to the variable _, which acts as a namespace for the library (you could assign it to any variable name, but the _ symbol is the convention, due to the name of the library). We then call the `now()` from Lodash and use `console.log()` to display the result in the console. The `now()` method simply returns the number of seconds since the Epoch.

On its own, this code won't work, but we can use Webpack to sort out importing the Lodash library from the `node_modules` directory. To do this, we simply need to run the following command in the terminal:

```
./node_modules/.bin/webpack main.js bundle.js
```

The first argument is the file that contains our code ("main.js"), and the second argument is the file that we want the output to be written to ("bundle.js").

After you run this code, you should notice that a new file called `budle.js` has been created. Now, if you open `webpack.html>` and open the console, it should display a number that represents the number of seconds since the epoch (at the time of writing, it was around 1,500,000,000,000). This means the Lodash library has been successfully imported into our `main.js` file and can now be used.

To make things simpler, going forward, we can create a webpack configuration file called `webpack.config.js`. This is actually just a standard JavaScript file and should be saved in the root of the directory and contain the following code:

```
module.exports = {
entry: './main.js',
output: {
```

```
    filename: 'bundle.js',
    path: __dirname
  }
};
```

This can be run using the following line of code in the terminal:

```
./node_modules/.bin/webpack
```

We can use npm to simplify this. Update the "scripts" property in your `package.json` file to the following:

```
  "scripts": {
  "test": "echo \"Error: no test specified\" && exit
↪ 1",
    "build": "webpack"
}
```

Now you can run Webpack using the following command:

```
npm run build
```

 Running Other Processes, Too

The technique above can be used to run other processes, by adding them as properties of the **scripts** object. npm's **run** command can then be used to run the code specified.

The property name **build** is arbitrary (although it is the convention), and it could be named anything ... even **webpack**.

Quiz Ninja Project

We'll now put some of the ideas we've learned in this chapter into practice in our quiz project. First of all we'll move our code into separate modules. We'll create a module for the `view` object, another for the `game` object and one more for our utility functions, `random()` and `shuffle()`. We'll also update our file structure to keep all our source files in a `src` folder then use Webpack to compile them all together into a `dist` folder.

To get started, create a folder called `quiz` (or something similar), navigate to it in the terminal and enter the following code:

```
npm init
```

Answer all the questions to create a `package.json` file that is similar to the one below.

```
{
"name": "quiz-ninja",
"version": "1.0.0",
"description": "A JavaScript quiz.",
"main": "main.js",
"scripts": {
 "test": "echo \"Error: no test specified\" && exit
↳ 1"
},
"keywords": [
    "quiz",
    "ninja",
    "javascript"
],
"author": "DAZ",
"license": "MIT"
}
```

Now we need to create our directory structure. Create a folder called `dist` at the root of the directory and copy the `index.html` and `styles.css` files inside it.

 A Simulated Example

> The `dist` directory is normally only used for files that have been compiled from the `src` directory. In reality you would probably use some sort of pre-processors to create your HTML and CSS files. In this example, we're just going to pretend that this has happened and `index.html` and `styles.css` have been compiled into the `dist` directory.

We will also need to make a small update to the `index.html` file so that it loads a JavaScript file called `bundle.min.js` in the `dist` directory, which is the file that Webpack will build:

```html
<!doctype html>
<html lang='en'>
<head>
<meta charset='utf-8'>
 <meta name='description' content='A JavaScript Quiz
↪ Game'>
<title>Quiz Ninja</title>
<link rel='stylesheet' href='styles.css'>
</head>
<body>
<section class='dojo'>
    <div class='quiz-body'>
    <header>
 <div id='timer'>Time:
↪ <strong>20</strong></div>
 <div id='score'>Score:
↪ <strong>0</strong></div>
 <div id='hiScore'>High Score:
↪ <strong></strong></div>
        <h1>Quiz Ninja!</h1>
    </header>
    <div id='question'></div>
    <div id='response'></div>
    <div id='result'></div>
```

```
    <div id='info'></div>
    <button id='start'>Click to Start</button>
    </div>
</section>
<script src='bundle.min.js'></script>
</body>
</html>
```

Now we're going to create our JavaScript modules in the src directory. Create src folder in the root directory and save the following in a file called utilities.js:

```
function random(a,b=1) {
  // if only 1 argument is provided, we need to swap the
↪ values of a and b
if (b === 1) {
    [a,b] = [b,a];
}
return Math.floor((b-a+1) * Math.random()) + a;
}

function shuffle(array) {
for (let i = array.length; i; i--) {
    let j = random(i)-1;
    [array[i - 1], array[j]] = [array[j], array[i - 1]];
}
}

export {
random,
shuffle
}
```

This contains our utility functions random() and shuffle() that we will use. Separating them into their own module is a good move as it will make it easier to update and use them in future projects.

The next module will include the code for the quiz itself. Save the following code in `quiz.js`:

```javascript
import { random, shuffle } from './utilities.js';

const view = {
score: document.querySelector('#score strong'),
question: document.querySelector('#question'),
result: document.querySelector('#result'),
info: document.querySelector('#info'),
start: document.querySelector('#start'),
response: document.querySelector('#response'),
timer: document.querySelector('#timer strong'),
hiScore: document.querySelector('#hiScore strong'),
render(target,content,attributes) {
    for(const key in attributes) {
        target.setAttribute(key, attributes[key]);
    }
    target.innerHTML = content;
},
show(element){
    element.style.display = 'block';
},
hide(element){
    element.style.display = 'none';
},
setup(){
    this.show(this.question);
    this.show(this.response);
    this.show(this.result);
    this.hide(this.start);
    this.render(this.score,game.score);
    this.render(this.result,'');
    this.render(this.info,'');
    this.render(this.hiScore, game.hiScore());
},
teardown(){
    this.hide(this.question);
    this.hide(this.response);
    this.show(this.start);
```

```javascript
        this.render(this.hiScore, game.hiScore());
    },
    buttons(array){
     return array.map(value =>
    ↪ `<button>${value}</button>`).join('');
    }
};

const game = {
start(quiz){
    console.log('start() invoked');
    this.score = 0;
    this.questions = [...quiz];
    view.setup();
    this.secondsRemaining = 20;
    this.timer = setInterval( this.countdown , 1000 );
    this.ask();
},
countdown() {
    game.secondsRemaining--;
    view.render(view.timer,game.secondsRemaining);
    if(game.secondsRemaining <= 0) {
        game.gameOver();
    }
},
ask(name){
    console.log('ask() invoked');
    if(this.questions.length > 2) {
    shuffle(this.questions);
    this.question = this.questions.pop();
 const options = [this.questions[0].realName,
↪ this.questions[1].realName, this.question.realName];
    shuffle(options);
 const question = `What is ${this.question.name}'s real
↪ name?`;
    view.render(view.question,question);
    view.render(view.response,view.buttons(options));
    }
    else {
    this.gameOver();
```

```
    }
},
check(event){
    console.log('check(event) invoked')
    const response = event.target.textContent;
    const answer = this.question.realName;
    if(response === answer){
    console.log('correct');
    view.render(view.result,'Correct!',{'class':'correct'});
    this.score++;
    view.render(view.score,this.score);
    } else {
    console.log('wrong');
 view.render(view.result,`Wrong! The correct answer was
↪ ${answer}`,{'class':'wrong'});
    }
    this.ask();
},
gameOver(){
    console.log('gameOver() invoked')
 view.render(view.info,`Game Over, you scored ${this.score}
↪ point${this.score !== 1 ? 's' : ''}`);
    view.teardown();
    clearInterval(this.timer);
},
hiScore(){
    const hi = localStorage.getItem('highScore') || 0;
 if(this.score > hi || hi === 0)
↪ localStorage.setItem('highScore',this.score);
    return localStorage.getItem('highScore');
}
};

export {
view,
game
}
```

This is the same code for the `view` and `game` objects that we used previously in `main.js`, but made into a module by using the `export` declaration at the end. We also imported the `utilities.js` module at the start, which allows us to use the `random()` and `shuffle()` functions in this module.

Now that we have our modules in place, we need to update `main.js` to import them:

```
import { view, game } from './quiz.js';

const url = 'http://spbooks.github.io/questions.json';

fetch(url)
.then(res => res.json())
.then(quiz => {
view.start.addEventListener('click', () =>
↳ game.start(quiz.questions), false);
view.response.addEventListener('click', (event) =>
↳ game.check(event), false);
});
```

This file will serve as an entry point, in that Webpack will look at this file and determine which modules to load.

Next, we'll use Webpack to prepare our code for deployment. This will involve transpiling our code into ES5 using Babel, and minifying the code using the Babili plugin[31]. The minified code will then be placed inside a single file in the `dist` directory.

To do this, we need to install Webpack locally, as well as Babel, some Babel modules and the Babili plugin:

```
npm install --save-dev webpack babel-core babel-loader
↳ babel-preset-env babili-webpack-plugin
```

[31.] https://babeljs.io/blog/2016/08/30/babili

We use the `--save-dev` flag to install these modules as all of them are only used in development.

Next, we need to configure WebPack. Create a file called webpack.config.js in the root directory and add the following code:

```javascript
const webpack = require('webpack');
const BabiliPlugin = require("babili-webpack-plugin");

module.exports = {
context: __dirname + '/src',
entry: './main.js',
output: {
    path: __dirname + '/dist',
    filename: 'bundle.min.js'
},

module: {
    rules: [
    {
        test: /\.js$/,
        exclude: /node_modules/,
        use: {
        loader: 'babel-loader',
        options: {
            presets: ['env' ]
        }
        }
    }
    ]
},
plugins: [
    new BabiliPlugin(),
    new webpack.DefinePlugin({
    'process.env': {
    'NODE_ENV': JSON.stringify('production')
    }
})
    ]
```

```
};
```

The context and entry properties tell WebPack to take the code found in /src/main.js, and the output property tells it to place the transpiled code in /dist/bundle.min.js. The rules property contains the standard rules to transpile from the latest version of ECMAScript into ES5 code. We have also added a reference to the Babili plugin in the plugins property that will minify the output.

To run this as a build script, add the following line to the "scripts" property of your package.json file:

```
"build": "webpack --progress --colors --profile"
```

 Flags

The flags used with the webpack command above are quite common when transpiling JavaScript. --progress will display what is happening as WebPack does its thing, and --colors will display it all in different colors. The --profile flag will make WebPack show how long each part of the build takes, which can be helpful in identifying any bottlenecks in the build process.

Our last job is to run the build script:

```
npm run build
```

This should create a file called bundle.min.js inside the dist directory. This contains all the JavaScript the application needs in just one, minified file without having to load any external libraries at runtime.

Have a go at playing the game by loading index.html in your browser:

15-2. Quiz Ninja

Although we haven't changed the functionality of the quiz game in this chapter, we have created a modular structure and separated the source files from the files that are deployed. If this project was to be deployed in public, then only the files in the `dist` directory would actually be distributed. The files in the `src` directory would only be used for development.

This makes the code easier to maintain in the future, as well as ensuring that the distributed code uses the optimal file size and works in a large number of browsers. These are both important tasks to consider when writing JavaScript that will be deployed to a server.

Chapter Summary

- JavaScript libraries provide methods to make common tasks easier to achieve.

- Libraries can make programming much easier, but you should think carefully about whether you require a library, and which one is best for your needs.

- jQuery and Lodash are two popular libraries that provide a large number of useful and well-tested functions.

- npm and Yarn are package managers that can be used to install JavaScript packages, as well as any dependencies that they require.

- A module is a self-contained piece of code that provides functions and methods that can then be used in other files and by other modules.

- ES6 added support for modules, allowing code to be abstracted into their own self-contained files and imported into another file.

- The MVC pattern is used to organize code into distinct sections that are responsible for different elements of an application.

- Template files can be used to separate view code from JavaScript; they also enable dynamic code and programming logic to be used to generate markup.

- React and Vue.js are popular JavaScript view libraries that render components and keep track of their state.

- Minification is the process of removing any redundant characters from the code in order to reduce its file size.

- Files can be compressed on the server using the gzip compression tool.

- Webpack can be used to bundle multiple files into a single bundle, and automate common tasks such as transpiling, minifying code and running tests.

- Before code is deployed, it should be concatenated into a single file, minified and compressed. The script tag should be placed just before the closing `</body>` tag to ensure that all elements on the page have loaded before the script runs.

In the next chapter, we'll be looking at some of the features in the next version of JavaScript, as well as some ideas of what you can build using JavaScript.

Chapter **16**

Next Steps

We are nearing the end of the road to becoming a JavaScript ninja. But as one journey finishes, a new one begins. Now it's time to level up your JavaScript ninja skills. In this final chapter, we're going to see what's in store for JavaScript in the future. We'll also look at how to become a better programmer, as well as offer some ideas of what to do with your newfound JavaScript programming skills.

In this chapter, we'll cover the following topics:

▓ The future of JavaScript

▓ Ninja skills to take you to the next level

▓ Project ideas for JavaScript development.

What's Next For JavaScript?

This is an exciting time for the JavaScript language. It is developing at a rapid rate and its new annual release schedule means that it's able to adapt quickly to the changing needs of developers. JavaScript engines are also getting quicker at implementing the latest features, so they become available sooner. The yearly release cycle means that not as many new features make it into each release, and so far, there aren't any big changes on the horizon for ES2018. The changes proposed so far include:

- Allowing dynamic importing of modules using conditional code.
- New features for the spread operator.
- A standard way of accessing the `global` object.
- Support for asynchronous iteration that will allow you to perform a loop asynchronously. This means that the code can move on to the next iteration in the loop before the last task has completed.
- Numerous other improvements, particularly with regular expressions.

As you can see, there are no major changes, but over time, JavaScript will continue to evolve as a language with each increment. The yearly release cycle should give developers time to learn any new features and keep their skills up to date.

WebAssembly

WebAssembly is an emerging standard that provides the ability to compile a low-level programming language such as C or C++ into code that can run in the browser. WebAssembly is significantly faster than JavaScript due to it being in a binary format. This means applications that require more raw speed and processing power can run in a browser without the need for a plugin.

WebAssembly is not a replacement for JavaScript. Rather it is a complementary technology. JavaScript will still be used for most web applications, but WebAssembly code will be able to run from within a JavaScript application when the need arises. WebAssembly offers the exciting prospect that the browser will be able to run even more powerful applications that operate on a similar level to native applications. It will be particularly useful for improving the standard of online gaming, as well as uses in scientific modeling and the Internet of Things. As WebAssembly becomes more available, there is a chance that, slowly but surely, it will start to replace JavaScript as a compile target. Developers will eventually start using tools to compile code into WebAssembly instead of JavaScript before deploying it.

JavaScript Fatigue

JavaScript fatigue is a term coined over the last few years to describe the explosive growth of JavaScript libraries, tools and frameworks, and the speed at which they come and go out of fashion. Keeping up to date with the current JavaScript trends can be very hard and tiring, especially when there's work to be done!

Many people, particularly beginners, can often feel overwhelmed by the sheer volume of different technologies that now need to be learned just to produce a simple web app. It is not uncommon to read an online tutorial that is overflowing with technical jargon and acronyms such as ES6, jQuery, React, Redux, WebPack, Babel, TDD, Jest, Git, async, OOP, functional-style, npm, Node.js, Yarn, SQL, NoSQL, Graph databases ... it's no wonder that some people find it all so confusing!

Hopefully, reading this book has gone a long way to explaining what a lot of the terms mean and how different libraries and frameworks fit into your workflow. You should also keep in mind that you can achieve a lot with just plain old vanilla JavaScript. You can go a long way with some HTML files, a sprinkling of CSS and a single JavaScript file.

Modern JavaScript certainly has a rich and diverse ecosystem, and this means there is a huge choice of tools to use. This can seem daunting at first, but in reality it's a good thing that there is a large choice on offer. You just need to be disciplined about when and how you choose which tools to use.

Of course, it's useful to keep up to date about modern JavaScript practices, but you also need to accept that you can't do it all. Try to keep up to date with any emerging trends and developments, but don't feel you have to adopt them straight away. If you start to develop *magpie syndrome* (when you can't help but be attracted to the latest shiny JavaScript framework) then you'll never have any time to master anything.

The best way to move forward is to avoid paralysis by analysis and get coding! The more code you write, the more you will start to recognise where a certain tool might help to improve your workflow. As you become more experienced, you will soon know when it's time to introduce a new tool into a project. And if everything is working fine with your current setup, there's no need to change it. The old adage of "if it ain't broke, don't fix it" still holds!

Some interesting thoughts on the matter can be found in the following articles:

Ninja Skills

At this stage of the book, you should be well on your way to becoming a proficient JavaScript programmer. But as JavaScript has matured, a whole ecosystem has built up around it, which means that a Ninja programmer needs to do more than just know the basics of the language. You'll need to develop further skills that set you apart from regular programmers. This section outlines a few key skills that are well worth mastering to help take your programming to the next level.

Version Control

Version control software allows you to track all the changes that are made to your code, because every version of your code is kept and can be recalled at any time. Many people use a crude form of version control by saving different versions of code with different file names such as "projectV1.js", "projectV2.js", "projectV3.js"... and so on. This is a reasonable method, but it can be error-prone. If you've used this method before, how many times have you forgotten to change the name before saving? It also doesn't offer the same benefits that can be gained by using a source control management tool.

One of the most popular source control management tools is Git[1], written by Linus Torvalds, the creator of Linux. Git enables you to roll back to a previous

---

[1] http://git-scm.com/

version of your code. You can also branch your code to test new features without changing the current stable codebase. Git is a distributed source control system, which means that many people can fork a piece of code, develop it independently, then merge any of their changes back into the main codebase.

Git uses the command line to issue commands, but there are a large number of GUI front ends that can be installed to give a visual representation of the code.

Source control is invaluable if you're working in a team, as it means that different developers can work on the same piece of code without worrying about causing any errors in the main codebase. If any mistakes do accidentally end up in the main codebase, they can easily be rectified by rolling back to the last stable version. It also prevents you from overwriting somebody else's code.

There are a number of online services that can host Git repositories, including GitHub[2], Kilnhttps://www.fogcreek.com/kiln/, Bitbucket[3] and Codeplane[4]. They can be used to host an online Git repository that can then be forked by other developers, making it particularly useful for team projects. Some of these services make all the code public, so they're often used by open-source projects to host source code; others keep the code private, and are used to host personal or business projects.

As a ninja JavaScript developer, your life will be made much easier by integrating Git into your everyday workflow. You can find out more about Git in *Jump Start Git* by Shaumik Daityari[5].

Keep Your Knowledge Up to Date

The world of JavaScript is fast-moving, and it's getting faster every year. You need to ensure that you keep up to date with recent developments and best practices. Here are some suggestions of how you can keep your knowledge current:

- Subscribe to blogs such as SitePoint's JavaScript channel.

[2.] https://github.com/
[3.] https://bitbucket.org/
[4.] https://codeplane.com/
[5.] https://www.sitepoint.com/premium/books/jump-start-git

- Write your own blog.

- Follow other JavaScript developers on Twitter.

- Attend conferences or local meetups.

- Read magazine articles.

- Contribute to an open-source project.

- Join a local or online user group.

- Listen to podcasts.

Use Common JavaScript Coding Patterns

A **pattern** is a piece of code that solves a common problem and represents best practice. In the time that JavaScript has existed, a number of patterns have emerged that help to write maintainable code that has been proven to work. In JavaScript development, a pattern is the generally accepted way of achieving a specific goal, often because it's the best way of doing it.

Another advantage of using standard coding practices is that it makes sharing code between developers far less painful. If you use the same style and terminology, developers will find it much easier to follow your code. Patterns often have names attached to them (for example, the IIFE pattern that we've seen previously). This makes it easier to discuss different patterns, since the name can be referred to explicitly.

An antipattern is a piece of code that's accepted bad practice. They generally cause more problems than they solve and should be avoided. Not using `const`, `let` or `var` to declare variables is an example of an antipattern. This pollutes the global namespace and makes the likelihood of naming collisions much more likely. Another example of an antipattern is to fork your code based on "browser sniffing' instead of user feature detection. Other examples that have been mentioned already in this book are declaring functions using the `Function()` constructor, using `document.write()`, using `new Array()` and `new Object()` constructor functions to create arrays and objects instead of the literals `[]` and `{}` and not ending statements with a semicolon. What is considered an antipattern can also become a little evangelical: Many developers consider extending `Object.prototype` (monkey patching) to be an antipattern, and a sizeable majority will argue that having complex, deeply nested classes is also an antipattern.

As you write more JavaScript, it's a good idea to try and follow as many patterns and conventions as possible. They'll save you from having to reinvent the wheel, and help you to write reusable code that is easier for others to read. A good resource for learning more about JavaScript patterns is >earning JavaScript Design Patterns by Addy Osmani[6].

Another good practice is to follow a coding style-guide. These are usually written by teams of developers to ensure they agree on how they write code. Airbnb make theirs publicly available[7] and it not only includes coding style recommendations, but also explains the justification behind them. It would certainly make a good starting point or template for your own style guide. You can also configure some code linters to help you stick to a particular style-guide.

The post Elements of Javascript Style[8] by Eric Elliot contains some excellent guidelines that will help to improve your coding style (and hopefully understand the reasoning behind them).

Build Things

You can learn all the theory you want, but the only way you'll actually develop your coding style is to go out and build things. By putting ideas into practice and solving real problems, you'll really start to get a feel for the language. There is nothing better for improving your technique than writing code. So get writing! In the next section, there are some ideas for what you could do.

Pair Programming

A great way to level up your skills is to **pair program**. This involves working together with another developer on a project, either sat together in person or

---

[6.] http://addyosmani.com/resources/essentialjsdesignpatterns/book/
[7.] https://github.com/airbnb/javascript
[8.] https://medium.com/javascript-scene/elements-of-javascript-style-caa8821cb99f

(more usually) by connecting machines remotely. It can be between a novice and a more experienced programmer, where the focus is on the experienced programmer helping the novice improve their programming style and teaching them new tricks. This might seem like a one-sided experience, but it can be tremendously helpful for an experienced programmer to try and explain difficult concepts, and often leads to them developing a deeper understanding themselves. It can also speed up the development of a beginner programmer as they can be guided away from common pitfalls by the more experienced programmer.

Pair programming can also be between two programmers of a similar ability where they are working together to try and solve a problem. The benefit here is that they can discuss the different strategies they would use, and compare different approaches to solving a problem. Having two sets of eyeballs looking over code can also help identify careless errors that can take a long time to find when you're on your own.

Codeshare[9] is a site that lets you connect with other programmers.

Contribute to Open Source Projects

The Open Source community is responsible for creating some excellent software that many of us use every day. It also gives us an excellent opportunity to give something back by contributing to a project, and provides the chance to gain some experience of working on a big project with a large number of users.

There are many ways you can contribute to an open-source project, which will help to develop your skills as a programmer and give you an appreciation of the processes involved in developing software. Here are some ideas of how you can get involved:

- Help fix a bug that has been identified
- Run benchmark tests
- Write documentation or help to translate it
- Suggest a new feature
- Implement a new feature
- Help to test a new feature

---

9. https://codeshare.io

- Moderate the project's message boards
- Provide unofficial support for the project.

If you want some ideas about what you can do then take a look at Contributor Ninja[10], which provides a running list of issues that need fixing.

JavaScript Development Ideas

Now that you've learned how to program in JavaScript, you might be thinking, 'what next?' You need a project! In this section, we'll look at what you can do with your newly acquired programming skills.

JavaScript has evolved so much in recent years. It's no longer considered just an easy scripting language used to add a drop-down menu and a few effects to a web page (although it is still perfectly fine to use it for this).

The following ideas are intended to get your creative juices flowing and, I trust, spark an idea for a project. It is by no means a complete list of what you can do with JavaScript — the possibilities are endless and only limited by your imagination.

HTML5 Game Development

The advent of HTML5 has heralded a massive growth in online games written in JavaScript and using other HTML5 technologies. Previously, most online games were written using Flash, as JavaScript was considered too slow. The adoption of Canvas as well as faster JavaScript engines now means that HTML5 games can compete with native applications. The development of WebGL and browser GPUs means that fast, rendered 3D games in the browser are now a realistic possibility.

Modern online classics such as HexGL[11] and Swooop[12] serve to highlight just what is possible using just HTML5 technologies.

---

10. https://contributor.ninja/js/
11. http://hexgl.bkcore.com
12. http://swooop.playcanvas.com

There are many libraries that help to write HTML5 game code. A couple of excellent examples are Jaws[13]

Single-page Web Applications

A **single-page web application** is an application that, as the name suggests, runs on a single web page in a browser. They aim to create a seamless experience as users navigate around the application and avoid the feeling that they are moving from one page to another. This is often achieved by preloading data in the background using data stored in a back-end database and retrieved as JSON using Ajax. Alternatively, the data can be stored locally using the Local Storage API that we met in Chapter 14. An MVC framework will often be used to ensure that the interface is updated quickly. Many applications are now using the single-page web application model, a couple of good examples are the Strike to-do list app[15] and the Stack Edit MarkDown editor[16].

Progressive Web Applications

Progressive Web Apps (PWAs) are an evolution of single-page web applications that are being developed by Google. The idea is that web applications can be made more reliable and responsive by caching key resources in advance. This will make them load quicker and appear snappier to use, without the need for a constant network connection. PWAs achieve this goal by using a variety of modern web APIs to make web applications feel more like a native application, resulting in a much better app-like experience for users.

Mobile App Development

Android and iOS don't use JavaScript as their native programming language. However, it's still possible to build an application using HTML5 technologies and JavaScript, then use a conversion tool such as CocoonJS.[17] These will convert an

---

[13.] http://jawsjs.com/ and Phaser[14].

[14.] http://phaser.io/

[15.] http://www.strikeapp.com/

[16.] https://stackedit.io

[17.] https://www.ludei.com/cocoonjs/

HTML5 application into native code that can be run on the Android and iOS platforms. So you can build using just HTML5 technologies and JavaScript, but then deploy on multiple devices.

Desktop App Development

Electron[18] is an open-source library that allows you to build desktop applications using just HTML, CSS and JavaScript. It uses Chromium (the open-source version of Google Chrome) and Node.js to create applications that can run on Windows, MacOS and Linux. This means that if you have an idea for a desktop application, you already have the skills needed to produce one.

Electron was developed by GitHub when they built their own text editor, Atom. Since then, it has become a popular option for developers who want to create a desktop version of a web app. It has been used to create desktop applications such as Slack, Microsoft Visual Studio Code and Insomnia.

Node.js Development

JavaScript has been traditionally thought of as a front-end programming language used for client-side programming in the browser. That all changed when Node.js was released and transformed the JavaScript landscape. Node.js means that JavaScript can be run without using a browser, so JavaScript can now be used to write server-side code or command-line tools that interact with the file system.

As a JavaScript ninja, you'll probably install Node anyway to use the many tools that will make your life easier (such as React and WebPack, which we saw in the previous chapter). Node.js can also be used to write your own tools that help to automate your workflow, or to build server-side applications, dynamic websites that link to back-end databases, and web API services. Node.js is increasingly being used to develop large-scale websites and applications, with companies such as PayPal, Groupon, and Yahoo using it to deliver parts of their sites.

Due to the asynchronous nature of JavaScript, Node.js has a number of advantages over traditional server-side languages such as PHP, Python and Ruby.

---

18. https://electron.atom.io

It's ideally suited for real-time update applications with lots of concurrent users as it's able to quickly deal with requests in a non-blocking way.

If you want to learn more about Node.js, you can learn more about it by reading *Node.js 8 the Right Way* by Jim R Wilsonhttps://pragprog.com/book/jwnode2/ node-js-8-the-right-way.

And There's More!

And it doesn't stop there — JavaScript is becoming the language of choice for communicating with devices via APIs provided by the manufacturers. The so-called "Internet of Things" includes a range of devices, from watches and virtual-reality headgear to home automation devices and even robots! Knowledge of JavaScript will enable you to program an ever-growing list of electronic devices.

Chapter Summary

- New versions of ECMAScript will continue to ship every year. Each version should help to make the language more expressive and easier to use. This rapid release cycle should mean that new features are implemented sooner in browsers.

- WebAssembly is a new low-level language that will allow browsers to run compiled code on the web. This will make it possible to run processor-heavy applications on the web.

- A JavaScript ninja should use version control such as Git to manage their projects.

- A JavaScript ninja's knowledge can be kept up to date by subscribing to mailing lists, listening to podcasts, attending talks and conferences, following developers on Twitter, and reading books and blog posts.

- A JavaScript ninja should use common JavaScript coding patterns that are proven best practice. This also makes it easier to communicate about code.

- A JavaScript ninja should write lots of code and build things!

▪ There are many different uses for JavaScript, such as HTML5 games, server-side development using Node.js, progressive web apps and even desktop apps using Electron.

▪ JavaScript is increasingly being used as a scripting language for the Internet of Things (IoT), meaning it can be used to program a variety of devices.

And that brings us to the end of our journey! I hope you have enjoyed learning JavaScript and will continue to develop your skills in the future.

JavaScript has moved beyond its humble beginnings as a basic scripting language for adding effects to web pages. It now occupies a unique position as a powerful language that can be used to program on the client-side *and* the server-side. JavaScript is now becoming increasingly available on several other platforms, extending its reach beyond the Web. The future certainly seems bright for the language as it offers various opportunities to interact with technology. The only limit to what you can do is your imagination. So what are you waiting for? Get programming, ninja!